Citizen-Driven Humanitarianism and the Bangladesh Liberation War

Citizen-Driven Humanitarianism and the Bangladesh Liberation War

Australian Aid during the 1971 Refugee Crisis

Rachel Stevens

BLOOMSBURY ACADEMIC
LONDON • NEW YORK • OXFORD • NEW DELHI • SYDNEY

BLOOMSBURY ACADEMIC
Bloomsbury Publishing Plc, 50 Bedford Square, London, WC1B 3DP, UK
Bloomsbury Publishing Inc, 1385 Broadway, New York, NY 10018, USA
Bloomsbury Publishing Ireland, 29 Earlsfort Terrace, Dublin 2, D02 AY28, Ireland

BLOOMSBURY, BLOOMSBURY ACADEMIC and the Diana logo are trademarks of
Bloomsbury Publishing Plc

First published in Great Britain 2024
This paperback edition published in 2025

Copyright © Rachel Stevens, 2024

Rachel Stevens has asserted her right under the Copyright, Designs and Patents Act, 1988, to be identified as Author of this work.

For legal purposes the Acknowledgements on pp. viii–ix constitute an extension of this copyright page.

Cover image © Courtesy of the National Archives of Australia. NAA: C4078, N41313.

This work is published open access subject to a Creative Commons Attribution-NonCommercial-NoDerivatives 4.0 International licence (CC BY-NC-ND 4.0, https://creativecommons.org/licenses/by-nc-nd/4.0/). You may re-use, distribute, and reproduce this work in any medium for non-commercial purposes, provided you give attribution to the copyright holder and the publisher and provide a link to the Creative Commons licence.

All rights reserved. No part of this publication may be: i) reproduced or transmitted in any form, electronic or mechanical, including photocopying, recording or by means of any information storage or retrieval system without prior permission in writing from the publishers; or ii) used or reproduced in any way for the training, development or operation of artificial intelligence (AI) technologies, including generative AI technologies. The rights holders expressly reserve this publication from the text and data mining exception as per Article 4(3) of the Digital Single Market Directive (EU) 2019/790.

Bloomsbury Publishing Plc does not have any control over, or responsibility for, any third-party websites referred to or in this book. All internet addresses given in this book were correct at the time of going to press. The author and publisher regret any inconvenience caused if addresses have changed or sites have ceased to exist, but can accept no responsibility for any such changes.

A catalogue record for this book is available from the British Library.

A catalog record for this book is available from the Library of Congress.

ISBN: HB: 978-1-3503-8144-5
PB: 978-1-3503-8147-6
ePDF: 978-1-3503-8145-2
eBook: 978-1-3503-8146-9

Typeset by Newgen KnowledgeWorks Pvt. Ltd., Chennai, India

For product safety related questions contact productsafety@bloomsbury.com.

To find out more about our authors and books visit www.bloomsbury.com and sign up for our newsletters.

Contents

List of Figures	vi
List of Tables	vii
Acknowledgements	viii
List of Acronyms	x
Key Figures	xii
Timeline	xvi
1 Introduction	1
2 The rise of citizen-driven humanitarianism	31
3 The federations: The Australian Council for Overseas Aid and Austcare	55
4 The establishment: The Red Cross movement	75
5 The religious: Organized church aid and Christian activists	99
6 The grassroots: Oxfam and the Freedom from Hunger Campaign	127
7 The individuals: Moira Dynon, Paul Poernomo and citizen letters of protest	151
8 Conclusion	187
Bibliography	197
Index	217

Figures

1.1	Map of northern South Asia at time of partition	6
2.1	Registration of Australian charities, 1880s–1990s	32
3.1	Relative position of Australian humanitarian organizations	58
3.2	Cash donations by humanitarian organization over time	60
4.1	Flow chart of donations to Bangladeshi refugees during 1971	81
5.1	Timeline of Australian government cash and in-kind donations	123
7.1	Mrs M. Dynon checks a load of milk at her Melbourne home	153
7.2	A hunger demonstration outside Parliament House Canberra	174
7.3	Citizen letters by number and date of sending, 1971	178
7.4	Geographical distribution of letters from citizens to Whitlam	182
8.1	Inter-network cluster analysis	190

Tables

1.1	Refugee Population by State on 1 December 1971	15
4.1	Donations from Red Cross National Societies	80
6.1	Top Fifteen Donating Municipalities in Victoria	148
7.1	Cash and In-Kind Donations, December 1970 to March 1972	156
7.2	Keywords from Letters	179
7.3	Letter Writers, Population Distribution and TV Access	183

Acknowledgements

This book began as an application for a National Library of Australia (NLA) fellowship in 2017, a funded scheme that, in its words, 'supports curious minds to create new knowledge'. I think this book has made good on the objectives of the fellowship programme. Without a doubt, my residency at the NLA provided me with the resources, supportive atmosphere and, importantly, time to read through and process many manuscript collections, which form the archival backbone of this book. I find it hard to imagine that this project would have ever gotten off the ground without the NLA fellowship. As many academic researchers will attest, starting a new project is easy yet completing it requires persistence, bloody-mindedness and institutional support. I am deeply grateful for the opportunities that the NLA offered me.

Intellectually, the genesis of this project stems from my work on Professor Joy Damousi's Australian Research Council-funded Kathleen Fitzpatrick Laureate Fellowship on child refugees and Australian internationalism. As her full-time research assistant, Joy provided me with extensive opportunities to visit archives and research libraries throughout Australia, the United States, Switzerland and the UK. In spending many months over five years examining the archival records of various humanitarian organizations, I developed a deep understanding of the histories of humanitarianism in Australia and abroad, knowledge that would shape how I framed this project. I thank Joy for her commitment to supporting early career researchers, women in academia and the humanities in wider society.

In 2020 I joined the Australian Catholic University's (ACU) newly established Research Centre on Refugees, Migration and Humanitarian Studies within the Institute of Humanities and Social Sciences. Appointed to a full-time research-only position, ACU has provided an outstanding intellectual environment that values humanities research and the transformative role it can play in society. I particularly note the visionary leadership of ACU's former deputy vice chancellor of research, Professor Wayne McKenna, who initiated the research intensification strategy at ACU and, in doing so, has helped cement the research careers of the next generation of scholars in Australia.

As part of the research for this book, I have attended numerous archives and libraries, and I thank the library and archive staff for accommodating me. Aside from the NLA, the National Archives of Australia has provided archival access in the Canberra, Sydney, Melbourne and Brisbane branches. Library staff at the University of Melbourne, University of Oxford and University of Birmingham provided me with access to the records of the Australian Red Cross, Oxfam and Save the Children Fund, respectively. The United Nations in New York and Geneva also granted me access to their records, materials that provided essential overviews of the contributions of various international voluntary agencies to the Bangladeshi refugee crisis.

Several people have provided me assistance throughout the completion of this project and deserve special mention. Anisa Puri analysed and catalogued approximately half of the 2,500 citizen letters to Gough Whitlam, which forms a major section in Chapter 7. The prospect of processing on my own such a large volume of letters was daunting, even overwhelming. Without Anisa's contribution, I can't imagine I would have had the endurance let alone the time to dissect all these letters. Mary Tomsic, a colleague at the University of Melbourne and, later, ACU, selflessly read numerous drafts, including of chapters that never made it into this book. She provided insightful feedback on my introduction and book proposal, not least of which was helping me see the forest from the trees. Jon Piccini, another ACU colleague, offered feedback on an early presentation and a journal article stemming from this research. His expertise on the Australian Left and post-Second World War political activism influenced how I thought about grassroots organizations and individual humanitarianism. Michael Thompson similarly provided advice on progressive Christian internationalism, a key component to understanding twentieth-century humanitarianism. Jacinta Efthim kindly granted me access to the Dynon family papers, a rich collection that is currently unavailable to the public but in the process of being transferred to the NLA. Jacinta also met with me on numerous occasions to discuss her mother's work, which would later inform my analysis in Chapter 7. G. B. Nath painstakingly translated Bengali language newspaper articles into English, evidence that appears in Chapter 5. Lastly, Maddie Holder, publisher in History at Bloomsbury, who immediately saw the value of this book and patiently shepherded this project to completion.

I particularly wish to thank the two anonymous referees who reviewed my book proposal and, later, the full manuscript. Both referees provided insightful and detailed feedback, which significantly improved the final book. Their advice was even more valuable than typical: because this book was written during the Covid-19 pandemic and resulting lockdowns, its research was not exposed to the usual 'socialization' that comes from presenting at academic conferences. The reports from the referees therefore played an important role in shaping the analysis, argument and scope of this book.

My partner, Romy, has been my sounding board throughout the writing of this book, and long before. This book is dedicated to Romy and our two 'little ladies', Whingey and Karli.

Acronyms

ACASR	American Committee for Armenian and Syrian Relief
ACC	Australian Council of Churches
ACFOA	Australian Council for Overseas Aid
ACT	Australian Capital Territory
AJWS	Australian Jewish Welfare Society
AL	Awami League
ALP	Australian Labor Party
BERRS	Bangladesh Ecumenical Relief and Rehabilitation Service
CAA	Community Aid Abroad
CASA	Christian Agency for Social Action (India)
CCIA	Commission of Churches on International Affairs
CICARWS	Commission on Inter-Church Aid, Refugee and World Service
CICR	Comité International de la Croix-Rouge
CPA	Communist Party of Australia
CSSM	Catholic Social Studies Movement
DEA	Australian Department of External Affairs (1901–16; 1921–October 1970)
DEC	Disasters Emergency Council (UK)
DFA	Australian Department of Foreign Affairs (November 1970–87)
DP	Displaced Persons
FAO	Food and Agriculture Organization
FCO	UK Foreign and Commonwealth Office
FFHC	Freedom from Hunger Campaign
GPO	General Post Office
ICRC	International Committee of the Red Cross
IGO	Intergovernmental organization
IRO	International Refugee Organization
ISS	International Shipwreck Society
LRCS	League of Red Cross Societies
MSF	Médecins Sans Frontières
NEF	Near East Foundation
NGO	Nongovernmental organization
NSW	New South Wales
ODA	Overseas Development Assistance
PPP	Pakistan People's Party
PTI	Press Trust of India
SCF	Save the Children Fund
UNAA	United Nations Association of Australia
UNHCR	United Nations High Commissioner for Refugees

UNICEF	United Nations International Children's Emergency Fund
UNRRA	United Nations Relief and Rehabilitation Administration
VOLAG	Voluntary Agency
WBCW	West Bengal Council of Women
WCC	World Council of Churches
WRY	World Refugee Year

Key Figures

Leaders in the Bangladesh War

Pakistan

Ayub Khan (Gen.)	Second president of Pakistan (1958–69)
Tikka Khan (Gen.)	Military governor of East Pakistan (April–August 1971)
Yahya Khan	Third president of Pakistan; chief martial law administrator (1969–71)
Zulfikar Ali Bhutto	Leader of Pakistan People's Party; fourth president of Pakistan (1971–3)

Bangladesh

Sheikh Mujibur Rahman	Leader of AL and first president of Bangladesh (1971–2) and prime minister of Bangladesh (1972–5)
Mukti Bahini	Bengali independence fighters
Mukti Fauj	Bengali liberation army
Razakars	Bihari volunteers of the Pakistani Army
Birangona	War heroines; rape survivors of the 1971 war

India

Indira Gandhi	Prime minister of India (1966–77; 80–4)
Sam Manekshaw (Gen.)	Chief of army staff
Swaran Singh	Minister for external affairs (1970–4)

Humanitarians

Australian Catholic Relief

Wm. C. Byrne	Executive director, Australian Catholic Relief
James W. Gleeson	Episcopal deputy for Australian Catholic Relief

Australian Council of Churches (ACC)/World Council of Churches (WCC)

Rev. Alan A. Brash	Director, Commission on Inter-Church Aid, Refugee and World Services, WCC
Rt. Rev. David A. Garnsey	President, ACC

Humanitarians

F. G. Engels	Secretary of ACC
Rev. Edmund (Ted) Arblaster	Director, Division of World Christian Action/Inter-church Aid, ACC
Vaughan Hinton	Secretary for Public Relations, ACC
Mr P. C. Joseph	Christian Agency for Social Action – Kolkata

Austcare

Major General Paul Cullen	Co-founder, president
Rev. Geoff Parish	Co-founder, first CEO, later executive secretary
Rev. Alan Prior	Co-founder and national director

Australian Council for Overseas Aid

Syd Einfeld, AJWS	Chairman (to September 1971)
Paul Cullen, UNAA	Delegate, later chairman (from September 1971)
Geoffrey D. Solomon	Executive director
Sir John Crawford	President
Moira Dynon, Aid India Campaign	Delegate
Rev. E. Arblaster, ACC	Delegate
Noreen Minogue, Red Cross	Delegate
Jim Webb, CAA	Delegate
Phyllis Frost, FFHC	Delegate
Adrian Harris, CAA	Observer
Alan Smith, FFHC	Observer

Community Aid Abroad (CAA)/Oxfam

Father Gerard Kennedy Tucker	Founder, Food for Peace
Jean Mackenzie	Secretary, Food for Peace
Leslie Kirkley	Director, Oxfam (1971–3)
Bernhard Llewellyn	Appraiser, Oxfam (1967–82); field director for Asia (1964–7)
Thea Foster	Executive director, Oxfam America
David Scott	Director, CAA (1969); chairman, CAA (1971)

Humanitarians

Jim Webb	Director, CAA (1971–3)
Adrian Harris	Acting director, CAA; field director Far East, Oxfam (1973)
J. W. Jackson	International secretary, Oxfam (1971)
Philip Jackson	Head of communications, Oxfam (1972)
Ken Bennett	Overseas aid director, Oxfam (1971)
Michael Harris	Deputy overseas aid director, Oxfam (1971)
Marilyn Sanders	International secretary (1973)
Raymond Cournoyer	Field director Bangladesh (1972); in West Bengal 1971
Frank Field	Field director Bangladesh (1973)
Donald Shields	Field director Far East, Oxfam (1969)
Bill Acworth	Field secretary for Asia, Oxfam (1973)

Freedom Fasters

Paul Poernomo	Thirty-six-year-old Indonesian-born poet and clerk
Steve Rooney	Nineteen-year-old truckdriver
Jim Rooney	Seventeen-year-old brother to Steve
Geoff Evans	Twenty-year-old student

Freedom from Hunger Campaign (FFHC)

Binay Ranjan Sen	Director-general, Food and Agriculture Organization (1956–67)
G. V. Hinton	Chairman, FFHC Australia
Phyllis Frost	National president, FFHC Australia
Alan Smith	National executive officer, FFHC Australia
Leo Kelly	National publicity officer, FFHC Australia
J. B. Singh	Deputy commissioner, FFHC India
H. F. Dawson	Chairman, FFHC Australia, Victorian branch
Ron Butt	State director, FFHC Australia, Victorian branch

Aid India Campaign

Moira Dynon	Founder and president
Jim Allen	Australian deputy high commissioner, Dhaka
Douglas Sturkey	Australian deputy high commissioner, Kolkata
Uptala Misra	West Bengal Council of Women

Humanitarians

N. Mukherji	President, West Bengal Council of Women

Red Cross movement

Henrik Beer	Secretary general, League of Red Cross Societies
Sir Geoffrey Newman-Morris	Vice chairman, League of Red Cross Societies
Jean-Pierre Robert-Tissot	Director, Relief Bureau, League of Red Cross Societies
Enrico Bignami	Commissioner, International Committee of the Red Cross
S. S. Maitra	Secretary general, Indian Red Cross Society
Leon G Stubbings	Secretary general, Australian Red Cross Society
Bill Deane	National director of public relations, Australian Red Cross Society
Noreen Minogue	Deputy secretary general, Australian Red Cross Society

The Society for Those Who Have Less

Len Reid	Founder and president

Timeline

1947
Dissolution of the British Raj and the creation of the self-governing dominions of Pakistan (including present-day Bangladesh) and India.

1948
Pakistani governor general and nationalist hero Muhammad Ali Jinnah declared Urdu and no other language as the official language of Pakistan.

1949
The Awami Muslim League, later known as the Awami League (AL), established in East Bengal.

1952
21 February: in response to continued government insistence on the primacy of Urdu in Pakistan, East Bengali protesters staged rallies demanding equal recognition of Bengali as an official language. Government forces suppressed the uprising by opening fire on protestors, resulting in the deaths of many civilians. The fallen dissidents were viewed by Bengalis as martyrs, further emboldening the nascent Bangla Language Movement in the years ahead. Each year thereafter, 21 February was commemorated as *Bhasha Andolan* (rebellion for language) as a day that recognized the sacrifices of those who fought for cultural and linguistic equality in Pakistan. In 1999 UNESCO recognized 21 February as International Mother Language Day, an annual observance still recognized to this day.

1954
Bengali recognized as an official language of Pakistan.

1955
One unit scheme implemented in Pakistan, a government programme that merged the four provinces and tribal areas in the western wing into one unit. This unit served to counter the demographic dominance of East Bengal over the western wing. East Bengal officially renamed East Pakistan.

1958
Pakistani armed forces stage a coup d'état, suspended the constitution and imposed martial law. General Ayub Khan became president of Pakistan until 1969 and embarked on a modernization programme that favoured development in Pakistan over East Pakistan.

1962
Martial law lifted.

1965
April to September: Second Indo-Pakistani war over Kashmir, resulting in a stalemate and no territorial changes. However, the war worsened relations between the neighbours. After the war the Indian government imposed greater restrictions on movement across the East Pakistani-Indian border, a region which hitherto had tolerated a porous boundary.

1966
Mujib and the AL launched their Six Points Programme outlining a vision for greater autonomy for East Pakistan. The policy advocated a loose federal government, separate currencies for the two provinces, fiscal autonomy, a separate militia for East Pakistan and parliamentary democracy.

1969
Pro-democracy protests widespread in West Pakistan and East Pakistan, forcing the military government to concede the need for democratic elections in 1970. Ayub resigned and Yahya Khan became president and commander-in-chief.

1970–November
Bhola cyclone and tidal bore, killing an estimated 500,000 people.

1970–December
National elections held in 300 constituencies. The AL won 160 of the 162 seats representing East Pakistan, while the Pakistan People's Party (PPP) won 81 of the 138 seats in Pakistan. Yahya and the PPP refused to allow the AL to form government despite it winning an absolute majority of seats.

1971–March
Talks broke down between the AL and PPP over forming government, prompting civil disobedience, strikes and protests throughout East Pakistan. On 25 March, the Pakistani armed forces launched Operation Searchlight in East Pakistan, targeting dissidents, intellectuals, AL members and Hindus in Dhaka. Mujib was arrested and detained in Pakistan for the duration of the war.

1971–August
India signed a Treaty of Friendship and Cooperation with the Soviet Union, abandoning its former policy of non-alignment.

1971–December
3 December: Indian armed forces intervened directly in the war in support of the Mukti Bahini.
5 December: The Indian government formally recognized the independence of Bangladesh.
16 December: Pakistan surrendered, and Bangladesh is liberated.

1

Introduction

The Bangladesh Liberation War and the resulting refugee crisis of 1971 captured global attention in 1971. For a moment in time, it was the cause célèbre: Beatle George Harrison and Indian sitar player Ravi Shankar organized the world's first benefit concert of the modern period on 1 August 1971 in New York City. The United Nations High Commissioner for Refugees (UNHCR) estimated that ten million refugees fled to neighbouring India within the space of ten months, the largest mass movement of people in the second half of the twentieth century. Even more remarkably, these refugees voluntarily returned to their homeland within three months after the cessation of hostilities, the largest repatriation programme after the Second World War.[1] The significance of the Bangladesh Liberation War was not lost on contemporaries. Throughout 1971 the Bangladesh war and the plight of the refugees in India received intense media coverage around the world. Shocked by images of famine, displacement and violence, the international community acted to ease the misery of Bangladeshi refugees.[2] This war acted as an accelerant for the democratization of aid giving and global expressions of solidarity, and propelled the well-established transnational humanitarian NGO movement in new directions during the late twentieth century.[3]

This book argues that the growth in the humanitarian NGO sector after 1945 triggered a popular backlash by 1971 that spurred a revival in individual and grassroots forms of charity. Mid-century advancements in the professionalization of the NGO sector, such as the employment of salaried staff, closer relationships with states and intergovernmental organizations, and an emphasis on scientific rationalism over emotive forms of discourse, may have shielded humanitarian organizations from public scrutiny or rebuke. However, in their efforts to demonstrate transparency and accountability, humanitarian NGOs presented a sanitized image that failed to resonate with a politically engaged, well-travelled and informed populace. The professionalization of NGOs may have granted them greater access to (and funding from) state actors, but it also created an emotional void for citizens unsure of the benefits

---

[1] United Nations High Commissioner for Refugees (hereafter UNHCR), *State of the World's Refugees* (Geneva: UNHCR, 2000), 59.
[2] Donald Beachler, 'The Politics of Genocide Scholarship: The Case of Bangladesh', *Patterns of Prejudice* 41 (2007): 468.
[3] Kevin O'Sullivan, *The NGO Moment: The Globalisation of Compassion from Biafra to Live Aid* (Cambridge: Cambridge University Press, 2021), 34–54.

of the post-Second World War economic boom and continued military conflicts in the execution of the Cold War. Furthermore, *Citizen-Driven Humanitarianism* illustrates the extent to which older, elite-driven NGOs were out of touch with contemporary sensibilities, clinging on to imperial and neo-imperial attitudes that offended aid recipients and failed to connect with cosmopolitan citizen donors.

This book also makes two further interventions into humanitarian historiography. First, despite arguments of the secularization of Western society since the 1960s, this research demonstrates the persistence of faith in Australia, especially Catholicism, in debates about humanitarianism, inequality and suffering. Second, rather than politicians guiding the public, in this case study we see how citizens led the political establishment and, on occasion, withstood government interference and intimidatory tactics. In many ways, we can view Australian humanitarian activism as another example of the wider protest movements of the 1960s and early 1970s. The capacity of civil society in this instance to force a change in government policy is inspiring and worth remembering when current times seem to dictate that populist politicians can only move in a rightward direction.

The title of this book, *Citizen-Driven Humanitarianism*, was deliberately phrased in this way for two reasons. First, it uses the term 'citizen' rather than 'people'. Here, I define the term 'citizen' expansively and not in a restrictive legal sense. The difference between 'citizen' and 'people' is more than mere semantics. A 'citizen' exists in relation, even opposition, to the state. Furthermore, 'citizen' is often associated with participation in democracy. Conversely, the term 'people' lacks these political connotations and is often associated with a national community and culture rather than a state apparatus. Because this book seeks to stress the intrinsically political and personal aspects of humanitarianism, it is therefore necessary to use terminology that reflects its partisan and ideological undercurrents. Second, it includes the suffix '-driven' as a way of emphasizing a dynamic process instead of a static state. Rather than seeing citizens as passive or reactive to elite leadership, I wish to underscore the extent to which individuals and civil society directed governments and NGOs associated with the state.

Conceptually, this book is interested in exploring variations of scale (individual, community, national, transnational and international) and the complex and muddled interactions between them. To do so, I have elected to focus on a singular event – the Bangladesh Liberation War and refugee crisis – and the humanitarian responses from a single country, Australia. As will be made apparent throughout this book, this study does not intend to restrict its analysis to one national unit. Rather, it explores in depth specific hubs of activity within Australian locales and their connections with contemporaries in India, Bangladesh, the UK and Switzerland. A central question of this book asks: how did these interactions hamper or enhance the outcomes of aid? As such, this book is structured in a way that logically moves from larger units of analysis, such as national federations and transnational organizations, through to smaller organizations and finally to individuals. By transitioning between scales from largest to smallest, we can assess which actors were most influential in the operation of humanitarianism at a time of increasing globalization through advancements in aviation and cross-cultural exchange.

Methodologically, *Citizen-Driven Humanitarianism* has been influenced by recent developments in global microhistory over the past dozen years. In a 2010 article, Tonio Andrade coined the term 'global microhistory', an approach that sought to shed light on 'individual lives in global contexts' as a way 'to understand the structures and processes of world history'.[4] Although this was an empirical article rather than a theoretical one, it stirred a methodological debate over the ensuing decade, including an *American Historical Review* 'Conversation' in 2013 and a *Past & Present* supplement in 2019.[5] Not all historians welcomed this new direction in scholarship; indeed, some were openly hostile.[6] Despite some criticism of global microhistory, historians have persisted with the approach and provided additional analytic rigour. In 2014 Oxford historian John-Paul A. Ghobrial published a convincing article that provided much needed sophistication to an otherwise analytically weak concept. Ghobrial framed global microhistory as a solution to the inherent problems of global history. Namely, in its search for connections and movement, global historians create narratives of 'faceless globetrotters, colourless chameleons and invisible boundary crossers, individuals stretched so far out of any local, confessional or personal context as to make them little more than panes of glass through which to view the worlds in which they live'.[7] As an alternative history, Ghobrial suggested that a close study of global life necessitates 'deep, local history'.[8]

Possibly the best way to understand global microhistory and its benefits is to unpack its component parts: microhistory and global history, both of which have existed for decades, and each has methodological limitations. First, microhistory was popularized in the 1970s and gained mainstream academic acceptance in the 1980s and 1990s. Its most prominent practitioners included Italian renaissance historians Carlo Ginzburg and Giovanni Levi, and French early modernists Jacques Revel and Natalie Zemon Davis. The core contribution of microhistory to wider historiography was the idea that the scale with which we analyse a historical phenomenon should be open to interrogation. In other words, microhistorians argue that there are no natural scales for analysis, whether they be nations, continents or villages.[9] Although national histories remain a typical container for analysis, microhistorians argue that by varying

---

[4] Tonio Andrade, 'A Chinese Farmer, Two African Boys, and a Warlord: Toward a Global Microhistory', *Journal of World History* 21 (2010): 574, 591.
[5] Sebouh David Aslanian, Joyce E. Chaplin, Ann McGrath and Kristin Mann, 'AHR Conversation. How Size Matters: The Question of Scale in History', *American Historical Review* 118 (December 2013): 1455; John-Paul A. Ghobrial (ed.), 'Global History and Microhistory', *Past & Present Supplement* 14 (2019): 1–383.
[6] Sigurður Gylfi Magnússon, 'Far-Reaching Microhistory: The Use of Microhistorical Perspective in a Globalized World', *Rethinking History* 21 (2017): 330; Jan de Vries, 'Playing with Scales: The Global and the Micro, the Macro and the Nano', *Past & Present* 242, Supplement 14 (November 2019): 29.
[7] John-Paul A. Ghobrian, 'The Secret Life of Elias of Babylon and the Uses of Global Microhistory', *Past & Present* 222 (2014): 59.
[8] Ibid. Similar arguments have been advanced by Agnieszka Sobocinska, *Saving the World? Western Volunteers and the Rise of the Humanitarian-Development Complex* (Cambridge: Cambridge University Press, 2021), 13; David Bell, 'This Is What Happens When Historians Overuse the Idea of the Network', *New Republic*, 26 October 2013, 6 and O'Sullivan, *The NGO Moment*, 179.
[9] Francesco Trivellato, 'What Differences Make a Difference? Global History and Microhistory Revisited', *Journal of Early Modern History* 27 (2023): 10.

scales, we can generate novel interpretations that eschew top-down, grand narratives.[10] The problem with microhistory, however, is with the veracity of its assertion for the generalizability of the specific. That is, microhistorians claim the individual is representative of a collective experience, yet this belief contradicts how individuals typically see themselves as unique, complex and with multiple not singular selves.[11]

Like microhistory, global history similarly resists the nation as a natural frame for analysis and seeks to elucidate networks of social relationships. Global history arrived on the North American academic scene with gusto in the 1990s, responding in part to the end of the Cold War, the desire to humanize the impersonal forces of globalization and counter Eurocentrism in historical narratives.[12] This genre is characterized by diplomatic and political histories, particularly those that chart imperial networks, trade exchanges and cross-cultural encounters. But in striving to narrate transborder crossings, global histories tend to privilege movement over rootedness.[13] There is also an implicit class bias within global history for it centres those with the means to travel, specifically, colonizers, entrepreneurs and the educated. Global history therefore has the tendency to overlook those who have been left behind, such as children, women and the working class.[14] Furthermore, by emphasizing movement across space, global historians negate the influence of place. As Mark Gamsa observes, 'everybody comes from somewhere and one's place of origin is seldom irrelevant, or put out of mind, however cosmopolitan, global, or transnational a life one later leads'.[15]

Global microhistory, therefore, seeks to combine the advantages of global history and microhistory while restricting the impacts of their respective methodological limitations. I employ microhistory for its capacity for focused analysis of individuals, organizations and institutions in their interactions and entanglements; I use global history for its orientation towards awareness of broader contexts and wider processes of change. This approach may be crudely reduced to its ability to zoom in and zoom out like a photographic lens.[16] A better way to summarize global microhistory would be to highlight its capacity to explore how global changes manifested in local environments using evidence, interpretation and contextualization to decipher meaning.[17] As Hans Medick writes, the goal of global microhistory is to balance narratives that depict individual agency while still acknowledging the impacts of wider structural forces. In short, if microhistory and its predilection towards biography grants too

---

[10] Francesca Trivellato, 'Microstoria/Microhistoire/Microhistory', *French Politics, Culture and Society* 33 (2015): 122.
[11] Mark Gamsa, 'Biography and (Global) Microhistory', *New Global Studies* 11 (2017): 233.
[12] John-Paul A. Ghobrial, 'Introduction: Seeing the World like a Microhistorian', *Past & Present* 242, Supplement 14 (2019): 1 and 9.
[13] Maxine Berg, 'Introduction: Global Microhistory of the Local and the Global', *Journal of Early Modern History* 27 (2023): 1, 4.
[14] Jeremy Adelman, 'Is Global History Still Possible, or Has It Had Its Moment?' *Aeon* (2017), accessed 6 May 2023, https://aeon.co/essays/is-global-history-still-possible-or-has-it-had-its-moment.
[15] Gamsa, 'Biography and (Global) Microhistory', 234.
[16] Harald Fischer-Tiné, 'Marrying Global History with South Asian History: Potential and Limits of Global Microhistory in a Regional Inflection', *Comparativ* 2 (2017): 54.
[17] Ghobrial, 'Seeing the World like a Microhistorian', 16.

much autonomy to individuals, and if global history is too distant from the human experience, then global microhistory can occupy the interstitial spaces.[18]

The remainder of this chapter has four sections. First, it presents a brief history of the Bangladesh Liberation War. Second, this chapter examines popular and scholarly accounts of the war as well as international humanitarian aid efforts. Third, because refugees were based in eastern India, it was the Indian state (not East Pakistan/Bangladesh) that was the recipient of international aid. As such, to understand humanitarianism during the Bangladesh Liberation War, the third section explores India's relations with foreign donor states. In this context, Australia emerges as an outlier, one of the few countries willing to side with India while risking Pakistani (and therefore American) retaliation, a risky calculation in the context of the Cold War. Lastly, the fourth section provides a chapter outline and scope of this book.

The path to war

The Bangladesh Liberation War was an outcome of the hasty partition of British India in 1947. Inspired by the theory that Indian Hindus and Muslims are two distinct nations, the Pakistan Movement advocated self-determination and independence from British-ruled India. Yet the borders of such a Muslim state or states were poorly demarcated. Sir Muhammad Iqbal (1877–1938) was a chief proponent of a separate federation of Muslim-majority provinces yet even he was uncertain about structures of governance or national borders. In his writings, Iqbal considered a loose federation of Muslim-majority provinces presumably with some degree of local autonomy; he also considered Bengal and north-west India as separate nations.[19] In the Lahore Resolution of 1940, Bengal and north-west India were deemed 'independent states' that should be 'autonomous and sovereign'.[20] Even three months before independence and partition in 1947, it was still uncertain if Bengal would be divided and if the territory would join India or Pakistan. With Indian support, Viceroy Louis Mountbatten implemented his 3 June Plan in which the legislative assemblies of West Bengal and East Bengal voted on the partition of Bengal. Revealingly, the Muslim-majority East Bengal legislators voted *against* partitioning Bengal (106–35). Meanwhile the non-Muslim-majority West Bengal voted in favour of partition (58–21), glad to 'rid themselves of the Muslim problem'.[21] Under the Mountbatten Plan, assent to partition only required majority support in one legislature not both nor a majority of votes overall. With Bengal set to

---

[18] Hans Medick, 'Debatte: Turning Global? Microhistory in Extension', *Historische Anthropologie* 24 (2016): 251. For an example of a global microhistory that focuses on the effects of worldwide transformation in a single locale and at a particular time, see Adam Mestyan, 'Domestic Sovereignty, A'yan Developmentalism, and Global Microhistory in Modern Egypt', *Comparative Studies in Society and History* 60 (2018): 415–45.

[19] Letter from Muhammad Iqbal to Muhammad Ali Jinnah, 21 June 1937, in Gulam Allana, *Pakistan Movement: Historic Documents* (Karachi: University of Karachi, 1967), 133.

[20] Ayesha Jalal, *The Struggle for Pakistan* (Cambridge, MA: Harvard University Press, 2014), 144.

[21] Ian Talbot, 'Partition of India: The Human Dimension', *Cultural and Social History* 6 (2009): 404; Rizwana Shamshad, *Bangladeshi Migrants in India* (New Delhi: Oxford University Press, 2017), chapter 3.

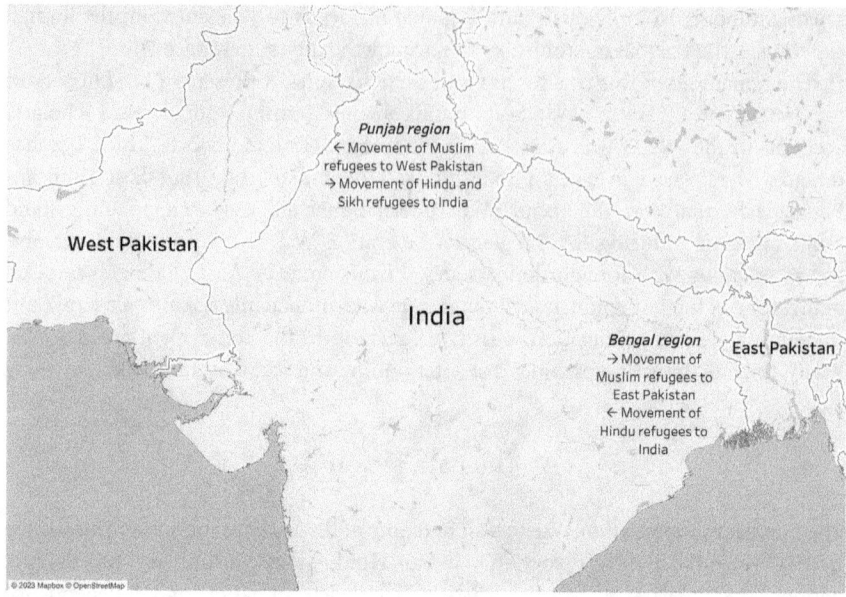

Figure 1.1 Map of northern South Asia at time of partition with migration flows, 1947. Created by author.

be split between two soon-to-be independent states, the task of demarcating territorial boundaries within six weeks was left to Sir Cyril Radcliffe.

In just a matter of months, then, the fate of East Bengal was determined by a handful of elites. Religious nationalism and pan-Islamic solidarity dictated that East Bengal would become a non-contiguous province of the newly independent Dominion of Pakistan. Separated by over 1,000 miles (or 1,600 kilometres), Pakistan's two wings were devised with a 'problematic territorial logic' that privileged Muslim solidarity above other forms of collective identity.[22] As is well known, the Partition of India resulted in the migration of nine million Hindus and Sikhs from Pakistan to India and a further five million Muslims moved from India to both wings of Pakistan (see Figure 1.1). Yet stories of communal violence, exile and resettlement are typically 'Punjabocentric' and focus on the swift, bloody and absolute partition of this province. In contrast, the partition of Bengal was not a singular event but rather a protracted process. Transborder communities existed in Bengal from 1947 to 1965 and it was commonplace for residents to move across the national boundary for work, education and familial reunification. Although passports and visas were introduced in 1952 (five years after partition), travellers rarely used them. It was not until after the inconclusive second Indo-Pakistani war over Kashmir in 1965 that the Indian–East Pakistan border hardened,

---

[22] Shelley Feldman, 'Displacement and the Production of Difference: East Pakistan/Bangladesh, 1947–1990', *Globalizations* 19 (2022): 190. Tahir Naqvi, 'Migration, Sacrifice and the Crisis of Muslim Nationalism', *Journal of Refugee Studies* 25 (2012): 475.

making transborder migration difficult.²³ Amidst coexistence in this borderland region, episodes of communal riots (or, more accurately, ethnic cleansing) occurred frequently in both India and East Pakistan. Not surprisingly, five million Hindus fled East Pakistan for India between 1947 and 1970. This migration reduced the Hindu population in East Pakistan from 30 per cent of the provincial total to 13 per cent by 1971.²⁴ Edward Said described partition as 'a parting gift of Empire', one that instilled rituals of violence, ethnic chauvinism and religious intolerance into postcolonial Asia.²⁵ East Pakistan was therefore born into a volatile, fractious environment that was made even more precarious by misgovernance and discrimination.

The causes of the Bangladesh Liberation War remain contested, and scholars are divided on the relative significance of governance, economic, ethnic and religious factors. For Ayesha Jalal, the dismemberment of Pakistan was caused by unpopular military rule rather than an inevitable division based on cultural and linguistic differences between the two provinces.²⁶ In its first decades of existence, the Pakistani state governed in the tradition of colonial bureaucratic authoritarianism, seeking to extract maximum resources from the economy for the benefit of the few. The military coup in 1958 replaced one set of authoritarian rulers with another, and they imposed martial law until 1962. Although more than half (54.5 per cent) of Pakistanis lived in East Pakistan, Bengalis were under-represented in the civil service and armed forces. In the 1950s, East Pakistanis accounted for just 1 per cent of those enlisted in the armed forces. By the late 1960s, Bengalis represented 5 per cent of the officer class and 7 per cent of all other ranks in the military. With such political marginalization, East Bengali nationalists thought 'they were trapped in a system of internal colonialism' not that dissimilar to the British rulers they had evicted two decades prior.²⁷ The ineptitude and indifference of Pakistan's military junta towards its eastern province was highlighted after the 1970 Bhola cyclone and resulting tidal bore. In estimates from the US State Department, 500,000 people perished during the calamity. What was even more shocking for Bengalis was that their central government did little to ease their suffering. In the days following the disaster, no Pakistani leader visited the eastern wing. At most, the president of Pakistan, Yahya Khan, flew over the affected areas en route from a trip to China. In a drunken haze, Yahya concluded the reports out of East Pakistan 'had been blown out of all proportion', thereby justifying his government's decision to provide minimal aid to the survivors.²⁸ While the central government dismissed East Pakistani needs for assistance, international aid poured in.

---

[23] Md. Mahbubar Rahman and Willem van Schendel, '"I Am Not a Refugee": Rethinking Partition Migration', *Modern Asian Studies* 37 (2003): 557; Haimanti Roy, *Partitioned Lives: Migrants, Refugees, Citizens in India and Pakistan, 1947–65* (Oxford: Oxford University Press, 2013), 3.

[24] Feldman, 'Displacement and the Production of Difference', 191.

[25] Willem van Schendel, *The Bengal Borderlands: Beyond State and Nation in South Asia* (London: Anthem Press, 2005), 35.

[26] Jalal, *The Struggle for Pakistan*, 145–6.

[27] Aqil Shah, *The Army and Democracy* (Cambridge, MA: Harvard University Press, 2014), 102; Ahsan Butt, *Secession and Security: Explaining State Strategy against Separatists* (Ithaca, NY: Cornell University Press, 2017), 46–7.

[28] Srinath Raghavan, *1971: A Global History of the Creation of Bangladesh* (Cambridge, MA: Harvard University Press, 2013), 32.

Suppressive, authoritarian rule no doubt contributed to East Pakistani resentment towards West Pakistan. However, West Pakistanis too were victims of the military dictatorship, particularly those outside the Punjabi heartland. Secessionist movements arose in the western province, such as in Baluchistan and the unruly tribal areas of the north-west frontier.[29] Yet these regions were ultimately unsuccessful in gaining independence. What made the Bangladeshi liberation movement so effective was that it was a reaction to systemic economic discrimination and the deliberate impoverishment of the eastern province by military leaders in Islamabad. At partition, East Bengal was under-developed: transportation and trade links between East Bengal and the neighbouring states of West Bengal and Assam had been curtailed. The few industrial areas in united Bengal were allocated to the Indian side of the border by Radcliffe. The need for development in East Bengal was urgent but the Pakistani government directed development funds (including American development aid) to the western province at an average ratio of 3:1.[30] The industrialization of the west at the expense of the east came at a time when East Bengal harvested Pakistan's most profitable export: the production and sale of jute. Foreign earnings from jute exports were transferred to West Pakistan, and consequently, per capita income was 61 per cent higher in the west than in the east throughout the 1950s and 1960s.[31] Wealth was also highly concentrated. According to Mahbubul Haq, Pakistan's chief economist in the Planning Commission, twenty-two families in Pakistan controlled two-thirds of industrial assets, 80 per cent of banking and 79 per cent of insurance.[32] The Hindu minority in East Pakistan encountered a loss of wealth by way of government-enforced land grabs and property acquisition after communal riots in 1964 and the Indo-Pakistani war in 1965.[33] As a result of these economic policies, opposition to the central government spread across many sectors of society, from upper class landlords and businessmen to middle class civil servants, teachers and lawyers and, finally, workers, peasants and students.

Although Pakistan was premised on the notion of Islamic solidarity, this nation state was built on a foundation of division and mutual animosity. Even the presumed religious affinity among all Pakistanis proved erroneous as it assumed that Islam represents a monolithic culture. Yet what it means to be Islamic is shaped by local cultural idioms and practices. Muslims of West Pakistan distrusted Bengali Muslims as they had converted to Islam relatively recently during the Mughal conquest in the sixteenth century. West Pakistanis denigrated their eastern compatriots as 'Muslims in name only' and essentially 'Hindu at heart'.[34] Furthermore, the secularist inclinations and communist leanings of many Bengali nationalists undermined the religious

---

[29] Butt, *Secession and Security*, 63–82.
[30] Wardatul Akram, 'Atrocities against Humanity during the Liberation War in Bangladesh: A Case of Genocide', *Journal of Genocide Research* 4 (2002): 547.
[31] Butt, *Secession and Security*, 47; Akram, 'Atrocities against Humanity during the Liberation War in Bangladesh', 546.
[32] Shah, *The Army and Democracy*, 101.
[33] Feldman, 'Displacement and the Production of Difference', 196.
[34] Sufia Uddin, *Constructing Bangladesh: Religion, Ethnicity and Language in an Islamic Nation* (Chapel Hill: University of North Carolina Press, 2006), chapter 4; Md. Maidul Islam, 'Secularism in Bangladesh: An Unfinished Revolution', *South Asia Research* 38 (2018): 21; Beachler, 'The Politics of Genocide Scholarship', 477.

credentials of the province.³⁵ In contrast, West Pakistanis considered themselves authentically Islamic. Ethnic chauvinism also divided East and West Pakistanis. West Pakistani political and military elites disparaged Bengalis as effeminate and uncivilized. During the 1971 war, West Pakistani soldiers dehumanized Bengalis by referring to them as monkeys or chickens. One West Pakistani army commander, Major Nazir Baig, summed up this derogatory attitude to a *New York Times* journalist in 1971: 'The Bengalis are very, very soft and chicken-hearted people ... They have no guts.' But despite this alleged cowardice, Major Baig warned that Bengalis could not be trusted: 'They are lambs in front of you, tigers behind your back. They are a people who never miss a chance to stab you in the back.'³⁶ The problem was that as a young nation, Pakistan sought to create one unifying identity (that of religion) in a population with multiple and competing identities. Pakistani nationalism therefore created the parallel imaginaries of an 'us' and a 'them'.³⁷ Injected with a sense of foreboding and fearing that the new nation was riven with internal enemies, Bengalis became an easy target for West Pakistani anxieties.

Language differences further exacerbated tensions between the two provinces. Specifically, the one-nation, one-language policy meant that Urdu was designated the official language of Pakistan. With Perso-Arabic script, Urdu was popularly viewed as connected to the Koran despite its close linguistic association with Devanagari scripted Hindi. In addition to its perceived links with Islam, Urdu was used by educated Muslim elites in South Asia. Yet Urdu was not a language for the masses. According to the 1961 census (the last census before the 1971 conflict), in West Pakistan more than two-thirds spoke Punjabi (67 per cent), followed by Urdu (14.6 per cent) and Sindhi (14.2 per cent). Meanwhile in East Pakistan, 99 per cent of the population spoke Bengali.³⁸ The initial refusal of the central Pakistani government to bestow official status on Bengali was widely viewed by East Pakistanis as a hostile act and an affront to the rich literary tradition among Bengalis.³⁹ From the beginning of independence, Bengali leaders sought to elevate the position of their language to at least official status within their province. These ambitions were quashed by the founding father and first governor general of Pakistan, Muhammad Ali Jinnah, in 1948, who insisted that Bengalis learn to speak Urdu. The refusal of the central government to recognize the cultural significance of Bengali sowed the seeds of a nationalist movement. When university students began preparations for a mass protest in 1952, officials banned all public meetings. The dissidents ignored the ban and were met with violent police suppression, leading to the deaths of four students. Bengalis viewed the fallen students as heroic martyrs whose sacrifices inspired a language movement that appealed to East Pakistanis regardless of

---

³⁵ Yasmin Saikia, 'Insāniyat for Peace: Survivors' Narrative of the 1971 War of Bangladesh', *Journal of Genocide Research* 13 (2011): 484.
³⁶ Sydney H. Schanberg, 'A Pakistani Terms Bengalis "Chicken-Hearted"', *New York Times*, 17 July 1971, 6. See also Beachler, 'The Politics of Genocide Scholarship', 478.
³⁷ Feldman, 'Displacement and the Production of Difference', 191.
³⁸ Pakistan Census, 1961, cited in Bina D'Costa, *Nationbuilding, Gender and War Crimes in South Asia* (London: Routledge, 2011), 87.
³⁹ The most famous Bengali literary figures include Rabindranath Tagore, the first non-European to win the Nobel Prize for Literature, and the poet Nazrul Islam.

class or religious background. To quell civil unrest and nascent Bengali nationalism in the eastern province, the Pakistani government capitulated, designating Bengali nominally as an official language in 1954, which was constitutionally recognized in 1956. Yet in practice, Urdu maintained its privileged position in society. Bengalis were encouraged to learn Urdu, aspiring civil servants – the gateway to the middle class – required fluency in Urdu, and in 1958, the Pakistani government attempted to introduce Arabic script to replace the Sanskritized Devanagari Bengali script to make it appear more Pakistani.[40] These government efforts at cultural assimilation and marginalization led many Bengalis to feel like 'strangers in their own land'.[41]

Aside from official recognition of Bengali, the 1956 Pakistani constitution was important for other reasons, too. First, it declared Pakistan as an independent Islamic republic rather than a dominion of the British Empire. This move further cemented the centrality of Islam in Pakistani nationalism, leaving little doubt about the tolerance of the state towards religious minorities. Second, the constitution ushered in a period of heightened political instability. Due to a constitutional clause that permitted the president to dismiss prime ministers and rule by decree, a tradition carried over from the post-partition period, there were four prime ministers in two years. Unhappy with growing civilian and military unrest and political instability, in October 1958 Pakistani President Iskandar Mirza declared martial law, rescinded the 1956 constitution and appointed military general Ayub Khan as chief martial law administrator. In a bloodless coup, Ayub forced Mirza to resign as president and consolidated his position by combining the offices of president and prime minister. These tumultuous two years ended Pakistan's brief flirtation with democracy, a system that theoretically favoured the numerically dominant East Pakistan. The reign of Ayub was dictatorial: political parties were banned, the press censored and hundreds of mostly Bengali politicians were disqualified from holding public office. Without the possibility of seizing control via the ballot, East Pakistanis became alienated and began to consider alternative forms of governing, such as greater regional autonomy. The Awami League, founded as the Awami Muslim League in 1949, capitalized on these rumblings of discontent. Its charismatic leader, Sheikh Mujibur Rahman, launched the Six Points movement in 1966, a policy platform that mobilized the masses in East Pakistan. In general terms, the movement sought to limit the powers of the Pakistani central government to defence and foreign affairs; all other matters, including a provincial militia, would fall under the remit of individual federating states, such as East Pakistan.[42] Importantly, this movement did not call for independence from Pakistan.

Meanwhile, Ayub's control over the western wing was beginning to unravel. By 1969 and after a decade of repressive, authoritarian rule, various groups within West Pakistan vented their rage. Sub-national groups, such as Pashtuns, Sindhi and the Baloch, resented the dominance of Punjabis, particularly since the installation of the One Unit scheme in 1955 that federated all West Pakistani provinces into one. Class

---

[40] Feldman, 'Displacement and the Production of Difference', 190; Uddin, *Constructing Bangladesh*, 120–1.
[41] Saikia, '*Insāniyat* for Peace', 480–6.
[42] Shah, *The Army and Democracy*, 104.

cleavages also became apparent. Student protests and union strikes crippled the West Pakistani economy in early 1969, for example, by bringing the port city of Karachi to a standstill. Unable to calm the unrest and fearing the military may stage yet another coup, Ayub resigned and invited his protégé, the commander-in-chief of the Army General Yahya Khan, to succeed him as president. Ayub trusted Yahya and knew he had the fortitude to suppress rising dissent. Not surprisingly then, President Yahya quickly reimposed martial law on 26 March 1970. Alongside the army's crackdown, Yahya insisted his government 'had no political ambition' but simply sought to create the conditions conducive to representative government.[43] To reach that end, Yahya pledged to hold a general election based on universal adult suffrage by the end of 1970. However, these public promises concealed the true intent of the president who was determined to maintain the pre-eminent position of the military in Pakistan. Elections would be held but only under contrived circumstances that preordained the outcome. The Yahya regime employed a divide-and-conquer strategy, patronizing and financing Islamist parties to undermine the popularity of the Awami League in East Pakistan. This strategy assumed that the major political party in West Pakistan, the Pakistani People's Party (PPP), would win most seats in the western wing. As the PPP was most popular in Punjab, an army stronghold, Yahya calculated that a PPP election victory would reinstate military rule, if not in name then at least in deeds.[44]

Although the 1970 general election was supposed to stabilize Pakistan, its impact marked the beginning of the end of a united country. Yahya and his advisors grossly underestimated the appeal of the Awami League. The failure of the central government to offer sufficient aid in the wake of the Bhola cyclone no doubt enhanced the appeal of the Awami League and the Six Point programme for greater regional autonomy. Despite efforts of the military junta to boost the electoral chances of Islamist parties in East Pakistan, these parties made little headway in the eastern province, indicating the limited appeal of religious nationalism there. Conversely, the electoral success of the Awami League was stunning. Of the 162 electorates in East Pakistan, the Awami League won all but two. Even though the Awami League did not win a single seat in West Pakistan, because of East Pakistan's numerical majority over West Pakistan, the Awami League ended up with an absolute majority of seats in the national parliament (160 out of 300 seats). Holding most seats in the national assembly also meant that Mujib, leader of the Awami League, could rightfully claim the office of prime minister. As Ayub had feared years earlier, East Pakistanis were using their sizeable population to seize control of the government via the ballot. But the main opposition to the Awami League, the PPP, made their own claims to the highest office. Like the Awami League, the PPP won most seats in their provincial heartland but on a less convincing scale. The PPP won 81 of the 138 seats in West Pakistan, with 62 of these seats from Punjab.

The 1970 election had presented a clear electoral mandate for the Awami League, yet West Pakistani elites refused to relinquish their grip on power. In the ensuing three months, Yahya, Mujib and Zulfiqar Ali Bhutto, leader of the PPP, met frequently to negotiate a mutually acceptable agreement of the formation and composition of the

[43] Ibid., 105.
[44] Raghaven, *1971*, 34.

national assembly.⁴⁵ Ostensibly conducted in good faith, these negotiations obscured the desire of Yahya and his military cabinet to install a Turkish-style civil–military regime that would perpetuate the army's tutelage over the state.⁴⁶ From 12 December 1970 to 25 March 1971, the three parties also debated the finer details of a new civilian constitution and, again, were unable to find common ground. Without a new constitution that designated powers and responsibility, Yahya insisted that the national assembly based on the 1970 election outcome could not convene. Alongside the public negotiations for a political resolution, behind the scenes Yahya was preparing the military for intervention in East Pakistan. As early as December 1970, Yahya's regime began plans for 'Operation Blitz', an armed campaign that was eventually abandoned after the chief commander resigned in opposition.⁴⁷

With negotiations still deadlocked by late February 1971, Yahya committed to the use of military force on his own people. At this time, Mujib and the Awami League were frustrated with the stalling tactics of Yahya and impatient extreme elements within the party were openly calling for independence. At a memorial service for the martyrs of language movement, Mujib declared, 'We will die but we will not surrender.'⁴⁸ When Yahya announced on 1 March 1971 that he would indefinitely postpone convening the national assembly; within minutes hundreds of thousands of people took to the streets in Dhaka. Government workers went on strike, businesses ceased operating and universities shut. To channel the rambunctious energies of the protestors and avoid a civil uprising, Mujib called a general strike for the province, bringing life in East Pakistan to a halt. Over the coming days, the military regime sought to quash the dissent by imposing a curfew and the armed forces violently clashed with protestors, killing 172 people according to state figures.⁴⁹ With chaos on the streets of Dhaka and an intransigent Bengali leader committed to regional autonomy, Yahya gave the orders to senior army officers to 'fully restore the authority of the Government' in the wayward province.⁵⁰

War and liberation

At 11.30 pm on 25 March 1971, Pakistani armed forces entered East Pakistan under the codename 'Operation Searchlight'. Yahya justified this military action to the public as a necessary step to 'save' Pakistan.⁵¹ In his radio address, Yahya asserted that the Awami League had attacked the solidarity of the republic, a treacherous act that could not go unpunished. All political activity was subsequently prohibited and the Awami League banned. For Pakistani armed forces entering East Pakistan, the primary objective was to arrest Mujib and other Awami League leaders, disarm East Pakistani militias

---

⁴⁵ Butt, *Secession and Security*, 47–8.
⁴⁶ Shah, *The Army and Democracy*, 109; Jalal, *The Struggle for Pakistan*, 167.
⁴⁷ Ibid., 171–2.
⁴⁸ Raghaven, *1971*, 40, 44.
⁴⁹ Ibid., 43.
⁵⁰ Butt, *Secession and Security*, 50.
⁵¹ Raghaven, *1971*, 51.

and police, and 'neutralize' radical and student organizations.⁵² Government rhetoric concealed the full extent of military brutality on civilians. Commanding officer Major General Khadim Hussain Raja made clear the true nature of the incursion: 'I will muster all I can – tanks, artillery, and machine guns – to kill all the traitors and, if necessary, raze Dacca to the ground. There will be no one to rule; there will be nothing to rule.'⁵³ This violent mindset filtered from the top brass through to the boots on the ground. On the first night of what would become a nine-month-long war, Pakistani soldiers entered dissident enclaves, such as Dhaka University, executing students, intellectuals, journalists and Hindus. Alongside known rebels, Pakistani troops also unleashed a maelstrom of violence against East Pakistani society, for example, by raping women and girls, looting properties and destroying villages.⁵⁴ In fact, rape and sexual assault of Bengali women were so widespread that these victims were honoured in the post-war rehabilitation period as 'war heroines' (*birangona*), although subsequently they were shamed by men as prostitutes (*barangona*) and criminal responsibility is still denied in Pakistan.⁵⁵ With Pakistani troops committing atrocities against their own people, one may reasonably ask: did the international community consider a humanitarian or military intervention to stop the bloodshed? In short, no. National governments were unwilling to intervene in the internal affairs of a sovereign country, particularly one as unpredictable as Pakistan. As the months rolled on, and without foreign intervention or the deployment of UN peacekeepers, the violence continued unabated.

The first stage of the war, from March to May, was characterized by Pakistani sweeps of cities and towns, spanning out from Dhaka to the rest of the country as they gradually eliminated dissenters. In these months, Pakistani soldiers began occupying seized towns while urban Bengalis fled to the countryside or neighbouring India for safety. After the arrest and detention of Mujib in West Pakistan, Awami League leaders evaded capture by escaping to India. In the case of Awami League General Secretary Tajuddin Ahmed and Amirul Islam, a close associate of Mujib, the pair travelled for five days incognito on horseback and on foot, reaching India on 31 March. Within days, the two leaders met with senior Indian officials in New Delhi and, on 13 April, announced their Bangladesh government in exile.⁵⁶ The fact that India provided a haven to Awami League leaders and served as the initial seat of a Bangladeshi government in exile proved crucial for setting up the second stage of the war during

---

[52] Ibid.
[53] Cited in Butt, *Secession and Security*, 51.
[54] D'Costa, *Nationbuilding, Gender and War Crimes in South Asia*, 95.
[55] Nayanika Mookherjee, *The Spectral Wound: Sexual Violence, Public Memories, and the Bangladesh War of 1971* (Durham, NC: Duke University Press, 2015), xv; Yasmin Saikia, 'War as History, Humanity in Violence: Women, Men and Memories of 1971, East Pakistan/Bangladesh', in *Sexual Violence in Conflict Zones: From the Ancient World to the Era of Human Rights*, ed. Elizabeth Heineman (Philadelphia: University of Pennsylvania Press, 2011), 157; Nayanika Mookherjee, '1971: Pakistan's Past and Knowing What Not to Narrate', *Comparative Studies of South Asia, Africa and the Middle East* 39 (2019): 220.
[56] Sarmila Bose, *Dead Reckoning: Memories of the 1971 Bangladesh War* (London: Hurst, 2011), 162; Raghaven, *1971*, 53, 64; Caf Dowlah, *The Bangladesh Liberation War, the Sheikh Mujib Regime, and Contemporary Controversies* (Lanham, MD: Lexington Books, 2016), 55.

the monsoonal months of June to October. In this second phase, Bengali guerrillas were harboured, supplied and trained in India with the goal of creating a quagmire for Pakistani forces in East Pakistan. The monsoonal rains caused mudslides and floods, which favoured nimble guerrilla warfare over traditional military tactics. Pakistani forces were also outnumbered by their opponents. At the height of the war, there were 80,000 regular soldiers in East Pakistan who were supported by a paramilitary force of 25,000, a civil armed force of 25,000 and 50,000 auxiliary paramilitary forces, including the Razakars, Al-Badr and Al-Shams units. In total, the number of fighters on the side of Pakistan numbered around 180,000, albeit with varying degrees of training, discipline and access to weaponry. The Bangladeshi freedom fighters, known as the Mukti Bahini, numbered 175,000, which included defectors from East Pakistan Rifles, East Bengal Regiment and the Bengali police force. When India entered the conflict on 1 December, marking the final stage of the war, they added an additional 250,000 ground troops in East Pakistan along with a superior air force.[57] Outgunned by their rival, Pakistani forces retreated from its eastern province and surrendered on 16 December 1971. Formally liberated from Pakistani rule, East Bengalis claimed independence as a sovereign state and adopted the name Bangla Desh (Land of Bengal). India was the first country to recognize Bangladesh as a sovereign nation, doing so pre-emptively on 5 December before the war had ended. In the months that followed, other nations followed suit, including the Australian government that initiated and led worldwide recognition and advocated for Bangladesh membership of the United Nations.

Throughout 1971 Bangladeshis discovered that freedom would come at a high price. During the war nearly ten million Bangladeshi civilians sought sanctuary in neighbouring Indian states. As shown in Table 1.1, West Bengal attracted most Bangladeshi refugees, especially those able to stay with family and friends, which was indicative of long-standing ties between East and West Bengal. Many refugees also settled in the states of Tripura, Meghalaya, Assam, and Madhya Pradesh.

Because most international journalists were restricted to West Bengal by Indian authorities, the refugee crisis in India was often depicted as a West Bengal problem, a simplification that elides significant humanitarian problems faced by other states, especially in the mountainous and isolated areas of Assam, Meghalaya, and Tripura.

The refugee crisis captured international attention not just because of the scale of the exodus but also due to the speed with which refugees arrived in India. Within the first three weeks of the war, over 100,000 refugees had arrived in India. One week later, this figure increased tenfold to over one million people. In May, the rate of arrivals increased again, reaching three million refugees by 22 May. To put this statistic another way: each day in May 102,000 refugees entered India, or 71 refugees every minute.[58] The rapid growth continued through June, and by the month's end, there were six million refugees.[59] With the arrival of monsoon rains, conditions in the camps deteriorated

---

[57] D'Costa, *Nationbuilding, Gender and War Crimes in South Asia*, 97.
[58] Raghavan, *1971*, 74. Statistics originally sourced at the National Archives of India, New Delhi.
[59] Sonia Cordera, 'India's Response to the 1971 East Pakistan Crisis: Hidden and Open Reasons for Intervention', *Journal of Genocide Studies* 17, no. 1 (2015): 51–3.

Table 1.1 Refugee Population by State, Subdivided between Refugees in Camp and Out of Camp on 1 December 1971. Government of India statistics

State	Number of camps	Living in camps	Living with friends or family	Total
West Bengal	492	4,849,786	2,386,130	7,235,916
Tripura	276	834,098	547,551	1,381,649
Meghalaya	17	591,520	76,466	667,986
Assam	28	255,642	91,913	347,555
Bihar	8	36,732	---	36,732
Madhya Pradesh	3	219,298	---	219,298
Uttar Pradesh	1	10,169	---	10,169
Total	825	6,797,245	3,102,060	9,899,305

Source: UNHCR, *State of the World's Refugees 2000. Fifty Years of Humanitarian Action* (Geneva: UNHCR, 2000), 65.

quickly, triggering a cholera outbreak. Not only did the refugees require shelter, food and clothing, they now needed cholera vaccines en masse to avoid contracting this waterborne and potentially fatal disease. Indeed, the UNHCR estimated that 46,000 refugees died from cholera by September 1971.[60]

For the country of temporary resettlement, India, its government officials worried about the arrival of refugees from the beginning of the war. On 29 March 1971, India's UNHCR representative communicated with the high commissioner about the probability of a large influx of evacuees. On 23 April 1971, the Indian government requested UN aid to assist with the unfolding humanitarian crisis. Six days later, the UN secretary general announced the UNHCR would act as a focal point, coordinating UN, bilateral and most but not all NGO aid. Importantly, although the Indian government requested international aid, it insisted that it alone would be responsible for the distribution of relief. As we will see in Chapter 4, the Indian government prohibited the involvement of foreigners, especially international aid workers, and only permitted foreign journalists in state-sanctioned environments, thereby controlling the narrative to an international audience. The Indian government was particularly hostile towards the UN. Indian External Affairs Minister Swaran Singh lamented in June 1971, 'I am fully convinced about the total ineffectiveness of the UN organization ... whether they are political, social, or human rights. They talk and talk and do nothing.'[61] From the Indian perspective, since partition its eastern states had resettled over five million Hindu refugees and the Indian government was disinclined to welcome further migrants on a permanent basis.[62] For this reason, from the beginning of the war the Indian government insisted that East Pakistani arrivals were not refugees with a prospect of permanent resettlement but rather were temporary evacuees. To ensure

---

[60] UNHCR, *State of the World's Refugees*, 64.
[61] Raghaven, *1971*, 155; UNHCR, *State of the World's Refugees*, 60, 62.
[62] Raghaven, *1971*, 75.

that these evacuees could not vanish into the countryside, the Indian government established settlement camps by the East Pakistani border and provided inexpensive temporary shelter that could not be transformed into permanent homes.[63] Of the 825 refugee camps, only 17 were run by the central Indian government; the remainder were operated by state governments, including 486 in West Bengal and 273 camps in Tripura. The devolved nature of administering these camps added another layer of bureaucracy for international humanitarian organizations that had to liaise with the UN, the Indian government, Indian state governments and possibly also their home government.[64]

State of the field

Academic histories of the Bangladesh Liberation War are relatively few, especially in comparison to other contemporaneous wars with global impacts, such as the American wars in Vietnam, the Cambodian genocide and the Biafran war in Nigeria. Professional historians have neglected the examination of South Asian history after the 1947 partition, leading one prominent historian to describe the third quarter of the twentieth century as 'the least studied in the modern history of South Asia'.[65] This scholarly blind spot is partly due to practical reasons. Access to official archives remains difficult: (West) Pakistani archives on this episode are closed and East Pakistani archives were destroyed by retreating Pakistani armed forces before their surrender. Indian central and state government files are gradually being transferred to the National Archives or state archives, but these archival materials are 'fragmented, erratic, kept in dilapidated archival storage' across different cities or different locations within the same city. As historian Haimanti Roy notes, 'destroyed by white ants and water' is an all-too-common descriptor in archival catalogues in West Bengal.[66] Without access to textual material, historians are left with oral testimonies of protagonists and their written memoirs, an approach employed by the authors of the three most widely read texts on the Bangladesh Liberation War: Richard Sisson and Leo Rose's *War and Secession* (1990), Srinath Raghaven's *1971* (2013) and Gary Bass's *The Blood Telegram* (2013).[67] Interestingly, more recent publications, such as Zorawar Singh's *Power and Diplomacy* (2019), have challenged the arguments presented in these authoritative works by questioning the veracity of source material, such as oral history interviews and publicly available published memoirs, and noting the gap between public rhetoric

---

[63] Antara Datta, *Refugees and Borders in South Asia: The Great Exodus of 1971* (New York: Routledge, 2012), 65; Zorawar Daulet Singh, *Power and Diplomacy: India's Foreign Policies during the Cold War* (New Delhi: Oxford University Press, 2019), 286.
[64] Datta, *Refugees and Borders in South Asia*, 58.
[65] Rahman and van Schendel, '"I Am Not a Refugee"', 553.
[66] Roy, *Partitioned Lives*, 19.
[67] Richard Sisson and Leo E. Rose, *War and Secession: Pakistan, India, and the Creation of Bangladesh* (Berkeley: University of California Press, 1990); Raghaven, *1971*; Gary J. Bass, *The Blood Telegram: Nixon, Kissinger, and a Forgotten Genocide* (New York: Alfred A. Knopf, 2013).

and private intentions, as evidenced in recently declassified archives.[68] Alongside scholarly debates among diplomatic and political historians, social and cultural historians have made significant interventions in analysing the lived experiences of the Bangladeshi war, particularly sexual violence against women. Through lengthy field trips and with proficiency in local languages, historians such as Yasmin Saikia, Nayanika Mookherjee and Sarmila Bose have uncovered subaltern memories of war, subverting the established elite-oriented narratives.[69]

Furthermore, historians have examined the extent to which violence committed during the Bangladesh Liberation War amounted to genocide. The question of whether Pakistani armed forces singled out and deliberately sought to exterminate Bengalis as an ethnic group or Hindus as a religious group is more than an academic debating point. Should the actions of the Pakistani military be deemed as constituting genocide, then Bangladeshi survivors could seek justice through international war crimes tribunals.[70] The definition of genocide is well documented as a historically and politically contingent concept: although 'born from the Holocaust', scholars in recent decades have considered the extent to which the term applies to other human-induced atrocities, particularly outside of Europe.[71] The term 'genocide' was first applied to the Bangladesh Liberation War on 28 March 1971. Here, US Consul-General to Dhaka, Archer Blood, cabled a telegram to the US State Department with the subject heading 'Selective Genocide'. In this telegram, Blood stressed to his indifferent superiors:

1. Here in Dacca we are mute and horrified witnesses to a reign of terror by the Pak military. Evidence continues to mount that the MLA [martial law administration] authorities have a list of Awami League supporters whom they are systematically eliminating by seeking them out in their homes and shooting them down.

2. Among those marked for extinction in addition to the A.L. hierarchy are student leaders and university faculty. Also on list are bulk of MNAs-elect [members of national assembly] and number of MPAs [members of provincial assembly].

---

[68] Singh, *Power and Diplomacy*, 302–6.
[69] For example, Yasmin Saikia, *Women, War and the Making of Bangladesh: Remembering 1971* (Durham, NC: Duke University Press, 2011); 'Insāniyat for Peace'; 'War as History, Humanity in Violence'; 'Beyond the Archive of Silence: Narratives of Violence of the 1971 Liberation War of Bangladesh', *History Workshop Journal* 58, no. 1 (2004): 275–87. Mookherjee, *The Spectral Wound*; '1971: Pakistan's Past and Knowing What Not to Narrate'; Nayanika Mookherjee, 'Historicising the Birangona: Interrogating the Politics of Commemorating the Wartime Rape of 1971 in the Context of the 50th Anniversary of Bangladesh', *Strategic Analysis* 45 (2021): 588–97. Sarmila Bose, 'History on the Line: Fragments of Memories: Researching Violence in the 1971 Bangladesh War', *History Workshop Journal* 73 (2012): 285–95; *Dead Reckoning*; 'The Question of Genocide and the Quest for Justice in the 1971 War', *Journal of Genocide Research* 13 (2011): 393–419.
[70] Bose, 'The Question of Genocide', 395.
[71] Frank Jacob, 'Genocide and Mass Violence in Asia: An introduction', in *Genocide and Mass Violence in the Age of Extremes*, ed. Frank Jacob (Berlin: De Gruyter, 2019), 3. For historiographical and conceptual debates on genocide, see David Moshman, 'Conceptual Constraints on Thinking about Genocide', *Journal of Genocide Research* 3 (2001): 431–50; Dan Stone, ed. *The Historiography of Genocide* (London: Palgrave Macmillan, 2008); Adam Jones, *The Scourge of Genocide. Essays and Reflections* (New York: Routledge, 2013).

3. Moreover, with support of Pak military, non-Bengali Muslims [i.e., Biharis] are systemically attacking poor people's quarters and murdering Bengalis and Hindus.[72]

Within weeks, the American diplomat backtracked from his provocative allegation of genocide, commenting that 'the term genocide was not appropriate to characterize all killings of Muslim Bengalis. Atrocities were being committed on both sides.'[73] Despite the reappraisal of Blood, the idea that the Pakistani army and their collaborators committed genocide took hold, particularly in contemporary journalist reporting and subsequent nationalist histories in Bangladesh and India.[74] Indeed, Bose contends that the claim of '"genocide of three million" took on the status of a sacred mantra' for these countries.[75]

In academic circles, the question of genocide remains unresolved. For Wardatul Akram, Pakistani actions and intentions during the Bangladeshi war were 'genocidal in scope'. He cites the atrocities committed against Bengalis as an ethnic nation and against Bengali Hindus as a religious minority. Interestingly, Akram includes mass rapes as further evidence of 'acts of genocide' as this sexual violence aimed to destroy the victim group.[76] Donald Beachler concurs that 'genocide did occur' and reflects on why this atrocity has received scholarly 'neglect, even denial' in the West.[77] Beachler argues that 'all genocide victims are not remotely equal' because of the uneven distribution of academic, financial and political capital around the world. In other words, American academics choose to ignore the alleged genocide in Bangladesh because the US government was complicit in arming the Pakistani military. To devote academic resources to examining atrocities in Bangladesh will inevitably raise uncomfortable questions about American involvement in the war. Beachler contends that Western scholars prefer to concentrate on oppositional regimes that committed genocide, such as Pol Pot's Cambodia, the Ottoman Empire or Stalinist Russia, as doing so reinforces Western ideological and political assumptions of superiority.[78]

On the other hand, Sarmila Bose rejects allegations of genocide, explaining that the situation on the ground was far more complicated than simple narratives of Pakistani atrocities committed against Bengali civilians. Echoing the sentiments of Blood four decades prior, Bose insists that 'violence was apparently the weapon of choice for all sides'.[79] Criticized by some as a Pakistani apologist, the Kolkata-born American academic documents that many civilian deaths were due to hunger and disease rather than systemic extermination. She also notes that allegations of Pakistani

---

[72] Archer Blood, *The Cruel Birth of Bangladesh: Memoirs of an American Diplomat* (Dhaka: University Press Limited, 2002), 213.
[73] Ibid., 216.
[74] A. Dirk Moses, 'The United Nations, Humanitarianism and Human Rights: War Crimes/Genocide Trials for Pakistani Soldiers in 1971', in *Human Rights in the Twentieth Century*, ed. Stefan-Ludwig Hoffman (New York: Cambridge University Press 2011), 261.
[75] Bose, 'The Question of Genocide and the Quest for Justice in the 1971 War', 394.
[76] Akram, 'Atrocities against Humanity during the Liberation War in Bangladesh', 544.
[77] Beachler, 'The Politics of Genocide Scholarship', 467–8.
[78] Ibid., 469–71.
[79] Bose, 'History on the Line', 290.

genocide against Bengalis conceal Bengali atrocities against Biharis and against each other.[80] Perhaps in her greatest contribution to the scholarly debate, Bose reminds us, 'ultimately, neither the numbers nor the labels matter', notwithstanding Bangladeshi claims to international justice. It is easy to become lost in debates about what types of violence constitute genocide and disagreements over the death toll. What is undeniable is that the Bangladesh Liberation War was a complex struggle for power among multiple groups. Collectively, the war had a devastating human toll that left a legacy of violence and inter-ethnic antipathy. Debates about numbers and terminology can sanitize narratives, distancing the reader from the horrors of civil war. In her interviews with victims and perpetrators, Yasmin Saikia uncovers how urban, guerrilla warfare leads to the dehumanization of people in which long-accepted boundaries of mutual human respect break down. Through a brutalization of the mind, individuals become capable of gruesome acts, such as the decapitation and dismemberment of enemy combatants.[81] Thus, Bose and Saikia draw our attention to the seemingly incomprehensible and indiscriminate violence that became part of everyday life in Bangladesh during 1971.

International actors

The Bangladesh Liberation War influenced, and was impacted by, worldwide trends and ideological fault lines. Global factors that affected the war included Cold War allegiances, decolonization, ethnic nationalism, transnational humanitarianism and nascent globalization, among others. Given the international dimension of this conflict, scholars have considered how states and citizens responded to the war and resulting refugee crisis. Historians have focused especially on the actions and rhetoric of the Indian government. As previously stated, Indian officials provided a haven for the Awami League leadership and recognized it as the legitimate Bangladesh government in exile on 13 April 1971. Around the same time, American diplomats reported that 'Indians are providing small arms and communications equipment' to the Mukti Bahini. Within a few weeks, British diplomats recorded that Indian munition supplies to the freedom fighters were 'substantial'. Additionally, training camps were established by the Bangladeshi border by mid-May.[82] Publicly, Indian Prime Minister Indira Gandhi escalated her rhetoric towards Pakistan in a speech on 24 May. In the address, Gandhi equated the arrival of millions of refugees as threatening the peace and security of India. Accordingly, Gandhi asserted that India would be justified 'to take all measures as may be necessary to ensure our own security'.[83] At this stage, then, Gandhi was preparing her domestic constituents and international observers for an Indian military response to the refugee crisis.

---

[80] Bose, 'The Question of Genocide and the Quest for Justice in the 1971 War', 398.
[81] Saikia, 'War as History, Humanity in Violence', 152–4.
[82] Butt, *Secession and Security*, 59–60.
[83] Cited in Raghaven, *1971*, 78.

Yet the Indian government had to wait months until conditions were suited to a successful Indian invasion. Monsoonal rains prevented Indian intervention from May to September, a time in which low-lying areas throughout Bangladesh were waterlogged. During this time Indian armed forces rectified concerns that they would be outgunned by Pakistan in an open conflict and redirected matériel to protect its western flank.[84] Diplomatically, the Indian government also sought to harness international support to offset any threat posed by the United States and China, Pakistan's two closest allies. On 9 August 1971, India signed a treaty of 'Peace, Friendship and Cooperation' with the Soviet Union. This treaty, some two years in the making, took on a greater sense of urgency and relevance, particularly Article IX that acted as a mutual defence pact.[85] Recently declassified Indian government files reveal that Indian officials chose to exercise military restraint in these early months of the conflict for self-serving political reasons, too. Initially, conservatives within the Indian Ministry for External Affairs wanted the Awami League in power but did not support a secessionist movement. Their reasoning was that an independent Bangladesh may embolden pro-China Naxalites, a radical Maoist movement that had wreaked havoc in West Bengal. The Indian government only intervened militarily once it became clear that independence for Bangladesh was the only viable solution to the humanitarian crisis and it sought to make strategic geopolitical gains in the process.[86]

Alongside India, the US government played an important, if covert, role in the war by providing military and political support to the Pakistani regime. The close relationship between the United States and Pakistani governments was long-standing. In 1954, Pakistan joined the SEATO defence pact, an American-led treaty designed to limit the spread of communism in Asia. As Pakistan fell within America's sphere of influence, it also benefitted from American aid and military supplies throughout the Cold War. To be sure, after the 1965 Indo-Pakistani war the Johnson Administration imposed an arms embargo on both countries. However, in practice the American arms embargo only applied to India, not Pakistan. Under President Johnson, arms were covertly sold to Pakistan, albeit in small numbers, through third parties. When Richard Nixon came to power, the embargo was relaxed even further for Pakistan. In October 1970, Pakistan procured US$50 million worth of replacement aircraft and three hundred armed personnel carriers, all at a time when selling military equipment to Pakistan was still illegal under US law.[87] At the time of *Operation Searchlight*, the American influence on the Pakistani military was apparent. West Pakistani troops were shuttled to East Pakistan on American C-130 transport planes, bombs were dropped from American F-86 sabres, US made Jeeps bore American .50 calibre machine guns and Pakistani forces patrolled the streets of Dhaka in American M-24 tanks.[88] The

---

[84] Singh, *Power and Diplomacy*, 284.
[85] Raghaven, *1971*, 108–10; Singh, *Power and Diplomacy*, 296.
[86] Sonia Cordera, 'India's Response to the 1971 East Pakistan Crisis: Hidden and Open Reasons for Intervention', *Journal of Genocide Research* 17 (2015): 45; Singh, *Power and Diplomacy*, 271. For a history of the Naxalite movement, see Dipak K. Gupta, 'The Naxalites and the Maoist Movement in India: Birth, Demise and Reincarnation', *Democracy and Security* 3 (2007): 157–88.
[87] Raghaven, *1971*, 84; Bass, *The Blood Telegram*, 12.
[88] Ibid., 68.

complicity of the American government in Pakistani atrocities was not lost on their diplomats. American ambassador to India, Ken Keating, wrote in a cable to the State Department on 3 April 1971:

> Am deeply shocked at massacre by Pakistani military in East Pakistan, appalled at possibility these atrocities are being committed with American equipment, and greatly concerned at United States vulnerability to damaging allegations of association with reign of military terror.[89]

In the United States, there was a clear divide between State Department advice and the belligerence of the Nixon Administration, especially the National Security Advisor Henry Kissinger. In June 1971, the Nixon White House provided further supplies of military equipment for Pakistan, all at a time when Bengali refugees in India were starving and threatened with a cholera outbreak.[90] The close allegiance between the American and Pakistani governments can be explained by two reasons. First, in 1971 the Nixon Administration was in the process of establishing diplomatic relations with Mao's China and the Pakistani government served as a crucial conduit between the two states. The Nixon Administration was loath to upset Pakistani officials should it jeopardize the possibility of rapprochement with the PRC. Second, Nixon and Kissinger exhibited a profound hatred of India and Indians. In private, recorded conversations, Kissinger described Indians as 'such bastards' while Nixon suggested that all Indians 'really need is a mass famine'.[91]

Although the Indian and American governments were most involved, albeit supporting competing sides, other nations also played a part in this conflict. Most notably, the UK, the former imperial power of South Asia, adopted a contradictory stance. At the government level, official rhetoric remained committed to neutrality, insisting that the conflict was a civil war and an internal matter for Pakistan alone. On 22 April 1971, British Foreign Secretary Sir Alec Douglas-Home informed the cabinet that 'hideous atrocities were being committed on both sides', information that was used to justify international non-intervention.[92] The British government was reluctant to meddle in the affairs of its former colony because it was preoccupied with its accession into the European Economic Community (EEC) in 1973 and had since 1968 gradually reduced its military presence 'east of Suez'.[93] However, the British government increased aid for refugees in response to public pressure. This policy change was arguably caused by an activist print news media that shaped community attitudes and expectations of government.[94] On 13 June 1971, the *Sunday Times* published a first-hand account of Pakistani atrocities in East Pakistan by Pakistani journalist Anthony Mascarenhas.

---

[89] Blood, *The Cruel Birth of Bangladesh*, 215.
[90] Raghaven, *1971*, 102.
[91] Bass, *The Blood Telegram*, xv, 144.
[92] Angela Debnath, 'British Perceptions of the East Pakistan Crisis 1971: "Hideous Atrocities on Both Sides"', *Journal of Genocide Research* 13, no. 4 (2011): 421, 429; O'Sullivan, *The NGO Moment*, 46.
[93] Simon C. Smith, 'Coming Down on the Winning Side: Britain on the South Asia Crisis, 1971', *Contemporary British History* 24, no. 4 (2010): 451–70.
[94] O'Sullivan, *The NGO Moment*, 48.

Under the headline 'Genocide', Mascarenhas reported on his state-sanctioned tour of East Pakistan where he was told by top officers 'they were seeking a final solution'. This provocative news report was syndicated widely, including in Australia, and triggered further reporting on Bangladesh that was sympathetic to their liberation struggle and the plight of refugees in India.[95] British press coverage of Pakistani atrocities therefore posed a direct challenge to the neutral position of the British government. By the year's end, the British government had contributed £14.75 million to the UNHCR, and British humanitarian NGOs raised a further £1 million.[96] Alongside mainstream British demands for increased government aid, eleven radicals launched Operation Omega, a high-profile campaign involving illegal crossings into Bangladesh to distribute food and clothes. Blurring the line between humanitarianism and activism, the Omega group challenged the primacy of the state in established humanitarian practices by engaging in publicity stunts, a strategy similarly employed by Greenpeace, which was established at this time.[97]

British government and citizen aid only tells part of the story, however. At the time Britain was home to a sizeable and established South Asian diaspora. According to Ceri Peach, in 1971 there were 22,000 Bangladeshis, 119,000 Pakistanis and 375,000 Indians permanently settled in the UK.[98] Conversely, there were just 6,182 Pakistanis (East and West) in the United States and 1,658 Pakistanis in Australia, a consequence of their racially restrictive immigration policies.[99] Many of these migrants in Britain maintained close ties with the homeland and participated in diasporic political activism. Throughout 1971 migrants from Bangladesh and Pakistan in Britain staged opposing public demonstrations, some of which became violent. These protests illustrate a gap between elite efforts to depoliticize the crisis and local activists who inflamed pre-existing animosities across migrant communities.[100]

Many states avoided siding with the Bangladesh independence movement for fear that doing so would animate secessionists within their own borders. Here, Canada is a case in point. In the wake of the rising (and increasingly militant) Front de libération du Québec, the Canadian government opposed the separatist movement in Pakistan. Although the Canadian government and Canadian citizens provided significant humanitarian aid for the refugees in India, this country was also responsible for facilitating the conditions that caused the refugee exodus in the first place.[101] For years, the Canadian government was the second largest donor of aid and military

---

[95] Anonymous, 'Policy of Genocide', *Canberra Times*, 14 June 1971, 5; Debnath, 'British Perceptions of the East Pakistan Crisis 1971', 434–5.
[96] Raghaven, *1971*, 140; Debnath, 'British Perceptions of the East Pakistan Crisis 1971', 439.
[97] Florian Hannig, 'Negotiating Humanitarianism and Politics: Operation Omega's Border-Breaching Missions During the East Pakistan Crisis of 1971', in *Dilemmas of Humanitarian Aid in the Twentieth Century*, ed. Johannes Paulmann (Oxford: Oxford University Press, 2016), 330, 343.
[98] Jed Fazakarley, 'Multiculturalism's Categories and Transnational Ties: The Bangladeshi Campaign for Independence in Britain, 1971', *Immigrants and Minorities* 34 (2016): 53; Ceri Peach 'Contrasting Patterns of Indian, Pakistani and Bangladeshi Settlement in Britain', *Migracijske teme* 13 (1997): 16.
[99] Campbell Gibson and Kay Jung, *Historical Census Statistics on the Foreign-Born Population of the United States, 1850 to 2000* (Washington, DC: US Census Bureau, 2006), 28; Commonwealth of Australia, *Bulletin 4. Birthplace. Part 9. Australia* (Sydney: Ambassador Press, 1973), 4.
[100] Fazakarley, 'Multiculturalism's Categories and Transnational Ties', 55.
[101] O'Sullivan, *The NGO Moment*, 50.

equipment to the Pakistani government after the United States. Notwithstanding the outpouring of Canadian compassion at the individual level, the actions of consecutive Canadian governments led Richard Pilkington to conclude that Ottawa's policy had 'an unfortunate absence of principle and an uncomfortable air of appeasement'.[102] Similarly, in Josip Tito's Yugoslavia, fears of stirring secessionist sentiment within the federation precluded the non-aligned nation from intervening, even after a direct request was made by Indira Gandhi to the marshal on 4 September 1971.[103] Furthermore, during the war Bangladeshis discovered they had few friends in the Arab world. Arab leaders worried about separatism in their own lands, particularly given the heterogeneous nature of their populations. Moreover, Arab leaders were anxious about the role of Hindus in Bangladesh and creeping secularization. When Israel announced it supported Bangladesh on 2 July 1971, the Arab world in unison turned against Bangladesh, if only to oppose Israel. Arab countries also aided Pakistan. Saudi Arabia provided weapons and cash, and funnelled embargoed US supplies to Pakistan, as did Libya.[104]

For international NGOs, the Bangladesh Liberation War was transformative and contributed to the globalization of compassion. In *The NGO Moment*, Kevin O'Sullivan demonstrates how several humanitarian NGOs in Canada, the UK and Ireland who worked in the refugee camps employed modernist solutions to narrowly defined medical problems, and in doing so, decontextualized and depoliticized the refugee crisis. The erasure of local social, political and cultural factors meant that the humanitarian practices first utilized in Bangladesh could then be applied in any conflict zone in the years to come.[105] O'Sullivan astutely identifies this universalizing force as critical to understanding how humanitarianism became truly global in the final decades of the twentieth century. The ways that professional, technical and volunteer NGO staff redefined aid to satisfy government, intergovernment and donor interests help explain the rapid rise of this sector.[106] This book builds on the research of O'Sullivan and others by exploring how citizens – particularly those outside the NGO sector – reacted to this ideological convergence across the foreign aid industry.

Australia–India relations

Initially, the official position of the Australian government echoed the impartiality expressed elsewhere in the world. Behind the scenes, however, the Australian government demonstrated itself to be a close ally of India and, by extension, Bangladesh. The reasons why the Australian government sought an uncharacteristically independent path can be explained by historical, cultural,

---

[102] Richard Pilkington, 'In the National Interest? Canada and the East Pakistan Crisis of 1971', *Journal of Genocide Research* 13, no. 4 (2011): 451.
[103] Raghaven, *1971*, 179, 242.
[104] Redowanul Karim, 'The Role of the Arab World in the Liberation War of Bangladesh', *International Journal of Innovative Science and Research Technology* 4 (2019): 331–41.
[105] O'Sullivan, *The NGO Moment*, 35, 41–7.
[106] Ibid., 111–23.

geographic and political reasons. From the mid-nineteenth century, Australian–Indian relations were characterized by affection and compassion. During the 1876–8 Indian famine, Australian colonies provided £52,000 of citizen-funded humanitarian aid to victims. In comparison, a contemporaneous Chinese relief drive raised just £3,600 and a Persian aid committee raised £1,087. The fact that the Australian famine relief committee raised significantly higher funds for Indian victims compared with competing causes was due to Australians' sense of loyalty to the British imperial order of which Indians were a part.[107] From the 1880s, Australia sent hundreds of missionaries to British India who would later be joined by academics, cultural travellers and soldiers who served alongside Indians in both world wars.[108] In the early to mid-twentieth century, prominent Australians established Australia–India associations that promoted better understandings of India, organized cultural events and promoted a sympathetic approach to India's struggle against colonial rule in the Australian press. When the Bengal famine struck in 1943–4, these associations were prepared to raise funds and send wheat to India. These associations included an unlikely coalition of academics, politicians, Christians, socialites and communists.[109] In the post-1945 period, Australian countercultural networks such as the Theosophical Society assisted individuals to travel to, read about and engage with India in a way that challenged the imperial consensus.[110] The influence of people-to-people connections and civil society organizations cannot be overstated, even if their impacts are difficult to measure.

Two imperial decisions in 1943 fundamentally altered Australian–Indian relations. First, dominion governments established high commissions across the empire. Previously, direct dominion-to-dominion representation was restricted to non-diplomatic trade commissioners who lacked customary diplomatic immunities and privileges.[111] The arrival of Australian and Indian high commissions in their respective countries created a truly bilateral relationship between the nations. With direct diplomatic channels now in place, Britain was no longer a central node in intra-imperial communications. Over the following decades, a series of Australian diplomats stationed in India became 'absorbed' and deeply engaged with the country, always seeking deeper understandings of India's complexity, and relaying this knowledge to their superiors in Canberra.[112] Given the close affinity between India and Australian diplomats, some of whom became senior officials within the Australian Department

---

[107] Christina Twomey and Andrew J. May, 'Australian Responses to the Indian Famine, 1876–78: Sympathy, Photography and the British Empire', *Australian Historical Studies* 43 (2012): 250.

[108] Meg Gurry, *India and Australia: Mapping the Journey* (Melbourne: Melbourne University Press, 2015), 3; Margaret Allen, ' "White Already to Harvest". South Australian Women Missionaries in India', *Feminist Review* 65 (2000). 92–107; Kama Maclean, *British India, White Australia: Overseas Indians, Intercolonial Relations and the Empire* (Sydney: UNSW Press, 2020), 239.

[109] Maclean, *British India, White Australia*, 19–20, 207–8.

[110] Ibid., 239.

[111] Lorna Lloyd and Alan James. 'The External Representation of the Dominions, 1919–1948: Its Role in the Unravelling of the British Empire', *The British Year Book of International Law* 67 (1997): 492; Lorna Lloyd, ' "What's in a Name?" The Curious Tale of the Office of High Commissioner', *Diplomacy & Statecraft* 11 (2000): 56.

[112] Gurry, *India and Australia*, 9.

of External Affairs, it is little wonder that India was the leading recipient of Australian aid from 1951 to 1969.[113]

Second, in December 1943 Britain's Secretary of State for India, Leo Amery, appointed Australian Richard Casey as governor of Bengal, a position he served from January 1944 to February 1946. On the surface, the appointment of Casey to the governorship was a safe choice: despite his colonial roots, Casey was accepted into the British establishment by virtue of his personal wealth, his Cambridge education and his decorated military service. Yet Casey's tenure as governor at the challenging time of famine and Japanese occupation of nearby Burma led him to question his previous support of imperialism. In a letter to Viceroy Wavell, Casey reflected that after 150 years of rule, in Bengal at least 'we can point to no achievement'.[114] Although Casey's appointment to governor was initially criticized widely in India, he endeared himself to his constituents, particularly nationalist leaders. Casey remained detached from the British establishment, symbolized by his refusal to accept a peerage or knighthood prior to his appointment and his insistence that, as an Australian, he 'had no imperial past' and was not dependent on the continuance of empire for employment.[115] Most notably, from late 1945 to early 1946 Casey held a series of meetings with Mohandas Gandhi at a critical time in negotiations over Indian decolonization. A close, respectful relationship developed between the governor and the mahatma, an association that was recognized by future prime minister Jawaharlal Nehru. Alongside his diplomatic manoeuvres in Bengal, Casey endeavoured to educate the Australian public on India through the Australian press. During his governorship, Casey was extensively interviewed by the press and penned articles himself that provided detailed explanations about Indian politics.[116] Casey would later serve as Australia's Minister for External Affairs from 1951 to 1960. As Australia's leading diplomat, Casey maintained a special interest in India's economic development and, like Nehru, 'was not an admirer of all things American'.[117] As he had done with Gandhi, Casey maintained close relationship with Nehru, exchanging detailed letters in the lead up to the Asian-African Bandung conference in 1955, for example.[118] Even in retirement, Casey offered counsel to Australian high commissioners stationed in India and Bangladesh.[119]

Indian attitudes towards Australia, however, were at best lukewarm initially. Indians rightly took offense to the maintenance of Australia's racially exclusionary white Australia immigration policy. The white Australia policy was official legislation

---

[113] Teesta Prakash, 'Strategic Reassessments: Aid and Bureaucracy in Australia-India Relations 1951–70', *Australian Journal of Politics and History* 67 (2021): 2.
[114] Cited in Kama Maclean, 'A Colonial in the Colonies: Governor Casey, Mahatma Gandhi and the Endgame of Empire', *Journal of Colonialism and Colonial History* 19 (2018): 4.
[115] Ibid., 24.
[116] Maclean, *British India, White Australia*, 197.
[117] Cited in Prakash, 'Strategic Reassessments', 8.
[118] India-Australia: 1955 – Casey-Nehru letters, M3401/55, National Archives of Australia (henceforth NAA).
[119] See Casey's diary entries 12 April 1969, 9 September, 22 December 1971 in 'R. G. C. 1969, 1970, 1971', no. 29 and 5 February 1974, 8 April 1974 in 'R. G. C. 1972, 1973, 1974, 1975 and to 17 June 1976', no. 30 in Box 31a, R. G. Casey (series 4), Casey Family papers, National Library of Australia (henceforth NLA); Philip Flood, *Dancing with Warriors: A Diplomatic Memoir* (Melbourne: Australian Scholarly, 2011), 79.

until 1973, although its application in practice had been curtailed since 1966. Still, the existence of an anti-Asian immigration law in Australia created barriers to formal and people-to-people relationships throughout the twentieth century.[120] As an independent republic, Indian foreign policy concerns rarely extended to the antipodes. If Indian officials did contemplate Australia, their perspectives were usually unfavourable. As two-time Australian high commissioner to India Walter Crocker (1952–5; 1958–62) commented, Indians viewed Australia as a 'backwater'. Casey informed Australia Prime Minister Robert Menzies that Australia was seen as 'an American satellite'.[121] When Australian armed forces joined the American war in Vietnam in 1965 – a conflict that India fiercely opposed – this military intervention further distinguished Australian and Indian foreign policies in Asia. Yet Australian involvement in Vietnam was not the fatal blow to Australia–India relations one may have expected. When Prime Minister Indira Gandhi visited Australia in 1968, her private discussions with the Australian cabinet focused heavily on Vietnam. Despite differing approaches to international affairs, the Australian and Indian prime ministers found common ground in desiring political stability in Asia, whether governments were communist or otherwise.[122] Publicly, Gandhi declared she wished to see Australia become a 'bridge' between the developing countries of Asia on one side and the Pacific and affluent New World on the other.[123]

The 1960s witnessed shifting global allegiances that reconfigured Australian–Indian relations. James Plimsoll, Australian high commissioner to India (1962–5) and later secretary of the Department of External Affairs (1965–70), interpreted India's war with China in 1962 as a turning point. At this time, while Indian officials viewed the United States and UK as pro-Pakistan, Prime Minister Nehru recognized Australian military aid to the Indian cause. The 1965 Indo-Pakistani war only exacerbated Indian perceptions of their allies and enemies. As previously stated, the UK government ceased defence aid to India and the US government embargoed future military supplies to both India and Pakistan, although it continued to supply Pakistan covertly. Indian officials perceived with bitterness the British and American policy to 'cut [India] off in our hour of need'. Meanwhile, Australian non-intervention escaped India's wrath.[124] Furthermore, Australian officials worried about the increasingly close relationship between the Pakistani and Chinese governments, and resented Pakistani ingratitude towards Australian aid.[125] If the Australian government had to choose between India and Pakistan, long-serving Australian high commissioner to India Arthur Tange made the calculation clear:

---

[120] Maclean, *British India, White Australia*, 4–6.
[121] Gurry, *India and Australia*, 74–7; Andrea Benvenuti, 'Difficult Partners: Indo-Australian Relations at the Height of the Cold War, 1949–64', *Australian Journal of Politics and History* 57 (2011): 67.
[122] 'Discussions between Prime Minister of India (Mrs. Indira Gandhi) and Prime Minister of Australia (Mr. Gorton) and other Cabinet Ministers on 22nd May 1968', NAA: M3401/55.
[123] David Goldworthy, *Facing North: A Century of Australian Engagement with Asia* (Melbourne: Melbourne University Press, 2001), 313.
[124] Arthur Tange, Australian High Commission, New Delhi. Despatch No. 3/70. 'What Australia can expect from India', 11, 23 January 1970. NAA: M3401/55; Gurry, *India and Australia*, 89.
[125] Ibid., 86–9.

One of Australia's longest lasting misconceptions is that we must treat India and Pakistan identically: visit for visit, dollar for dollar, concession for concession. This policy lacks rationality ... The countries are different. One is substantially bigger than the other – in most ways. One is a friend of China and one is not. One is a parliamentary democracy and one is not. One does better with agriculture (and maybe foreign capital) than the other.[126]

In this comparison, Australian diplomats decided that it was in their country's best interest to side with India, which put it at odds with its Cold War allies. The Indian government, too, found itself increasingly aligned with Australian interests if only because it was being marginalized by other countries. In the words of Patrick Shaw, Tange successor, 'India has remarkably few friends and it values its friendship with Australia.' Shaw reflected, 'it is strange perhaps, but true, that Australia occupies quite a favoured position in the Indian government's political thinking'. Shaw explained India's stance towards Australia as a reaction against the 'great imperialist powers' of the United States and UK, memories of violent Japanese expansion through southeast Asia, the fact that Australia was too small to pose a threat to India and Australia's established record of goodwill through economic development aid and humanitarian relief.[127]

By the early 1970s, the Australian government had made a conscious decision to pivot towards India in an effort to secure regional stability. At the time, Australian political and military officials were war-weary after fighting conflicts in Korea (1950–3), Malaysia–Indonesia (1962–5) and Vietnam (1962–73), with underwhelming results. Australian officials were increasingly willing to hedge their bets on a partnership with India to counter the perceived threat of an expansionistic communist China. In his final despatch from New Delhi in 1970, Tange listed the reasons why 'India is important to Australia'. These included India's strategic location on the Indian Ocean, which geographically connects the two countries, India's immense population, its industrial capacity (second only to Australia in the Indian basin) and its commitment to moderate politics despite long-running revolutionary skirmishes. Tange concluded emphatically, 'I cannot think of another country which has a greater national interest than has Australia in the productive employment in India itself of the growing mass of frustrated and politically awakened people.' Revealingly, Tange declared that Australia should ally with India because it was in the best interests of both countries to do so. Tange made clear he was not motivated by morality or ethical compulsions, commenting, 'My argument does not rely upon either Christian charity or United Nations Resolutions.'[128] Thus, when millions of Bangladeshi refugees began arriving in India, the Australian government viewed the unfolding crisis through the prism of the need to maintain stability and social order rather than purely humanitarian

---

[126] Tange, 'What Australia Can Expect from India', 5.
[127] Patrick Shaw, Australian High Commission, New Delhi. Letter to K. C. O. Shann, Deputy Secretary, Department of Foreign Affairs, 28 September 1971, 6–7. 'Relations with India', NAA: A1838/16/10/1 Part 19. Note that from November 1970 the Australian Department of External Affairs was renamed the Department of Foreign Affairs.
[128] Tange, 'What Australia Can Expect from India', 3.

concerns. These geopolitical considerations put Australia in an unusual position, unlike other developed nations that were preoccupied with Cold War allegiances, fears about awakening internal secessionist movements or economic factors, such as the UK's accession to the EEC.

Throughout the Bangladesh Liberation War, the official position of the Australian government was to maintain neutrality to avoid an escalation in the conflict. While Australian words were conciliatory, their deeds revealed where their true allegiances lay. The Australian government was one of the first Western governments to denounce Pakistani atrocities.[129] On 6 April 1971, Foreign Minister Leslie Bury (22 March to 2 August 1971) conveyed to the Australian parliament 'our concern at the reported scale of the loss of life and suffering'. Acknowledging that he could only speak 'in the most general terms' 'until a sufficient picture of the facts has been authoritatively established', the foreign minister nevertheless blamed the military for 'bloodshed and destruction'.[130] These restrained comments were in marked contrast to the position of the British government, which insisted that atrocities were being committed by both sides. During a diplomatic visit from West Bengali politician Siddhartha Shankar Ray in June, Bury went further, declaring to the Indian that he 'hoped the Awami League could set up government' in an independent Bangladesh. In making these private comments, Bury went against conventional protocol that endorsed the inviolability of territorial borders of nation states. As early as June, Indian government records show Australian officials as 'sympathetic' to their concerns, especially on the resettlement of refugees. Furthermore, the Australian government acknowledged there could only be a military rather than political solution to the conflict but urged the Indian government to practice restraint to avoid a drastic escalation.[131] As the war dragged on, the Australian government position remained steadfast. When the Indian government signed its provocative Treaty of Peace, Friendship and Cooperation with the Soviet Union in August 1971, the Australian government was one of the few countries to be sympathetic to Indian needs. Indeed, Australian diplomats sought a friendship treaty with India at this time, only to be thwarted by risk-averse bureaucrats in Canberra.[132] When Bangladesh was liberated from Pakistani rule, the Australian government was the first Western country to recognize the new state and lobbied other countries to do the same and by supporting the application of Bangladesh to join the UN.[133] Australian Foreign Minister Nigel Bowen (2 August 1971–5 December 1972) was one of the first foreign dignitaries to visit independent Bangladesh (as well as India) in May 1972. When Australian Prime Minister Gough Whitlam visited Bangladesh in January 1975,

---

[129] Flood, *Dancing with Warriors*, 79.
[130] Leslie Bury, 'International Affairs, ministerial statement', 6 April 1971, Australian House of Representatives.
[131] 'Note on visit to Australia by Ray', 25 June 1971, Subject File 168, P. N. Haskar Papers (III instalment), Nehru Memorial Museum and Library; record of conversation between S. S. Ray and L. H. E. Bury, 11 June 1971, 20-India-1-3-Pak Vol. 11 RG 25, 8914 Library and Archives, Ottawa, cited in Raghaven, *1971*, 171.
[132] Gurry, *India and Australia*, 92–4.
[133] NAA: A1838, 1506/22 PART1; NAA: A1838, 1500/2/82/2 PART1. For a firsthand account from a junior Australian diplomat in New Delhi, see Ric Smith, *India, the United States, Australia and the Difficult Birth of Bangladesh* (Canberra: Australian Institute of International Affairs, 2019).

father of the nation Mujibur Rahman said, 'we count Australia as one of our best friends'.[134] The affection was mutual.

The 1971 Bangladesh Liberation War presented Australians and their government with a unique opportunity to imagine an Asia that respected human rights, parliamentary democracy and an inclusive form of nationalism. For a moment, the Australian government adopted an independent and activist policy, seeking to shore up international support for a liberated Bangladesh. Arguably, this activist stance was only possible because it occurred when Australian diplomats and foreign ministers had influence over the ineffectual prime minister, William McMahon (1971–2). But government policy and political rhetoric is only one side of the coin; the flip side is the effects of civil society. In this book I show that the groundswell of popular support for Bangladeshi refugees in India was the result of significant social change, including the popularization of social movements, the empowerment of previously marginalized groups, the democratization of overseas travel and a reorientation towards fostering new regional connections over old imperial-based ones.[135]

Chapter structure

Rather than taking the humanitarian NGO as a monolith, this book is careful to examine specific aid agencies at various levels of scale. We begin with the national federations, Austcare and the Australian Council for Overseas Aid, in Chapter 3, bodies that ostensibly acted as coordinating agencies but in practice operated in self-serving ways to consolidate power and access to funds. Chapter 4 turns to the largest humanitarian organization, the Red Cross movement. As the oldest, and arguably most esteemed, humanitarian NGO, the Red Cross enjoyed privileged access to power brokers and, in the case of the Australian Red Cross Society, direct funding from the Australian government. But in 1971, the Red Cross movement faced challenges and a loss of credibility. In a moment of weakness, this organization revealed itself to be vulnerable, struggling to maintain relevance in an overcrowded market and lacked the pizzazz of newer, more nimble NGOs. Chapter 5 examines Christian aid efforts, both at the level of organized religion and the actions of individuals. This chapter demonstrates that despite common claims of secularization in the Western world during the 1960s, citizen giving was still motivated by Christian notions of charity. Chapters 6 and 7 pivot towards grassroots NGOs and individual aid, respectively. In Chapter 6, we examine the evolution of two international NGO movements, Oxfam and the Freedom from Hunger Campaign. In Australia, these organizations were driven by volunteers and a handful of paid staff, who were inspired by calls for social justice and a redistribution of wealth. Chapter 7 studies citizen-driven humanitarianism at its logical extreme: that of the lone humanitarian. It explores the motivations and actions of Melbourne trained chemist and housewife Moira Dynon, a Catholic internationalist. It also examines the

---

[134] Flood, *Dancing with Warriors*, 92.
[135] David Thackeray, *Forging a British World of Trade: Culture, Ethnicity and Market in the Empire-Commonwealth* (Oxford: Oxford University Press, 2019), 15.

actions of individuals who participated in life-threatening hunger strikes and analyses over 2,500 citizen letters of protest to Australian prime minister-in-waiting, Gough Whitlam. But first, the next chapter provides an outline of the origins and histories of humanitarianism, exploring how acts of charity evolved from a local practice to one global in scale.

2

The rise of citizen-driven humanitarianism

In the contemporary world, charity is big business. In 2020, the Australian Charities and Not-for-profits Commission (ACNC) reported over 49,165 registered charities in Australia, or one charity for every 500 Australians.[1] Australian charities and not-for-profits received A$12.7 billion in direct donations from citizens who typically financially supported smaller charities over government-backed large NGOs.[2] Donations in 2020 increased by 8 per cent despite the economic uncertainty surrounding extended Covid-19 lockdowns throughout the country. The size and continued growth of the Australian NGO sector is remarkable, but like many countries, it has its roots in the nineteenth century. Figure 2.1 charts the registration of new Australian charities from the late nineteenth century through to the 1990s.

The left axis illustrates numerical increases for all charities (dark line); the right axis shows growth for charities that operated internationally – that is, overseas aid agencies (pale line). Despite the differing scales on both vertical axes, the trendline is approximately the same: steady growth during the early twentieth century and then sudden, exponential growth after the 1940s. The Australian experience is not unique. The number of registered charities in the UK grew from 56,000 in 1948 to over 80,000 by 1971; at the UN, its Economic and Social Council (ECOSOC) recognized forty-one NGOs with consultative status in 1948.[3] By 1971, this figure had risen to over five hundred. Similar trends were evident in the United States.[4] To put the dominance of NGOs in the humanitarian sector into context, by the early twenty-first century, international NGOs funded over 50 per cent of all foreign aid expenditures.[5] How

---

[1] Australian Charities and Not-for-profits Commission (ACNC), *Australian Charities Report, 8th Edition*, 7 June 2022, 4, accessed 12 May 2023, https://www.acnc.gov.au/tools/reports/australian-charities-report-8th-edition.
[2] Ibid., 3.
[3] UK data sourced from Matthew Hilton, 'Commentary: Politics Is Ordinary: Non-Governmental Organizations and Political Participation in Contemporary Britain', *Twentieth Century Britain* 22 (2011): 238; UN data sourced from Marlou Schrover, Teuntje Vosters and Irial Glynn, 'NGOs and West European Migration Governance (1860s until Present): Introduction to a Special Issue', *Journal of Migration History* 5 (2019): 209.
[4] Michael Barnett and Janice Gross Stein, *Sacred Aid. Faith and Humanitarianism* (New York: Oxford University Press, 2012), 5; David P. King, *God's Internationalists: World Vision and the Age of Evangelical Humanitarianism* (Philadelphia: University of Pennsylvania Press, 2019), introduction.
[5] Michael Barnett, *Empire of Humanity: A History of Humanitarianism* (Ithaca, NY: Cornell University Press, 2011), 7.

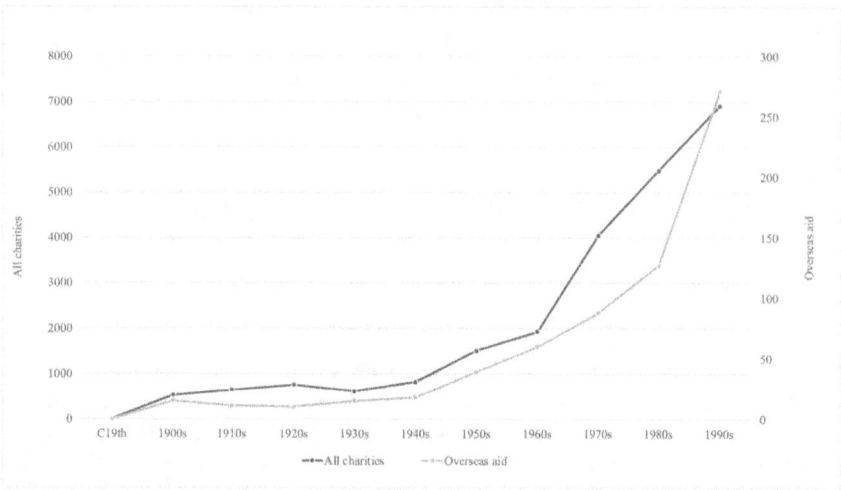

Figure 2.1 Registration of Australian charities, 1880s–1990s.

Source: https://www.data.gov.au.

do we explain the emergence and growth of non-state actors in humanitarianism? If nineteenth-century humanitarianism centred on actions of governments, what caused citizens to care and intervene to help those in distress in distant lands? This chapter outlines the ideological foundations that rationalize, even mandate, individual acts of charity and identifies political, social and cultural developments that accelerated the role of NGOs in the global delivery of aid.

Origins

Although humanitarianism may seem intuitive, it is a historically contingent construct, shaped by specific events, intellectual trends and cultural movements of the early modern period. At its core, humanitarianism is an idea with three central tenets. First, that humanitarianism in general seeks to improve the lives of those perceived as victims in a material sense, including the provision of disaster relief, economic development and, more recently, the promotion of human rights.[6] Second, humanitarianism is based on a shared sense of humanity; that we care for the well-being of others outside of our own ethnic, religious or national group. In this sense, humanitarianism promotes compassion for those significantly different from us and with whom we may otherwise rarely identify.[7] Third, humanitarianism is international, and often, but not necessarily,

---

[6] Enrico Dal Lago and Kevin O'Sullivan, 'Introduction: Towards a New History of Humanitarianism', *Moving the Social* 57 (March 2016): 7.
[7] Keith Watenpaugh, *Bread from Stones: The Middle East and the Making of Modern Humanitarianism* (Oakland: University of California Press, 2015), 2.

global in reach.⁸ Consequently, humanitarianism fundamentally is about distance, not proximity: aid donors remain distant from harm, from aid recipients and, arguably, from an interrogation of their activities. The distance between humanitarian actors and the subject of their concern is a theme that will recur throughout this book.

Humanitarianism is grounded in both secular and religious intellectual traditions. Continental philosophers in the eighteenth century argued that all individuals have intrinsic value and therefore every life is sacred. Most notably, in *Groundwork in the Metaphysics of Morals* (1785), Immanuel Kant theorized the dignity or worth (*würde*) that all humans possess.⁹ Although Kant did not discuss humanitarianism or charity explicitly, his concept of human dignity had profound consequences. At the time, the notion that all humans have value implicitly presented a challenge to the autocratic rule of religious and monarchic leaders, believed to be morally and spiritually above their subjects, which contributed to the American and French revolutions. These seismic events had impacts well beyond the political; it gave credence to the protection of all human life and, concomitantly, justified the pursuit of advancing and regenerating humanity. European Enlightenment philosophes supported a range of reforms to improve the human condition, including banning war, torture and slavery, and promoting religious tolerance, education and hygiene. To be sure, these public intellectuals were preoccupied with outlining the ethical obligations we owe to each other and pursuing moral causes, rather than being concerned with the practicalities of aid. Still, these thinkers can be credited for laying the foundations of what Davide Rodogno calls, 'the humanitarian spirit', which would shape contemporary iterations of benevolence in the years ahead.¹⁰

Alongside secular thought, all world religions advocate or dictate assisting those in need. In Hinduism, the concept of *seva* directs believers to give alms and ritually feed the poor as a matter of religious duty.¹¹ Similarly, the Buddhist principle of *dāna* promotes altruistic, non-reciprocal giving to 'worthy recipients'.¹² Among the Abrahamic religions, their holy texts explicitly call on adherents to offer charity to the impoverished and disadvantaged on the basis that we are all created in God's image.¹³ In Christian thought, the concept of love is universal in scope and expansionistic in intent, compelling disciples to seek the most marginalized in society as a practical manifestation of the Gospel. Furthermore, notions of resurrection and personal salvation are particularly salient. In this sense, Christian charity is informed by an

---

⁸ Thomas Davies, 'Rethinking the Origins of Transnational Humanitarian Organizations: the Curious Case of the International Shipwreck Society', *Global Networks* 18 (2018): 467.
⁹ Jeremy Waldron, 'Dignity and Rank', in *Dignity, Rank, and Rights*, ed. Meir Dan-Cohen (New York: Oxford University Press, 2012), 24–7. For a philosophical analysis of the interpretations of Kant's concept of human dignity, see Oliver Sensen, *Kant on Human Dignity* (Berlin: De Gruyter, 2011).
¹⁰ Davide Rodogno, *Against Massacre: Humanitarian Interventions in the Ottoman Empire, 1815–1914* (Princeton, NJ: Princeton University Press, 2011), 5–6.
¹¹ Elizabeth Ferris, 'Faith and Humanitarianism: It's Complicated', *Journal of Refugee Studies* 24 (2011): 608.
¹² Sara Ann Swenson, 'Compassion without Pity: Buddhist Dāna as Charity, Humanitarianism, and Altruism', *Religion Compass* 14 (2020): 3–4.
¹³ Rodogno, *Against Massacre*, 4; Watenpaugh, *Bread from Stones*, 8.

almost revolutionary commitment to social uplift, compassion for the poor and the quest for justice, as well as evangelization.[14] In Islam, *zakat*, the obligatory practice of charity for fellow Muslims, is one of its five pillars.[15] Furthermore, orphans occupy a central place within Islam as the Prophet Muhammad himself was an orphan. In the hadith on orphans, Abu Hurairah narrated that the Prophet Muhammad said, 'I and someone who cares for an orphan will become like this (index and middle finger intertwined) in paradise'.[16] The Torah similarly instructs Jews to visit orphans (and widows) in their distress (James 1.27). Within the Jewish tradition, the principle of *tzedakah*, or righteousness and charity, is viewed as a central commandment of the Hebrew Bible. Since the Talmudic period, Jewish charities became an ingrained part of Jewish life. This informal arrangement was codified when Moses Maimonides (1138–1204) penned his influential *Hilkhot Mattenot Aniyyim* ('Laws of Giving to the Poor'), thereby adding a legal structure to Jewish aid that transcended communal but not religious lines.[17] Further to humanitarian acts, these religions and their denominations either require or request tithes (donations), such as *sadaqah* in Islam.

The concepts of charity and human dignity were well established by the early modern period. But it was European imperialism that converted abstract ideas into global practice. From the expansion of the British and French empires, and the related imposition of Western political, cultural and economic hegemony on overseas colonies, the first humanitarians emerged with a focus on remediating the ill effects of trans-Atlantic trade.[18] By the 1780s, humane societies were widespread in the Anglosphere and these bodies circulated knowledge that many slaves were drowning crossing the Middle Passage. When humane societies joined forces with the emerging anti-slave trade movement, their close association strengthened the abolitionist cause by bringing the horrors of enslavement into the consciousness of white Americans.[19] Abolitionism was an important development in the history of humanitarianism: it

---

[14] Daniel Laqua, 'Inside the Humanitarian Cloud: Causes and Motivations to Help Friends and Strangers', *Journal of Modern European History* 12 (2014): 176.

[15] The Koranic interpretation that *zakat* only be given to Muslims is widespread although contested among the Islamic humanitarian community. See Ferris, 'Faith and Humanitarianism', 615.

[16] Jonathan Benthall, 'The Care of Orphans in the Islamic Tradition, Vulnerable Children and Child Sponsorship Programs', *Journal of Muslim Philanthropy and Civil Society* 3 (2019): 5–6.

[17] Mirjam Thulin and Björn Siegel, 'Transformations and Intersections of *shtadlanut* and *tzedakah* in the Early Modern and Modern Period', *Jewish Culture and History* 19 (2018): 3.

[18] Abigail Green, 'Humanitarianism in Nineteenth Century context: Religious, Gendered, National', *Historical Journal* 57 (2014): 1159; Lago and O'Sullivan, 'Towards a New History of Humanitarianism', 7. Although the anti-slavery movement is often credited as the first, well-organized humanitarian movement, the lifesaving movement – with its roots in Qing China – predates abolitionism. See Davies, 'Rethinking the Origins of Transnational Humanitarian Organizations', 465–6.

Davies's research reveals a more complex origin story that destabilizes celebratory, Western-centric narratives that inaccurately declare nineteenth-century British abolitionists as founders of modern humanitarianism. For the abolitionist origin story, see State of the Field essay by Rob Skinner and Alan Lester, 'Humanitarianism and Empire: New Research Agendas', *Journal of Imperial and Commonwealth History* 40 (2012): 729–47, 731; Matthew Hilton, Emily Baughan, Eleanor Davey, Bronwen Everill, Kevin O'Sullivan and Tehila Sasson, 'History and Humanitarianism: A Conversation', *Past & Present* 241 (2018): e1–e38; Michelle Tusan, 'Humanitarianism, Genocide and Liberalism', *Journal of Genocide Research* 17 (2015): 83–105.

[19] Amanda B. Moniz, *From Empire to Humanity: The American Revolution and the Origins of Humanitarianism* (Oxford: Oxford University Press, 2016), 131–4.

was fundamentally transnational, with close ties between activists in Britain and the American Republic, between Britain and France, and between Britain and Brazil.[20] The abolitionist cause also formalized public protests and methods of advocacy, for example, through the introduction of mass petitions, publications of periodicals, staging public meetings and harnessing the power of public opinion, which became increasingly important as democracies enfranchised greater sectors of society in the Western world.[21]

Even after Britain's formal abolition of the trans-Atlantic slave trade in 1807 and outlawing of slavery in 1833, slavery itself continued. For slaves of African descent in the Americas, emancipation mainly came through revolution and war rather than British legislative reforms.[22] Western powers defined slavery narrowly to permit the continued use of bonded labour throughout their empires – for example, Britain's deployment of Indian indentured workers in the British Caribbean, southern Africa and Pacific Islands. Despite ongoing slave-like conditions throughout the world, during the nineteenth century, European abolitionists chose to focus on slavery within Africa, arguably for self-serving reasons. After the Partition of Africa among Europe's Great Powers, new European actors engaged in the anti-slavery movement as it justified colonization of African territory on humanitarian grounds. The so-called 'neo-abolitionism' targeted Arab slave traders throughout Africa and, in turn, incorporated notions of a Western civilizing mission to protect Africans against Muslims.[23] The Catholic Church was especially active in the neo-abolitionist cause, overturning its previous practice of 'a massive silence' on anti-slavery until the mid-nineteenth century.[24] Anti-slavery societies in Catholic-majority European states, including France, Italy, Austria, Spain, Portugal and, to a lesser extent, Germany, all maintained close associations with the Catholic hierarchy and Catholic missionary organizations.[25] These European societies shared information amongst themselves about their activities through a range of periodicals. Yet despite this information sharing, there were occasions of open competition between national groups, most evidently among missionary-aligned anti-slavery societies. Nevertheless, mainland European anti-slavery societies demonstrated the rise of Christian internationalism, a trend that accelerated at the fin de siècle.

Apart from imperial expansion, domestic economic, social and cultural developments provided fertile ground for the growth of citizen-driven humanitarianism during the eighteenth and nineteenth centuries. Industrialization from the late eighteenth century provided the necessary economic structures for humanitarianism to take hold among the masses. As nations industrialized, rural workers migrated to

---

[20] Daniel Laqua, 'The Tensions of Internationalism: Transnational Anti-slavery in the 1880s and 1890s', *International History Review* 33 (2011): 705.
[21] Rodogno, *Against Massacre*, 7.
[22] Joel Quirk and David Richardson, 'Anti-slavery, European Identity and International Society: A Macro-historical Perspective', *Journal of Modern European History* 7 (2009): 82.
[23] Laqua, 'The Tensions of Internationalism', 707.
[24] Ibid., 708.
[25] Amalia Ribi Forclaz, *Humanitarian Imperialism: The Politics of Anti-Slavery Activism, 1880–1940* (Oxford: Oxford University Press, 2015), introduction.

cities for employment opportunities. But in the process, these labourers endured a deterioration of working conditions and witnessed a widening gap between them and their employers. With rising inequality and squalid living conditions concentrated in cities for all to see, social reformers-cum-humanitarians mobilized to address the ill effects of industrialization.[26] Concomitantly, the expansion of the market economy offered the burgeoning middle classes discretionary income for the first time, some of which could be allocated to philanthropic pursuits.[27] Thus, from the late eighteenth century in the Anglosphere, economic conditions created sufficient demand and supply of charitable resources for citizens to disperse among the needy. Advances in travel and telecommunications networks gave individuals a greater capacity to explore foreign lands and, importantly, send reports of their discoveries back home. Improvements in telegraphy also supported the development of transnational advocacy networks, which helped to reduce the distance between aid donor and recipient, while further cementing the narrative of a shared humanity across national, religious and ethnic boundaries.[28] Meanwhile, literacy rates among citizens were on the rise, supplementing a growing print culture that provided ordinary people with the means to learn about distant lands and the hardships of strangers. As Amanda Moniz observes, the increasing popularity of reading narratives (whether novels or non-fiction books) helped develop individuals' 'imaginative connections' to sympathize with those suffering far away, thereby broadening the remit of concern from local to international.[29]

The intersection of imperialism and humanitarianism is also evident in the changing perceptions of children during the nineteenth century throughout the English-speaking world. From the 1830s and as a development of the abolitionist movement, children increasingly became viewed not as a source of labour but as vulnerable and in need of protection. During the 1830s and 1840s, the British Parliament passed legislation imposing tighter regulations on child labour. In 1880, British laws mandated compulsory schooling.[30] British working class families were immediately affected by these reforms, which would later fan out across the British settler colonies, including Australia, New Zealand, South Africa and the British Caribbean.[31] Furthermore, British social reformers tried to save local children from urban poverty and a life of destitution by initiating child emigration schemes. Proponents argued that it was a

---

[26] Tony Ballantyne, 'Moving Texts and "Humane Sentiment": Materiality, Mobility and the Emotions of Imperial Humanitarianism', *Journal of Colonialism and Colonial History* 17, no. 1 (2016): 1–21, accessed 23 April 2021, doi:10.1353/cch.2016.0000.

[27] Moniz, *From Empire to Humanity*, 5.

[28] Davies, 'Rethinking the Origins of Transnational Humanitarian Organizations', 462, 467; David, 'Transnational Advocacy in the Eighteenth Century', 367.

[29] Moniz, *From Empire to Humanity*, 5; Andrew C. Thompson, 'The Protestant Interest and the History of Humanitarian Intervention, c.1685–1756', in *Humanitarian Intervention: A History*, ed. Brendan Simms and D. J. B. Trim (Cambridge: Cambridge University Press, 2011), 67.

[30] Ellen Boucher, *Empire's Children: Child Emigration, Welfare, and the Decline of the British Empire* (Cambridge: Cambridge University Press, 2014), 34.

[31] Rebecca Swartz, *Education and Empire: Children, Race and Humanitarianism in the British Settler Colonies, 1833–1880* (Cham: Palgrave Macmillan, 2019), 224. See also Ulduz Salmanova, 'The Coal Mines Regulation Act of 1862: The Beginnings of the Child Labor Debate in Australia', *Journal of the History of Childhood and Youth* 13 (2020): 359–83; Jane Humphries, *Childhood and Child Labour in the British Industrial Revolution* (Cambridge: Cambridge University Press, 2010).

'humanitarian imperative' to rescue children and offer 'hopeless youth' the prospect of a better life in the settler colonies.[32] The emigration of children to British colonies reinforced British claims to these lands, helping grow the settler population with 'good British stock' while also engraining British values of hard work, Christianity and loyalty to the Crown in the new societies.[33]

Alongside emigration schemes, children were at the centre of numerous humanitarian campaigns in the nineteenth and twentieth centuries. For humanitarian activists, the desire to rescue young children, assumed to be a 'blank slate' in the Western imagination, offered an uncontroversial gateway to providing relief to overseas communities, some of whom were in hostile or enemy territory.[34] Crucial for fundraising and publicity efforts, humanitarian campaigners constructed narratives of war orphans and child survivors as innocent victims of war, deserving of Western philanthropy. This growing interest in child welfare in war-torn countries led to the creation of a raft of humanitarian organizations, many focusing exclusively on providing aid to children. Most notably, in May 1919, bourgeois British social reformers Eglantyne Jebb and her sister, Dorothy Buxton, founded the Save the Children Fund, a 'mainstay' of the humanitarian project and at the centre of apolitical European humanitarianism during the interwar years.[35] Save the Children Fund established a vast network of colonial and European branches, connected by the Save the Children International Union in Geneva (founded in 1920) and communicating via a twice-monthly periodical, *The Record*, from 1920.[36] Save the Children Fund found a natural ally in the International Committee for the Red Cross, which, as we will see in Chapter 4, shared their values of impartiality, universality and political neutrality.[37]

These European endeavours were complemented by American initiatives. Philanthropist and future US President, Herbert Hoover, was instrumental in introducing relief for civilians in occupied Belgium from 1914 to 1917, then more broadly across the continent from 1917 until the armistice in November 1918. From that date until the signing of the Treaty of Versailles in June 1919, Hoover redirected

---

[32] Boucher, *Empire's Children*, 67 and 79.

[33] Nick Frost, 'Historical Themes in Child Welfare: The Emergence of Early Child Welfare Structures', in *The Routledge Handbook of Global Child Welfare*, ed. Pat Dolan and Nick Frost (New York: Routledge, 2017), 26.
  There is a voluminous literature on British child emigration, most notably, Shurlee Swain and Margot Hillel, *Child, Nation, Race and Empire: Child Rescue Discourse, England, Canada and Australia, 1850–1915* (Manchester: Manchester University Press, 2017); Janet Sacks and Roger Kershaw, *New Lives for Old: The Story of Britain's Home Children* (London: Bloomsbury Academic, 2008); Philip Bean and Joy Melville, *Lost Children of the Empire*, 2nd edn (New York: Routledge, 2019).

[34] After 1900 the 'innocent child' motif replaced previous Christian depictions of infants tainted with original sin. Note that other cultures held different views of childhood, for example, Islamic and sub-Saharan African cultures. Linda Pollock, 'Childhood, Parents and the Family, 1500–1900', in *The Routledge Handbook of Global Child Welfare*, ed. Pat Dolan and Nick Frost (New York: Routledge, 2017), 4.

[35] Emily Baughan and Juliano Fiori, 'Save the Children, the Humanitarian Project, and the Politics of Solidarity: Reviving Dorothy Buxton's Vision', *Disasters* 39 (2015): s130.

[36] In 1922, *The Record* was replaced with a quarterly journal, *The World's Children*, see 'SCF Publications', Box A0670, Save the Children Fund Archive, Cadbury Research Library, University of Birmingham, UK.

[37] Baughan and Fiori, 'Save the Children, the Humanitarian Project, and the Politics of Solidarity', s133.

his relief activities to the European Children Fund. It is estimated that American aid for European children during the First World War and its immediate aftermath fed more than 10 million children.[38] Beyond Europe, American organizations led the humanitarian response to victims of the Armenian genocide. Founded in 1915, the American Committee for Armenian and Syrian Relief (ACASR), later known as the Near East Foundation (NEF), concentrated on providing relief to Armenian orphans. Through the advocacy work of theologian William Walker Rockwell and American public officials, Armenian orphans became a leading humanitarian cause throughout the Christian-majority world from 1915 to 1927. Armenian aid agencies emerged throughout Europe, North America, Russia, South America, Australia and southern Africa.[39] ACASR treasurer Cleveland H. Dodge recorded that between 1 October 1915 and 1 June 1918, the organization had received over $10,500,000 in donations from across the world 'to help 3,000,000 destitute people in Bible Lands [Palestine, Mesopotamia, Persia, Syria, Greece, Egypt and Anatolia]'.[40] In the aftermath of the First World War and the Allied occupation of the Ottoman Empire, the NEF as well as the League of Nations extended their relief activities to overpopulated refugee centres and orphanages in Istanbul. In this post-genocidal context, child rescue meant rehabilitation, re-conversion (from Islam) and re-Armenization (from Turkification).[41]

Western humanitarianism in the Ottoman Empire had lasting significance, the remnants of which are evident to this day. It began an era of American influence in the Middle East, thereby overturning its previous commitments to restrict foreign entanglements to the western hemisphere. To be sure, American missionaries have had a long presence in the Middle East. However, it was Ottoman massacres of Armenians that led to secular American philanthropists and political elites taking a proactive role in international humanitarian crises.[42] During the early twentieth century, humanitarian ideologies and practices shifted from earlier precedents. If late eighteenth- and nineteenth-century humanitarians were influenced by Protestantism, colonialism, sentimentalism and transnationalism, then twentieth-century aid workers were explicitly secular, bureaucratic and global and held a commitment to social progress through scientific advancement.[43] Finally, Western relief efforts to save minority Christian Armenians in the Ottoman Empire put beyond doubt what many had long suspected: the highly selective nature of aid disbursement based on race,

---

[38] Dominque Marshall, 'Humanitarian Sympathy for Children in Times of War and the History of Children's Rights, 1919-1959', in *Children and War: A Historical Anthology*, ed. James Marten and Robert Coles (New York: New York University Press, 2002), 184.
[39] See chapters in Joanne Laylock and Francesca Piana, eds, *Aid to Armenia: Humanitarianism and Intervention from the 1890s to the Present* (Manchester: Manchester University Press, 2020).
[40] 'Map 1918', Missionary Research Library Archives: Section 2. Near East Relief Committee Records, 1904-1950, series 1, box 5, folder 1-2, The Burke Library at Union Theological Seminary, Columbia University in the City of New York.
[41] Nazan Maksudyan, 'The Orphan Nation: Gendered Humanitarianism for Armenian Survivor Children in Istanbul, 1919-1922', in *Gendering Global Humanitarianism in the Twentieth Century*, ed. Esther Möller, Johannes Paulmann and Katharina Stornig (Cham: Palgrave Macmillan, 2020), 119, 142.
[42] Charlie Laderman, *Sharing the Burden: The Armenian Question, Humanitarian Intervention and Anglo-American Visions of Global Order* (Oxford: Oxford University Press, 2019), introduction.
[43] Watenpaugh, *Bread from Stones*, 5.

religion or ethnicity. Armenian aid campaigners overtly championed the cause by calling to a shared Christian identity.[44] Yet Armenians were not the only minority group subjected to massacres and expulsions in the Ottoman Empire. Balkan Muslims were victims of atrocities perpetrated by (Christian) nationalists who wished to 'homogenize their populations' while 'Europe indulgently looked on'.[45] Western humanitarianism in the Ottoman Empire demonstrated that despite claims of universality and common humanity, aid advocates invariably target groups in need, especially those who will appeal most in popular fundraising campaigns.[46]

State-based humanitarian intervention in foreign lands has deeper roots than citizen-driven humanitarianism. During the European wars of religion, humanitarian intervention involved statesmen and elite commentators who endeavoured to protect minority Christian populations in 'unfriendly' empires. At first, it was the newly created Protestant states, such as England and the Netherlands, which sought to save their co-religionists in Catholic empires. English intervention in the French Wars of Religion and the Dutch Revolt against the Spanish Empire are two cases in point. During the seventeenth and eighteenth centuries, English politicians extended their hawkish position to protect Protestants throughout Catholic-majority states in continental Europe – most notably, the Cromwellian intervention in Savoy/Piedmont (modern-day Italy) in 1655 to halt persecution of the Waldenses. Subsequent interventions similarly occurred in Heidelberg (1719), Thorn (1724) and Salzberg (1731).[47] In the nineteenth century, Catholic, Protestant and Orthodox European states united against a common concern: Christian persecution in the Muslim-majority Ottoman Empire, which at various points throughout its existence included extensive territories throughout southern and eastern Europe. Until its downfall during the First World War, European powers intervened on humanitarian grounds in a range of territories, including during the Greek War of Independence (1821–32), Lebanon and Syria (1860–1), Bulgaria (1875–8), the Balkans (1875–8) and Armenia (1877–1914).[48] These interventions became part of what was labelled 'the Eastern Question' for the Great European powers, a diplomatic concern defined by the Orientalist 'civilization-barbarity dichotomy'.[49]

---

[44] For the Australian example, see Joy Damousi, 'Humanitarianism in the Interwar Years: How Australians Responded to the Child Refugees of the Armenian Genocide and the Greek-Turkish Exchange', *History Australia* 12 (2015): 98–103; and Joy Damousi, *The Humanitarians: Child War Refugees and Australian Humanitarianism in a Transnational World, 1919–1975* (Cambridge: Cambridge University Press, 2022), chapter 2.

[45] M. Hakan Yuvuz and Hakan Erdagöz, 'The Tragedy of the Ottomans: Muslims in the Balkans and Armenians in Anatolia', *Journal of Muslim Minority Affairs* 39 (2019): 274, 276.

[46] Nazan Maksudyan, *Orphans and Destitute Children in the Late Ottoman Empire* (Syracuse, NY: Syracuse University Press, 2014), 146.

[47] D. J. B. Trim, 'If a Prince Use Tyrannie towards His People: Interventions on Behalf of Foreign Populations in Early Modern Europe', in *Humanitarian Intervention: A History*, ed. Brendan Simms and D. J. B. Trim (Cambridge: Cambridge University Press, 2011), 29–30 and Thompson, 'The Protestant Interest and the History of Humanitarian Intervention', 67–68.

[48] Alexis Heraclides and Ada Dialla, *Humanitarian Intervention in the Long Nineteenth Century: Setting the Precedent* (Manchester: Manchester University Press, 2015); Gary J. Bass, *Freedom's Battle: The Origins of Humanitarian Intervention* (New York: Vintage Books, 2008); Michelle Tusan, *The British Empire and the Armenian Genocide: Humanitarianism and Imperial Politics from Gladstone to Churchill* (London: Bloomsbury, 2017).

[49] Heraclides and Dialla, *Humanitarian Intervention in the Long Nineteenth Century*, x.

Although state-based humanitarian intervention may in many cases overlap with citizen-driven humanitarianism, it is important to highlight the difference between the two concepts. Specifically, humanitarian intervention can only be initiated by states and their militaries that have the capacity to invade sovereign nations. Humanitarian intervention explicitly involves the use of unilateral coercion of one state (or an alliance of states) by another, and therefore, unequal power relationships come into play. Conversely, non-state actors typically engage in humanitarian activities from afar, and if they wish to enter the host society to distribute aid, they first require permission, a barrier that blocked the International Committee of the Red Cross (ICRC) from Bangladesh, as we will explore in Chapter 4.

War and global governance

As we have seen, wars of religion, colonialism and the First World War all created conditions for a boon in humanitarian activities. But arguably, it was the Second World War and the subsequent emergence of the United Nations (UN) that served as significant watershed moments. First, existing international humanitarian organizations, such as the ICRC and its affiliated national societies, as well as the Save the Children Fund, benefitted from total war. As Matthew Hilton explains, the Second World War created opportunities for these organizations to expand their operations, providing medical and emergency relief to combatants, prisoners of war (POWs), internees, destitute children and the civilian population more broadly.[50] Second, the war prompted the establishment of additional humanitarian organizations, most notably the Oxford Committee for Famine Relief in England (Oxfam) in 1942, discussed in Chapter 6, and CARE, a consortium of twenty-two American charities that funnelled food packages to war-ravaged Europe.[51] Third, during the postwar period, humanitarian organizations were drawn into a rapidly expanding global humanitarian regime, all of which were created by states to advance reconstruction. The establishment of the United Nations Relief and Rehabilitation Administration (UNRRA) in 1943, followed by the United Nations Children's Emergency Fund (UNICEF) in 1946, the International Refugee Organization (IRO) in 1946 and succeeded by the United Nations High Commission for Refugees (UNHCR) in 1950, all offered humanitarian agencies leadership, opportunities and experience in the field.[52] In a symbiotic relationship between NGOs,

---

[50] Matthew Hilton, 'Ken Loach and the Save the Children Film: Humanitarianism, Imperialism, and the Changing Role of Charity in Postwar Britain', *Journal of Modern History* 87 (2015): 392.

[51] Matthew Hilton, 'International Aid and Development NGOs in Britain and Human Rights since 1945', *Humanity: An International Journal of Human Rights, Humanitarianism, and Development* (hereafter *Humanity*) 3 (2012): 451; Daniel Roger Maul, 'The Rise of a Humanitarian Superpower: American NGOs and International Relief, 1917–1945', in *Internationalism, Imperialism and the Formation of the Contemporary World*, ed. Miguel Bandeira Jerónimo and José Pedro Monteiro (Cham: Palgrave Macmillan, 2018), 146; Heike Wieters, *The NGO Care and Food Aid from America 1945–80: 'Showered With Kindness'?* (Manchester: Manchester University Press, 2017), chapter 1.

[52] Silvia Salvatici, '"Help the People to Help Themselves": UNRRA Relief Workers and European Displaced Persons', *Journal of Refugee Studies* 25 (September 2012): 428–51.

intergovernmental organizations and the states that funded them, humanitarian agencies became 'a recognizable cog in the aid machine', a trend that only accelerated in the second half of the twentieth century.[53]

Decolonization in the post-Second World War era similarly facilitated the expansion and entrenchment of international humanitarianism. With former colonies no longer under the exclusive purview of imperial powers, newly independent states throughout Asia and Africa became accessible and, in some cases, required international aid to reverse centuries of neglect or exploitation due to colonial rule. Wars of independence and civil strife also exacerbated the need for emergency relief, as did natural disasters and famines. Within the space of a few decades, humanitarian sensibilities were now truly global.[54] Ideologically, decolonization ushered in a period of optimism in which previously occupied nations could sustain hopes for self-determination, economic self-sufficiency and the resolution of conflicts through cooperative fora, such as the UN.[55] Scandinavian nations, for their part, actively supported national liberation movements in the Global South, eschewing Cold War allegiances and *realpolitik* that constrained their European neighbours.[56]

In 1959, the UN instituted two publicity-driven programmes that galvanized the international community, shifting the concept and practice of humanitarianism from elites and states to civil society. The UN's World Refugee Year (WRY) from 1959 to 1960 was designed to inform the world about refugees, drawing attention to human stories of suffering and long-term destitution. With this increased global awareness, WRY branches across the world fundraised US$92 million by 1961, with which they hoped to provide humanitarian solutions to established refugee populations in Europe, Palestine/Israel and China.[57] The WRY was not a mere publicity campaign though. In Britain, Sweden and Australia, the WRY compelled hitherto intransigent governments to resettle the so-called 'hard core' displaced persons (DPs) who were previously rejected by immigration intake officers based on disability or illness.[58] Britain admitted seven hundred DPs with multiple conditions, including tuberculosis (TB); Australia

---

[53] Kevin O'Sullivan, 'A "Global Nervous System": The Rise and Rise of European Humanitarian NGOs, 1945–1985', in *International Organizations and Development, 1945–1999*, ed. Marc Frey, Sönke Kunkel and Corinna Unger (London: Palgrave Macmillan, 2014), 219.

[54] Barnett, *Empire of Humanity*, 132.

[55] Neville Wylie, Melanie Oppenheimer and James Crossland, 'The Red Cross Movement: Continuities, Changes and Challenges', in *The Red Cross Movement: Myths, Practices and Turning Points*, ed. Neville Wylie, Melanie Oppenheimer and James Crossland (Manchester: Manchester University Press, 2020), 10.

[56] Sabina Widmer, 'Neutrality Challenged in a Cold War Conflict: Switzerland, the International Committee of the Red Cross, and the Angolan War', *Cold War History* 18 (2018): 203–20. Nikolas Glover has demonstrated the role of Swedish corporations in aiding African development in the 1960s, see 'Between Order and Justice: Investments in Africa and Corporate International Responsibility in Swedish Media in the 1960s', *Enterprise & Society* 20 (2019): 401–44. See also Kevin O'Sullivan, *Ireland, Africa and the End of Empire: Small state identity in the Cold War 1955–75* (Manchester: Manchester University Press, 2012), 133, 142.

[57] Joy Damousi, 'World Refugee Year 1959–60: Humanitarian Rights in Postwar Australia', *Australian Historical Studies* 51 (2020): 212–13; Peter Gatrell, *Free World? The Campaign to Save the World's Refugees, 1956–63* (Cambridge: Cambridge University Press, 2011).

[58] Holger Köhn, 'Jewish Life in Camps after 1945. Displaced Persons Camps in the US Zone of Germany', in *Catastrophes*, ed. Andreas Hoppe (Cham: Springer, 2016), 64.

resettled two hundred refugee families with at least one 'handicapped' member; Sweden accepted five hundred refugees with TB.[59] The admission of chronically ill DPs during the WRY demonstrated a moment in time when public pressure to resettle the destitute eclipsed narrow economic interests of the receiving state. Importantly, the WRY led to the establishment of refugee-focused humanitarian organizations, such as Austcare in Australia, which is the subject of Chapter 3.

In addition to WRY in 1959, the UN designated the 1960s as the first 'Development Decade' with the intent of reorienting aid from providing emergency short-term relief towards long-term economic development, particularly in the decolonizing world.[60] The UN Development Decade was idealistic and unenforceable, yet it provided the ideological foundation that promoted global economic restructuring to lift underdeveloped countries out of poverty.[61] Unfortunately, such idealism failed to manifest practical gains. By the end of the first development decade, government overseas aid was in free fall. In 1969, the Nixon Administration rejected the UN-proposed official aid target of 0.7 per cent of Gross National Product (GNP). In financial year 1969–70, the United States ranked last among developed nations, contributing just 0.5 per cent of GNP to overseas aid. Among other nations, only the Swedish and Dutch governments agreed unconditionally to committing 0.7 per cent of GNP to overseas development assistance (ODA). Elsewhere in Europe, the British, West German, French and Swiss governments agreed to a target of 1 per cent GNP, although the figure included private philanthropy, not just ODA. Meanwhile, the Japanese and Australian governments dismissed the target of 0.7 per cent of GNP as 'unrealistic', and the Canadian government remained uncommitted, even though its former Prime Minister, Lester Pearson, headed the UN commission responsible for setting ODA targets.[62] As Matthew Wright documents, by the end of the 1960s, there was 'widespread dissatisfaction with aid' among both donor and recipient countries. Even the President of the World Bank, George Woods, described the UN's Development Decade as 'faltering'.[63] Disappointed and impatient with state inertia, humanitarian organizations increasingly adopted the language of justice-based solidarity activism to pursue their goals, as will be shown in Chapters 6 and 7.[64]

[59] Becky Taylor, 'A Change of Heart? British Policies towards Tubercular Refugees during 1959 World Refugee Year', *Twentieth Century British History* 26 (March 2015): 97–121; Veronika Flegar, 'UNHCR's Shifting Frames in the Social Construction of Disabled Refugees: Two Case Studies on the Organization's Work During the World Refugee Year (1959–1960) and the International Year of Disabled Persons (1981)', *Diplomatica* 1 (2019): 157–79, 167–9. See also contemporary newspaper coverage, for example, Neilma Sidney, 'Is Australia Passing-by in World Refugee Year'? *Canberra Times*, 19 December 1959, 2.

[60] Matthew Hilton, 'Oxfam and the Problem of NGO Aid Appraisal in the 1960s', *Humanity* 9 (2018): 2; Andrew Jones, 'The Disasters Emergency Committee (DEC) and the Humanitarian Industry in Britain, 1963–85', *Twentieth Century British History* 26 (2015): 585.

[61] Text of Resolution 1710 is available online, accessed 12 May 2023, https://undocs.org/en/A/RES/1710%20(XVI).

[62] Kevin Brushett, 'Partners in Development? Robert McNamara, Lester Pearson, and the Commission on International Development, 1967–1973', *Diplomacy and Statecraft* 26 (2015): 94.

[63] Matthew Wright, 'The Pearson Commission, Aid Diplomacy and the Rise of the World Bank, 1966–1970', PhD dissertation, University of Durham, 2017, 74, 102.

[64] Peter Van Dam, 'No Justice Without Charity: Humanitarianism after Empire', *International History Review* 44 (2020): 653–74.

While some UN initiatives were short-lived, its establishment of the UNHCR was long-lasting and consequential. Established in December 1950 to succeed the IRO, the UNHCR initially had a small budget and just thirty-three workers. This restricted influence of the UNHCR was by design: Western governments instructed that this UN agency did not impinge on state sovereignty nor impose financial obligations on them. It was also the only UN agency *not* to receive funding from the US government until 1955, putting the UNHCR at a considerable disadvantage compared to more established NGOs, such as the Red Cross or the Inter-governmental Committee for European Migration.[65] In its early days then, the remit of the UNHCR was merely to provide legal protection of refugees in European DP camps and not deliver any material assistance.[66] The UNHCR adhered strictly to its mandate and statute in its early years, adopting a narrow, legalistic definition of who qualified as a refugee. For example, it did not recognize internally displaced people en masse as refugees until the late 1980s.[67] Politically, the UNHCR maintained a non-judgmental and non-political stance, going to great lengths to avoid controversy. This timid institutional approach was in part due to its limited mandate and because it required permission from host countries to initiate its activities.[68] The administration of the UNHCR is funded by member states of the UN, and with UN General Assembly assent, it can act as a coordinating body for government and non-government aid. It is a non-operational agency, meaning that it facilitates and redirects funds to support relief activities implemented by NGOs.[69] The UNHCR does not perform practical tasks, such as establishing refugee camps. Rather, it employs operational partners (namely, NGOs) to implement its plans. As a result, there is a symbiotic relationship between states, the UNHCR and a myriad of refugee aid agencies, each dependent on another for financial, technical or practical support. The arrival of the UNHCR as a central actor in the international humanitarian regime is nowadays almost taken for granted, but in 1971, this central position was far from inevitable.

During the 1960s, the UNHCR responded to more crises affecting more people in more places, gaining global exposure and credibility as an institution above the political fray. The growing role of the UNHCR was, to be sure, a reaction to increased instability during episodes of decolonization and Cold War machinations. It also reveals the expansionist aspirations of its charismatic and well-connected High Commissioner at the time, Prince Sadruddin Aga Khan. Born the second son to an Iranian heredity Imam of Nizari Ismaili Muslims (a sub-sect of Shi'a Islam), Sadruddin enjoyed a

---

[65] Florian Hannig, 'The Power of the Refugees. The 1971 East Pakistan Crisis and the Origins of UN's Engagement with Humanitarian Aid', in *The Institution of International Order: From the League of Nations to the United Nations*, ed. Simon Jackson and Alanna O'Malley (New York: Routledge, 2018), 120.

[66] Gil Loescher, 'UNHCR's Origins and Early History: Agency, Influence, and Power in Global Refugee Policy', *Refuge* 33 (2017): 78.

[67] Phil Orchard, *Protecting the Internally Displaced* (London: Routledge, 2019), 96.

[68] Anne Hammerstad, *The Rise and Decline of a Global Security Actor: UNHCR, Refugee Protection and Security* (Oxford: Oxford University Press, 2014), 103–6.

[69] Peter Gatrell, 'The World-Wide Web of Humanitarianism: NGOs and Population Displacement in the Third Quarter of the Twentieth Century', *European Review of History: Revue européenne d'histoire* 23 (2016): 102.

privileged upbringing that straddled Eastern and Western cultures. As his mother was French, Sadruddin was raised in France and Francophone Switzerland before moving to Boston to pursue his undergraduate and postgraduate degrees at Harvard University. While at Harvard, Sadruddin befriended descendants of doyens of European culture, including Paul Matisse, the grandson of French painter Henri Matisse, and Stephen Joyce, grandson of Irish writer James Joyce. Sadruddin also lived with a young Edward Kennedy, who would later become an outspoken critic of the Nixon Administration's indifference to the plight of Bangladeshis during their liberation war. Sadruddin was an erudite man, speaking French and English fluently, and was conversant in German, Italian, Farsi and Arabic. Alongside his formal, Western-style education, Sadruddin was well versed in Islamic art and culture, travelling extensively throughout the Muslim world. He also completed postgraduate research in Middle Eastern studies while at Harvard.[70] The capacity of Sadruddin to oscillate between Islamic and Western traditions with ease was unusual: at this time, UN agencies were staffed by European internationalists still tarnished with the legacies of colonialism. Sadruddin was different. He became the first non-European to head the UNHCR in 1966 and, to date, remains the longest-serving high commissioner, with his tenure lasting a day under twelve years. During his term, Sadruddin turned the UNHCR into a truly global agency, responding to refugee crises as diverse as those in Indochina, Uganda and Chile. Along with the increased geographic scope, the UNHCR under Sadruddin also increased the number of individuals it sought to assist. The definition of a refugee was broadened from its previously narrow focus on European DPs fleeing persecution to incorporate the internally displaced in specific cases and those uprooted by human-made disasters.

During the Bangladesh Liberation War, the UNHCR played a critical role, coordinating state and non-state assistance for the refugees in India at the behest of the Indian government.[71] As mentioned in Chapter 1, within one month of the onset of hostilities (23 April 1971), the Indian government made a direct appeal to the United Nations for assistance. On 29 April, the UN Secretary General U Thant announced that the UNHCR would act as the focal point, coordinating aid but leaving the distribution of aid in the hands of Indian authorities.[72] In preparation for the most significant undertaking of the UNHCR's short history, the organization sent a three-man team, including Deputy High Commissioner Charles Mace, on a thirteen-day discovery tour of India, meeting with officials in New Delhi and inspecting the makeshift refugee camps near the Bangladeshi border. At the culmination of this fact-finding trip on 19 May, the UNHCR began soliciting funds directly from governments around the world. The UNHCR maintained permanent contact with Indian officials in New Delhi throughout the war, stationing Thomas Jamieson, the UNHCR Director of Operations,

---

[70] Gil Loescher, *The UNHCR and World Politics: A Perilous Path* (Oxford: Oxford University Press, 2001), 141–2.

[71] Note that the USSR bypassed the UNHCR and disbursed funds directly to the Indian government. Hannig, 'The Power of the Refugees', 124.

[72] UNDP/UNICEF/UNHCR Office, Sydney, 'Notes for Information: East Pakistan Refugees in India', 10 June 1971, Box 117, folder 'Pakistan, East and West – 1964–71'. Records of the Australian Council of Churches (ACC), NLA.

in the Indian capital.[73] Although Jamieson may have been close to the centre of power in India, he, and the UNHCR by extension, remained over 1,500 kilometres away from Kolkata, which was the principal city for receipt and disbursement of aid. Furthermore, in Geneva, the UNHCR arranged weekly meetings with international aid agencies, including the League of Red Cross Societies, which is the focus of Chapter 4. In these weekly meetings, the UNHCR exchanged 'information on assistance needs', ensured 'interagency cooperation', agreed on a 'common position' and took 'advice on the handling of contributions' to avoid duplication.[74] Just as the Red Cross movement benefitted from the Second World War, the UNHCR gained legitimacy and visibility during the Bangladeshi refugee crisis. As the coordinating agency connecting state actors, NGOs and the Indian government, the UNHCR became responsible for the largest operation in its history, with a relief budget sixty times its own operations budget.[75]

Cultural developments

The growth in citizen-driven humanitarianism is also an outcome of cultural advancements. First, the human rights movement had a profound impact on Western notions of equality and progress in the second half of the twentieth century. With its origins in the American and French revolutions, the human rights movement advanced a belief in a shared, common humanity, and equality was fundamental to this understanding.[76] Political rights in the Western, democratic tradition were first to be sought in the developing world. The establishment of Amnesty International in 1961 is illustrative of the movement to protect political prisoners specifically and challenge authoritarianism generally.[77] In the 1960s, human rights discourse appealed to left-leaning humanitarians, activists, and academics who were frustrated with older notions of paternalistic charity. An elastic concept, human rights activists drew upon strong theoretical foundations, the most prominent of which was John Rawls's theory of justice as fairness.[78] Academics and writers entered the debate, critiquing the effectiveness and morality of charity to developing countries in the early 1970s. The arguments ran the gamut of the political spectrum, with books published by Thatcherite economist Peter

---

[73] United Nations Press Section, Office of Public Information, New York, 'Contributions Through United Nations for Relief of East Pakistanis in India Exceed $34 Million', 11 June 1971, Box 117, folder 'Pakistan, East and West – 1964–71', Records of the ACC.
[74] United Nations Press Section, Office of Public Information, New York, 'Contributions through United Nations for Relief of East Pakistanis in India Exceed $34 Million', 11 June 1971, Box 117, folder 'Pakistan, East and West – 1964–71', Records of the ACC.
[75] Loescher, *The UNHCR and World Politics*, 157.
[76] Lynn Hunt, *Inventing Human Rights: A History* (New York: W. W. Norton, 2007).
[77] Silvia Salvatici, *A History of Humanitarianism, 1755–1989: In the Name of Others* (Manchester: Manchester University Press 2020), 192.
[78] John Rawls, *A Theory of Justice* (Cambridge, MA: Harvard University Press, 1971) and Kevin O'Sullivan, 'The Search for Justice: NGOs in Britain and Ireland and the New International Economic Order, 1968–82', *Humanity* 6 (2015): 178.

Bauer, British activist Teresa Hayter and BBC journalist C. R. Hensman.[79] To be sure, it is tempting to exaggerate the effects of the human rights movement. When one looks beyond aspirational documents such as the Universal Declaration of Human Rights (1948) to examine lived experiences, the so-called global human rights movement of the twentieth century was, in fact, a Western-centric campaign that was closely intertwined with the institutions of global governance.[80] The movement advanced the rights of the individual within a liberal, capitalist economy and was primarily concerned with the promotion of negative liberty – that is, freedom from external constraints.[81] This allegiance to liberalism, capitalism and individualism made sense to a Western audience, but for developing postcolonial states, the human rights movement was far from a panacea. Human rights discourse seldom spoke to questions of sovereignty and self-determination. On the issue of territorial integrity, UN member states agreed that national borders were inviolable. This consensus was strongest within the Soviet bloc and among newly independent and fragile African states, many of which had battled secessionist movements during the 1950s and 1960s. During the Cold War, the US government similarly stymied national liberation movements, although they did so based on the assumed socialist inclinations of the secessionists.[82] It is important to note the limitations of the human rights movement as it demonstrates the tensions that arose from an inherently contradictory discourse that privileged individual rights over group rights. As we will see, these tensions were evident during the Bangladesh Liberation War in which Western NGOs decontextualized the crisis to avoid granting legitimacy to a secessionist state. The socialist leanings of Bangladeshi freedom fighters were also problematic for some Western NGOs as they wished to sustain the liberal economic order.[83] Notwithstanding these criticisms, the human rights movement aided humanitarianism as it drew attention to underdevelopment, poverty and inequality, problems that humanitarians sought to solve.

Second, advancements in media during the twentieth century drastically collapsed time and space, so that citizens could promptly bear witness to overseas disasters.

---

[79] Peter Bauer, *Dissent on Development: Studies and Debates in Development Economics* (Cambridge, MA: Harvard University Press, 1971); Teresa Hayter, *Aid as Imperialism* (London: Penguin, 1971); C. R. Hensman, *Rich against Poor: The Reality of Aid* (London: Penguin, 1971).

[80] Hilton, 'International Aid and Development NGOs in Britain and Human Rights since 1945', 451. There are numerous works that examine the impact of the human rights movement in the developed world, see Akira Iriye, Petra Goedde and William I. Hitchcock, eds, *The Human Rights Revolution* (New York: Oxford University Press, 2012); Samuel Moyn, *The Last Utopia: Human Rights in History* (Cambridge, MA: Harvard University Press, 2010). To be fair, Moyn reconsiders his North Atlantic orientation in his recent book, *Not Enough: Human Rights in an Unequal World* (Cambridge, MA: Harvard University Press, 2018). For counter-narratives that place the Global South at the centre rather than at the periphery, see Steven L. B. Jensen, *The Making of International Human Rights: The 1960s, Decolonization and the Reconstruction of Human Values* (Cambridge: Cambridge University Press, 2016); Roland Burke, *Decolonization and the Evolution of International Human Rights* (Philadelphia: University of Pennsylvania Press, 2013); A. Dirk Moses, Marco Duranti and Roland Burke (ed.), *Decolonization, Self-Determination and the Rise of Global Human Rights Politics* (Cambridge: Cambridge University Press, 2020).

[81] Bradley Simpson, 'Self-Determination, Human Rights, and the End of Empire in the 1970s', *Humanity* 4 (2013): 252.

[82] Ibid., 247–9.

[83] O'Sullivan, 'The Search for Justice', 176 and 181.

Beginning with the emergence of the Kodak handheld camera and related printing technologies during the late nineteenth century, media advancements revolutionized how disasters were recorded and disseminated.[84] Such 'atrocity photography' changed distant crises into proximate emergencies, which in turn, could be harnessed by humanitarian movements to raise awareness and funds to ease the suffering of others.[85] By the First World War, colonial administrators and missionaries had established a consistent, internationally recognizable visual discourse that centred on tropes of emaciated, naked bodies, squalid material conditions and anguished facial expressions. Unlike textual representations, photography presents the appearance of a realistic, impartial depiction that is above dispute or denial.[86] Photography therefore creates documentary evidence that suffering exists, providing the visual medium to arouse a desired emotional or behavioural response from the audience. Since the twentieth century, humanitarian organizations have relied on photography to disseminate knowledge of disasters and rally the audience into action. The French humanitarian organization Médecins Sans Frontières (MSF) arguably pioneered the use of photojournalism to elicit outrage to provoke activism and raise funds.[87] The use of photography to mobilize the masses has its critics, however. Specifically, photography emphasizes the victimhood of the sufferer rather than their agency. Such condescending portrayals are remnants of colonial times in which the inflated self-regard of donors takes precedence over the empowerment and autonomy of recipients.[88]

The advent of television added a layer of spectacle to humanitarian fundraising activities. The inclusion of moving images and sound bites of unfolding crises created the sense of watching events in real time, impelling viewers to act. The uptake of television among Western consumers during the 1950s and 1960s was staggering, particularly when the cost of purchasing a new television set is considered (roughly equivalent to ten weeks of the average wage).[89] British TV ownership grew exponentially during the 1950s, and by 1960, more than 70 per cent of households had access to the public broadcaster, the BBC, and commercial network ITV. By comparison, Australia was slow to introduce television relative to other Western nations. Delayed by extensive political debates over the control, purpose and funding of television, Australians had to wait an additional eight years (from 1948 to 1956) before consensus was reached

---

[84] Joanna Simonow, 'The Great Bengal Famine in Britain: Metropolitan Campaigning for Food Relief and the End of Empire, 1943–44', *Journal of Imperial and Commonwealth History* 48 (2020): 177; for a comprehensive collection of essays on photography and humanitarianism, see Heide Fehrenbach and Davide Rodogno, eds. *Humanitarian Photography: A History* (Cambridge: Cambridge University Press, 2015).

[85] Christina Twomey, 'Framing Atrocity: Photography and Humanitarianism', *History of Photography* 36 (2015): 255; Kevin Grant, 'Anti-slavery, Refugee Relief, and the Missionary Origins of Humanitarian Photography ca. 1900–1960', *History Compass* 15 (2017): 2.

[86] Simonow, 'The Great Bengal Famine in Britain', 185.

[87] Salvatici, *A History of Humanitarianism*, 192.

[88] Michael Ignatieff, *The Warrior's Honor: Ethnic War and the Moral Conscience* (London: Chatto & Windus, 1998), 16.

[89] Kate Darian-Smith and Paula Hamilton, 'Part of the Family: Australian Histories of Television, Migration and Memory', in *Remembering Television: Histories, Technologies, Memories*, ed. Kate Darian-Smith and Sue Turnbull (Perth: Boffin Books, 2012), 38.

in the nation's parliament. Australia's first television broadcasts were transmitted in September 1956 to coincide with Melbourne hosting the Summer Olympic Games. Initially, only residents of Sydney and Melbourne enjoyed television service (one public broadcaster and two commercial stations); residents of the other state capital cities of Brisbane, Adelaide, Hobart and Perth had to wait a further three years, and for country residents, the wait was even longer.[90] Still, once services began, Australians embraced television culture. Between 1956 and 1965, TV ownership in Sydney grew from 1 per cent of the population to nearly 90 per cent; in Melbourne, the ownership rate rose from 4 per cent to over 90 per cent.[91]

Humanitarian NGOs capitalized on this emerging cultural phenomenon, gaining greater access to the mass public through entertaining and informative programming. The charity telethon in which celebrities and TV personalities urge viewers to donate money to a worthy cause has become a staple of network television. Although first established in the United States in the late 1940s, it was humanitarian organizations in the UK that utilized the charity telethon most systematically. In 1963, the five main humanitarian NGOs formed the Disasters Emergency Committee (DEC) to coordinate with the BBC televised fundraising appeals. By entering a formal arrangement with the national broadcaster, these British charities pre-emptively ensured access to a trusted media outlet to raise funds whenever a disaster struck.[92] The synergetic relationship between television, humanitarian agencies and fundraising extended to televised news coverage. Although the Vietnam War is widely recognized as the first televised war, the Nigeria–Biafra secessionist conflict and resulting famine (1967–70) began 'the age of televised disaster' in which catastrophe was broadcast across the globe through modern media.[93] Given the relative novelty of television and the limited number of entertainment alternatives, televised news broadcasts in the 1960s and 1970s enjoyed wide viewership, with audiences of news programmes in the UK double or even triple what they are today, in relative and raw terms. Early television audiences also had a tolerance for extended news stories, screened across several bulletins over multiple days. As a result, news coverage was widespread, detailed and repeatedly available.[94]

Foreign news content became increasingly available in the mid-twentieth century in two main ways. First, new recording and transmission technologies during the 1960s and 1970s granted foreign correspondents greater freedom and access to unfolding events in previously remote corners of the world. Portable video recorders replaced

---

[90] Darian-Smith and Hamilton, 'Part of the Family', 35; Bridget Griffen-Foley, *Australian Radio Listeners and Television Viewers: Historical Perspectives* (Cham: Palgrave Pivot, 2020): 109–10.

[91] Michelle Arrow, *Friday on Our Minds: Popular Culture in Australia since 1945* (Sydney: University of New South Wales Press, 2009), 29.

[92] In the 1960s, DEC membership included the British Red Cross, Save the Children Fund, Oxfam, Christian Aid and War on Want. See Jones, 'The Disasters Emergency Committee (DEC) and the Humanitarian Industry in Britain, 1963–85', 573–601.

[93] For details on the role of television during the Vietnam War, see Michael Mandelbaum, 'Vietnam: The Television War', *Daedalus* 111, no. 4 (1982): 157–69. For the Nigerian-Biafran conflict, see Lasse Heerten and A. Dirk Moses, 'The Nigeria-Biafra War: Postcolonial Conflict and the Question of Genocide', *Journal of Genocide Research* 16 (2014): 169 and Lasse Heerten, *The Biafran War and Postcolonial Humanitarianism: Spectacles of Suffering* (Cambridge: Cambridge University Press, 2017), 3.

[94] Suzanne Franks, 'How Famine Captured the Headlines', *Media History* 12 (2006): 306–7.

cumbersome film cameras; improved satellite capabilities shrunk the time between capturing and broadcasting footage. Consequently, televised news became more immediate, a feature that only accelerated in the years ahead. Still, in the early 1970s, these technological changes were groundbreaking, creating an editorial and viewer appetite for instant news from across the globe.[95] Second, national press associations entered agreements with world news agencies to reduce overseas operational costs while still maintaining access to global news stories. The rise of syndicated news services was a highly competitive market in the mid-twentieth century: UK company Reuters endeavoured to make itself the news agency of choice among member nations of the British Commonwealth but with mixed results. Well-funded US company Associated Press (AP) extended its global reach after the Second World War, creating a fierce rivalry for supremacy with Reuters.[96] Meanwhile, state-subsidized Agence France Presse (AFP) provided a French perspective that gained traction in Francophone Africa and the Middle East.[97] In sum, news coverage of humanitarian crises from the 1960s became more accessible and more vivid than in earlier decades, all the while being packaged within the nightly televised news bulletins habitually watched by families around the dinner table.

Third, the onset of the jet age in the early 1960s revolutionized travel and democratized international tourism, which in turn increased public awareness of suffering in foreign lands. Previously, intercontinental travel was restricted to slow and, for most, arduous passage by ship. Replacing the older, piston-powered engines, jet airliners could travel further and faster, drastically reducing travel times from weeks or days to hours. With reduced transit times, international travel for the first time became a viable holiday option for many Westerners. Importantly, jet planes could also carry more passengers on the aircraft than older planes. Due to economies of scale, international airlines reduced the price of airline tickets, which in turn made overseas trips affordable to the middle class.[98] Mass market tourism and the packaged holiday became commonplace during the 1960s. Full employment and strong economic growth in many Western nations put upward pressure on wages and entitlements for workers, such as paid vacation leave. In an era of prosperity and economic security, Northern Europeans and Australians specifically had the financial means and the opportunity to take extended breaks from work for a holiday. Thus, the traditional social categories of the leisure class and the working class were no longer relevant in some developed countries during post-Second World War boom years.[99] Through their travels in the

---

[95] Jones, 'The Disasters Emergency Committee (DEC) and the Humanitarian Industry in Britain, 1963–85', 590.

[96] Peter Putnis, 'Reuters and the Idea of a British Commonwealth News Agency in the Aftermath of World War II', *Media History* 27 (2021): 314–30.

[97] Barbara Vignaux, 'L'Agence France-Presse en guerre d'Algérie', *Vingtième Siècle. Revue d'histoire* 3 (2004): 121–30.

[98] Per Catharina Backhuis, '"Noble Helpers of Evil Exploiters?" Contesting and Negotiating West German Mass Tourism to the Global South, 1970-1985', *Journal of Tourism History* 14 (2022): 47–8; Hillary Kaell, 'Pilgrimage in the Jet Age: The Development of the American Evangelical Holy Land Travel Industry, 1948–1978', *Journal of Tourism History* 2 (2010): 28–31.

[99] Thomas Kaiserfeld, 'From Sightseeing to Sunbathing: Changing Traditions in Swedish Package Tours; from Edification by Bus to Relaxation by Airplane in the 1950s and 1960s', *Journal of*

developing world, middle class Westerners were forced to face their own complicity or indifference to the creation of vast global inequality. For some, such revelations triggered moral outrage and an unwavering commitment to redress injustice and minimize suffering.

Australian tourists in the 1960s and 1970s had cultural, economic and geographic peculiarities that distinguished them from other Western travellers. Culturally, Australians are accustomed to long distance travel by virtue of the size of the country itself, and its isolation from other Western nations, making 'mobility' a national habit.[100] Although most countries in the Anglo world have, to varying degrees, embedded the Protestant work ethic within their cultures, Australia has maintained 'Mediterranean attitudes' to leisure and work.[101] Economically, Australians had the financial means and the time to take extended breaks. Like Nordic countries, Australian workers in the mid-twentieth century were entitled to paid annual leave; by the 1970s, the average Australian worker enjoyed four weeks of paid vacation time.[102] Importantly, workers were encouraged to take their annual leave in extended blocks to ensure they had adequate time for rejuvenation. Moreover, the unique Australian tradition of long service leave – where workers are granted extended paid leave for continued service to an employer every seven to ten years – is further evidence of the high priority Australians place on lengthy time away from work. Geographically, Australian experiences of overseas travel were particularly shaped by trips to its closest neighbours in Asia. Whereas Europeans and North Americans could relatively easily travel to Latin America, Africa, the Middle East and Asia, for many Australian tourists, an Asian holiday was a practical solution to the tyranny of distance. For example, in 1973, for the first time, more Australians visited an Asian country than visiting Europe, a trend that has continued without break since 1981. This pivot to Asia is remarkable because, since European colonization in the late eighteenth century, settlers in Australia have historically sought to return to the Mother Country (Britain or Ireland) or alternatively conducted grand tours of Western Europe. A reorientation towards Asia represented a historical as well as a cultural break from past practices.

There are historically contingent reasons why Australians travelled in increasing numbers to Asia. Military engagements after 1945 entangled Australian lives with Asia. The Allied occupation of Japan from 1945 to 1952 involved many Australian men, some of whom engaged in intimate relationships with Japanese women. Most of these interactions were fleeting, while others led to marriage and emigration of Japanese brides to Australia.[103] Importantly, some of these encounters bore children. Despite having a paternal connection to Australia, these children remained stuck

Tourism History 2 (2010): 150–1; Richard White, *A History of Getting Away* (Melbourne: Pluto Press, 2005), 125.

[100] Yves Rees, 'Reading Australian Modernity: Unsettled Settlers and Cultures of Mobility', *History Compass* 15: e12429 (2017): 5, accessed 9 October 2022, https://doi.org/10.1111/hic3.12429.

[101] White, *A History of Getting Away*, xiv.

[102] Agnieszka Sobocinska and Richard White, 'Travel and Connections', in *The Cambridge History of Australia*, vol. 2, ed. Alison Bashford and Stuart McIntyre (Cambridge: Cambridge University Press, 2015), 483.

[103] Rachel Stevens and Seamus O'Hanlon, 'Intimate Oral Histories: Intercultural Romantic Relationships in Postwar Australia', *Australian Historical Studies* 49 (2018): 369–70.

in Japan and, in the words of Moira Dynon in a public address, lived 'in varying degrees of poverty, neglect and social ostracism'.[104] Although the numbers of children fathered by Australian servicemen in Japan were only in the hundreds, their plight captured the interest of Australians who lobbied unsuccessfully for their admission into Australia. These 'abandoned' 'waifs' triggered public outrage and attracted significant press coverage in the 1950s and 1960s and public appeals for aid.[105] Intimate relationships between Australian servicemen and Asian women continued throughout the eleven-year deployment in Vietnam (1962–73). These initial romantic encounters arguably facilitated the growth in sex tourism from the 1970s, particularly in liberal destinations such as Bali, Hong Kong, the Philippines and Thailand. As Richard White observes, although these carnal interactions were undeniably exploitative and unequal, they did humanize Asian workers, thereby negating the appeal of ignorant stereotypes.[106] Increasing trade networks between Australian and Asian nations was another important factor. Historically, Australian exports of raw materials were mostly destined for the UK; in exchange, Australians imported manufactured goods from Europe. But by 1967, Japan became Australia's largest export market. Australian consumers also enjoyed the benefits of cheaper products manufactured in Japan, and later Korea, Taiwan, Indonesia and China. Trade therefore necessitated business travel to the region, further entwining Australian futures with those of its closest neighbours.

Australian travel to Asia boomed during the 1960s and 1970s as it offered both spiritual and hedonistic pursuits, all within Australia's 'pleasure periphery'. The term 'pleasure periphery' was coined by Louis Turner and John Ash in 1975 to describe the 'tourist belt surrounding the great industrialized zones of the world'. They explained that the pleasure periphery is typically two to four hours by aeroplane from major urban centres, generally towards the equator and the sun. I would add that a lower cost of living – relative to home – also seduced many would-be tourists who could not afford a grand tour of Europe. For North Americans, their pleasure periphery included the Caribbean islands, Mexican resorts and Hawaii. Northern Europeans sought pleasure along the Mediterranean Sea. Although Turner and Ash did not mention Australia, their definition is appropriate in this instance. The Pacific Island of Fiji is just over four hours from Sydney and the tourist mecca of Bali, six hours. Significantly, what constitutes a nation's pleasure periphery is dynamic not static, often expanding outwards to locations more and more remote and deemed exotic. For example, an American who holidayed in Hawaii may the next year travel to Tahiti; a Swede who visited Majorca may next time fly to a Greek island.[107] For Australians, their

---

[104] Moira Dynon, 'Australian-Japanese Children in Japan', address, Melbourne, February 1964, 3. Held at NLA.

[105] For two examples of citizens writing to the prime minister on this issue, see Gordon Goring, letter to Prime Minister Robert Menzies, 13 January 1960, NAA: A463, 1957/1908 and Miss Edith Pulsford, letter Edward St John, MP, 28 June 1968, NAA: A1209, 1965/10193. For examples of news coverage on this issue, see NAA: A1209, 1965/10193 and NAA: A463, 1963/2728; for Australian government deliberations on this issue from 1955 to 1962, see NAA: A1838, 3103/10/12/1 PART 1 and NAA: A1838, 3103/10/12/1 PART 2.

[106] White, *A History of Getting Away*, 179.

[107] Louis Turner and John Ash, *The Golden Hordes: International Tourism and the Pleasure Periphery* (London: Constable, 1975), 11–13.

pleasure periphery expanded from Southeast Asia to South Asia, a transition aided by the introduction of overland trips across the continent that made ground travel comfortable, affordable and accessible, even for cash-strapped backpackers. Here, India was central to the counter-cultural image of the East, a country often romanticized as free from the materialism and conformity that beset Western societies.[108] Australian newspapers advertised India as the 'ultimate love story', encouraging air travellers en route to Europe to take a stopover in India to see 'mystic' sights, such as the Taj Mahal.[109] Meanwhile, national carrier Air India advertised in Austcare's quarterly *News Bulletins*, paying for full page, back cover advertisements with the slogan, 'The new place is India'.[110]

Technological advancements in aviation, the mass marketed package holiday and favourable economic conditions conducive to vacationing all contributed to a sharp spike in overseas travel in the second half of the twentieth century. After the Second World War, Australia experienced negative net migration because outward travel exceeded migrant and refugee arrivals, an unusual occurrence for a settler society.[111] Between 1960 and 1970, Australian outbound tourism nearly quintupled in size, from 77,000 Australians departing Australia on a short-term basis in 1960 to 353,000 by 1970. This figure nearly quadrupled again over the next decade, eclipsing 1.2 million short-term departures in 1980.[112] To put it another way, in 1980, over 8 per cent of Australians travelled abroad in one year alone, notwithstanding the possibility of a small minority taking multiple overseas trips that year.

The proclivity of Westerners to travel to traditional recipient countries of aid contributed to the expansion in the NGO sector and citizen-driven humanitarianism. The symbiotic relationship between international travel and overseas aid was made explicit from the 1950s with the introduction of overseas graduate volunteer programmes. Development volunteering, such as Peace Corps in the United States and Voluntary Service Overseas in the UK, became popular among university graduates at the same time as budget travel to the developing world became commonplace. In the case of the Volunteer Graduate Scheme in Australia, graduates cited altruistic internationalism, spiritual growth and adventure as reasons for applying to the programme.[113] Of course, these volunteer schemes only recruited idealistic and youthful university graduates and were not open to members of the general public. To fill this void, two leading Australian humanitarian NGOs – Community Aid Abroad (CAA) and the Freedom from Hunger Campaign (FFHC) – began organizing annual tours of South Asia for interested citizens and donors in the late 1960s. These trips were designed to promote cross-cultural understanding, improve Australians' knowledge of Asia and enable donors to see first-hand the impact of their donations. The organized tours also

---

[108] Agnieszka Sobocinska, *Visiting the Neighbours: Australians in Asia* (Sydney: UNSW Press, 2014), 124–6, 150–1. For a personal memoir, see Asta Gray, *Travelling Rough on the Hippie Trail: Drugs, Danger and Dysentery* (Santa Cruz: CreateSpace, 2016).
[109] For example, see *The Age*, 13 October 1971, 12.
[110] See Austcare News Bulletins in February, May, August, November 1972 and February 1973.
[111] Sobocinska, *Saving the World?* 116.
[112] Sobocinska and White, 'Travel and Connections', 481.
[113] Sobocinska, *Saving the World?* 117.

included meetings with representatives of international aid agencies, including UNICEF, the Food and Agriculture Office and the local branch of the Freedom from Hunger Campaign. In marketing these educational tours, CAA made it clear that participants were not tourists in foreign countries 'but visiting friends overseas'.[114]

Conclusion

Despite its long secular and religious roots, humanitarianism is a very modern idea. Arguably, it was European imperialism that converted abstract ideas regarding charity and human dignity into a global practice of humanitarianism. The trans-Atlantic life-saving and abolitionist movements cemented new forms of political activism. These nascent movements formalized methods of advocacy and protest – for example, by using petitions, staging public meetings and publishing informative periodicals with the goal of shaping public opinion. In an era when Western nations enfranchised increasing segments of their citizenry, public opinion on controversial issues gained a new importance for those seeking political office. Concomitantly, economic developments, such as industrialization and the shift to market-based economies, and cultural advancements in travel and literacy meant that large sections of the public were informed of suffering in foreign countries and had the capacity to contribute to humanitarian causes. Emergent NGOs in the nineteenth and early twentieth centuries were, for the most part, led by elites, such as Herbert Hoover in the case of the United States and Eglantyne Jebb in the UK. These individuals understood the power of imagery and how to elicit sympathy from the public. In this context, children were widely used in numerous de-politicized humanitarian campaigns to project innocence and victimhood.

Alongside such overt sentimentalism, the early decades of the twentieth century witnessed a shift away from the archetypal humanitarian as Christian do-gooder towards the technical expert. Secular NGOs grew in prominence at this time, although Christian charities never ceded completely before a mid-century revival. From the 1940s, humanitarian NGOs bureaucratized and were staffed with technocrats committed to social progress through scientific advancement. The professionalization of the NGO sector may have addressed concerns over volunteer amateurism, but they also opened avenues for new criticisms and cynicism. By 1970, it had long been clear that states alone could not remedy global inequality nor respond to crises. What was new, however, was growing public dissatisfaction with some of the largest, most established humanitarian NGOs, which created a vacuum for new players to emerge. Inspired by the rights-based and protest movements of the 1960s, individuals and development-oriented humanitarian NGOs grew in importance. Furthermore, advancements in media – particularly news media – and the democratization of overseas travel created the conditions for a well-informed, culturally aware and

---

[114] CAA, *Now*, August 1972, cover in Folder 179 'Miscellaneous Reports, Newsletters and Correspondence 1971–72', Box 32 'Folders 177–180', Records of the Australian Freedom from Hunger Campaign [henceforth AFFHC], 1961–73, NLA.

politicized Australian public. This chapter has outlined significant developments in the evolution of humanitarianism and explained how and why citizens practised humanitarianism. The remainder of this book documents humanitarian activities from multiple perspectives: from established, esteemed NGOs such as the Red Cross, to faith-based charities; from elite advocacy to grassroots activism; from career humanitarians to schoolchildren. As we will see, in the case of Australian citizen humanitarianism during the 1971 refugee crisis, this event captured the attention of large sections of the Australian public, leaving no sector of society unaffected.

3

The federations: The Australian Council for Overseas Aid and Austcare

Histories of humanitarianism, particularly in the post-Second World War period, often observe the tensions between the conflicting approach of depoliticized emergency relief and radicalized development aid. This chapter illustrates how this division manifested in the Australian context and the ways that debates about humanitarianism materially impacted aid delivered to Bangladeshi refugees. To begin this story, we first need to take a step back and explore the humanitarian landscape in Australia in the early 1970s. What we find is a highly competitive market, arguably with an oversupply of aid agencies, all seeking funds from a small population base. Given this congested aid environment, humanitarian leaders established in the 1960s centralized, umbrella organizations that aimed to drive efficiency, professionalization and transparency in the sector. This chapter focuses on two such organizations active during the Bangladesh Liberation War: Australian Council for Overseas Aid (ACFOA) and Austcare (short for Australians Caring for Refugees).

Both ACFOA and Austcare served as federations that crossed political and religious divides. But they were not impartial intermediaries. In the sphere of refugee assistance, Austcare and ACFOA coordinated aid delivery, solicited donations from the public (in the case of Austcare) and lobbied the Australian government for assistance, too (ACFOA). Their leaders were elite public figures with decades of civil and military service and, consequently, enjoyed access to the highest levels of government, both domestically and internationally. Austcare and ACFOA wielded considerable power, controlling how donated funds were dispersed among humanitarian NGOs and what aid projects were financially supported. Arguably, these two organizations influenced the trajectories of the Australian aid scene, selecting with little oversight which humanitarian agencies would flourish and which would struggle. Given the primacy of Austcare and ACFOA, this chapter deliberately precedes the following chapters that cover secular, faith-based and grassroots organizations. Austcare and ACFOA were dominated by a handful of leaders who imposed their ideas of what humanitarian aid should aim to achieve and who it served to benefit. Acting like gatekeepers, Austcare and ACFOA commanded the power to marginalize organizations it deemed too radical, much to the irritation of emerging development agencies. NGOs sidelined by Austcare or ACFOA found themselves forming closer alliances with parent organizations abroad or opted out of this process entirely, which in turn facilitated the growth of grassroots bodies and individual activism.

The Australian aid environment

Before examining two distinctly Australian humanitarian organizations and their involvement during the Bangladesh Liberation War, it is important to underscore the extent to which these aid agencies maintained an international outlook that were inspired and influenced by global trends. Many Australian aid organizations were branches of pre-existing charities first established abroad, especially in the UK. For instance, the Australian Red Cross was established in 1914 with the onset of the First World War and was formally part of the British Red Cross Society until 1927. Save the Children Fund (UK) similarly established an Australian branch in 1919.[1] Although Community Aid Abroad was founded as an independent development agency in 1953, by 1971, it was working hand in glove with the left-of-centre Oxfam UK before a formal merger in 1972. Other prominent Australian relief agencies were established from earlier UN initiatives, such as Austcare and the UN World Refugee Year 1959, and Australia's Freedom from Hunger Campaign stemming from the UN's World Food Programme and Food and Agriculture Organization. Christian humanitarian organizations were similarly internationalist, affiliated with global federations that were typically based in Europe. For example, World Christian Action, the relief arm of Australian Council of Churches, closely collaborated with the Geneva-based World Council of Churches' Commission on Inter-Church Aid, Refugee and World Service. Australian Catholic Relief, now known as Caritas Australia, likewise fell under the remit of Caritas Internationalis, the global Catholic aid agency based in Vatican City. When Lutherans established their own humanitarian agency, World Service, in Geneva in 1947, an Australia branch was quickly established by a German migrant and pastor at a migrant resettlement centre in rural Australia in the same year. Australian aid agencies were therefore deeply entangled with their parent organizations in Western Europe. This chapter may concentrate on Australian humanitarians, but their experiences speak indirectly to wider trends across the Western world during the peak of decolonization.

Surveying Australian humanitarian organizations over the past century, it is possible to make a demarcation on three criteria. The first is between NGOs established in the early twentieth century, which in turn flourished during the two world wars, and those founded after 1945. For instance, in the former category, we may include the Red Cross movement, the subject of the next chapter, and the Australian branch of Save the Children Fund. These organizations were typically founded by elites, were informed by Christian ethics even if they eschewed explicit references to religion, and given their longevity, maintained a gravitas and prestige, evident in their cosy relationships to power brokers and government officials. In contrast, Australian

---

[1] Save the Children Fund, *Annual Report 1924*, 7, Box A0680, File 'Annual Reports, 1922/3–1934/5', Save the Children Fund Archive (SCF), Cadbury Research Library, University of Birmingham, UK.

aid organizations founded after 1945 were a diffuse bunch, with some motivated by faith and others unabashedly secular. Some of these agencies were established and run by elites, while others were led by ordinary men and women with little prior experience in the field. After decades of seemingly unbounded growth in the mid-twentieth century, the Australian aid sector experienced a period of consolidation, caused in large part by increasing public demands for efficiency, transparency and professionalization by the 1980s and 1990s. Consequently, some of the post-1945 organizations ceased to exist by the late twentieth century due to lack of funding, the retirement of a founding leader or confusion about the direction of the organization. Paradoxically, the older, pre-1945 humanitarian organizations have proved most resilient to modernization and maintain their positions as pre-eminent bodies within the Australian aid sector. This chapter uses the Bangladeshi refugee crisis to explore changing tides within this landscape, with older organizations uncertain and reactive, while the newer, bolder aid agencies took proactive steps to mobilize the public, solicit funds and enhance their brand awareness in the community.

Second, we can place humanitarian NGOs along a secular/faith spectrum. This book deliberately includes *both* secular and faith-based humanitarian organizations in its analysis and acknowledges that some agencies display elements of both traditions. Although it is tempting to treat secular and religious relief agencies as fundamentally distinct, each with their own motivations, causes and methods of intervention in the field, this assumption is false. Even the most avowedly secular organization may have religious origins – for instance, Oxfam and Community Aid Abroad, discussed in Chapter 6. Andrea Paras and Janice Gross Stein argue that the line between religious and secular humanitarian organizations is 'fuzzy rather than sharp'. To them, Judaeo-Christian religious traditions bring centuries of thought on the problems of humanity and how they are best solved. Indeed, Judaeo-Christian ethics are at the core of many humanitarian principles – for example, the respect for all life, equality and justice. Even if secular humanitarians refrain from employing biblical references, their goals remain influenced by religious morality. Thus, when we imagine a clear division between faith-based and secular humanitarianism, we incorrectly limit the impact of religion on society to religious *practices*, such as church membership or attendance, which is studied in more detail in Chapters 5 and 7.[2] Rather than thinking in terms of dichotomies, Olivia Wilkinson's *Secular and Religious Dynamics in Humanitarian Response* (2020) offers a framework that acknowledges that secular and religious humanitarian organizations exist in an intertwined dynamic that is relational and dialogic.[3] Indeed, the differences between faith-based aid agencies can be greater than those between secular and religious humanitarian NGOs.[4]

Our inclination to distinguish between secular and religious aid may have more to do with marketing and branding of the aid agencies than sound ontological reasons.

---

[2] Andrea Paras and Janice Gross Stein, 'Bridging the Sacred and the Profane in Humanitarian Life', in *Sacred Aid: Faith and Humanitarianism*, ed. Michael Barnett and Janice Gross Stein (New York: Oxford University Press, 2012), 211.
[3] Olivia Wilkinson, *Secular and Religious Dynamics in Humanitarian Response: Routledge Research in Religion and Development* (Oxford: Routledge, 2020), 12–13.
[4] Ferris, 'Faith and Humanitarianism', 621.

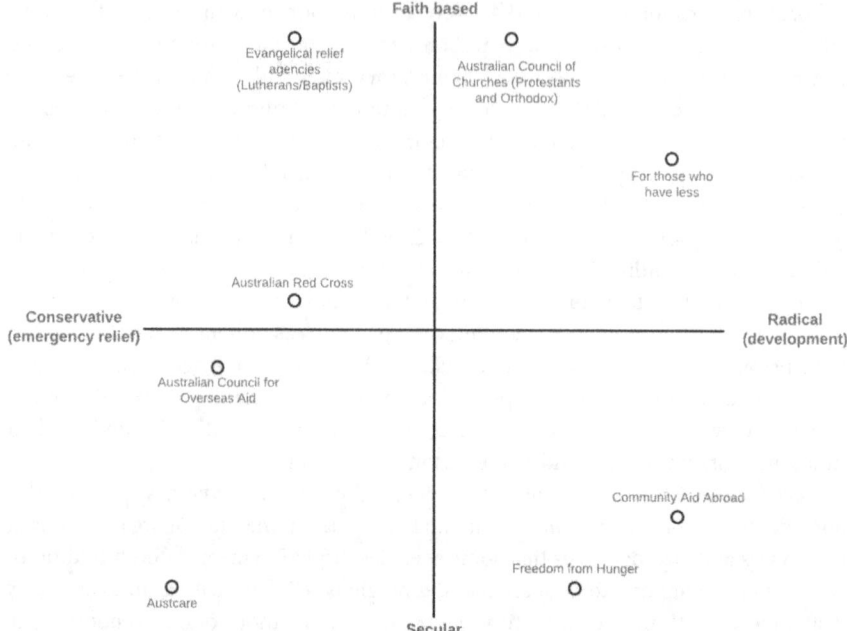

Figure 3.1 Relative position of Australian humanitarian organizations along radical/conservative and secular/faith-based spectra. Created by author.

Stephen Hopgood and Leslie Vinjamuri observe in the American context that faith-based organizations may choose 'to secularize' to access government funds, even if this orientation alienates private donors who identify strongly with the more strident, evangelical humanitarian organizations. Christian Children's Fund (now known as ChildFund International) is one example of this secularizing marketing strategy.[5] But the secularizing impulse is not universal, as demonstrated by the localized marketing strategy of World Vision International, an evangelical American Baptist agency with its origins in 1950s Asia. World Vision is one of the largest and most expansive US aid agencies, with offices in 100 countries, 40,000 employees and a budget over US$2.6 billion. Its growth arguably is due to understanding local circumstances to solicit funds. For example, in Ghana, World Vision presents a neo-Pentecostal image and embraces evangelism. Meanwhile in Australia, World Vision's Christian doctrine is silenced.[6] Thus, not only can humanitarian organizations oscillate between faith-based and secular orientations, but they can also maintain both identities simultaneously to be all things to all people.

---

[5] Stephen Hopgood and Leslie Vinjamuri, 'Faith in Markets', in *Sacred Aid: Faith and Humanitarianism*, ed. Michael Barnett and Janice Gross Stein (New York: Oxford University Press, 2012), 46.

[6] David P. King, 'World Vision: Religious Identity in the Discourse and Practice of Global Relief and Development', *Review of Faith and International Affairs* 9 (2011): 23–5.

Third, in addition to humanitarian organizations fluctuating on a faith/secular spectrum, they also operate on a radical/conservative continuum. The oscillation between radical and conservative poles is not just a philosophical stance as it has had real-world impacts. Generally, conservative (or status quo) organizations, such as the Red Cross (Chapter 4), wanted to provide aid reactively to emergencies – for example, after an earthquake or helping in refugee camps. Such aid was depoliticized, decontextualized and oriented to remediation not prevention. Conversely, radical organizations were more focused on development – that is, preventing crises and addressing the root causes of poverty. Figure 3.1 plots on a quadrant chart eight Australian humanitarian agencies that were active in the Bangladeshi refugee crisis and post-war reconstruction. The motivations and activities of two of these organizations will be examined in this chapter. Christian relief agencies will be discussed in Chapter 5, and Community Aid Abroad (CAA) and the Australian Freedom from Hunger Campaign will be covered in Chapter 6. The purpose of this chart is to show the extent of diversity in this field and to illustrate that the humanitarian landscape in Australia in 1971 was congested; agencies also held very different – and at times conflicting – ideas about who to help and why. As we will see throughout this book, they had to work together out of necessity, but in many ways, the individual organizations found greater support in and affinity with their federating agencies overseas – for instance, CAA and Oxfam UK, the Australian Red Cross and the League Red Cross Societies, and the Australian Council of Churches (ACC) and the World Council of Churches.

Perhaps the most revealing way to examine the Australian humanitarian landscape in 1971 is to calculate the cash donated by citizens to aid Bangladeshi refugees in Indian camps. Figure 3.2 illustrates the citizen donated funds to seven of the main humanitarian organizations from June 1971 to January 1972. As explained in Chapter 2, the UNHCR served as a focal point during the crisis, coordinating both state and voluntary agency (VOLAG) aid activities. In its archives, the UNHCR maintained comprehensive records of cash and goods, both pledged and received. The records consistently show a discrepancy between cash and goods pledged and those received, and it is important to note that some earmarked funds were never received. For this reason, data in Figure 3.2 includes *only* cash received. The Australian Red Cross and Austcare both provided substantial in-kind donations (A$2m and A$1.13m respectively), but as we will see in the next chapter, often, the goods donated were inappropriate or unable to be used for a variety of reasons. Thus, to avoid incorrectly inflating the cumulative amount of aid donated, the graph in Figure 3.2 omits dollar values of in-kind donations. The graph illustrates received donations by month, not cumulative totals. For example, Austcare received A$482,000 for each month of October, November and January, not A$482,000 overall. Austcare received large cash amounts over the three-month period because, as the central fundraiser for Bangladeshi refugee aid in Australia, other aid agencies directed their donors to contribute to Austcare's fundraising appeals. After each appeal, Austcare dispersed funds to its member organizations, as well as setting aside cash donations for its own activities, which explains the seemingly fixed amount for the months of August, October, November and January.

Aside from the centrality of Austcare in fundraising activities, the figure also reveals several trends. First, Australian Catholic Relief received cash donations

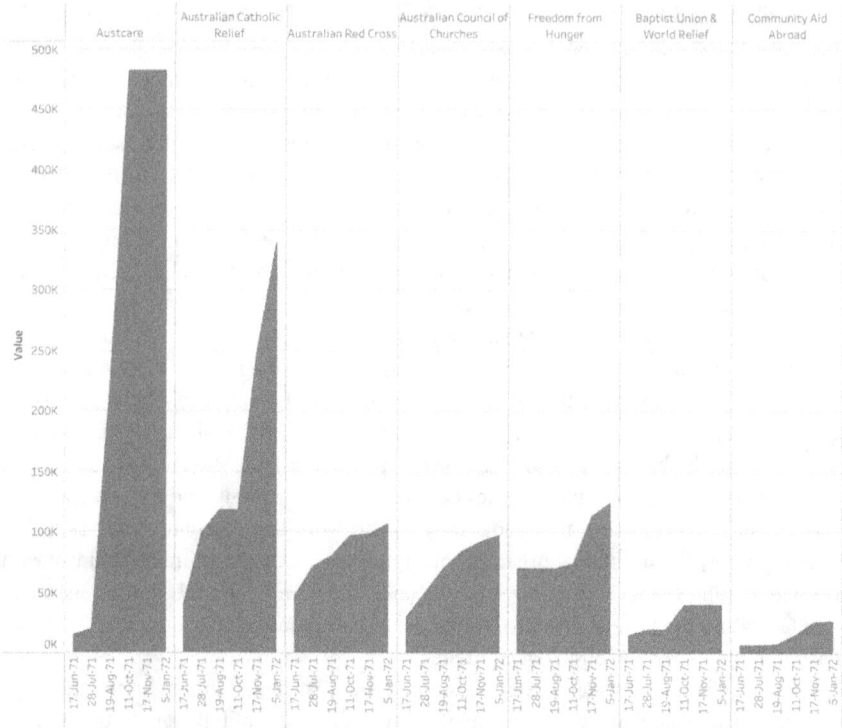

Figure 3.2 Cash donations by humanitarian organization over time in Australian dollars. Created by author from Records of the UNHCR, Geneva, Fonds 11, Box 372, File 11/1-27/3/43/AUL Contributions from NGOs to the Focal Point – Australia 06/1971-1/1972.

greater than that of the Australian Council of Churches. To avoid raising sectarian tensions, Austcare dispersed equal funds to the two religious federations. The gap, therefore, was due to Australian Catholic Relief receiving cash donations outside of its arrangement with Austcare. As we will see in Chapter 5, direct cash contributions from Catholics to Australian Catholic Relief indicates a faith-based community unwilling to engage with a secular organization, preferring instead to deal directly with the Catholic aid agency and its associated overseas bodies, such as Caritas Internationalis. Presumably, this inclination to donate within one's community was not shared with the interdenominational Protestant and Orthodox Australian Council of Churches. When one considers that there were twice as many mainstream Protestants and Orthodox Christians as Catholics in Australia in 1971, the extent of intra-Catholic giving is even more pronounced.[7]

---

[7] According to the 1971 census, 27 per cent of Australians identified as Catholic and 55 per cent identified as mainstream Protestant (Anglican, Methodist, Presbyterian, Lutheran, etc.) and Orthodox. See Commonwealth of Australia, *Census of Population and Housing, Bulletin 1. Summary of Population. Part 9. Australia*, 30 July 1971, 3.

Second, as we will see in the next chapter, the Australian Red Cross did not solicit funds direct from the public, instead, relying on government grants and Austcare allocations. Lastly, by examining donations over a six-month period, we see peaks and troughs in the donation cycle: funds were slow to come in at the beginning, perhaps due to public ignorance of the unfolding crisis or because of compassion fatigue stemming from fundraising campaigns after the 1970 Bhola cyclone. Yet from June, increased press coverage of swelling refugee camps and the beginnings of a cholera outbreak and humanitarian disaster (discussed later) captured the public's imagination, mobilizing aid agencies and the donors on which they rely. There was also an uptick in October for each organization to varying degrees, the result of a combination of factors, including Austcare's Bangladeshi refugee appeal in September, the annual Freedom from Hunger campaign activities in the final quarter of 1971 and public hunger strikes in September to November, which is examined in Chapter 7. Australian humanitarian organizations may have been slow to act at the beginning of hostilities, but by midyear, civil society galvanized, reaching fever pitch by November.

The Australian Council for Overseas Aid

The rapid growth in the humanitarian sector after the Second World War led to a congested landscape, with each agency competing for access to decision-makers, donor dollars and brand recognition. In the early 1960s, establishment figures with secular and/or faith backgrounds endeavoured to streamline the process, avoid public confusion and share resources by creating coordinating bodies. For example, Vaughan Hinton, publicity officer for the ACC, advocated that Austcare should be presented to the public as the sole avenue for donations. He warned that if each agency had their own appeal, 'utter chaos would be the result'.[8] The idea of Australian humanitarians to create an umbrella organization was not original; at the same time and in similar circumstances in the UK, the five largest humanitarian organizations in that country established the Disasters Emergency Council (DEC) in 1963.[9] In both countries, these peak bodies were staffed with veterans of the humanitarian sector, politicians, bureaucrats or religious leaders reflecting its right-of-centre orientation and predisposition towards emergency relief over development assistance. In the Australian context, the rationale for establishing these coordinating bodies was valid. Yet in practice, these councils simply created another layer of bureaucracy and concentrated power in an elite group. ACFOA and Austcare determined how to disburse funds to member organizations, a process that privileged existing humanitarian agencies over emerging ones.

From its origins, ACFOA was closely associated with the Australian government, particularly its departments of external affairs and trade. The impetus for creating ACFOA was driven by Sir John (Jack) Crawford, an esteemed public servant, and

---

[8] Vaughan Hinton, circular letter to all state staff, 9 June 1971, Box 117, folder 'Pakistan, East and West – 1964–71', Records of the ACC.
[9] Jones, 'The Disasters Emergency Committee (DEC) and the Humanitarian Industry in Britain, 1963–85', 578.

from 1960 a scholar at the Australian National University. As a bureaucrat, Crawford was introduced to the development scene through his work as secretary for the departments of commerce and agriculture and, later, trade. Importantly, Crawford was not a humanitarian worker but rather an internationalist who witnessed at close range the challenges and demands of a quickly decolonizing Asia. Over lunch in Canberra in late 1963, Crawford outlined his proposal of a coordinating body to David Scott, chairman of CAA, and Jim Webb, who then led the Overseas Service Bureau (the successor to the Volunteer Graduate Scheme) and would lead CAA himself in 1971; see Chapter 6. Webb later recounted that he suspected the lunch was arranged by the Minister for External Affairs, Sir Garfield Barwick. Regardless, Crawford gained sufficient support from Webb and Scott to expand his remit and solicit interest from additional humanitarian actors. In April 1964, Crawford organized a two-day workshop that included leaders from sixteen humanitarian agencies. The proposal to establish a coordinating body met with a degree of resistance from the attendees, who were wary about relinquishing some autonomy in exchange for sector-wide synergies. Negotiations continued throughout 1964 between Crawford, aid agencies and the Department of External Affairs, which was renamed the Department of Foreign Affairs in November 1970. After much back-and-forth, agreements were reached with twenty-one humanitarian organizations, and ACFOA was formally established in April 1965. The fact that a disparate group of competing organizations eventually formed a coalition has been attributed to Crawford, who 'charmed them into cooperation'.[10]

By 1971, the establishment roots of ACFOA were cemented. Its membership base was concentrated in the Sydney–Canberra–Melbourne triangle of power and had no representation from other states or regional areas. ACFOA reinforced a state-centric approach to humanitarian issues, which was notably at odds with burgeoning grassroots activism at this time, which is the subject of Chapter 6, and was oblivious to the demands of individual humanitarians; see Chapter 7. With a close association with government, ACFOA ensured diversity by mandating that the chairmanship would rotate between members of the centre-left Australian Labor Party (ALP) and members of the centre-right Liberal Party of Australia.[11] Of course, by requiring that the leadership position rotate between the two major political parties in Australia, the design of ACFOA ensured that marginalized or dissenting voices were not heard, let alone empowered.

During the 1971 refugee crisis and post-war reconstruction, ACFOA assisted Bangladeshi refugees in two ways. First, ACFOA focused on lobbying government politicians and bureaucrats for an increase in official aid to India and Bangladesh, which is unsurprising given the organization's close relationship with state actors. Familiarity and friendliness between ACFOA leaders and government officials is evident in the language used in letters. For instance, a Department of Foreign Affairs letter to ACFOA Executive Director Geoffrey Solomon, began with the casual, familiar greeting, 'Dear

---

[10] Patrick Kilby, *NGOs and Political Change a History of the Australian Council for International Development* (Canberra: ANU Press, 2015), 33–46.

[11] Major-General Paul Cullen, interviewed by Diana Ritch, 1983, accessed 3 September 2018, https://nla.gov.au/nla.obj-195610045, transcript, 38.

Geoff'.[12] Letters from government to ACFOA were lengthy and their prose original, and they were signed by the official in charge rather than an assistant. Prime Minister William McMahon personally signed a two-page detailed response to a letter from ACFOA chairman Major General Paul Cullen. Typically, letters from constituents or MPs to the prime minister would receive a standardized response from a staffer that simply acknowledged the receipt of the letter and reiterated government policy on aid to Bangladeshi refugees.[13] In contrast, McMahon's letter to Cullen explained and justified government policy and acknowledged the specific objections of Cullen.[14] The gravitas of ACFOA office bearers, therefore, enabled a dialogic relationship with government. While other agencies courted citizen or corporate donations, ACFOA mostly focused on soliciting an increase in official Australian aid for refugees as well as securing the provision of government logistical support for the disbursement of aid.

ACFOA urged the Australian government to increase its aid for Bangladeshi refugees and post-war reconstruction from A$5.5 million to A$20 million (A$245 million in 2022). In a letter to Foreign Minister Nigel Bowen, ACFOA chairman Cullen observed that many figures for Australian government aid had been bandied about, including at one end of the spectrum, A$10 million or, alternatively, A$1 per head of the Australian population (approximately A$12 million). At the other end of the spectrum, proposals included donating A$50 million immediately followed by giving an additional A$50 million at a later date. Reflecting the centre-right position of Cullen and ACFOA more broadly, the chairman advocated a figure (A$20 million) that was closer to the lower end of the range. Cullen justified this figure based on some creative accounting. According to Cullen, he reasoned that 'the response of the Australian government and other governments should be related to their assessed contribution to the operation of the UN organisation'. If we accept this assumption, then it followed that the Australian government donation should be commensurate with Australia's ongoing financial support of the UN, which at that time was 1.47 per cent of the total UN budget. This percentage equated to A$15 million donated over a twelve-month period. Cullen then added a 'regional loading' of A$5 million, 'which would have taken cognizance of the fact that India lies very much in the area of our interest and is a country to which, on all counts, an additional neighbourly contribution would have been entirely appropriate'.[15] The Cullen formula (annual UN contribution plus a regional loading) reveals two interesting world views so prevalent in mid-twentieth-century Australia: one, the centrality of the UN to the international world order; two, a deliberate realignment away from Europe towards Asia.

---

[12] Brian Burke, bureaucrat in the Department of Foreign Affairs, letter to Geoffrey Solomon, 17 April 1973, Box 40 'Refugees', file 201 'Aid to Bangladesh 1971-5', Records of the Australian Council for Overseas Aid (ACFOA), NLA.

[13] See letters to constituents from the Prime Minister's Office in Box 442 and 443, and letters to MPs in Box 447, 448, 449, 450, and 451 in Subseries 17/8 Correspondence 1971/2, Series 17 Prime Minister, 1967-72, Papers of Sir William McMahon, NLA.

[14] William McMahon, letter to Major General Paul Cullen, 2 May 1972, Box 40 'Refugees', file 201 'Aid to Bangladesh 1971-5', Records of ACFOA.

[15] Paul Cullen, letter to Nigel Bowen, 15 February 1972, file 201, Records of ACFOA and ACFOA, Minutes of Executive Committee Meeting, 24-25 March 1972, Minutes journal, 15 August 1971-25 August 1973, File 301, Box 57, Records of ACFOA.

Furthermore, Cullen was a confident, some would say brash, internationalist who felt emboldened in a decolonizing region and wished the Australian government to distance itself from the legacies of European imperialism in Asia. Cullen attempted to persuade the foreign minister to increase government aid by claiming that A$20 million was 'something commensurate with our influence and worthy of our international image'. He also rebuked previous government rationales for limiting aid to A$5.5 million on the basis that it was comparable to the contributions of other similar governments. Cullen dismissed the government's rationale, stating, 'we would certainly expect the Australian government to do no less comparatively than any other government similarly placed'. Cullen pleaded with the foreign minister to take the lead on matters of foreign aid rather than meekly following the (low) standard set by other countries. He wrote, 'Our hope has always been, and will continue to be, that the Australian government would do considerably more and in doing so give a lead to others'.[16] The position of Cullen, and by extension ACFOA, was an optimistic and assertive one in which he imagined his government would take a principled stance in helping new nations emerge from wars of decolonization.

The second way in which ACFOA assisted Bangladeshi refugees was by organizing essential logistical support for other aid agencies, acting as a conduit between NGOs, the government and Indian officials. Although logistical support rarely captures the headlines, it presents the crucial link between goods donated and goods received. This is even more true in the case of the Bangladeshi refugee crisis in which there were millions of displaced people scattered in clusters across eastern India, many of whom located in hard to access mountainous areas. In order to reach refugees in remote locations, ACFOA lobbied the Australian government to secure the use of small and nimble aircraft that had the capacity to land and take off on small runways. In practice, this meant that aid could be dispensed in locations other than Dum Dum airport in Kolkata, which as we will see in Chapter 5, was receiving aid at a rate faster than local workers could dispense.[17]

ACFOA worked closely with the Australian Department of Foreign Affairs, with the government chartering flights to ship donated goods from Australia to India. Working in collaboration with Austcare and the Australian Red Cross, ACFOA and the Australian government organized the use of Royal Australian Air Force aircraft, an arrangement that became vital after national carrier Qantas abandoned its commercial cargo service to Kolkata earlier in 1971.[18] By late September 1971, the monsoon season – and all the logistical and health challenges it had created in refugee camps – was coming to an end. New challenges, however, would emerge in the winter come November, creating fissures between the previously cosy relationship between ACFOA and the Australian government. The refugees in camps in the high-altitude hills in Assam, Meghalaya and Tripura faced freezing

[16] Paul Cullen, letter to Nigel Bowen, 15 February 1972, file 201, Records of ACFOA.
[17] Dum Dum airport in Kolkata was renamed Netaji Subhas Chandra Bose International Airport in 1995.
[18] Paul Cullen, letter to Hon. Walter L. Rice, American Ambassador to Australia', 18 November 1971, Box 2, file 13 'ACFOA Chairmen, Paul Cullen and Neil Batt, 1971–1977', Records of ACFOA.

conditions and lacked adequate clothing. Paul Cullen, Chairman of ACFOA and National President of Austcare, wrote to the Deputy Secretary of the Department of Foreign Affairs, Sir Keith (Mick) Shann, on 27 September 1971, suggesting that Australia rapidly manufacture woollen blankets, a product that was in excess supply at that time.[19]

Shann was a likely sympathetic ally for ACFOA. As a diplomat, he was posted across decolonizing Asia, stationed at embassies in Manila and Jakarta from 1955 to 1966, and on returning to Australia, ran the department's aid and economic division before becoming deputy secretary in 1970.[20] Although Shann may have supported exporting woollen blankets to India in principle, in practice, logistical disputes soured the relationship between ACFOA and the foreign affairs department. Specifically, Shann and Cullen disagreed on the type of aircraft to airlift the aid: Cullen and ACFOA favoured the Caribou with its agile short take-off and landing capability. Conversely, Shann and the foreign affairs department offered the Hercules aircraft, which had a longer range, faster speeds and larger cargo capacity than the Caribou. Shann replied to Cullen's letter on 30 September, explaining that 'our studies at the time (some months ago) showed that in terms of payload and cost effectiveness that the Caribou did not compare favourably with the Hercules'.[21] In response, Cullen was incredulous. In his 14 October letter, Cullen wrote,

> With regard to the aeroplanes, I must say that I am surprised at your comments.
> The cost effectiveness of the Hercules must be very much better than the Caribou.
> But this is not the point at all.
> If it were the only point, then of course no nation would include in its service aircraft, Caribous.
> But they nearly all do carry this aeroplane, or a similar type.
> The reason is of course that the Caribou can land in about 100 times as many places as Hercules.
> Furthermore, it is not necessarily economic per flight to use Hercules as compared with the Caribous, even though if theoretically both were full and both use a particular airstrip, then per lb. there would be cost effectiveness.
> No doubt your Defence colleagues will confirm this view.[22]

The concerns raised by Cullen were valid as the greatest need for blankets was at the foothills of the Himalayas, a significant distance from the nearest major airstrip that could accommodate Hercules planes.

---

[19] Paul Cullen, letter to K. C. O. Shann, 27 September 1971, file 13 'ACFOA Chairmen, Paul Cullen and Neil Batt, 1971–1977'.
[20] Sir Keith Shann, interviewed by Ken Henderson, 21–23 August 1985, accessed 29 October 2021, https://nla.gov.au/nla.obj-196345662, transcript, 155–7, NLA.
[21] K. C. O. Shann, letter to Paul Cullen, 30 September 1971, file 13 'ACFOA Chairmen, Paul Cullen and Neil Batt, 1971–1977'.
[22] Paul Cullen, letter to K. C. O. Shann, 14 October 1971, file 13 'ACFOA Chairmen, Paul Cullen and Neil Batt, 1971–1977'.

Frustrated at government resistance, Cullen sought alternative routes to India – namely, through the American Embassy in Australia. At this point, the US government had offered to charter and fund the cost of airfreighting blankets from any country of origin to the refugee camps. The American gesture was significant. Over recent months, ACFOA had secured 200,000 blankets, weighing 300 tonnes, and as such, the cost of airfreight would have been considerable.[23] The following week, Cullen and Shann engaged in a curt telephone exchange about the proposed American offer. According to conversation notes penned by Cullen, Shann was 'very cross' when Cullen outlined the American airlift of Australian blankets. Cullen documented their conversation:

I [Cullen] said:	We have to get the blankets to India and Mr Spratt [the American diplomat in Australia] says there will only be the three plane loads.
He [Shann] said:	I think you are playing the game both ways. I agreed to your request the moment you asked me.
I said:	You did, and thank you, but when Mr Spratt said there would be no more planes, I had no alternative but the repursue the matter with the American Government
He said:	You obviously did so before you approached us.
I said:	Yes, in a general sense, to test the validity of the offer made in the circular, but I only pursued it when informed that the Australian Government would not be providing more than three planes.
I said:	Please don't be cross Mr Shann.
He said:	I am very cross indeed.
I said:	There is no need to be. I am only trying to get the blankets to India.[24]

Cullen concluded with the comment, 'I didn't want him [Shann] to think that I was a B.S. [bullshitter] because I really wasn't. All I was trying to do was get the blankets to India.'[25] In this clearly one-sided account, Cullen presented himself as selfless and altruistic, seemingly oblivious to how his actions would impact the perceptions of the Australian government in India. As a veteran public campaigner, Cullen would not have been so naïve but in fact was a shrewd negotiator with contacts in the highest levels of government. The experience, skill and networks of Cullen is perhaps why ACFOA member organizations paid him A$1,500 for his lobbying to government, which was equivalent to three months' salary for the average male in 1971.[26] This consultancy fee was not publicly disclosed and only available in the archival records of CAA. Arguably,

---

[23] Paul Cullen, letter to Hon. Walter L. Rice, American Ambassador, 18 November 1971, file 13 'ACFOA Chairmen, Paul Cullen and Neil Batt, 1971–1977'.
[24] Paul Cullen, memorandum: re: Blankets for Refugees, telephone conversation between Cullen and Mr Shann, 3.15 pm, 26 November 1971, file 13 'ACFOA Chairmen, Paul Cullen and Neil Batt, 1971–1977'.
[25] Ibid.
[26] Minutes of meeting, National Committee, Community Aid Abroad, 10 May 1972, Folder 5, 'Community Aid Abroad', Records of Community Aid Abroad, NLA. ABS, 'Average Weekly Earnings. June 1971', accessed 24 February 2022, https://www.ausstats.abs.gov.au/ausstats/free.nsf/0/743DBDA3F3F797D0CA25751600108605/$File/63020_JUN1971.pdf.

this fee-for-influence represents the worst aspects of professionalization – namely, that leaders within humanitarian organizations could award themselves inflated salaries commensurate with the commercial world rather than what was accepted practice across the charity sector.

As we can see in the example of the ACFOA debates with the Department of Foreign Affairs, Paul Cullen was front and centre in this exchange over logistical support for Australian humanitarian agencies. The influence of Cullen also extended to Austcare in which he was national president. Both ACFOA and Austcare were coordinating organizations, albeit with distinct remits: as we have seen, ACFOA focused on negotiating with government. Austcare, conversely, ran annual and special fundraising appeals on behalf of thirteen humanitarian organizations, soliciting donations from individuals and corporations, and then disbursed the monies raised to agencies to fund specific aid projects. The fact that one man led two coordinating agencies that controlled the purse strings of numerous humanitarian organizations was never raised as a concern, at least according to the archived documents. With this concentration of power, Cullen wielded vast influence, and his perspectives reigned over alternative viewpoints, which as we will see, caused friction with some of the more political and younger humanitarians. Furthermore, the dominance of one man, with antiquated world views and prejudices, was problematic. Yet Cullen's hubris blinded him to his shortcomings.

Paul Cullen (born Cohen) was born into a wealthy, aristocratic Jewish family with roots in Australia since the early nineteenth century. Cullen's ancestors played critical roles in the colonization of Australia, including in politics, with three of Cullen's great grandfathers serving as members of Australian parliaments – two in New South Wales and one in Victoria – and in business. His maternal grandfather, Alfred David Hart, was a founder of the modern tobacco trade in Australia and chairman of the Foster's Brewing Company that eventually conglomerated in 1907 to form part of the Carlton and United Breweries beverage behemoth.[27] Beyond politics and business, by the twentieth century, the Cohen family entered the humanitarian and civic sphere. Sir Samuel Cohen, Paul's father, was a key figure within the Sydney Jewish community, serving as president of the orthodox Great Synagogue of Sydney, founding president of the Australian Jewish Welfare Society (AJWS) in 1937, founding president of the Australian Fund for German Refugees in 1938 and patron of the Zionist Mizrachi Palestine Committee in New South Wales. Sir Samuel was also active in non-Jewish causes, supporting a suite of orphan aid organizations and hospitals.[28]

Paul Cullen followed in his father's footsteps, mixing business interests with humanitarianism throughout his life. A decorated soldier during the Second World War, Cullen fought in the Greek campaign. In a newspaper interview in 1971, Cullen explained why he changed his surname, 'We spent a lot of time dodging Germans … I thought it would be mad to be caught by the Germans with a name like Cohen, so

---

[27] Paul Cullen, interviewed by Diana Ritch, 2.
[28] Martha Rutledge, 'Cohen, Sir Samuel Sydney (1869–1948)', in *Australian Dictionary of Biography*, accessed 24 February 2022, https://adb.anu.edu.au/biography/cohen-sir-samuel-sydney-5718/text9671.

I decided to change it', which he did by deed poll at the Australian consular office in Palestine.[29] Like his father, Cullen was active in Jewish humanitarian organizations during the 1930s, although he 'increasingly became non-receptive to the dogmatic and strict orthodox Jewish rituals and ideas'.[30] To reconcile his ambivalence towards the Jewish community in Sydney, Cullen channelled his humanitarian endeavours towards universal refugee relief rather than exclusively Jewish aid and helped establish a liberal synagogue in Sydney that aligned with his progressive attitudes. He also embraced internationalist causes, such as the League of Nations and various United Nations agencies, including working for the UN's World Refugee Year, from which Austcare was established.

Cullen's upbringing and life experiences directed him to humanitarian work, but arguably, it was his temperament that enabled him to have a lasting impact on the Australian aid sector. Academically gifted in a range of subjects, Cullen trained in accountancy, which he took to 'like a duck to water'.[31] He worked in a range of industries: taxation law, merchant banking, pastoral land holding and horse thoroughbred breeding. Cullen's varied interests bestowed upon him even greater affluence, adding to his significant inherited wealth. Described as 'straightforward, business-like but affable and outgoing', Cullen was an effective leader, lobbyist and visionary, and comfortable in high society.[32] In an interview late in life, Cullen reflected on what motivated him. His answer was disarmingly simple, saying, 'I just feel that I must do something about improving the current situation in whatever field of endeavour I am operating'. Cullen self-identified as 'an interventionist', acknowledging that he was 'not really a very meek man ... I think I know better than other people, often, about what should be done'. Cullen conceded that such a gung-ho approach may be viewed as a defect but insisted his intentions were always good.[33] In interviews and his biography, Cullen was seldom immobilized with self-doubt. For him, what mattered was doing something, especially in a crisis. His interventionist approach was typical of the times, although Cullen lacked the self-awareness that influenced his contemporaries – for example, Oxfam's Bernhard Llewellyn (see Chapter 6). Perhaps the arrogance of Cullen was due to his station in life or his cumulative successes in the army, business and civic life. Regardless, Paul Cullen wielded considerable power through ACFOA and Austcare, influencing how funds would be raised from the public and how donations would be disbursed and lobbying government officials.

Austcare

Austcare was a product of the post-1945, UN-driven international order and from its birth appears out of place in the activist political milieu of 1970s Australia. During the

---

[29] Vincent Smith, 'Army to Austcare and Beyond', *National Times*, 14–19 June 1971, 34.
[30] Paul Cullen, interviewed by Diana Ritch, 26.
[31] Ibid., 4.
[32] Smith, 'Army to Austcare and Beyond'.
[33] Paul Cullen, interviewed by Diana Ritch, 44.

late 1950s and early 1960s, individuals, NGOs, governments and the UN campaigned to aid refugees as part of the UN's World Refugee Year (WRY) in 1959–60. In Australia, leading figures in the humanitarian sector established a local WRY committee to lead operations – namely, through campaigns to raise awareness, understanding, empathy and material support.[34] As an active member of the United Nations Association of Australia and AJWS, Paul Cullen was deeply involved in WRY events. But as the WRY committee approached its natural conclusion, Cullen and other supporters lamented that the 'good work' and public profile of the WRY organization would fade into irrelevance, lest the committee cease its work. With the UN's WRY now long gone, Cullen, Baptist minister Rev. Alan Prior and Rev. Harvey Perkins, then head of the ACC, discussed a new coordinating body that would raise and distribute funds on a permanent basis. Austcare was thus established in 1967. Its first CEO was Baptist minister Rev. Geoff Parish, and its first chairman, and later president, was Paul Cullen who would lead the organization in some capacity at least until retirement in 1990, aged eighty-one.[35]

Austcare was a central fundraising body as well as financially supporting its own operations in the field. It began with an annual nationwide door knock appeal, which was a popular method of fundraising at the time. Austcare's initial raison d'être was simple: to coordinate fundraising appeals for disparate NGOs to free limited resources of member organizations. However, soon into its existence, Austcare began accepting unsolicited donations throughout the year and took responsibility for lobbying the Australian government about refugee issues, thereby negating any claims of impartial management and distracting it from its singular purpose. With religious leaders central to the establishment of Austcare, it is no surprise that ACR and ACC received generous allocations, receiving 20 per cent each of the donated funds. The remaining 60 per cent was shared between eleven other humanitarian organizations.[36] Austcare attempted to address critiques that plagued humanitarian work, such as the wasting or misuse of donated funds. To do so, Austcare only financially supported refugee aid projects in which the member body could guarantee supervision 'at the grassroots level', a process that Austcare described as 'genius'.[37]

By the time of the Bangladesh Liberation War, Austcare was just four years old but primed to dominate the Australian civilian response to the refugee crisis. Austcare scheduled its standard annual door knock appeal on 13 May 1971, raising A$1,078,558. Within weeks, a second, specific appeal for Bangladeshi refugees was launched on 9 June 1971 and coincided with similar collective appeals launched in Britain, Ireland and Canada.[38] By the end of 1971, Austcare had raised A$1,251,523 during the second appeal for Bangladeshi refugees. In total, in 1971, Austcare raised A$2,335,251, a record for the young organization.[39] As Cullen recalled in his 1983 interview, 'Austcare

---

[34] For the Australian campaign, see Damousi, 'World Refugee Year 1959-60'; for the global campaign, see Gatrell, *Free World*.
[35] Kevin Baker, *Paul Cullen: Citizen and Soldier* (Hong Kong: Everbest Printing, 2002), 204–5. Walt Secord, 'Refugee Head Retires', *The Australian Jewish News*, 14 September 1990, 8.
[36] Baker, *Paul Cullen. Citizen and Soldier*, 204.
[37] Austcare, *Austcare News Bulletin*, May 1972, 10.
[38] O'Sullivan, *The NGO Moment*, 39.
[39] *Austcare News Bulletin*, August 1972, 10.

had its peak year in 1971, when I think three million dollars was collected, which was a lot of money in those days'.[40] The fact that Cullen recalled donations of three million dollars, some 30 per cent above the actual receipts, reveals the lingering positive effect of 1971 and his propensity for self-congratulation.

As we will see in Chapter 4, some humanitarian agencies such as the Red Cross struggled to source up-to-date information from the refugee camps for publicity and fundraising. Austcare, however, was spared these frustrations. Paul Cullen visited West Bengal twice in May and October 1971, trips that were organized and sponsored by the Australian foreign affairs department, the Indian High Commission in Australia, the government of West Bengal and Austcare. Unlike other aid agencies that simply could not justify sending personnel abroad merely for 'observational' tours, Cullen leveraged his networks and high standing in society, so that governments paid for most of his travel costs. Moreover, Cullen's contacts in government ensured access to key figures and decision-makers in West Bengal. During his six-day tour, Cullen met with thirty-one individuals, including the governor, chief secretary, first secretary of West Bengal, the cabinet secretary of the Indian government, the director and deputy director of refugee relief and rehabilitation as well as numerous aid workers, including individuals representing Oxfam UK, the Indian Christian Agency for Social Action (CASA) and local Catholic agencies.[41] On arrival, Cullen was treated 'like royalty': he was greeted on the tarmac by Australian Deputy High Commissioner Douglas Sturkey and granted a full police escort to his accommodation, the Raj Bavan, or governor's mansion. As Cullen settled into his suite, the butler offered wine, whisky and 'female companionship', which were all declined.[42] In his biography, Cullen was noted as feeling 'trapped, having to stay in opulent surroundings although he [Cullen] had come to see what could be done for the poor'.[43] In this instance, Cullen was ambivalent about his privileged position, yet it was this social standing that enabled him access to the refugee camps in the first place.

As a result of his tour, Cullen made three recommendations. First, he proposed 'maximum publicity … emphasizing humanitarian aspects' and 'avoiding but not shunning political aspects'.[44] All humanitarian organizations must decide the extent to which they will acknowledge the political (i.e. human and therefore avoidable) causes of disaster. As will be shown in Figure 4.1, overt discussions of politics were seldom an either/or proposition but rather a spectrum in which agencies oscillated between opposing poles that reflected the ideological orientation of the organization and its leadership. In the case of Austcare and Cullen, their strategy was to decontextualize the refugee crisis from wider events to avoid attributing blame, a decision that was opposed by Community Aid Abroad, as we will see in Chapter 6. Moreover, the decision of Austcare to focus on humanitarian aspects enabled them to elicit emotions

---

[40] Cullen, interviewed by Diana Ritch, 37.
[41] Paul Cullen, 'Visit to India – West Bengal Calcutta & Districts', in Folder 'Pakistan, East and West, 1964–71', Records of Australian Council of Churches.
[42] Baker, *Paul Cullen. Citizen and Soldier*, 204.
[43] Ibid.
[44] Cullen, 'Visit to India – West Bengal Calcutta & Districts', 2.

in the Australian public, such as compassion and pity, which could prompt acts of charity if not sentiments of political solidarity.[45]

Second, Cullen recommended establishing a medical centre in West Dinajpur, a West Bengal district that shares a border with north-eastern Bangladesh. Cullen noted that West Dinajpur was home to 300,000 refugees in need of medical care to treat cholera, small pox, typhoid and general emergencies. The proposed medical centre would be operated by CASA (aligned with WCC) and the Indian Catholic Relief Services, employing four doctors and sixteen nurses. All personnel would be Indian and the centre financed by Austcare to the value of A$15,000 per quarter. This medical centre became the symbol of Austcare intervention during the Bangladesh war, showcasing practical assistance, administered by local staff, overseen by local agencies and governments and funded by Australians.[46] The decision of Austcare to employ local staff rather than send Australian volunteers to India demonstrates financial nous as well as an appreciation for independence in postcolonial India. As we will see in the next chapter, the Australian Red Cross lacked this cultural understanding of the countries in which they operated.

Lastly, during his tour, Cullen witnessed that 'people were living in the open in terrible wet conditions', which contributed to the transmission of disease and deaths. The need for shelter was obvious, so the question was, what material would provide shelter all the while being sufficiently light to allow for transportation and malleable to permit customization to specific environments? The Indian government suggested tarpaulins, even though this material is heavy and therefore would increase the cost of freight. Conversely, Cullen believed plastic sheeting would be better than tarpaulins as it was lightweight and sufficiently durable to protect against monsoonal rains. Cullen recalled,

> It was my idea to import from Australia vast rolls of ten-foot-wide plastic sheeting, which was issued and cut up into lengths, ten feet by thirty feet, to make some sort of tent shelter for these people. This has since become common practice in refugee crisis situations, but Austcare bought hundreds of thousands of linear yards of this and it was air freighted free, by Qantas, to Bengal, and taken right up and down the area.[47]

In this quotation, Cullen takes credit for the introduction of plastic sheeting as a form of shelter and its legacy use. Cullen failed to mention that such material would only suffice during monsoon conditions in warm climes and would offer inadequate protection in winter, particularly in the chilly foothills of the Himalayas. Still, Cullen demonstrated the practical advantages of a strong leader in a humanitarian

---

[45] For historiography on the history of emotions in humanitarianism, particularly through media outlets, see Johannes Paulmann, ed., *Humanitarianism and Media: 1900 to the Present* (New York: Berghahn Books, 2018); Heide Fehrenbach and Davide Rodogno, eds, *Humanitarian Photography: A History* (Cambridge: Cambridge University Press, 2015) and Brenda Lynn Edgar, Valérie Gorin and Dolores Martín-Moruno, eds, *Making Humanitarian Crises: Emotions and Imagery* (Cham: Springer, 2022).

[46] Ibid. and *Austcare News Bulletin*, November 1971, cover.

[47] Cullen, interviewed by Diana Ritch, 37.

organization: his autocratic style of decision-making facilitated a rapid response to weather conditions; he also used his influence to ensure free freight passage from Qantas while it was still operating cargo flights to Kolkata.

Most of the funds raised through the Austcare appeals were distributed to member organizations. According to Austcare publications, the process for securing Austcare funds had two stages. First, member bodies submitted proposed projects for funding, which were evaluated by the management committee of Austcare. It is unclear how projects were assessed and on what criteria. The committee recommended specific projects for funding, subject to approval of the national council during the annual general meeting. Again, there was no mention of why some projects were approved over others.[48] The first round of allocations occurred in November 1971. As mentioned earlier, ACC and ACR were automatically granted 20 per cent each. In this case, they received A$215,300 for their projects. Australian UN committees, such as UNICEF and UNHCR, also fared well, receiving A$100,000 and A$216,500, respectively, and likely reflected Cullen's close association with UN agencies in Australia. Evangelical Christian agencies received substantial funds, including the Baptists (A$43,060) and Lutherans (A$66,325).[49] These funds and subsequent allocations were used to sponsor a range of reconstruction and rehabilitation programmes in 1972 and 1973. For example, Austcare allocated funds to Baptist World Aid that in turn financed the reconstruction of the Joyramkura hospital near Mymensingh, emergency feeding of children, the repair of contaminated or damaged wells and ongoing support for returning refugee farmers who had lost land, cattle, and equipment during the war. For ACR, Austcare funds sponsored the relocation and return of refugees to former farmlands in Bangladesh, thereby assisting with food production. As we will see in Chapter 5, ACC worked closely with CASA and, later, the Bangladesh Ecumenical Relief and Rehabilitation Service to help with the reconstruction, specifically through boring wells to ensure access to clean drinking water. Lutherans meanwhile provided funds to pay for seed crops, cattle and the reconstruction of schools and homes. The many reconstruction programmes are too numerous to mention. Awash with donated funds, Austcare seemingly could support a suite of social and economic aid programmes. What is striking is that among these riches, CAA was only allocated A$15,000 from the Austcare appeals. Why CAA was granted such a miserly amount is the subject of Chapter 6.

Conclusion

This chapter has demonstrated the long-term impacts of the post-Second World War growth in humanitarian organizations. With a proliferation of budding aid agencies, each with their own specific causes, political agendas and donor base, established organizations agreed to pool their resources for the greater good. To avoid overt

---

[48] *Austcare News Bulletin*, May 1972, 10.
[49] *Austcare News Bulletin*, November 1971, 10.

competition in an industry aspiring to the lofty ideals of charity and self-sacrifice, the umbrella organizations of Austcare and ACFOA were established in the mid-1960s. The idea of creating a peak body to lobby government and citizens for money was nothing new and borrowed from existing practices in Britain. In Australia, both federations justified their existence on their ability to cut costs and minimize duplication of publicity and fundraising campaigns, which could create public confusion. The creation of Austcare and ACFOA was, in essence, an outcome in the pursuit of the sector to professionalize the industry, add transparency to their processes and hold humanitarian organizations to account to the donors from which they solicited funds. However, this chapter has shown the extent to which ACFOA and Austcare attempted to shape the direction of humanitarian practices and curtail the power of NGOs that were ideologically and politically oppositional to these centre-right federations.

In this chapter, Austcare particularly fared worse than ACFOA. Austcare may have had its peak fundraising year in 1971, but it belonged to a different era. Cullen was a humanitarian with imperialist impulses and reflected the aspirations and actions of early-twentieth-century philanthropists rather than the political activism of the early 1970s. Although Austcare and Cullen funded local medical centres staffed by Indians rather than despatching Australian volunteers, arguably he did so for financial rather than cultural reasons. For agencies that did not share the political orientation of Cullen, the dominance of this individual during the Australian response to the refugee crisis was particularly acute. The insistence of Cullen that aid agencies raise funds by emphasizing the humanitarian aspects of the crisis while overshadowing the political roots of the war illustrates his myopic world view. As such, Cullen wilfully minimized the postcolonial struggle for liberation and was oblivious to minority rights movements that were gaining traction across the globe at this time. In conclusion, Cullen was tone-deaf to emerging trends, yet he still controlled the purse strings for many Australian humanitarian organizations. For faith-based and secular radicals, this was an intolerable scenario.

4

The establishment: The Red Cross movement

On 8 June 1971, Henrik Beer, Secretary General of the League of Red Cross Societies (LRCS), and Jean-Pierre Robert-Tissot, the Director of its Relief Bureau, issued a circular memorandum to all national societies. In this seven-page memorandum, the Geneva-based LRCS leadership outlined the 'enormous humanitarian needs of refugees' in India. At that time, the LRCS noted that there were already four million refugees in India and that this displaced population was increasing at a rate of 60,000 refugees per day. The LRCS leaders announced that the total cost to the international community would be US$60 million, equivalent to approximately US$450 million in today's money.[1] In the memorandum, Beer and Robert-Tissot listed their proposed relief activities for the refugees in India, including feeding stations, medical care and providing shelter. But to provide such relief, the LRCS required ongoing cash and in-kind assistance from national societies across the world.[2] The way in which the LRCS framed the problem (Bangladeshis fleeing civil war to seek safety in India) seems uncontroversial at first glance. However, the Pakistani Red Cross Society held a different view.

One week later, on 15 June 1971, Pakistani Red Cross Secretary General Safdar Ali Khan sent a letter to the LRCS and all national societies 'to set the record right'. In the letter, Safdar reiterated comments by the Pakistani President, Yahya Khan, that all Pakistani citizens 'who had fled across the border [into India] during the recent upheaval in East Pakistan will be accepted back in the country and rehabilitated'. Safdar argued that his government and the UNHCR were working together to assist refugee repatriation and, indeed, that refugees were already beginning to return to Bangladesh. The true culprit, Safdar alleged, was the Indian government. Safdar wrote,

> The Government of India is using the present situation to its political advantage and for maligning Pakistan. The refugees are being discouraged from returning to their homes by giving publicity to the fabricated stories about the situation in

---

[1] 'Inflation Calculator', US Official Inflation Data, accessed 30 April 2023, https://www.officialdata.org.

[2] League of Red Cross Societies (henceforth LRCS) – Relief Bureau Circular No. 471, 'Refugees from East Pakistan in India', 8 June 1971, Box (Unit) 426, Folder 10 'Divisions Pakistan Conflict, Vol - 1+ 2, R - T', 1971', Records of the Australian Red Cross – National Office, 2015.0033. Correspondence Files, National Headquarters, University of Melbourne Archives, Melbourne, Australia.

East Pakistan. Further, ... a number of training camps have been set up in India for giving military training to the miscreant and secessionist elements. India also continues to send infiltrators across the border.[3]

The divergence of opinion between the LRCS and the Pakistani Red Cross even on a basic definition of the problem at hand and its causes demonstrates the fissures inherent in the Red Cross movement in the late twentieth century. More accustomed to conventional wars between states, the civil war for Bangladeshi liberation left the oldest ongoing international humanitarian organization fumbling, both ignorant of local conditions and uncertain of its role in complex postcolonial conflicts.

Chapter 4 unpacks the role and activities of the Red Cross movement in Bangladesh, concentrating on the Australian Red Cross Society and its working relationships with the LRCS, the Indian Red Cross, the International Committee of the Red Cross (ICRC) and, from 1972, the Bangladesh Red Cross Society. It charts a complex constellation of relationships among the various Red Cross agencies as well as conflicting interests. At a time of heightened political activism, liberation movements and debate over the politics of development, the Red Cross movement was unwilling to adapt to this new, postcolonial environment. Despite good intentions, Australian Red Cross workers implicitly reinforced colonial power structures and resisted the growing autonomy of their South Asian partners.

The International Committee of the Red Cross and the League of Red Cross Societies

The Red Cross movement is a behemoth. In 2020, the Red Cross and Red Crescent movement involved 165,822 local branches and employed 473,514 paid workers and 11.5 million volunteers.[4] It is both the largest volunteer organization and the longest-serving humanitarian body, with over 150 years of service.[5] As a result of these accolades, the Red Cross is widely held in high regard, enjoying access to powerbrokers and endowed with vast budgets. The Red Cross movement has two distinct, yet associated, bodies: the ICRC and the LRCS, which in 1991 was renamed the International Federation of Red Cross and Red Crescent Societies. National Red Cross societies are affiliated with the LRCS, though member societies remain independent and have varying levels of autonomy from government. Although the Red Cross movement is treated as a monolith, it is important to note the distinction between the ICRC, the LRCS and national Red Cross societies as they all had distinct roles to play during the Bangladesh Liberation War.

---

[3] Letter from Pakistan Red Cross Society, Karachi, to LRCS, Geneva, 15 June 1971, in Folder 10 'Divisions Pakistan Conflict'.
[4] Wylie et al., 'The Red Cross Movement', 1.
[5] Melanie Oppenheimer, Susanne Schech, Romain Fathi, Neville Wylie and Rosemary Cresswell, 'Resilient Humanitarianism? Using Assemblage to Re-evaluate the History of the League of Red Cross Societies', *International History Review* 43 (2021): 579.

The ICRC is the older of the two federating institutions, forming in 1863 in Geneva, Switzerland. Culturally, the ICRC reflects the ideals of its birthplace and time. Colloquially known as the Rome of Protestantism, Geneva offered a cosmopolitan and liberal environment for the ICRC to flourish.[6] Despite its insistence on secularism, the ICRC has never been able to shake its Protestant roots, leading to the subsequent formation of Red Crescent, Red Lion and Red Shield of David societies in the non-Christian world.[7] The ICRC was also a product of its time. In the mid-nineteenth century, conflicts such as the American Civil War, the Crimean War (1853–6) and the German/Danish Schleswig wars (1848–51, 1864) led militaries and the medical professions to reconsider how the war wounded and sick ought to be treated and what legal protections should be offered to prisoners of war. Consequently, since the mid-nineteenth century, the ICRC has been at the forefront of advancements in international humanitarian law, which provides the framework for the lawful execution of war between states. While mid-nineteenth-century Europe witnessed some progress, there were other developments that were far from ideal. First, the ICRC implicitly sanctioned war as a legitimate means to resolve disputes between nation-states. ICRC advocacy was limited to codifying the rules of war; the morality or efficacy of war itself was never questioned.[8] Second, the ICRC accepted the supremacy of the nation-state over the individual and eschewed intervening in revolutionary or civil wars, particularly in its first fifty years.[9] Third, in its first 100 years, the ICRC was largely complicit in sustaining European imperialism. Historians have documented numerous cases where the ICRC deliberately or inadvertently aligned with imperial powers to quell colonial uprisings, including the Rif War in Morocco (1921–6), the Italo-Ethiopian War (1935–6), Indonesian War of Independence (1945–9) and Kenya's Mau Mau rebellion (1952–60).[10] The wars of decolonization illustrated that the ICRC was powerless to act when

---

[6] Wylie et al., *The Red Cross Movement*, 7.
[7] The Red Crescent first appeared during the Russo-Turkish War, 1876–8, although it was not officially recognized by the ICRC until 1929; the Red Lion with Sun was used during the Western-backed Pahlavi dynasty in Iran, 1924–80. After the Islamic Revolution, Iran adopted the Red Crescent. The Red Star of David was first proposed by Jewish settlers in Palestine and was only officially recognized in 2006.
[8] Tessa Morris-Suzuki, 'Unconventional Warfare: The International Committee of the Red Cross and Humanitarian Dilemmas in Korea 1950–53', *History Australia* 10 (2013): 32; Mark F. N. Franke, 'Responsible Politics of the Neutral: Rethinking International Humanitarianism in the Red Cross Movement via the Philosophy of Roland Barthes', *Journal of International Political Theory* 6 (2010): 143.
[9] Kimberly Lowe, 'Humanitarianism and National Sovereignty: Red Cross Intervention on Behalf of Political Prisoners in Soviet Russia, 1921–3', *Journal of Contemporary History* 49 (2014): 655.
[10] Yolana Pringle, 'Humanitarianism, Race and Denial: The International Committee of the Red Cross and Kenya's Mau Mau Rebellion', *History Workshop Journal* 84 (2017): 89–107; Pablo La Porte, 'Humanitarian Assistance during the Rif War (Morocco, 1921–6): The International Committee of the Red Cross and "an Unfortunate Affair"', *Historical Research* 89 (2016): 114–35; L. van Bergen, 'Medical Care as the Carrot: The Red Cross in Indonesia during the War of Decolonization, 1945–1950', *Medicine, Conflict and Survival* 29 (2013): 216–43; Boyd van Dijk, 'Internationalizing Colonial War: On the Unintended Consequences of the Interventions of the International Committee of the Red Cross in South-East Asia, 1945–1949', *Past & Present* 250 (February 2021): 243–83.

faced with opposition from European powers and that international humanitarian laws were hopelessly inadequate in a rapidly changing world.[11]

The ICRC is distinctive from other humanitarian organizations in that it proclaims seven 'fundamental principles' to which their workers must adhere. Four are relatively uncontroversial: humanity, independence, voluntary service and unity. Conversely, the remaining three (impartiality, neutrality and universality) have attracted ongoing debate. The impartiality and universality principles in particular mean that ICRC workers find themselves providing aid to all sides and, as such, risk becoming 'bystanders at best, collaborators at worst' or 'feeding the killers'.[12] There are numerous examples of a seemingly neutral ICRC attempting to help the victims of conflict zones while simultaneously enabling warfare. Two events stand out above the rest: The Holocaust and the Nigerian Civil War. The decision of the ICRC at a plenary meeting in 1942 *not* to condemn Nazi plans to exterminate the Jews irredeemably tarnished the organization. Furthermore, the ICRC provided only limited aid to civilians (especially Jews) and Russian POWs, even when the Nazi regime was in retreat.[13] Over twenty years later, the ICRC similarly failed to denounce publicly the alleged Nigerian genocide against Biafrans during the Nigerian Civil War (1967–70). The problematic actions (or inactions) of the ICRC during the Biafran crisis also contributed to the establishment of Médecins Sans Frontières (MSF) by disgruntled activist French doctors working with the ICRC.[14] Frustrated by the rigidity of the ICRC's fundamental principles, these rebel doctors splintered from the Red Cross movement and, in December 1971, established an overtly political humanitarian agency that valued bearing witness (*témoignage*) and revolutionary Third Worldism (*tiers-mondiste*).[15]

The LRCS was by design different from the ICRC in fundamental ways. Established on 5 May 1919, the LRCS was created as a coordinating body to which national societies reported, but from which they were independent. The founding of the LRCS by 'pushy'

---

[11] Two additional protocols were added to the Geneva Conventions in 1977 that addressed human rights in armed conflicts. Fabian Klose, 'The Colonial Testing Ground: The International Committee of the Red Cross and the Violent End of Empire', *Humanity* 2 (2011): 118–19.

[12] Christine Winter, 'Limits of Impartiality: The Delegates of the International Committee of the Red Cross in Australia during the Second World War', *History Australia* 10 (2013): 74. 'Feeding the killers' quotation is in reference to the ICRC feeding Rwandan refugees in Zaïre (Democratic Republic of the Congo) camps in 1994–6. But in doing so, the ICRC nourished Hutu militias keen on vengeance against the Tutsi-led Rwandan government. Neville Wylie, 'The Sound of Silence: The History of the International Committee of the Red Cross as Past and Present', *Diplomacy & Statecraft* 13 (2002): 199.

[13] For the authoritative account, see Jean-Claude Favez, *The Red Cross and the Holocaust* (Cambridge: Cambridge University Press, 1999). Also, Gerald Steinacher, *Humanitarians at War: The Red Cross in the Shadow of the Holocaust* (Oxford: Oxford University Press, 2017).

[14] Florian Hannig, 'The Biafra Crisis and the Establishment of Humanitarian Aid in West Germany', in *German Philanthropy in Transatlantic Perspective*, ed. Gregory R. Witkowski and Arnd Bauerkämper (Cham: Springer 2016), 207. Marie-Luce Desgrandchamps, 'Dealing with "Genocide": the ICRC and the UN during the Nigeria-Biafra War, 1967–70', *Journal of Genocide Research* 16 (2014): 282; A. Dirk Moses and Lasse Heerten, 'The Nigeria-Biafra War: Post-colonial Conflict and the Question of Genocide', *Journal of Genocide Research* 16 (2014): 169–203.

[15] For a detailed account of the origins and politics of MSF, see Eleanor Davey, *Idealism Beyond Borders: The French Revolutionary Left and the Rise of Humanitarianism 1954–1988* (Cambridge: Cambridge University Press, 2015), chapter 1. See also Degrandchamps, 'Dealing with "Genocide"', 282 and Wylie, 'The Sound of Silence', 282.

American banker-turned-philanthropist Henry P. Davison was in part an attempt to usurp Swiss dominance of the ICRC. Davison wished to create 'a real international Red Cross', albeit one led by the American national society. Thus, from its early days, the LRCS posed an existential threat to the ICRC. In response, the ICRC limited the influence and mandate of the LRCS, and many national societies refused initially to join the federation, including those from Nordic countries. Tensions between the ICRC and LRCS were formally resolved with the 1928 Statute of Movements that effectively divided the responsibilities between the two organizations and, importantly, reinforced the autonomy of the ICRC from any other Red Cross institution.[16] Whereas the ICRC addressed wartime activities, the LRCS was firmly committed to peacetime relief, particularly medical research, public health education and disaster assistance.[17]

Established in 1914, the Australian Red Cross Society had aristocratic and colonial roots, socio-economic characteristics that would continue to shape the organization during the Bangladeshi refugee crisis. British emigrants Lady Helen Munro Ferguson, the wife of the incoming Governor-General Sir Ronald Munro Ferguson, initiated the formation of an Australian branch of the Red Cross. Lady Helen was the daughter of the former viceroy of India and like her mother, Lady Hariot Dufferin, believed in the principles of duty, service and philanthropy, values that were typical of upper class and titled women during the Victorian and Edwardian eras. Lady Helen had been active in the British Red Cross society and, once in Australia, was committed to establishing a national branch. This desire quickly gained pace with the outbreak of war in Europe on 4 August 1914. Within a week Lady Helen was canvassing support for an Australian Red Cross across the upper echelons of Australian society. Within two weeks, the Australian Red Cross was officially formed at Government House among dignitaries, and Lady Helen was appointed founding president.[18] For the next thirteen years, the Australian Red Cross was technically a branch of the British Red Cross Society until 1927 when it was recognized by the ICRC as a separate, national society.

By the time of the Bangladesh Liberation War, there were over one hundred national societies affiliated with the LRCS.[19] During the conflict and refugee crisis, the LRCS and ICRC called for donations from all member societies. During the war, fifty-one national societies offered cash or in-kind assistance to the LRCS, the top twenty of which are listed in Table 4.1. Surprisingly, small to mid-sized nations topped the table rather than the superpowers of the time. These contributions also had diverse provenances, including direct government grants, donations from citizens, either independently or as part of a fundraising drive, and offerings from other NGOs. In the case of the Australian Red Cross – the third largest donor society – it received funds

---

[16] David P. Forsyth, *The Humanitarians: The International Committee of the Red Cross* (Cambridge: Cambridge University Press, 2005), 35–7.
[17] Kimberly Lowe, 'The League of Red Cross Societies and International Committee of the Red Cross: A Re-Evaluation of American Influence in Interwar Internationalism', *Moving the Social* 57 (2017): 38. See also Julia F. Irwin, *Making the World Safe: The American Red Cross and a Nation's Humanitarian Awakening* (New York: Oxford University Press, 2013).
[18] Melanie Oppenheimer, *The Power of Humanity: 100 Years of Australian Red Cross 1914-2014* (Sydney: HarperCollins, 2014), 12–5.
[19] Hans Haug, *Humanity for All: The International Red Cross and Red Crescent Movement* (Berne: Paul Haupt,1993), 633–45.

Table 4.1 Donations (Cash and In-Kind) from National Societies to the League of Red Cross Societies for Disbursement to Refugee Camps via the Indian Red Cross Society, 3 November 1971. In Swiss Francs

Rank	National society	Donations	Rank	National society	Donations
1	Netherlands	6,284,885	11	USSR	649,171
2	West Germany	2,266,842	12	USA	627,119
3	Australia	2,181,644	13	Italy	549,313
4	United Kingdom	2,076,535	14	Denmark	500,843
5	Sweden	2,033,805	15	Hungary	467,000
6	Norway	1,393,424	16	Belgium	414,445
7	Switzerland	1,300,733	17	France	313,177
8	Japnan	707,359	18	Poland	255,000
9	Finland	692,158	19	Ireland	209,044
10	Canada	680,694	20	New Zealand	167,379

Source: LRCS Relief Bureau. Progress Report. Circular No. 486. 3 November 1971, Box (Unit) 426, Folder 10 'Divisions Pakistan Conflict, Vol - 1+ 2, R - T', 1971'.

from government and other aid agencies. As was its custom at the time, the Australian Red Cross did not solicit funds directly from the public. Instead, cash donations were channelled through other NGOs.

Throughout 1971, national societies forwarded their cash or in-kind donations either to the ICRC or the LRCS, which was then transferred to local national societies – that is, the Indian or Pakistani Red Cross societies, for disbursement. This Red Cross process differentiated it from other NGOs that funnelled their funds through the UNHCR focal point, which was discussed in Chapter 2. For the moment, it is worthwhile highlighting the complex network of humanitarian aid as it flowed from donor to distributor to recipient. The flow of aid from Red Cross, NGO and government sources to Bangladeshi refugees is illustrated in Figure 4.1.

Red Cross Activity during the Bangladeshi Refugee Crisis

When Operation Searchlight began at 11.30 pm on 25 March 1971, ICRC leadership in Geneva wasted little time in preparing humanitarian assistance. Because the ICRC requires approval for admission from the host government, the ICRC delegation flew into Karachi, the largest city in Pakistan, its commercial hub and the nation's first capital city from 1947 to 1957, rather than into Dhaka. The first team left Geneva on 28 March, arriving in Karachi on 29 March. The second team, which included ICRC Assistant Director Pierre Gaillard, departed Geneva on 30 March. The delegation arrived in Pakistan carrying 8 tonnes of medical supplies and, judging by the telegrams, seemed optimistic about securing government permission to execute its humanitarian mission in Bangladesh. Their hopes were quickly dashed, however. Within a day of the arrival of the

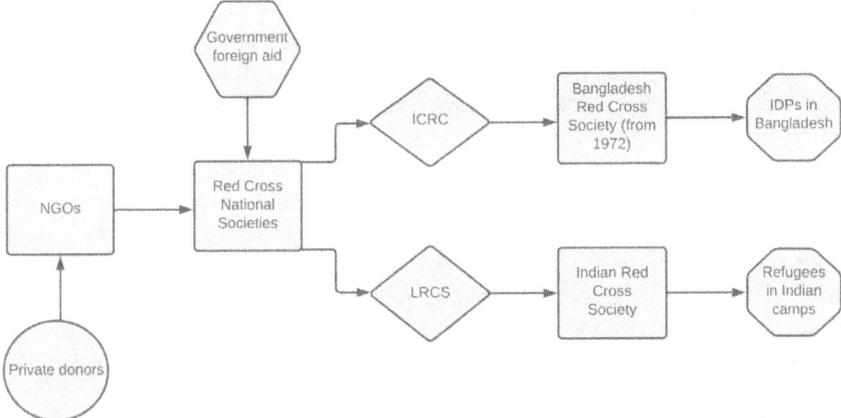

Figure 4.1 Flow chart of Red Cross donations to Bangladeshi refugees during 1971. Created by author.

second team, ICRC delegates left Karachi ingloriously and frustrated that the Pakistani government refused them access. The ICRC intervention was in vain, and all the delegates could do was leave their medical supplies with the local Pakistani Red Cross Society. From the Pakistani perspective, they had witnessed how ICRC aid allegedly enabled the separatists during the Biafran War, an event all too similar to the Bangladesh liberation movement.[20]

The world's oldest and most respected humanitarian organization, then, was marginalized during the Bangladesh Liberation War. Its century-long profession that it was always neutral in conflict and its medical aid was impartial appeared unconvincing in the light of recent wars. Unwilling to accept Pakistani intransigence, in the early months of the war, the ICRC continued to negotiate access with Pakistani authorities, reaching a breakthrough agreement in late July to enter Bangladesh from late August. The Pakistani concession was, however, restrictive, limiting ICRC activities in Bangladesh to establishing a tracing service for missing persons and reuniting dispersed families. It was not until hostilities ceased on 16 December that substantive humanitarian aid could again be offered to the newly independent Bangladesh, which will be discussed later in this chapter.

With the ICRC sidelined, the LRCS spearheaded Red Cross relief activities and focused its relief efforts on refugees displaced by the war who had fled to India. As outlined in Chapter 1, the refugee exodus from Bangladesh to makeshift camps in

---

[20] ICRC circular cables to National Red Cross societies 30 March 1971 and 5 April 1971, Box (Unit) 426, Folder 10 'Divisions Pakistan Conflict, Vol - 1+ 2, R - T', 1971'; 'External Activities. Pakistan', *International Review of the Red Cross*, no. 121 (April 1971), 208; 'For the Benefit of the Indo-Pakistan Conflict Victims', *International Review of the Red Cross*, no. 131 (February 1972): 82. Corroborating material also held at the ICRC archives in Geneva, Switzerland, see *Notifications et offres de service aux États en cas de conflit* (B AG 201), specifically *Offre de services du 30 mars 1971, refuse par les autorités pakistanaises jugeant que l'intervention du CICR* (B AG 201 154–001.01).

the neighbouring Indian states of West Bengal, Assam, Meghalaya and Tripura was staggering. Within six weeks from the outbreak of hostilities, there were over one million refugees (3 May). Within another fortnight, refugee numbers more than doubled, reaching 2.3 million (17 May). This rapid growth continued through the monsoon season (June and July). By mid-July, the Indian government estimated nearly 6.9 million refugees, with the vast majority (5.3 million) camping in West Bengal.[21] As the months rolled on, the arrival of refugees was unrelenting. In late September, there were 8.7 million (27 September); by mid-October, there were 9.3 million evacuees, with two-thirds in camps. The remaining 3.3 million were living with family or friends.[22] Refugees in camps required food, shelter and medicines during the crisis. The Indian government (with some UN assistance and bilateral government aid) provided refugees with daily food rations and a small stipend, with an average daily cost of 2.77 rupees per day, per refugee, as shown in Figure 4.1.[23]

The LRCS directed humanitarian aid from all national societies to the Indian Red Cross, specifically the West Bengal branch in Kolkata. Red Cross aid was therefore designed to *supplement* the services provided by the Indian government. Throughout 1971, the Indian Red Cross provided emergency medical care, complementing existing offerings provided by the Indian Ministry of Health and the World Health Organization. The Indian Red Cross also granted refugees clothing, blankets and shelter. The most significant Red Cross contribution, however, was its Child Nutrition Programme, which targeted children under eight, pregnant women and nursing mothers. Under this programme, the Indian Red Cross established feeding centres in refugee camps, offering target populations access to daily rations of 75 grams of the high-protein food bal-ahar or 50 grams of skim milk powder, plus 25 grams of sugar.[24] This programme fed approximately 600,000 refugee children under five and a further 1.2 million children aged between five and eight years. In total, the Indian Red Cross established 963 feeding centres across eastern India; see Figure 4.2. Given the scale of this food programme, the Indian Red Cross enlisted the logistical support of other volunteer agencies and sourced the high-protein food from United Nations' agencies UNICEF and the World Food Programme. Milk powder and sugar (essential to making the food palatable) were sourced from national Red Cross societies. The central role of the Indian Red Cross proved crucial to the effective rollout of humanitarian aid in the refugee camps. The LRCS, as a federating body, simply did not have the personnel

---

[21] These statistics sourced from files in the Records of the Australian Red Cross – National Office' collection. Specifically, Ligue des Sociétés de la Croix-Rouge, 'Refugees from East Pakistan in India', 3 May 1971; Ligue des Sociétés de la Croix-Rouge, 'Refugees from East Pakistan in India', 17 May 1971; LRCS, 'Refugees from East Pakistan in India', 8 June 1971; Statement of the United Nations High Commissioner for Refugees, 16 July 1971.
[22] Henrik Beer, Secretary General, LRCS, letter to Leon G. Stubbings, Secretary General, Australian Red Cross, 27 September 1971 and LRCS, 'Refugees from East Pakistan in India', 18 October 1971, Box (Unit) 426, Folder 10 'Divisions Pakistan Conflict, Vol - 1+ 2, R - T', 1971.
[23] Datta, *Refugees and Borders in South Asia*, 58.
[24] Bal-ahar is a weaning food common in food programmes. It contains 22.31 per cent protein and 360 calories per 100 grams. It is made up of wheat flour, groundnut flour and bengalgram flour. LRCS, 'Refugees from East Pakistan in India', 17 September 1971, Box (Unit) 426, Folder 10 'Divisions Pakistan Conflict, Vol - 1+ 2, R - T', 1971.

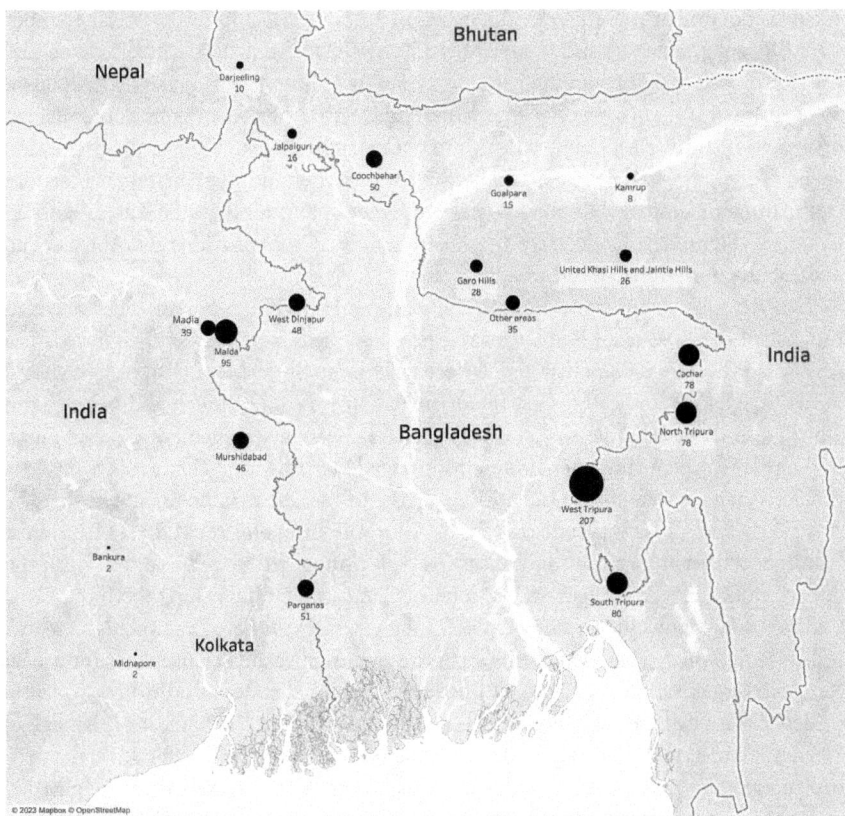

Figure 4.2 Red Cross feeding centres in Indian refugee camps. Size of circle reflects number of feeding centres in region/town. Created by author from data in LRCS, 'Refugees from East Pakistan in India', 17 September 1971, 4–5. Box (Unit) 426, Folder 10 'Divisions Pakistan Conflict, Vol - 1+ 2, R - T', 1971.

to provide practical assistance. Indeed, only one representative from the LRCS was ever present in India at any one time, and in New Delhi no less, some 1,600 kilometres from Kolkata. The Indian Red Cross not only had the human resources necessary to undertake such a large feeding programme, but it also had the local knowledge to navigate India's notorious labyrinthine customs processes and established working relationships with other voluntary groups on the ground.[25]

The LRCS and Indian Red Cross explicitly called on all national societies routinely throughout 1971 to donate cash, multivitamins, sugar, powdered milk and vaccines for cholera and typhoid. Circulars from the LRCS headquarters in Geneva to all national

---

[25] Henrik Beer, Secretary General, LRCS, confidential letter to Sir Geoffrey Newman-Morris, Vice Chairman, LRCS, 1 July 1971, 2. Box (Unit) 426, Folder 10 'Divisions Pakistan Conflict, Vol - 1+ 2, R - T', 1971.

societies document these specific requests on 3 May 1971, 8 June 1971, 1 September 1971, 17 September 1971 and 3 November 1971.[26] Throughout 1971, the Australian Red Cross provided cash incrementally to the Indian Red Cross, reaching nearly A$100,000 by November 1971. However, when compared with other Australian humanitarian organizations, this cash donation pales in comparison. As explored in Chapter 3, aid agencies including Austcare, Australian Catholic Relief and the Australian Freedom from Hunger Campaign all donated cash in larger quantities than the Australian Red Cross; see Figure 3.2. Conversely, the Australian Red Cross provided two-thirds of all Australian goods donated to India.[27]

Despite such unequivocal appeals for cash and specific goods in most need, in the case of the Australian Red Cross at least, these pleas were frequently ignored. The Australian Red Cross demonstrated itself to be blind to the needs of both recipients and local aid agencies, indicating that the organization was out of touch and belonged to a bygone era. For example, on 1 July 1971, Acting Secretary General of the Australian Red Cross, Noreen Minogue, wrote a four-page letter to Major General S. S. Maitra, the Secretary General of the Indian Red Cross. In the letter, Minogue noted that the Australian Red Cross was soliciting funds from supporters for the refugees from East Pakistan. Rather than donating the cash raised, Minogue declared that 'we think the donors would like Australian goods to be sent'. Again, without asking the Indian Red Cross on what goods they needed most, Minogue wrote, 'we have in mind high protein milk biscuits which have been produced by the Commonwealth Scientific and Industrial Research Organisation'. Minogue outlined the nutritional benefits of the biscuit, citing evidence from experience in donating the biscuits to a South Vietnamese orphanage in 1969. Appended to the letter was a report from Sister Francoise of the South Vietnamese orphanage. She noted the orphans 'ate the biscuits willingly' and their weight had increased. In this example, we see the Australian Red Cross ignoring LRCS appeals for cash, specific medicines and milk powder. Moreover, Noreen Minogue seemed more concerned about appeasing the wishes of the donors and supporting Australian biscuit manufacturers than seeing to the needs of destitute and malnourished refugees.[28] As we will see throughout this chapter, the Australian Red Cross attempted to appeal to two audiences during this crisis: internationally, the LRCS and, domestically, donors in Australia. Unfortunately, these two groups had distinct, and at times opposing, interests.

With LRCS circulars routinely disregarded, the LRCS on one occasion directly communicated with the Australian Red Cross for suitable in-kind support. Cognizant of Australia's food growing capacities, on 15 October 1971, the LRCS Relief Bureau Director, Jean-Pierre Robert-Tissot, asked if the Australian Red Cross 'might be able to help with the [urgent] provision of sugar'. In this proposal, the British Red Cross offered to fund the delivery of 800 tonnes of sugar, amounting to nearly 60 per cent of

---

[26] All circulars sourced from Records of the Australian Red Cross – National Office, Box (Unit) 426, Folder 10 'Divisions Pakistan Conflict, Vol - 1+ 2, R - T', 1971.

[27] Data from the Australian aid coordinating body, Australian Council for Overseas Aid, 'Contributions to East Pakistan Refugees (on 27 October 1971)', in Box (Unit) 426, Folder 10 'Divisions Pakistan Conflict, Vol - 1+ 2, R - T', 1971.

[28] Noreen Minogue, letter to Major General S. S. Maitra, 1 July 1971, in Box (Unit) 426, Folder 10 'Divisions Pakistan Conflict, Vol - 1+ 2, R - T', 1971.

the monthly requirement for the administration of the Child Nutrition Programme. Despite the clear sense of urgency in Robert-Tissot's letter, the Australian Red Cross took an additional five days to consult the Australian Department of Foreign Affairs about this proposal. The Department replied on 10 November, stating that the Australian government already had plans to donate 600 tonnes of caster sugar in mid-December and an additional 300 tonnes of caster sugar and 4,000 tonnes of ordinary sugar in early January 1972. These consignments of sugar were at the request of the Indian Ministry of Rehabilitation in support of the feeding programme of the Indian government. It in no way benefitted the Red Cross Child Nutritional Programme. With this knowledge, the Australian Red Cross Secretary General Leon Stubbings informed the Secretary General of the LRCS, Henrik Beer, that the LRCS-British Red Cross proposal was 'complex' because 'in Australia all export sugar in this country is based in a quota system' in which 'only the Commonwealth Government can pronounce on the availability of existing stocks'.[29] Stubbings deduced that the pre-arranged consignment of 900 tonnes of caster sugar and 4,000 tonnes of ordinary sugar in December and January were 'the amount of sugar that they [the government] would be prepared to release from the quota'. From the records then, the Australian Red Cross was not only slow to act in an emergency; they were also unable to secure essential foodstuffs for the central LRCS aid programme during the refugee crisis of 1971.

Early in the crisis, the LRCS cabled a telegram to all national societies. The title of the telegram, 'PURCHASING LOCALLY WITH CASH GIFTS', made the contents of the message abundantly clear. Nevertheless, the LRCS elaborated to ensure their request was understood. The telegram read, 'RELIEF CAN BE PURCHASED LOCALLY DELEGATES STRESS IMPORTANCE OF CASH GIFTS STOP NATIONAL SOCIETIES REQUESTED REFRAIN SENDING PERSONNEL WHICH INDCROSS AND LEAGUE DELEGATES ADVISE NOT PRESENTLY REQUIRED'.[30] Academics and practitioners have studied extensively the relative efficacy of cash versus material aid, such as food. Research shows that cash donations offer several advantages over in-kind donations. For example, cash reduces supply chain costs, such as transport and warehousing, and is therefore more cost-effective than goods.[31] Cash is more efficient than in-kind donations, ensuring faster response times during a crisis.[32] There are also financial advantages of using cash rather than food aid: foreign currency offers greater value for money as goods purchased in-country are typically cheaper than in the sending country; the purchasing of local goods with donated cash can stimulate the domestic economy and improve livelihoods for the host society.

---

[29] L. G. Stubbings, Secretary General, Australian Red Cross Society, letter to Henrik Beer, Secretary General, LRCS, 15 November 1971, in Box (Unit) 426, Folder 10 'Divisions Pakistan Conflict, Vol - 1+ 2, R - T', 1971.

[30] LRCS telegram to all national societies, 7 May 1971, in Box (Unit) 426, Folder 10 'Divisions Pakistan Conflict, Vol - 1+ 2, R - T, 1971.

[31] Jenny Aker, 'Cash or Coupons? Testing the Impacts of Cash versus Vouchers in the Democratic Republic of Congo', *Center for Global Development Working Paper* 320 (2013): 1–51.

[32] Wojciech D. Piotrowicz, 'In-kind Donations, Cash Transfers and Local Procurement in the Logistics of Caring for Internally Displaced Persons. The Case of Polish Humanitarian NGOs and Ukrainian IDPs', *Journal of Humanitarian Logistics and Supply Chain Management* 8 (2018): 374.

Despite these measurable advantages of cash over in-kind donations, traditionally, most aid is dispensed as goods not cash. This is because donors have long suspected cash to be misused, stolen or used to corrupt those in power. An injection of large amounts of cash into a local economy can also trigger inflation and distort local market conditions.[33] Additionally, there are cases where goods may only be available outside the recipient country, such as multivitamins and medicines, thus warranting in-kind donations under specific conditions. Even so, the Australian Red Cross made numerous miscalculations when they disbursed in-kind aid to the Indian refugee camps, errors that in many cases rendered the goods useless.

For example, on 9 June 1971, the West Australian Trades and Labour Council offered the Indian Red Cross a shipment of 200,000 dressed sheep mutton. The offer – which was sent through the Australian Red Cross headquarters – was met with a polite rejection. In a cable on 16 June, the LRCS reported that the Indian Red Cross 'IN CONSULTATION WITH GOVERNMENT REGRETS CANNOT HANDLE AT THIS TIME BUT OFFER GREATLY APPRECIATED'.[34] It is unclear why the West Australian Trades and Labour Council offered a specific amount of fresh mutton at this time. Most likely, West Australian sheep meat producers encountered an oversupply of stock, hence the offer of mutton (mature sheep) rather than lamb (sheep under one year of age). In Australia, mutton is widely considered inferior to lamb because it has a tough texture and strong, gamey taste. Consequently, mutton sells at prices considerably lower than lamb. In Indian cuisine, mutton typically refers to goat meat, not sheep meat. Thus, the offer of (sheep) mutton, an undesirable, low-cost meat with little customary use in India, arguably was an attempt by West Australian meat producers to offload excess stock that had little value to them, all the while reaping Indian goodwill, crucial in any export-oriented market. On 5 July 1971, the LRCS Secretary General Henrik Beer wrote a letter to Sir Geoffrey Newman-Morris, the Australian who was the Vice-Chairman of the LRCS from 1969 to 1973. In the letter, Beer outlined that the Indian Red Cross was the intermediary responsible for distribution of food to refugees and that donated food should consider cultural sensitivities. He wrote,

> The fact that the new chairman is a vegetarian and that there is always a superstitious feeling that foreign meat, even if it is mutton, could come from pigs (which Muslims can't take) or cows which the Indou (sic.) can't take might play a role, but this is a purely personal speculation.[35]

---

[33] Graham Heaslip, Ira Haavisto and Gyöngyi Kovács, 'Cash as a Form of Relief', in *Advances in Managing Humanitarian Operations*, ed. Christopher W. Zobel, Nezih Altay and Mark P. Haselkorn (Cham: Springer, 2018), 59; David Peppiatt, John Mitchell and Penny Holzmann, *Cash Transfers in Emergencies: Evaluating Benefits and Assessing Risks* (London: Overseas Development Institute, 2001), 1.

[34] Australian Red Cross telegram to Indian Red Cross, New Delhi, 9 June 1971 and LRCS telegram to Australian Red Cross, 16 June 1971, in Box (Unit) 426, Folder 10 'Divisions Pakistan Conflict, Vol - 1+ 2, R - T', 1971.

[35] Henrik Beer, Secretary General LRCS, letter to Sir Geoffrey Newman-Morris, Vice-Chairman LRCS, 5 July 1971, in Box (Unit) 426, Folder 10 'Divisions Pakistan Conflict, Vol - 1+ 2, R - T', 1971.

The notion that starving, malnourished children should accept any food offered to them, however religiously inappropriate, appears to be the implicit logic behind the West Australian offer. But this is not the only case of cultural insensitivity exhibited by the Australian Red Cross.

By September 1971, the monsoon season and subsequent cholera outbreak had passed, only to make way for new dangers: the onset of winter and the threat of hypothermia, particularly for refugees in the elevated, mountainous states of Assam, Meghalaya and Tripura. In a 1 September 1971 circular, LRCS Director of the Relief Bureau, Jean-Pierre Robert-Tissot, informed the national societies of the urgent need for warm clothing. He explained that 'the clothing the refugees had with them when they arrived is already worn out and that some of the women refugees are unable to come out of their shelters in camps due to lack of clothing'. Robert-Tissot requested 'that as far as possible assistance be provided in the form of cash' to enable the local purchase of clothing. With 'extremely serious transportation problems' after the monsoon rains, cash would negate the need to transport the goods. Furthermore, cash would also 'facilitate the provision of the type of clothing which the refugees are accustomed'. The circular listed the required items. For males over twelve, they required one *dhoti* (loose trousers) or for Muslims, a *lungi* (sarong) for their lower half plus a *kurta* (collarless top). For females over twelve, they required one *sari* and one blouse. For boys under twelve, the requirements were similarly specific, needing one grey shirt with shorts of blue or green colour. Clothing for girls under twelve was more general, requiring one frock and underwear. Given the cooling temperatures, the LRCS also requested sweaters, pullovers and blankets.[36] The call for cash to purchase local clothing was reiterated on 5 October 1971. In an article by LRCS-supported journalist Paul Eptaine, the reporter noted that the sending of 'light European clothing' would be inappropriate and 'would involve losing the goodwill gained' from past donations. Eptaine affirmed the call of the LRCS for cash because 'it would make possible to purchase the <u>dhotis</u> and <u>saris</u> generally worn by the refugee men and women' [underline in original].[37] The records indicate that the Australian Red Cross did heed some of this advice, providing nine thousand cotton blankets, two thousand saris, seven cases of boys' shirts and shorts (colours unknown), six cases of girls' frocks and five cases of men's trousers (presumably Western style). Cash was also offered, although not specifically earmarked for clothing. The preference for cash over goods to avoid the logistical challenges of ground transportation in mountainous areas was generally ignored, as was the request for warm clothing and ethnic-specific men's trousers.

Furthermore, on one occasion, the Australian Red Cross sent medical supplies that had passed their expiry date. As Jean-Pierre Robert-Tissot wrote in an August letter to Leon Stubbings, 'many of the medical supplies sent by the Australian Red Cross had considerably passed their expiry date and were therefore useless'. The deleterious effects of this mistake were threefold: one, the expired medical supplies consumed

---

[36] LRCS Relief Bureau Circular No. 478, pp. 2–3, 1 September 1971, in Box (Unit) 426, Folder 10 'Divisions Pakistan Conflict, Vol - 1+ 2, R - T', 1971.
[37] Paul Eptaine (on behalf of LRCS), 'Refugees from East Pakistan in India', 5 October 1971, pp. 1–2, in Box (Unit) 426, Folder 10 'Divisions Pakistan Conflict, Vol - 1+ 2, R - T', 1971.

scarce financial resources that could have been allocated to more productive supplies; two, Red Cross workers in India had to identify and discard any expired goods from a mass of donated items, which 'takes time and effort'; three, the medical supplies were transported to and within a disaster area, which again, 'utilizes badly needed transport and the limited space available from airlines'. The LRCS Relief Director was diplomatic, insisting that 'we are of course most grateful for your many other valuable contributions'. Nevertheless, Robert-Tissot concluded that they 'do feel the necessity of strongly stressing the above points'.[38] The sending of expired medical goods may well have been a simple oversight. But when viewed within the context of other such errors in judgement, the Australian Red Cross appeared more interested in how their work was perceived by other donors (domestically and internationally) rather than the effectiveness of their aid in the field.

This predilection towards self-gratification or self-promotion was also evident in the issue of sending overseas personnel to the refugee camps. As noted earlier, from early May, the LRCS explicitly stated that it did not need overseas aid workers. Yet curiously, within a month, the Australian Red Cross initiated preparations to send Australian medical personnel to India. In a memorandum to all state divisions, Leon Stubbings acknowledged that the LRCS 'continues to state that personnel are not required'. Notwithstanding LRCS assertions, Stubbings deduced that 'further assistance may be required' and therefore 'has seemed to us wise to prepare for the possibility that we may be asked to send a medical team' [underline in original]. Stubbings noted that state divisions had already received offers to assist in India from Australian doctors and nurses. In his role as head of the coordinating Red Cross body in Australia, Stubbings requested from all division leaders a compilation of demographic and medical information of interested medical practitioners, such as age, address, nationality and inoculation history. Replying the same day, R. S. Maclean, the General Secretary of the New South Wales division, provided a detailed list of five medical officers and three trained nurses. Meanwhile, the Victorian division offered details of five medical doctors and nine nurses.[39]

Two days later, on 10 June 1971, Noreen Minogue received a telegram from the Australian Department of Foreign Affairs. In it, the Department of Foreign Affairs relayed a message from Indian government officials about the prospect of the Australian Red Cross sending medical professionals who would 'supervise and train others in the operation of the mass injection equipment'. According to the telegram, Australian officials had discussed this Red Cross proposal with Indian officials from the ministries of External Affairs and of Rehabilitation. According to A. B. Malik, the Joint Secretary, Ministry of Health and Family Planning in the Indian government, there were already sufficient Indian doctors who were familiar with the injector guns,

---

[38] Jean-Pierre Robert-Tissot, Director, Relief Bureau, LRCS, letter to Leon Stubbings, Secretary General, Australian Red Cross Society, 30 August 1971, in Box (Unit) 426, Folder 10 'Divisions Pakistan Conflict, Vol - 1+ 2, R - T', 1971.

[39] R. S. Maclean, General Secretary, Australian Red Cross Society. New South Wales Division, memorandum to Secretary General, Australian Red Cross Society, 8 June 1971 and 'Medical Doctors and Nurse Volunteers', General Secretary, Australian Red Cross, Victoria Division, in Box (Unit) 426, Folder 10 'Divisions Pakistan Conflict, Vol - 1+ 2, R - T', 1971.

both in terms of operating them and training others. The telegram read, 'MALIK WAS EMPHATIC THAT AUSTRALIAN DOCTORS ARE NOT REQUIRED'.[40] To be fair, the Australian Red Cross was not the only national society – or indeed overseas aid agency – that continued to insist on sending foreign aid workers to the Indian refugee camps. As was the case with the Australian proposals, other foreign aid workers in India were not only not welcomed, but they were also asked to leave. For instance, on 19 August, Jean-Pierre Robert-Tissot informed Leon Stubbings in a letter that 'medical and para-medical personnel were asked to leave their area of operation as soon as possible and had handed over their duties to Indian personnel'.[41] It seems that the Australian Red Cross alongside many other international aid agencies made two incorrect assumptions. First, they assumed that local Indian medical workers were insufficient in number, thus necessitating a need for overseas workers. Second, the Australian Red Cross assumed that even if there were sufficient medical workers in India, they lacked the training and skills necessary in a refugee crisis. As a result, the Australian Red Cross failed to understand how their offers of medical personnel – and the implicit assumption of Western superiority – were offensive to Indian ears.

The Australian Red Cross also failed to grasp *why* the use of local, Indian personnel would be preferable to introducing foreign workers. In a confidential letter from Henrik Beer to Sir Geoffrey Newman-Morris, the Secretary General explained the advantages of local workers. 'Many of them speak the language [Bengali], they understand the conditions, they can adapt the relief to local standards, which foreigners cannot do'.[42] Furthermore, Beer acknowledged that the Indian government feared the political consequences should a non-Indian aid worker be injured or killed in the conflict zone. Beer explained, 'there is shooting around the border, there is also a rather higher than normal criminality on account of the difficult conditions', and thus, the Indian authorities wished to avoid any chance of a non-Indian becoming a martyr or used as a political weapon. Unsurprisingly, in July 1971, the Indian government expelled foreign aid workers.[43] And it was not just humanitarians causing problems. Beer noted that there had been 'a lot of "loose" persons offering their aid, going around as adventurers or journalists, some of them have already caused a lot of difficulties'.[44] Despite the consistent insistence of the LRCS that foreign workers were not needed or even welcome, the issue of sending medical personnel remained contentious throughout 1971. Putting aside diplomacy, the Secretary General of the Indian Red Cross, S. S. Maitra, cabled the following message to all national societies in mid-November: 'GOVERNMENT OF INDIA WILL NEVER ALLOW FOREIGN

---

[40] Australian Department of Foreign Affairs, telegram to Noreen Minogue, Deputy Secretary General, Australian Red Cross Society, 10 June 1971, in Box (Unit) 426, Folder 10 'Divisions Pakistan Conflict, Vol - 1+ 2, R - T', 1971.

[41] Jean-Pierre Robert-Tissot, Director, Relief Bureau, LRCS, letter to Leon Stubbings, Secretary General, Australian Red Cross Society, 19 August 1971, in Box (Unit) 426, Folder 10 'Divisions Pakistan Conflict, Vol - 1+ 2, R - T', 1971.

[42] Henrik Beer, 'Notes from voyage India', letter to Sir Geoffrey Newman-Morris, 1 July 1971, in Box (Unit) 426, Folder 10 'Divisions Pakistan Conflict, Vol - 1+ 2, R - T', 1971.

[43] O'Sullivan, *The NGO Moment*, 46.

[44] Henrik Beer, 'Notes from Voyage India', letter to Sir Geoffrey Newman-Morris, 1 July 1971, in Box (Unit) 426, Folder 10 'Divisions Pakistan Conflict, Vol - 1+ 2, R - T', 1971.

DELEGATES AND TEAMS TO COME TO INDIA TO DO RELIEF WORK ON BEHALF OF PAKISTANI REFUGEES'.[45]

These insistent offers of medical personnel from the Australian Red Cross demonstrate two points: one, persistent *cultural* insensitivity among certain segments of the Australian public towards its Asian neighbours and, two, a gross misunderstanding by the Australian Red Cross of the precarious *political* situation in postcolonial South Asia. First, records from the Australian Red Cross show an organization that was more than merely ignorant of cultural practices in India but was wilfully oblivious to non-Western perspectives. Arguably, the Australian Red Cross – despite its well-intentioned humanitarian practices – was attempting to reinforce racist notions of Western superiority. If Paul Cullen was an imperialist and an arrogant interventionist (see Chapter 3), then the Australian Red Cross staff behaved like neo-imperialists, superficially engaging in dialogue with Indian humanitarian organizations but maintaining assumptions of Western righteousness. As we will see in the following chapters, the behaviours of the Australian Red Cross, Austcare and ACFOA were increasingly at odds with religious and grassroots humanitarian organizations that imagined a symbiotic relationship between aid agencies in the global north and south, all the while resisting the outdated donor/recipient binary.

Second, Australian Red Cross workers lacked the knowledge or imagination to understand the political impacts and legacies of two hundred years of British colonialism on Indians. As Sumit Ganguly and Manjeet Pardesi have argued, the concept of national autonomy dominated Indian political culture in the second half of the twentieth century. In the conduct of Indian foreign affairs, Indian officials desired 'the greatest possible independence' and public opinion would find any deference to external powers 'intolerable'.[46] It is well known that India's first prime minister, Jawaharlal Nehru (1947–62), pioneered non-alignment, a foreign policy concept rooted in a deep mistrust of international institutions and a result of 'collective trauma' from the decades of the Indian independence struggle.[47] His daughter, Prime Minister Indira Gandhi, articulated her suspicions of foreign powers during a speech in 1971, declaring that superpowers have 'wanted to keep India weak ... And they wanted to keep the subcontinent divided'.[48] Indira Gandhi's determination to keep foreign powers out of India was more than mere rhetoric. As noted in Chapter 1, on 9 August 1971, the Indian government signed the Indo-Soviet Treaty of Peace, Friendship and Cooperation. This agreement ensured that foreign powers – namely, the United States and China – would be deterred from intervening in the Bangladesh Liberation War,

---

[45] Telegram cited in Henrik Beer, 'Notes from voyage India', confidential letter to Leon Stubbings, 16 November 1971, in Box (Unit) 426, Folder 10 'Divisions Pakistan Conflict, Vol - 1+ 2, R - T', 1971.
[46] Sumit Ganguly and Manjeet S. Pardesi, 'Explaining Sixty Years of India's Foreign Policy', *India Review* 8 (2009): 5.
[47] Adam B. Lerner, 'Collective Trauma and the Evolution of Nehru's Worldview: Uncovering the Roots of Nehruvian Non-Alignment', *The International History Review* 41 (2019): 1294.
[48] Indira Gandhi, *India and BanglaDesh: Selected Speeches and Statements, March to December, 1971* (New Delhi: Orient Longman, 1972), 161.

thereby continuing India's long-standing policy of excluding extra-regional powers from gaining a foothold in South Asia.[49]

Indian officials not only wished to assert national autonomy from foreign nations, they also aimed to distance their country from the injustices of colonialism. Post-independence India rejected domination and aggression towards others. In its place, Indian postcolonial modernity was shaped by pacificism, anti-imperialism, secularism, socialism and democracy. The aim of this ideological distancing was not to prove that India was equal to its colonial masters. Rather, as shown by Priya Chacko, Indian postcolonial modernity was an attempt to demonstrate Indian *superiority* over the great colonial powers.[50] Thus, the refusal of the Indian Red Cross and Indian government to accept foreign aid workers can be understood within this context of assertive Indian nationalism that sought its own path rather than blithely emulating Western policies or conceding to Western demands.

Yet this example was not the first instance of India asserting postcolonial autonomy. In 1953, the Press Trust of India (PTI), the largest news agency in India, terminated its working relationship with Reuters on the basis that the British news agency was too closely aligned with British colonialism and the Western prosecution of the Cold War. This rupture ended eighty-seven years of Reuters in India, the most profitable market for the British news agency in the Commonwealth.[51] In 1970, the Gandhi government abruptly expelled the BBC in India, forcing British employees to depart the country, closing their New Delhi office and releasing locally engaged staff from their BBC contracts. The Indian government had long believed the BBC to hold anti-Indian sentiment, especially vis-à-vis Pakistan and the Kashmir dispute. Long simmering diplomatic tensions escalated in mid-1970 with the BBC broadcast of *Calcutta*, a documentary film by French director Louis Malle. Indian audiences rejected the film's bleak (and misrepresentative) portrayal of life in Kolkata, which focused on poverty and destitution at the expense of the industriousness and creativity of the city. The snap decision of the Indian government to expel the BBC came from Gandhi's office, but she was responding to public pressure and community outrage at a film that maligned postcolonial India.[52] Sensitivities about India's image were not just from government but from the wider populace, too. Given the controversy surrounding the Louis Malle film, it is no wonder that the Indian Red Cross refused to admit foreign aid workers to ensure they could control how India was portrayed internationally during the refugee crisis.

The decision to exclude foreign aid workers created a new problem for the Australian Red Cross, the LRCS and other donor national societies. Without their own personnel

---

[49] Sinderpal Singh, *India in South Asia: Domestic Identity Politics and Foreign Policy from Nehru to the BJP* (New York: Routledge, 2013), 75.

[50] Priya Chacko, 'Indian Foreign Policy and the Ambivalence of Postcolonial Modernity', PhD dissertation, University of Adelaide, 2007, 234.

[51] Peter Putnis, 'Reuters and the Idea of a British Commonwealth News Agency in the Aftermath of World War II', *Media History* 27 (2021): 321–2.

[52] Alasdair Pinkerton, 'A New Kind of Imperialism? The BBC, Cold War Broadcasting and the Contested Geopolitics of South Asia', *Historical Journal of Film, Radio and Television* 28 (2008): 537–8, 550–1; Alasdair Pinkerton, 'The BBC in South Asia: From the End of Empire to the Cold War', in *Diasporas and Diplomacy: Cosmopolitan Contact Zones at the BBC World Service (1932–2012)*, ed. M. Gillespie and A. Webb (London: Routledge, 2012), 151–4.

in the field, the LRCS and donor societies became reliant on the Indian Red Cross for publicity materials, a vital component of any fundraising campaign. However, the Indian Red Cross lacked the time, resources or inclination to provide such materials, noting that refugees in camps 'resent being visited by people as visitors to a zoo'.[53] Henrik Beer relayed the concerns of donor societies to the Indian Red Cross, writing that 'the prestige of Red Cross is inevitably damaged' and that some national societies were 'extremely concerned about their future position'. Specifically, 'national societies do not understand why so little information is available about one of the biggest relief operations'. The publicity problem was in fact twofold for national societies: first, they were unable to send personnel to Indian camps, and second, delegates from other aid agencies had successfully entered India. As such, national societies believed that 'their position in their own country is weakened while other relief agencies with delegates on the spot become more and more important'. Beer reasserted that the current situation was 'embarrassing and disadvantageous' for the Red Cross movement, concluding that without a change in position by the Indian Red Cross, the 'enthusiasm [read funding] of national societies will diminish'.[54]

The problem of inadequate publicity was felt acutely by the Australian Red Cross. Leon Stubbings explained that unlike other aid agencies in Australia, it was the policy of the Australian Red Cross to 'refrain from criticism of the government of the day or from engaging in gimmick-style publicity'. Instead, the Australian Red Cross provided information and materials to news outlets, which was then distributed as '"hard" news'.[55] This circuitous and indirect method of self-promotion rendered their need for written and visual materials from India more urgent. In a letter to Henrik Beer, Stubbings outlined the local restrictions on Red Cross publicity in Australia and that he feared 'that the Red Cross is falling behind in this barrage of publicity' from competing humanitarian organizations. Existential anxiety littered this letter. Stubbings mused, 'if our identity is not to be completely submerged, it is essential that we receive information, especially good pictures, which show the Indian Red Cross on the job'. Moreover, Stubbings warned, 'Frankly, the whole question of our role in International Disaster Relief in this country is critical at present', concluding that 'if Red Cross is to retain its position of pre-eminence in this field, we simply cannot do without a steady supply of information'.[56] Despite months of campaigning from donor societies and the LRCS, the Indian Red Cross refused to change its position on providing publicity materials, let alone allowing foreign personnel into the camps for publicity purposes. Exasperated, Henrik Beer wrote to Leon Stubbings: 'I share your concern entirely and can assure you that we have tried all possible means of obtaining

---

[53] S. S. Maitra, letter to Henrik Beer, 3 August 1971, in Box (Unit) 426, Folder 10 'Divisions Pakistan Conflict, Vol - 1+ 2, R - T', 1971.
[54] Henrik Beer, letter to S. S Maitra, 23 July 1971, in Box (Unit) 426, Folder 10 'Divisions Pakistan Conflict, Vol - 1+ 2, R - T', 1971.
[55] Leon Stubbings, memorandum, 'Public Appeals on Behalf of East Pakistan Refugees', to General Secretary (all state divisions), 5 November 1971, in Box (Unit) 426, Folder 10 'Divisions Pakistan Conflict, Vol - 1+ 2, R - T', 1971.
[56] Leon Stubbings, letter to Henrik Beer, 27 October 1971, in Box (Unit) 426, Folder 10 'Divisions Pakistan Conflict, Vol - 1+ 2, R - T', 1971.

the kinds of information our member societies need for fundraising purposes.'[57] Donor societies such as the Australian Red Cross benefitted from the movement's prestige and integrity; yet they were also hindered by these public expectations, especially in the competitive and increasingly crowded landscape of 1970s humanitarian organizations.

Throughout the 1971 refugee crisis, there were occasions when Indian perceptions were at odds with Western perspectives. In a confidential letter to Sir Geoffrey Newman-Morris, Henrik Beer reflected on his recent trip to India. Beer advised the Australian Vice-Chairman of the LRCS:

> It should also be remembered that the Indians do not regard the present relief actions as a help to India, it is a help to Pakistani refugees in India, and the basic responsibility ought to lie on the international community. Relief is welcomed, but not on the donor's conditions, [but] on the Indian conditions.[58]

In this extract, Beer corrected a fundamental misunderstanding among most of the donor community: who is the beneficiary of this aid? Beer explained that in north-east India, tensions had emerged between local communities and the refugees. For instance, when humanitarian organizations purchased locally the food to support the refugees, this increased consumer demand 'automatically drives prices up, causing irritation, justified indeed, of the civilian population'.[59] Moreover, in a September progress report, the LRCS Relief Bureau wrote that after the monsoonal floods that had affected locals and refugees alike, local communities were aggrieved that the refugees alone were receiving aid. The report stressed that 'the two categories are in the same area and must be helped equally'.[60] It should be noted that this report came after an inspectional tour by Indira Gandhi, accompanied by Indian Red Cross chairman Padmaja Naidu. In these examples, among the Indian audience, there were stark national cleavages between Indians and Bangladeshi refugees. In the Indian view, their country was shouldering most of the responsibility for feeding, sheltering and healing the ten million refugees, which it deemed was an international problem requiring an international response. It is also very clear that Indian officials wished to stress that they themselves were not benefitting from the aid. In fact, in the instance of monsoonal flooding, refugee flood victims received more aid by virtue of their refugee status than locals. These examples all demonstrate Indian frustration at donor assumptions and the desire of postcolonial India to demonstrate its autonomy, and arguably, its superiority, over the great powers of yesteryear. Misunderstandings and cross-cultural barriers would continue in the reconstruction period, especially in 1972 when international aid was at its peak, which is the focus of the final section of this chapter.

---

[57] Henrik Beer, confidential letter to Leon Stubbings, 16 November 1971, in Box (Unit) 426, Folder 10 'Divisions Pakistan Conflict, Vol - 1+ 2, R - T', 1971.
[58] Ibid.
[59] Ibid.
[60] LRCS Relief Bureau Progress Report, 'East Pakistan Refugees in India', 1 September 1971, 5, in Box (Unit) 426, Folder 10 'Divisions Pakistan Conflict, Vol - 1+ 2, R - T', 1971.

Red Cross activity during the reconstruction

By the time of the ceasefire, ICRC assistance this time was unequivocally accepted by the inaugural Bangladeshi Prime Minister Sheikh Mujibur Rahman. Unlike the experience of the ICRC in its dealings with the Pakistani Red Cross, the Bangladesh Red Cross welcomed the humanitarian organization into Bangladesh. From February to April 1972, the ICRC was the leading aid agency working in Bangladesh. To be sure, there was an initial six-week delay.[61] In a circular letter to all national societies, ICRC Commissioner Enrico Bignami attributed the delay to the foundation of the Bangladesh Red Cross, which 'has only been able to formulate its programme of activities within the last few days'.[62] From the outset, the ICRC planned to employ Bangladeshis as part of their medical and nutritional teams as a way 'to work in the closest possible collaboration with the local Red Cross'.[63]

The ICRC's mission in Bangladesh was ambitious. On 15 December 1971, one day before the Pakistani surrender, the ICRC released its first appeal to national societies for funds and in-kind donations. The initial appeal requested CHF 31 million, followed by a subsequent call for another CHF 8 million on 24 January 1972. Many national societies responded immediately, including those from countries as diverse as Iran, Ireland, Thailand and Guyana in South America.[64] By 31 January 1972, twelve national societies had contributed far above the rest. Major donor societies included Sweden, Belgium, Canada, the United States, Britain, New Zealand, Australia and Iceland.[65] It is noteworthy that these ICRC records tabulated donations in a range of currencies, making comparison between donor societies difficult, if not impossible, which contrasts with Table 4.1 earlier in this chapter, which listed all country donations in Swiss francs.

Unlike during the war, in the reconstruction period, foreign medical and technical personnel were welcomed into Bangladesh to work alongside ICRC and Bangladesh Red Cross staff. European and Japanese Red Cross medical teams were dispatched to Bangladesh in early January 1972 and assigned to districts across the country. A Swedish Red Cross medical team worked with Australian Baptist missionaries in Mymensingh in the north of the country after an unsatisfactory stint in Rājshāhi near the Indian border.[66] The Australian Red Cross provided technical personnel, including Miss

---

[61] *International Review of the Red Cross*, number 125, August 1971, 431; number 126, September 1971, 491, number 128, November 1971 614–15 and number 130, January 1972, 17–19.

[62] Enrico Bagnami, Circular letter, 'Bangla Desh Relief Operations, 26 January 1972', 2. Box (Unit) 440, Folder 10 'A - D.E.C. 1972 18a', Records of the Australian Red Cross – National Office, 2015.0033. Correspondence Files, National Headquarters, University of Melbourne Archives, Melbourne, Australia. Note that the name and emblem changed from Red Cross to Red Crescent on 4 April 1988.

[63] Ibid.

[64] Comité International de la Croix-Rouge (CICR), 'Minutes of Meeting on ICRC/League operation India-Pakistan with representatives of National Societies, held at ICRC Headquarters (Geneva) on January 7th, 1972', Box (Unit) 440, Folder 10 'A - D.E.C. 1972 18a'.

[65] Financial data from CICR, 'Bangla Desh Relief Operation, 4 February 1972', circular letter, 3. Box (Unit) 440, Folder 10 'A - D.E.C. 1972 18a'.

[66] According to ICRC correspondence, the Swedish medical team was stationed in the south-eastern towns of Kachua and Chandpur (from 8 January 1972). See CICR, 'Report to the National Societies of the Red Cross, Red Crescent and Red Lion and Sun. ICRC-League Operation India-Pakistan', 11 January 1972, Box (Unit) 440, Folder '10. A-D.E.C. 1972 18a'. For corroborating evidence

Noreen Minogue, Deputy Secretary General of the Australian Red Cross, who assisted with coordination of the ICRC relief activities in Geneva from December 1971 to May 1972. Sydneysider Kevin Baldwin was seconded to Kolkata to serve as quartermaster supervising the on-shipment of relief goods to Bangladesh from February to April 1972. Meanwhile, National Director of Public Relations at the Australian Red Cross, Bill Deane, joined the ICRC in Bangladesh as a PR and information officer, a function that the Indian Red Cross refused to do in 1971.[67]

The ICRC mission in Bangladesh lasted three months, from 4 February to 18 April 1972, at which point the Bangladesh Red Cross Society assumed operational responsibility for an additional twelve-month relief programme, funded by national societies. The handover to the newly established Bangladesh Red Cross was not without its problems, however. Within one month of the transition, the Bangladesh Red Cross faced allegations that it was ignoring the needs of the Bihari minority population. Biharis, the Urdu-speaking Muslims who migrated from India to Bangladesh after the 1947 Partition, were seen by ethnic Bengalis as Pakistani collaborators during the 1971 war. After Pakistan's defeat, many Biharis were subjected to extra-judicial arrests and revenge killings at the hands of Bengalis. Bihari possessions and property were forcibly seized by the state or militias, and they were rounded up and settled in camps throughout Bangladesh. During 1972, over one million Biharis lived in these settlements, and when asked by the Bangladesh government, two-thirds of these residents requested repatriation to Pakistan via ICRC channels.[68] From the outset, the Pakistani government distanced itself from whom it called 'Bangladeshi-Biharis' and feared the cost of resettling a destitute and impoverished population. The ICRC, therefore, found itself in the position of aiding displaced people awaiting repatriation to a country that did not want them and collaborating with a national society unwilling to provide material relief to a former enemy.

Accusations that the Bangladesh Red Cross was mistreating Biharis was reported in Melbourne broadsheet *The Age* via a syndicated article in *The Times* of London. In the article, the award-winning international correspondent, Peter Hazelhurst, wrote,

> At the insistence of the military chauvinists in the Government, the International Red Cross has been forced to hand over supervision of food for the Biharis to Bengal nationalists belonging to the Bangladesh Red Cross. But the Bangladesh Red Cross is completely indifferent to its task.[69]

---

from Australian Baptists, see Grace Dodge, diary entry, 13 February 1972, Dodge family papers (accessed by author); Letter from Betty Salisbury to ABMS', Baptist Mission, Mymensingh, Bangla Desh, 4 June 1972, 6. Located in 'East Pakistan Crisis 1971 file, Archives of the Australian Baptist Missionary Society, held at Global Interaction Australian Headquarters, Melbourne, Australia.

[67] Leon G. Stubbings, Secretary General, Australian Red Cross, Letter to Len Reid, MP, President, For Those Who Have Less, 2 March 1972, 2. Box (Unit) 440, Folder 10 'A - D.E.C. 1972 18a'.

[68] A. Mantoo Shahnawaz, 'Bihari Refugees Stranded in Bangladesh since 1971', *Journal of South Asian Studies* 1, no. 2 (2013): 123–9, 124 and Eric Paulsen, 'The Citizenship Status of the Urdu-Speakers/Biharis in Bangladesh', *Refugee Survey Quarterly* 25, no. 3 (2006): 55. It was not until 2008 when the Bangladesh High Court ruled that Urdu-speakers (Biharis) should be entitled to Bangladeshi citizenship, thus ending nearly forty years of statelessness in the camps. Victoria Redclift, 'Abjects or Agents? Camps, Contests and the Creation of "Political Space"', *Citizenship Studies* 17 (2013): 311.

[69] Peter Hazelhurst, 'Bangladesh: for 1.5m It Now Spells Stark Terror', *The Age*, 10 May 1972: 10.

Concerned by the allegations, and the publicity surrounding them, the Australian Red Cross assured its state divisions that it would boycott sending 'any further supplies to the Bangladesh Red Cross' until the ICRC had confirmed that 'Red Cross relief was available to all in need without discrimination'.[70] Eight days passed before the Australian Red Cross received a curt reply from Geneva: 'ICRC AND LEAGUE SEE TO IT THAT BDRC ACTS ACCORDING [sic.] RED CROSS PRINCIPLES'.[71]

Notwithstanding the ICRC confirming that the Bangladesh Red Cross was adhering to their core values, negative press coverage continued. Two weeks later, another Hazelhurst article was syndicated in the Australian broadsheet newspapers, this time with the provocative title, 'Bangladesh "Massacres Biharis"'.[72] On 13 June 1972, an Associated Press article was syndicated across the Australian broadsheets, again, with an alarmist headline, 'Biharis face extermination, say Swiss'. In the anonymous article, the journalist reported that since the ICRC handover to the Bangladesh Red Cross, Biharis concentrated in camps had not received supplies and 'faced complete extermination unless international action' stopped the 'genocide'.[73] Once again, Australian state divisions required reassurance from the national office that the ICRC was maintaining Red Cross standards in Bangladesh. This time, though, the General Secretary of the Victorian Division, S. G. Goodard, suggested that the Australian Red Cross issue a press release to calm public concerns.[74] In his reply nine days later, Leon Stubbings politely deflected responsibility, noting that 'if you should receive a number of enquiries re this matter ... then you may well feel compelled to state the official stand that is being taken by the ICRC'. Leon Stubbings did offer to assist with drafting a statement and provide any new information that came to hand; however, it is evident in the letter that the Secretary General wanted to distance the national office from any controversy.[75]

The negative press coverage still continued. In early July, the national broadsheet, *The Australian*, ran another feature article by acclaimed politics professor and regular columnist, Henry Mayer. In the piece, Mayer claimed the ICRC had hastily vacated Bangladesh, leaving ethnic minorities at the mercy of the Bengali-led Bangladesh Red Cross. These assertions, once again, raised the ire of the Australian Red Cross leadership. Noreen Minogue, serving as Acting Secretary General of the Australian Red Cross, wrote to Mayer directly, requesting he correct his allegedly false claims. In the letter, Minogue noted that although the ICRC transferred rehabilitation and reconstruction responsibilities to the Bangladesh Red Cross in April, the ICRC maintained sixty-eight

---

[70] Australian Red Cross Memorandum. From Secretary General Leon G. Stubbings to General Secretary, All Divisions, 10 May 1972 and Australian Red Cross telegram to ICRC and LRCS, 10 May 1972, 10.50am. Box (Unit) 440, Folder 10 'A - D.E.C. 1972 18a'.

[71] Telegram, ICRC to Australian Red Cross, 18 May 1972, Box (Unit) 440, Folder 10 'A - D.E.C. 1972 18a'.

[72] *Canberra Times*, 23 May 1972, 4.

[73] *Canberra Times*, 13 June 1972, 4.

[74] Memorandum, S. G. Goddard to L. G. Stubbings, 14 June 1972, Box (Unit) 440, Folder 10 'A - D.E.C. 1972 18a'.

[75] Letter, L. G. Stubbings to S. G. Goddard, Victorian Division, 22 June 1972, Box (Unit) 440, Folder 10 'A - D.E.C. 1972 18a'.

delegates in Bangladesh. Minogue explained to Mayer, 'Among their other duties these delegates are responsible for providing food and shelter for the Biharis'. Minogue continued that bamboo huts housing 100,000 Biharis had been constructed under ICRC direction on the outskirts of Dhaka. Furthermore, the ICRC delegates continued to distribute some 4,000 tonnes of food grains to Biharis, according to Minogue. As such, the Acting Secretary General reiterated that the Australian Red Cross had received 'assurance that minority groups such as the Biharis were being cared for by the Bangladesh Red Cross'.[76] By the end of 1972, LRCS documents indicate that from the ICRC transfer of authority to the Bangladesh Red Cross in April, the number of feeding centres and beneficiaries had increased exponentially. For example, in April 1972, there were 300 feeding centres, assisting 120,000 individuals, mostly children under 13, pregnant women, nursing mothers and the elderly. By October, these figures had grown to 1,320 centres and 1,380,000 recipients, benefitting all districts and all segments of society.[77]

Despite the tangible and significant aid efforts of the ICRC in collaboration with the Bangladesh Red Cross during 1972, Australian newspapers remained preoccupied with publishing sensationalist allegations of ethnic cleansing. When Noreen Minogue wrote to Henry Mayer requesting a correction, she did so three weeks after the original article was published. In any case, her request was ignored, and Mayer's commentary was likely taken as fact by readers. What we have, then, is the largest humanitarian organization losing the battle for positive publicity in the public domain. Remarkably, at an international Red Cross meeting, American representative James Hickey argued that 'even negative reports are better than no reports' as they at least showed Red Cross workers active in the field.[78] By setting such a low bar for acceptable press coverage, it is evident that among Red Cross leadership, they were concerned about more than just the fate of Biharis. Indeed, at this time, the Red Cross faced an existential threat in which past errors had tarnished the image of the organization to such a point that they struggled to compete with emerging humanitarian organizations that enjoyed unblemished records.

By the 1970s, humanitarian organizations simultaneously cooperated and competed. They cooperated to share resources and maximize impact on the ground, but they also competed to leverage influence, champion specific causes and capture the imagination of the public. During the Bangladesh Liberation War and its aftermath, the ICRC was at a crossroads: the legacies of the Holocaust, Biafra and, more recently, limited involvement in Bangladesh during 1971 rendered the organization largely irrelevant; yet the ICRC still yielded significant resources and benefitted from close relationships with many governments, including in some nations acting as the de facto state aid agency. In January 1972, at a meeting between ICRC leadership and representatives from National Societies (including Minogue representing Australia), we see these tensions come to fruition. It was noted in the minutes that the Red Cross movement

---

[76] Noreen Minogue, Acting Secretary General, Australian Red Cross, letter to Henry Mayer, *The Australian* newspaper, 25 July 1972, Box (Unit) 440, Folder 10 'A - D.E.C. 1972 18a'.

[77] LRCS, Geneva, Relief Bureau. Circular No. 535, 8 December 1972, 1. Box (Unit) 440, Folder 10 'A - D.E.C. 1972 18a'.

[78] CICR, 'Minutes of Meeting on ICRC/League operation India-Pakistan with representatives of National Societies, held at ICRC Headquarters (Geneva) on January 7th, 1972', Box (Unit) 440, Folder 10 'A - D.E.C. 1972 18a', 4.

worried about the United Nations (UN) becoming 'the major relief organization in the world'. In this statement, it is implicit that the Red Cross feared losing its pre-eminence to the young, global and (relatively) representative body. In this light, the ICRC and national society representatives agreed that their competitive advantage over the UN was twofold: that unlike the UN, the ICRC could mobilize aid immediately pending host society approval and that, unlike the UN, the ICRC had existing, collaborative relationships with a range of voluntary and religious organizations. Consequently, the ICRC officials reassured national societies that despite emerging threats from the UN, the Red Cross movement was well positioned to maintain its leading role as a global coordinating body. But ICRC officials warned national society leaders that 'it [was] vital for the Red Cross to be a united group', a signal that conflicts within the movement posed more of a threat than external competition.[79]

Conclusion

The Australian Red Cross performed poorly in the Bangladesh Liberation War and subsequent reconstruction. Throughout the war, the in-kind goods donated by the organization reflected the demands of the Australian public rather than the needs of the refugees. From sending out-of-date medicines to culturally or weather-inappropriate clothing, the Australian Red Cross seemed more interested in self-promotion and maintaining its status as Australia's foremost charity than offering effective aid. Indeed, the question of publicity seemed to govern all Australian Red Cross decisions. Its insistence on providing Australian medical personnel was out of touch with Indian sensibilities and demonstrated ignorance of Indian aspirations in a postcolonial world. Through its neo-imperial mindset, the Australian Red Cross hindered rather than helped the global humanitarian effort to aid Bangladeshi refugees.

During the reconstruction period, the Australian Red Cross was left flat-footed, forced to respond reactively to press allegations of Bihari maltreatment. The controversy surrounding Bihari neglect reveals once again the fallacy of Red Cross neutrality and universalism, yet the Australian Red Cross could only deny and plead with the ICRC and Bangladesh Red Cross for assurances. What we have, then, is an organization out of step with cultural mores, operationally ineffectual and struggling to maintain relevance, let alone supremacy, in a highly competitive Australian aid sector. As we will see in the next two chapters, the Australian Red Cross was under threat from new, politically assertive and marketing-savvy humanitarian organizations that were established in the post-1945 period. Both Christian aid agencies and grassroots organizations were embedded within international federations and maintained close working relationships with humanitarian organizations in India. This integration meant that Christian and grassroots humanitarian NGOs were much more aware of the changing political tide in South Asia and sufficiently agile in their operations to respond to local needs. But, as we will see, these young and bold organizations, too, had their own struggles with which to grapple.

[79] Ibid., 10.

5

The religious: Organized church aid and Christian activists

In a letter to Reverend Ted Arblaster, the Director of the Australian Council of Churches Division of World Christian Action, Reverend C. Kingston Daws insisted that strident action was required to meet the demands of the Social Gospel, the liberal interpretation of the Bible that emphasizes equality of man and justice for all. Daws, who was also Australia's head Methodist, wrote,

> The plight of the refugees from East Pakistan is a human disaster of appalling dimensions … In such a crisis, it is not enough for us to be spectators, however concerned and sympathetic we may be. Nothing less than action which will be really costly to us individually and collectively will be sufficient to meet the claims of the Gospel on our compassion for those in need …
>
> In the face of such dire need, I would make a plea to all our people to respond with compassionate generosity. Countless lives can be saved if the aid is supplied quickly enough and in sufficient quantity. We have received very freely – let us give just as freely.
>
> Yours in the Fellowship of Christian Concern.[1]

In this extract, we can identify several themes that typified post-Second World War Christian humanitarianism, all of which will recur throughout this chapter. He insisted that feeling sympathy was not enough; given the scale of the refugee crisis, only sacrificial giving would suffice. This call to action was also universal in its coverage. Daws did not mention the religious background of the recipients of aid – who were mostly Hindu and some Muslims – because this was immaterial. What mattered to this Christian leader was that because everyone is made in the image of God, then all are deserving of charity. Daws also failed to mention proselytization: by the mid-twentieth century, Christian internationalists were distancing themselves from the missionary pasts of organized religion. Lastly, Daws urged Australian Methodists to

---

[1] C. Kingston Daws, 'An Urgent Appeal to the Methodists of Australasia from the President General. East Pakistan Refugees', 10 June 1971, Box 117, folder 'Pakistan, East and West – 1964–71'. Records of the ACC.

look beyond their immediate needs and turn outwards, taking responsibility for the complex problems facing the global community.

For some readers, the inclusion of a chapter on faith-based humanitarianism in Australia may appear unwarranted. Often described, even celebrated, as a secular nation, this chapter reminds us of the degree to which Christianity has permeated all aspects of Australian society for centuries. The dominance of Christian ethics and morality in Australia is arguably hegemonic and so normalized that it is hard to identify sometimes and separate out from overtly secular approaches to aid. Yet this chapter recalls how Christianity shaped the Australian response to the Bangladeshi refugee crisis in myriad ways.

This chapter focuses on the motivations, networks and activities of Australian faith-based aid agencies that were established after the Second World War, drawing comparisons with the more established Red Cross movement, which was examined in Chapter 4, and the elite umbrella NGOs covered in Chapter 3. It examines how these organizations understood the conflict, identified problems, debated possible solutions and considered what kind of world they sought to help create. Although Christian aid agencies are often associated with their missionary pasts, and thereby implicated in imperialism, this chapter shows that faith-based humanitarianism defied neat stereotypes. Indeed, in the early 1970s, Christian charities were the new outsiders and part of a wider counter-cultural movement that challenged individuals to reject consumerism and individualism, all the while supporting economic self-sufficiency and pacifism across the globe.

Religion in Australia: The most godless place under heaven?

Faith-based humanitarian organizations employ language, rationales and strategies that often, but not always, distinguish them from their irreligious colleagues. Scholars should examine not *whether* humanitarian organizations are religious but, rather, *how* religion shapes humanitarian organizations. Evangelical Christian scholar David King explains that religion is not just a static identity but a social tradition 'latent with its own cultural logics, meanings, symbols and organizational structures', which in turn influence how relief is conceived and disbursed.[2] Faith-based aid agencies can draw upon centuries of tradition, which indirectly bestows a legitimacy, authority and even righteousness on these organizations.[3] Religious relief bodies also benefit from dedicated donors who are committed to the scriptural rationale for aid. For example, the Hebrew Bible includes directives to care for the exiled and the stranger 'for you were once strangers yourself' (Leviticus 19.33–34). Importantly, in the Christian

---

[2] David King, 'World Vision: Religious Identity in the Discourse and Practice of Global Relief and Development', *Review of Faith and International Affairs* 9 (2011): 23; King, *God's Internationalists*, introduction. See also Heather D. Curtis, *Holy Humanitarians: American Evangelicals and Global Aid* (Cambridge, MA: Harvard University Press, 2018).

[3] Paras and Stein, 'Bridging the Sacred and the Profane in Humanitarian Life', 211, 214 and 218.

tradition such concern for the stranger extends beyond one's own community to include those who are different, even enemies. In Luke 10.25–37, Jesus tells the parable of the Good Samaritan who compassionately cares for a man who had been robbed, stripped and beaten and ignored by previous passers-by. The message of this parable is for Christians not only to offer aid without distinction, but to seek out the persecuted and marginalized who may be denied support within the community. Evangelical Christians also draw upon the Great Commission in Matthew 28.19–20, which calls on believers to 'go and make disciples of all nations', directing their ministry 'to the least of these' (Mark 25.31–46).[4] This distinctly evangelical internationalism identifies Christian responsibility as a mix of 'a quiet sharing of faith and an intense passion to alleviate the suffering' of the most impoverished.[5] Meanwhile, mid-twentieth century Catholics received contemporaneous papal instruction to address inequality. Most notably, the *Populorum Progressio* (1967) proposed a distinctly Catholic approach to development that addressed both material and spiritual needs of the disadvantaged.[6]

The Christian case for humanitarian aid is self-evident; the role that religion plays in Australian society, however, is complicated. In colonial Australia, a Scottish Presbyterian theologian James Denney allegedly described Australia pejoratively as 'the most godless place under Heaven'.[7] This theologian was despairing with what he found in the Antipodes, but his assessment was far from accurate in two ways. First and most blatantly, it negated indigenous spirituality that predates European conquest. Second, the quotation obscured the central yet informal role that Christianity played at the time of colonization. Wayne Hudson argues that religion was involved in the formation of national institutions.[8] Even the Australian Constitution, which denies federal parliament the power to legislate on matters of religion, has a theological bent.[9] Although section 116 seemingly creates a secular division between church and state, this provision was included at the behest of religious minorities. Specifically, Seventh Day Adventists (who observe sabbath on Saturday) wished to ensure that parliament could not legislate Sunday observance laws.[10] Furthermore, as a penal colony, Australia offered convicts an avenue for redemption through hard work and temperance. Thus, British convict transportation to Australia from 1788 to 1868 had overtones of

---

[4] Paul S. Rowe, 'The Global – and Globalist – Roots of Evangelical Action', *Review of Faith and International Affairs* 17 (2019): 36.

[5] King, *God's Internationalists*, 20.

[6] For a detailed analysis of this encyclical, see Mari Rapela Heidt, 'Development, Nations, and "The Signs of the Times": The Historical Context of Populorum Progressio', *Journal of Moral Theology* 6 (2017): 1–20.

[7] Joanna Cruickshank, 'Religious Freedom in "the Most Godless Place under Heaven": Making Policy for Religion in Australia', *History Australia* 18 (2021): 42.

[8] Wayne Hudson, *Australian Religious Thought* (Melbourne: Monash University, 2016): 1.

[9] Section 116 states, 'The Commonwealth shall not make any law for establishing any religion, or for imposing any religious observance, or for prohibiting the free exercise of any religion, and no religious test shall be required as a qualification for any office or public trust under the Commonwealth', accessed 14 April 2022, https://www.aph.gov.au/About_Parliament/Senate/Powers_practice_n_procedures/Constitution.

[10] Luke Beck, 'The Theological Underpinnings of Australia's Constitutional Separation of Church and State Provision', *Australian Journal of Politics & History* 64 (2018): 17.

Anglican Evangelical salvation during this 'age of atonement'.[11] Yet the perspectives of the convicts on religion was problematic: once emancipated, former convicts typically adopted anti-clerical attitudes. For the emancipated, their hostility was specifically targeted at the Anglican elite who were viewed as instruments of the British state.[12]

Since the nineteenth century, the relationship between church and state waxed and waned depending on the fears of the (mostly Anglican) Australian ruling class.[13] Initially, the Church of England enjoyed a privileged position among Christian denominations, and it seemed as though the young colony would follow the path of its metropole, cementing Anglicanism as the state religion. In the 1820s, the Church of England received grants of land and funds from the New South Wales (NSW) colonial government.[14] But this imitative trajectory was short-lived: fearing a sectarian rebellion in the young, religiously diverse colony, NSW Governor Richard Bourke introduced and the Legislative Council passed the Church Acts, which mandated equal funding for Anglicans, Catholics, Presbyterians and, later, Methodists, based on number of adherents.[15] Although this law was intended to subdue interdenominational tension, it had the opposite effect. As funding was determined by number of adherents, denominations sought conversions and implanted themselves in all aspects of Australian social life, including establishing confessional schools, orphanages, city missions and welfare services.[16] Schools became the next battleground. Protestant political leaders never accepted state funding for Catholic schools. From the 1890s, all Australian colonial governments ceased funding for denominational schools, a ban that would last until 1963.[17] The withdrawal of state funding of denominational schools had minimal impact on Protestant private schools, which were sustained by private tuition fees and philanthropy. Many Catholic schools, conversely, lacked private sources of funding and struggled financially, particularly those schools located in outer suburban and regional areas, further entrenching economic divides along religious lines. When the Catholic school system in NSW faced a financial collapse, the state government intervened, if only to prevent high numbers of Catholic students entering

---

[11] Hilary Carey, *Empire of Hell: Religion and the Campaign to End Convict Transportation in the British Empire, 1788–1875* (Cambridge: Cambridge University Press, 2019), 26–38, 306–19.

[12] Stephen Chavura, John Gasgoine and Ian Tregenza, *Reason, Religion and the Australian Polity: A Secular State?* (London: Routledge, 2019), 5; Shurlee Swain, 'A Long History of Faith-Based Welfare in Australia: Origins and Impact', *Journal of Religious History* 41 (2017): 82, 84.

[13] Australia's first Catholic Prime Minister, James Scullin, was in office from 1929 to 1932. He was succeeded by another Australian Labor Party (ALP) Catholic, Joseph Lyons, who served from 1932 to 1939. Subsequent ALP Catholic Prime Ministers included John Curtin (1941–5) and Ben Chifley (1945–9). Of the twenty-five prime ministers of Australia during the twentieth century, only five were Catholics. Of the remaining twenty, nine were Anglican, three Presbyterian, and one Methodist. Others were raised Methodist or Presbyterian as children but abandoned formal connections with the church in adulthood. Only two self-identified as lifelong agnostics. See Roy Williams, *In God they Trust? The Religious Beliefs of Australian Prime Ministers, 1901–2013* (Sydney: Bible Society, 2013).

[14] Cruickshank, 'Religious Freedom in "the Most Godless Place under Heaven"', 45.

[15] Chavura, Gasgoine and Tregenza, *Reason, Religion and the Australian Polity*, 2–3, 51–8.

[16] Swain, 'A Long History of Faith-Based Welfare in Australia', 84; Hudson, *Australian Religious Thought*, x–xi.

[17] Benjamin Edwards, *WASPS, Tykes and Ecumaniacs: Aspects of Australian Sectarianism, 1945–1981* (Sydney: Acorn Press, 2008), 223–4.

the public education system. Since 1964, denominational schools of all stripes have become ever more dependent on government grants. To this day, at least one-third of Australian children attend religious schools, a remarkably high figure in a country that professes to be secular.[18] In social services and healthcare, the role of religion is even more pronounced than in education, with Christian-related welfare organizations delivering 50 per cent of all social services in Australia.[19] Given the prevalence of faith-based social services in Australia, it is fair to say that 'deep layers of Christian sediment' remain in society, impacting a range of citizen behaviours, including humanitarian aid giving, and sustaining latent attitudes about ethics and responsibility.[20]

The global ecumenical movement during the post-Second World War years profoundly impacted Australian society. The Second Vatican Council (1962–5) permitted interfaith marriages, enabling Catholics to marry Protestants without fear of excommunication. As a result, mixed marriages became more common, if not completely welcomed. Offspring of these couples were raised with exposure to both faith traditions.[21] Residential patterns in Australian cities also changed, with upwardly mobile European immigrants moving from the inner city to the suburbs, thereby reducing geographical segregation between predominantly suburban British Protestants and urban Irish and Central European Catholics.[22] With greater community intermingling, old prejudices began to subside and a new Christian coalition formed, inclusive of both Western branches of Christianity and, to a lesser extent, of the Eastern Church, too.[23] During the 1960s, therefore, sectarianism was less of a divisive feature of Australian society than it had been in the nineteenth century.

The lingering role of faith in Australia cannot be overstated because it undermines the conventional wisdom that this country is more secular than most other Western societies.[24] Australian historians wrongly inherited the European secularization thesis, which theorizes that with industrialization, urbanization and modernization, societies inevitably become secular. During the twentieth century, the secularization thesis

---

[18] According to the Australian Curriculum, Assessment and Reporting Authority (ACARA), in 2020, 65 per cent of students (all levels/all states) attend government schools; 19.4 per cent attend Catholic schools and 15 per cent attend non-Catholic independent schools, mostly Protestant, but also Jewish and Islamic schools. The proportions for senior secondary schools are 59.4 per cent, 21.6 per cent and 20 per cent, respectively. See ACARA, 'National Report on Schooling in Australia Data Portal', accessed 14 April 2022, https://www.acara.edu.au/reporting/national-report-on-schooling-in-australia/national-report-on-schooling-in-australia-data-portal/student-numbers#view1.

[19] Cruickshank, 'Religious Freedom in "the Most Godless Place under Heaven"', 49; Swain, 'A Long History of Faith-Based Welfare in Australia', 96.

[20] Chavura, Gasgoine and Tregenza, *Reason, Religion and the Australian Polity*, 209; Hugh Chilton, *Evangelicals and the End of Christendom: Religion, Australia and the Crises of the 1960* (New York: Routledge, 2020), 10.

[21] Stevens and O'Hanlon, 'Intimate Oral Histories', 363.

[22] Seamus O'Hanlon and Rachel Stevens, 'A Nation of Immigrants or a Nation of Immigrant Cities? The Urban Context of Australian Multiculturalism, 1947–2011', *Australian Journal of Politics and History* 63 (2017): 563–5; Seamus O'Hanlon, *City Life: The New Urban Australia* (Sydney: New South, 2018), 90–2.

[23] Edwards, *WASPS, Tykes and Ecumaniacs*, 228.

[24] Shurlee Swain, 'Do You Want Religion with That? Welfare History in a Secular Age', *History Australia* 2 (2005): 79.2.

became a faith itself, caused in part by the academic influence of sociological doyens who promoted the theory, including Karl Marx, Emile Durkheim, Max Weber and Sigmund Freud.[25] The persistence and resurgence of faith in many parts of the developed world has led European scholars to openly challenge this thesis. Yet in Australia, the secularization thesis persists, routinely affirmed with every quinquennial census that documents increasing numbers of Australians who identify as having 'no religion, so described'.[26] The secularization thesis fails on broad, methodological grounds. Social scientists can support secularization based on measured behaviours in surveys and censuses. Church attendance and membership are two typical metrics. But the desire of the social scientist to quantify degrees of religiosity limits our understanding to institutional decline, as it is near impossible to survey how religion impacts behaviour. This book takes a broader view of religion by conceptualizing faith as a private matter and an internal state of mind that motivates and justifies humanitarian actions.[27] By drawing attention to more subtle forms of religious behaviour, we illuminate a more nuanced story of mid-twentieth-century humanitarianism than has been told before.[28]

National and international Protestant and Catholic aid organizations

By the time of the 1971 Bangladesh War, sectarian divisions were easing in Australian society, and there was a renewed commitment to interfaith dialogue, goodwill and international engagement. In a practical sense, Australian religious organizations worked cooperatively with each other and the humanitarian sector more broadly. The Australian Council of Churches (ACC) and its Division of World Christian Action, previously known as Inter-Church Aid, was emblematic of an optimistic and outward-looking conglomeration of various Christian churches in Australia. At the time, the ACC included Anglican, Protestant and Orthodox churches but not Catholics, Baptists or evangelical Anglicans.[29] Although not part of the association, Australian evangelicals were often in communication with the ACC leadership on matters relating to Bangladeshi aid. For instance, Baptist and ACC leaders exchanged letters and met in person while in Sydney. The tone of these letters reveals a folksy charm, with expressions such as 'have a yarn' used repeatedly, suggestive of a warm and relaxed friendship.[30] Relations with Australian Catholics and their relief agency were less

---

[25] J. C. D. Clark, 'Secularization and Modernization: The Failure of a "Grand Narrative"', *Historical Journal* 55 (2012): 163.

[26] In the 2021 census, 39 per cent reported 'no religion', up from 31 per cent in the 2016 census and 21.8 per cent in 2011. See ABS, 'Snapshot of Australia, 2021', 13 March 2022, https://www.abs.gov.au/statistics/people/people-and-communities/snapshot-australia/2021#religious-affiliation.

[27] Jeremy Morris, 'Secularization and Religious Experience: Arguments in the Historiography of Modern British Religion', *Historical Journal* 55 (2012): 197.

[28] Grant, 'Anti-slavery, Refugee Relief, and the Missionary Origins of Humanitarian Photography ca. 1900–1960', 20.

[29] The ACC now includes the Catholic Church within the association. Box 117, Folder 'Pakistan, East and West, 1964–71'.

[30] See letter from Arblaster to Rev. J. D. Williams, 23 June 1971 and letter from Williams to F. G. Engels, 2 June 1971. Box 117, Folder 'Pakistan, East and West, 1964–71'.

jovial, though still cooperative, as evidenced by their joint campaign in the Australian press to mobilize citizen activism in November 1971.

The ACC was part of a larger, global ecumenical movement, the World Council of Churches (WCC), which has its headquarters in Geneva. The WCC was a long time coming: the genesis of a worldwide pan-Protestant association was born at the time of the 1910 Missionary Conference in Edinburgh, but due to the world wars, the assembly only occurred in 1948.[31] At inception, the ambitions of the WCC went far beyond a fellowship of churches and included establishing a Commission of Churches on International Affairs (CCIA), which participated in drafts of the Universal Declaration of Human Rights.[32] Concerned by the displacement of Palestinians after the 1948 Arab-Israeli War, the CCIA approached the United Nations in 1949, advocating for a global response to refugee movements rather than the existing system that was limited to DPs in Europe. As explored in Chapter 2, when the UNHCR was founded in 1951, it had a skeleton staff and therefore relied on other aid agencies for operations. The WCC (along with the Lutheran World Relief) secured more funding than any other agency for operational support for UN refugee work in the post-war years.[33] During the 1950s and 1960s, the working relationship between the WCC and the UN was strengthened, with the ecumenical movement continuing to provide practical support in health, education, human rights and migration, as well as offering moral leadership on matters such as nuclear disarmament and peace negotiations.[34]

The centrist position of the WCC and its CCIA branch would, however, take a radical turn in the mid-1960s and 1970s. Inspired by left-wing Latin American Protestantism, the WCC became increasingly activist in its orientation, publicly supporting decolonization, anti-racism and democratic socialism, and funding liberation movements. Beyond specific issues, the WCC reinterpreted theological concepts along radical lines and advocated for collective social and economic rights, which was at odds with the liberal individualism that infused Western notions of human rights.[35] Under the second General Secretary, American Eugene Carson Blake (1966–72), the WCC became strident on 'soapbox' issues, such as its opposition to the war in Vietnam and support of Palestine. Blake had a long history in activism, most notably walking alongside Martin Luther King Jr during the March on Washington in 1963. For Blake, 'mere pious expressions of sympathy' were inadequate to address global injustice. Indicative of his radical leanings, Blake commented in 1968, 'the

---

[31] Katharina Kunter, 'Revolutionary Hopes and Global Transformations: The World Council of Churches in the 1960s', *Kirchliche Zeitgeschichte* 30 (2017): 344. For further reading on the 1910 Edinburgh Conference, see the work of Brian Stanley, particularly *The World Missionary Conference* (Grand Rapids, MI: William B. Eerdmans, 2009).

[32] Tal Zalmanovich, '"What Is Needed Is an Ecumenical Act of Solidarity:" The World Council of Churches, the 1969 Notting Hill Consultation on Racism, and the Anti-Apartheid Struggle', *Safundi* 20 (2019): 178.

[33] Katharina Kunter, 'Global Reach and Global Agenda: The World Council of Churches', in *The Changing World Religion Map: Sacred Places, Identities, Practices and Politics*, ed. Stanley D. Brunn and Donna Gilbreath (Dordrecht: Springer, 2015), 2915.

[34] Konrad Raiser, 'The World Council of Churches and International Civil Society', *Ecumenical Review* 46 (1994): 42–3.

[35] Zalmanovich, '"What Is Needed Is an Ecumenical Act of Solidarity"', 179–80; Kunter, 'Revolutionary Hopes and Global Transformations', 345–6; Kunter, 'Global Reach and Global Agenda', 218.

difference between a saint and a destructive revolutionary is not easy to discern'.[36] By this time, the membership base of the WCC was de-Westernizing: in 1954, 37 per cent of churches were based in the Global South; by 1975, this figure had increased to 54 per cent.[37] Blake therefore represented a political bridge from the first General Secretary, Dutch theologian Willem Visser't Hooft (1948–66), to the third General Secretary, Dominican Pastor Philip Potter (1972–84). Additional non-Western leaders of the WCC would follow Potter, reflecting the changing geographical membership of the body and subsequent shift in power towards Latin America, Africa and Asia.[38] It was during the 1970s that the WCC reoriented its focus to issues of most relevance to the developing world, including anti-colonialism, anti-racism, socialism and liberation movements, often at the expense of traditional Protestant issues, such as anti-communism, and the Niebuhrian realist approach to international relations.[39] It is in this context of radicalism that the ACC worked alongside the WCC in providing aid for Bangladeshi refugees in India.

When Reverend Daws made his appeal to his co-religionists in June 1971, as quoted at the beginning of this chapter, the number of refugees in India was approximately four million people.[40] With a swelling in the numbers of refugees, logistical challenges for aid agencies were mounting, especially given the monsoon season was approaching and the resulting floods and mudslides would restrict outside access to the camps. Fortuitously, the Indian government had by June already established a logistical network for the collection and disbursement of overseas aid. For the ACC, they channelled their funds through the WCC in Geneva, who would in turn disburse cash and goods to the Indian NGO, Christian Agency for Social Action (CASA). During the war, CASA operated in forty refugee camps throughout West Bengal and Meghalaya, providing milk to 64,000 children and nursing and expectant mothers and providing eight medical units that serviced 2,500 patients daily.[41] This interconnected national–global–local network was similarly applied with the Red Cross movement, as we saw in Chapter 4.

Churches within the ACC made direct appeals to their brethren. On 10 June 1971, Anglican Archbishop of Melbourne, Sir Frank Woods, sent a letter to all Anglican parishes in the diocese, urging them to donate funds to ACC in support of their aid

---

[36] Theodore A. Gill, 'Eugene Carson Blake: Renewal in Church and Society', *Ecumenical Review* 70 (2018): 84–8. For background on the American ecumenical Protestantism in the post-1945 period from which Blake emerged, see David A. Hollinger, 'After Cloven Tongues of Fire: Ecumenical Protestantism and the Modern American Encounter with Diversity', *Journal of American History* 98 (2011): 21–48.
[37] Kunter, 'Global Reach and Global Agenda', 2916.
[38] Zalmanovich, '"What Is Needed Is an Ecumenical Act of Solidarity"', 188.
[39] For further details on Niebuhrian realism, see Vassilios Paipais, 'Reinhold Niebuhr and the Christian Realist Pendulum', *Journal of International Political Theory* 17, no. 2 (June 2021): 185–202 and Michael G. Thompson, *For God and Globe: Christian Internationalism in the United States between the Great War and the Cold War* (Ithaca, NY: Cornell University Press, 2016), chapter 3.
[40] ACC, letter to Parish ministers, Box 117, folder 'Pakistan, East and West – 1964–71' and Len Reid, *The Tragedy of Those Who Have Less* (Melbourne: Society 'For Those Who Have Less', 1973), 19.
[41] World Council of Churches (WCC), Commission on Inter-Church Aid, Refugee and World Service (CICARWS), letter to all CICARWS related agencies, including Re. Edmund H. Arblaster of Inter-Church Aid Department, ACC, 21 June 1971, Box 117, folder 'Pakistan, East and West – 1964–71'.

programme. In this circular, the archbishop used inflammatory language, starting his letter, 'No doubt you are as appalled as I am at the shocking suffering and wastage of human life caused by the cholera epidemic, on a scale unimaginable to us in this country.'[42] In this opening statement, Archbishop Woods elucidated two points: first, the emotional impact of witnessing the suffering of distant others and the sheer size of the problem at hand. Second, the archbishop drew attention to the cholera outbreak in the refugee camps, which was part of the seventh cholera pandemic from 1961 to 1975. The arrival of millions of refugees, cramped in makeshift camps alongside the Bangladeshi border in squalid conditions, created the ideal environment for the transmission of water-borne illnesses such as cholera.[43] With the monsoon season expected to last for the following three months, thereby worsening conditions in the camps and facilitating further spread of the disease, it was feared a human catastrophe loomed. As it turned out, mass deaths were averted if only because staff at the Johns Hopkins University Center for Medical Research and Training in Kolkata implemented a full-scale rollout of orally administered electrolyte solution rather than the standard, but impractical, use of intravenous fluids. This approach revolutionized how cholera would be treated in the years ahead, enabling greater access to vital preventive measures and without the need for medical supervision. But at the time in June 1971, newspapers across the world reported on a cholera outbreak that was seemingly out of control in the overpopulated refugee camps. For example, the *New York Times* reported on 9 June 1971, 'Disease, Hunger and Death Stalk Refugees Along India's Border'.[44]

Arguably, the cholera outbreak in the refugee camps in June 1971, and subsequent news reporting across the world, was a key moment that stimulated the international community to increase humanitarian aid with a sense of urgency. In Archbishop Woods's letter to parishioners, he outlined his fundraising endeavours through his networks, including with the Anglican Missionary and Ecumenical Committee, telegraphing the Prime Minister of Australia and, finally, appropriating funds from the Diocesan account. Woods expressed disappointment with the government's response as it was deemed 'a great deal less than our rich nation could easily have afforded'. In his plea to the parishes, Woods acknowledged that even though the church is often called on to help those in distress, they had a duty to make 'a special effort to meet the present crisis in Pakistan and Bengal'. The fact that the refugees were mostly Hindu with a minority Muslim population did not impact decisions about the disbursement of aid. According to the evidence, the religious background of the refugees was insignificant, which demonstrates that mainstream Protestant charities were distancing themselves from the evangelistic traditions of their past.

Assuaging any concern about misuse or inappropriate use of funds, Woods assured readers that World Christian Action was in daily communications with relief workers in the refugee camps, and therefore, 'your gifts are translated into action literally in a

---

[42] Sir Frank Woods, Anglican Archbishop of Melbourne, letter to all parishes in the Melbourne Anglican Archdiocese, 10 June 1971, Box 117, folder 'Pakistan, East and West – 1964–71'.
[43] D. Mahalanabis, A. B. Choudhuri, N. G. Bagchi, A. K. Bhattacharya and T. W. Simpson, 'Oral Fluid Therapy of Cholera among Bangladesh Refugees', *WHO South-East Asia Journal of Public Health* 1 (2012): 106.
[44] Sydney H. Schanberg, *New York Times*, 9 June 1971, 3.

matter of minutes'.[45] Whether the archbishop could honestly make such a promise is unknown but improbable. His comment reflected the need of aid agencies to show donors that their generosity had direct, immediate and meaningful impacts to needy recipients. But in pandering to the emotional needs of donors, Woods also denied the need of humanitarian NGOs to pay personnel, fund ongoing projects or pay for administrative expenses. Arguably, Woods held his associated humanitarian agency to an impossible standard – that is, converting donated dollars immediately into aid. His loose language is perhaps because he, as archbishop, was not part of the humanitarian establishment, who typically tended to be more prudent about the promises they made to donors.

The President of the ACC, Rector Reverend David A. Garnsey, who was also Anglican Bishop of Gippsland in rural Victoria, similarly conveyed his concerns about the cholera outbreak to parish ministers. But unlike Archbishop Woods, Bishop Garnsey foresaw that the outbreak would pass only to give way to ongoing struggles of life in a refugee camp – namely, the provision of food, medicine and shelter. Furthermore, Garnsey foreshadowed that camp life, too, would end once hostilities ceased. When refugees returned to Bangladesh, they would need 'longer term rehabilitation', for which the ACC and the WCC were working on plans. By early June 1971, the ACC had already dispersed $30,000 in cash to the WCC and CASA, sourced by donations received and leftover funds from the previous year's Christmas Bowl fundraiser. Garnsey lamented, 'Clearly this amount is inadequate' and offered several avenues through which individual citizens and churches could donate.[46] Church members could donate to their local church, who would then forward funds to the ACC, *or* they could forward donations to Austcare, as we saw in Chapter 3. Austcare would then in turn distribute to its member bodies, one of which was the ACC. On receipt of funds from Austcare, the ACC would forward donations to WCC and then on to CASA in India. This convoluted method of dispersing funds was likewise echoed in the Australian Red Cross experience, as shown in Chapter 4, and indicates a need for the streamlining of processes. Even so, it is evident that humanitarian organizations were simply unprepared for the scale of the Bangladeshi refugee crisis and the need for urgent disbursement of aid.

Despite these limitations, the ACC bumbled on, continuing with their fundraising efforts throughout their organization and affiliates. Unlike the Australian Red Cross that lacked information from the field for publicity, the WCC supplied its national organizations ample material. Two of its leading aid workers Stanley Mitton and Frances Martin visited India from 26 May to 4 June 1971. After meeting with USAID and UN agencies in New Delhi, the two men toured CASA-operated aid sites in the refugee camps of West Bengal, noting that field officers were feeling 'overwhelmed with the magnitude of the problem' of 'refugees streaming along the roads in their thousands'.[47] In their nine-page report for national members of the WCC, Mitton and

---

[45] Woods, letter to all parishes in the Melbourne Anglican Archdiocese, 10 June 1971.
[46] The Rt. Rev. David A. Garnsey, Bishop of Gippsland, President, ACC, letter to parish ministers, 'East Pakistan Emergency', 9 June 1971, Box 117, folder 'Pakistan, East and West – 1964–71'.
[47] Stanley Mitton, Emergency Officer, CICAWRS, WCC, 'Refugees in India', 10 June 1971, 3, Box 117, folder 'Pakistan, East and West – 1964–71'.

Martin detailed the many challenges facing aid workers across the thousands of refugee camps in eastern India, thereby providing contextual justification for additional funds and goods. Compounding matters further on the ground, Mitton observed escalating tensions between refugees and locals, which he described as 'an explosive situation', as well as violent border incidents, including sniping and mortar shelling.[48]

Unlike foreign journalists who were restricted by Indian authorities to West Bengal, Mitton and Martin travelled to Dawki, Meghalaya, on the north-eastern border of Bangladesh. Here, the aid workers journeyed up the foothills to an altitude of 2,000 metres (6,400 feet) and encountered refugee camps very different from those in low-lying West Bengal. In West Bengal, the refugee population was dominated by the most vulnerable: women, children and the elderly. Conversely, the demographics of refugees in Meghalaya was skewed – they were young and male, reflecting a representative cross-section of society. With a younger, healthful population, camps in Meghalaya were well organized and administered. For example, refugee schoolteachers established a 'simple school room' and a children's play area, which was a far cry from the aimlessness and boredom documented in the West Bengal camps.[49] The topography of the two regions also varied greatly, which impacted weather conditions, water supplies and disease transmission. In West Bengal, clean drinking water was in short supply, which led to the use of contaminated water that in turn contributed to the cholera outbreak. In Meghalaya, by contrast, Mitton observed 'a great deal of running water', although this, too, facilitated the spread of water-borne disease, specifically dysentery. As Mitton wrote, 'In another camp, which we could smell about a mile away, the siting [sic.] was extremely bad and people were clearly drinking, washing and doing other things all in the same water'.[50]

In supplying aid to this mountainous region, CASA was venturing into new, and more challenging, territory. With the onset of the monsoon season, elevated areas in Meghalaya faced flooding and landslides, making the transport of donated goods difficult if not impossible. Mitton specified that 'Jeeps are at a premium' and that 'it is essential to have four-wheel drive vehicles for the monsoons'.[51] Based on these observations, the WCC wrote to all national members that they immediately needed funds to purchase fifty Jeeps and fifty light vehicles to cope with deteriorating soil conditions.[52] Mitton also noted the backlog of donated material aid 'piled up at Dum Dum airport' in Kolkata awaiting clearance, and once dispatched, goods would take an additional three to five weeks on the railways before reaching the refugee camps in Meghalaya and Assam.[53] The onset of the monsoon was a logistical challenge for the disbursement of aid and facilitated disease transmission; it also made living conditions

---

[48] Ibid., 3–4.
[49] See League of Red Cross Societies, 'Refugees from East Pakistan. Progress Report', 17 September 1971, 7, in Unit 426, Folder 10, 'Divisions Pakistan Conflict, Vol. 1 and 2. R – T'.
[50] Mitton, 'Refugees in India', 6.
[51] Ibid., 5.
[52] Stanley Mitton, telegram to all CICARWS related agencies, 7 June 1971, Box 117, folder 'Pakistan, East and West – 1964–71'.
[53] Mitton, 'Refugees in India', 5 and Stanley Mitton, telegram to all CICARWS related agencies, 15 June 1971, Box 117, folder 'Pakistan, East and West – 1964–71'.

in the camps intolerable. At this time, Mitton noted that 'the shelter situation is bad, there are not enough tarpaulins on the spot at the moment'. Without adequate shelter for protection from the rain, some refugees at Marshkela in the hills of Meghalaya 'have simply taken over the local bazaar. There is no question of a refugee camp. They have just moved in and established themselves'.[54] The integration of refugees at the expense of the local marketplace further escalated tensions with Indian residents and made it difficult for CASA to distribute aid to a refugee population indistinguishable from locals.

The weeklong tour by WCC officials of camps in West Bengal and Meghalaya was important as it provided specific information about CASA's humanitarian work in the field, details of which could be relayed to WCC affiliates across the globe. As we saw in Chapter 4, the Indian Red Cross was indifferent to Western demands for publicity materials, which severely hampered the ability of national Red Cross societies to raise awareness and donations among their publics. The WCC aid officers, in contrast, were cognizant of the value of real-time information from the field to member bodies. During a lunchtime meeting with the CASA advisory committee, Mitton and Martin reached agreements after a 'long discussion' with CASA representatives on six points. The first point stated, 'They [CASA] understand our need for publicity items and we urged that short films as well as photographs and written material must be made available (Photos are already on their way to you).'[55] Mitton concluded his nine-page report from India as follows:

P.S. Film
A sound colour film clip (5 – 10 minutes in length) will be made and should be in your hands within two or three weeks. It is hoped that interested agencies will contribute towards the production costs.[56]

The commitment of the WCC to ensure that national bodies had access to multimedia publicity materials illustrates the extent to which humanitarian organizations competed for scarce donor dollars. Furthermore, the inclusion of colour film, a relatively new technology, indicates that the WCC understood the power of television to bring the shocking conditions of the refugee camps into the homes of everyday citizens, mobilizing them to act.

Like the Australian Red Cross, the Australian Council of Churches received unsolicited offers of assistance from medical and nursing staff in Australia. As was the case with the Red Cross personnel (Chapter 4), the Indian government refused entry to foreign personnel, a fact reiterated by CASA and the WCC in a telegram to Ted Arblaster on 29 June 1971.[57] Nevertheless, Arblaster forwarded the names and details of individuals offering their services. The list included Mrs Caroline Clough

---

[54] Mitton, 'Refugees in India', 4.
[55] Ibid., 8.
[56] Ibid.
[57] Stanley Mitton, telegram to Ted Arblaster, 29 June 1971, Box 117, folder 'Pakistan, East and West – 1964–71'.

of Wollongong, NSW, a trained nurse who was born in Kolkata before emigrating in 1947. Now forty-one years, Mrs Clough maintained a knowledge of 'Hindustani' and had experience working with cholera patients. Others listed included doctors Peter Bass, aged forty, Beryl Barber, and nurses Betty Andersen and Dorothy Platt.[58] The offering of professional services was unnecessary and, as we have seen, unwelcomed by Indians. Nevertheless, the proposed contribution indicates that these individuals were willing to uproot themselves in service of a greater good, albeit one infused with overtones of racial superiority and a negation of Indian independence.

Although ACC leadership kept records of potential volunteer medics, at no point did the organization consider sending Australian personnel to India. Anecdotally, it appears that the ACC was more attuned to Indian sentiment than their Red Cross colleagues, who were incredulous that offers of voluntary service would be denied by Indian officials. As a member of the WCC, which at this point was undergoing de-Westernization and radicalization, the ACC was sensitive to third-world nationalism and the quest for postcolonial autonomy. As a Christian federation, the ACC was cognizant of its missionary past in Asia and the legacy of distrust due to attempts at proselytization. Bruce Best, the public relations officer and staff writer for the ACC, penned a brief report for the WCC and its affiliates after a short trip to the region in February 1972. Best visited (West) Pakistan, whose border regions with India were subject to war when India entered the conflict in December 1971 and opened a second front. He estimated that five hundred thousand Pakistani civilians were impacted by the war with India, specifically those evacuated from Indian-held villages and from towns destroyed by bombing and looting. Of the half million dispossessed, Best observed that fifty thousand were Christians in 'a convinced Muslim society'. Although the Christian minority were 'poor, if not starving', the Pakistan Christian Council urged the WCC to provide aid to *both* Christians and Muslims 'in equal numbers' and that the latter would receive donations via government officials rather than through the church to allay any concerns about Christian expansion in the Islamic republic. The insistence from the Pakistan Christian Council to provide humanitarian assistance to dispossessed Muslims, the majority group that routinely discriminated against Christians in employment and social standing, reflected a turning point: previously, Pakistani Christians were inwardly focused, using their 'meagre resources' to assist the Christian community rather than seeking to contribute to broader society. Now, Pakistani Christians were reorienting towards development aspirations across the country. As Best explained with a tone of alarm,

> Students growing up in Pakistan are dissatisfied with what they see as the pietism of the churches and the 'missionary' mentality. They are anxious to turn the churches toward social and economic development of the nation. They are speaking of

---

[58] Notes from telephone conversation between Mrs Caroline Clough and Ted Arblaster, undated; and letter from Ted Arblaster to Geoff Parish, Executive Secretary, Austcare, 22 June 1971, Box 117, folder 'Pakistan, East and West – 1964–71'.

Christian citizenship and their Christian duty to society. They are a growing group and may well become a radical force in the very near future.[59]

In this extract, Best reconceptualized traditional concepts such as Christian duty to suit the local environment that privileged notions of social and economic justice over evangelism. Although the WCC and ACC broadly supported Pakistani Christians to realign their focus towards issues of equality, they seemed concerned that the forces of militancy and radicalism had a growing momentum that could no longer be contained. As explained earlier in this chapter, by 1971, the WCC was moving in a left-wing direction, which was at odds with the centrism of their Western European post-Second World War founders and antithetical to its missionary roots, dating back to 1910. No wonder, then, that the changes were too much for the more conservative elements of the organization, and as such, some evangelical groups began leaving the federation in 1973.[60]

Aside from the radicalization of the WCC, the 1970s witnessed an ecumenical spirit never seen previously. In Australia, the ACC and Australian Catholic Relief (ACR) jointly established the short-lived 'Action for World Development', which is not to be confused with the British agency of the same name. By forming this cross-sectarian body, Australian Catholic and Protestant leaders united to lobby the Australian government to increase 'the East Pakistan aid programme'.[61] On 19 October 1971, Vaughan Hinton, publicity officer for the ACC, rang the prime minister's office, requesting a meeting between Prime Minister William McMahon and Archbishop James Gleeson and Bishop Garnsey, leaders of the ACR and ACC, respectively. In the noted telephone conversation between Hinton and the prime minister's secretary, Hinton offered multiple days, locations and times for the meeting: in Canberra on Monday 25 or Tuesday 26 October, or any time from Wednesday 27 to Friday 28 October in Sydney. These offers were rebuffed on account of McMahon needing 'breathing space' in preparation for an overseas trip, and the request was delegated to the Foreign Minister, Nigel Bowen.[62] At this point, McMahon was hunkering down and avoiding public discussion on contentious issues for fear that it could galvanize further public outrage at government indifference towards the unfolding crisis. Still, the extensive availability of leading figures in the Catholic and Protestant churches as shown in this example indicates not only a willingness to cooperate across the

---

[59] Bruce Best, 'East and West of a Disaster', 7 February 1972, File 'East Pakistan Refugees Relief Action 1972', Box 425.05.110 'Projects East Pakistan (Bangladesh); Christian Council (1969–71); East Pakistan refugees in India (1971); Bangladesh Ecumenical Relief and Rehabilitation Service 1972', Sub-series '425.05.102–425.05.113 Near East (1952–1971)', Series '425 Commission of Interchurch Aid, Refugee and World Service (CICARWS) (1948–1992)', Sub-fond Programmes (1911–), Fonds 'World Council of Churches paper archives, 1895 – ', Ecumenical Centre, Geneva, Switzerland.
[60] Kunter, 'Revolutionary Hopes and Global Transformations', 345.
[61] For an overview of Action for World Development, see Griff Foley, 'Action for World Development: An Australian Initiative in Development Education', *Journal of Christian Education* 21 (May 1978): 5–21.
[62] Telephone note to Prime Minister McMahon, 19 October 1971, from Box 444, File 'General Correspondence. A', in Subseries 17/8 Correspondence 1971/2, Series 17 Prime Minister, 1967–72, McMahon papers.

religious divide but also signifies the importance they placed on aid for Bangladeshi refugees.

In the case of the Bangladesh reconstruction in the post-war period, the WCC, the World Lutheran Federation and Roman Catholic aid agencies not only cooperated but also worked together under BERRS, the Bangladesh Ecumenical Relief and Rehabilitation Service. Best explained, 'Protestant and Roman Catholic agencies are working in close cooperation with each other and other voluntary agencies. Contact will also be maintained with the United Nations.'[63] In this quotation, it seems that the UN was an afterthought for Best; what mattered and deserved emphasis was that the WCC was deeply engaged with Catholic aid agencies. This ecumenical relationship is even more remarkable given that, at this time, the Pope had only visited the WCC headquarters once, in 1969.[64] The combined efforts of the ACC and ACR are evidence of declining sectarianism in Australian society by the early 1970s, representing a break from over a century of distrust and competition. Furthermore, the easing of interfaith tension had positive effects on the capacity of Australian Catholics and Protestants to deliver humanitarian aid: in a spirit of collaboration, Christians of both traditions were able to achieve more together than they could separately and in opposition to each other.

For Catholics in Australia, the early 1970s was a time of renewal and optimism. Ill will and distrust along sectarian lines were dissipating; the Australian government was finally supporting Catholic education, thereby easing financial pressures on the church. In late 1970, Australians received their first papal visit, a significant milestone aided by advancements in aviation. The visit by Pope Paul VI included a large ecumenical service at Sydney Town Hall, once again demonstrating Christian unity on a range of moral and social issues, notwithstanding residual dogmatic issues.[65] As Benjamin Edwards argues, in the 1970s, moderate Catholics and Protestants found that they had more in common than with evangelical Christians, and certainly more than with secular humanists.[66] As the WCC, and by extension the ACC, experienced a rise in radicalism mid-century, so too did Australian Catholics, especially in Melbourne. Here, since the 1940s, B. A. Santamaria's Catholic Social Studies Movement (CSSM) offered fertile ground for an intellectual movement that sought to promote an equal and just Christian social order. Distinct from materialistic Marxism, Australian Catholic leaders built upon previous social principles enunciated in the encyclicals *Quadragesimo Anno* (1931) and *Rerum Novarum* (1891), and henceforth developed by European writers and philosophers such as Hilaire Belloc, G. K. Chesterton and Jacques Maritain.[67] Catholic reformers desired a softer form of socialism that eschewed godless totalitarianism, all the while avoiding the casualties of unregulated capitalism. The CSSM advocated equal ownership of property, worker control of industry and the traditional family. In short, mid-century Australian Catholics fought against the

---

[63] Best, 'East and West of a Disaster', 7 February 1972.
[64] J. C. Willebrands and E. C. Blake, 'Patterns of Relationships between the Roman Catholic Church and the World Council of Churches', *Ecumenical Review* 24 (1972): 247–9.
[65] Edwards, *WASPS, Tykes and Ecumaniacs*, 218.
[66] Ibid., 216.
[67] Chavura, Gasgoine and Tregenza, *Reason, Religion and the Australian Polity*, 217–18.

reduction of human spirit to economic ends. The *Catholic Worker*, the main outlet for Catholic intellectuals, stated that their enemies were both capitalism and communism, which were considered the 'illegitimate offspring of the same diseased materialism'.[68]

ACR (now known as Caritas Australia) is the official Australian member of Caritas Internationalis. Like the WCC, Caritas Internationalis traces its origins to *fin-de-siècle* Europe but was not formally established until after the Second World War in 1954. As a confederation of more than 165 Catholic humanitarian agencies headquartered in Rome, Caritas represents a global network centred on the fundamental and sacred Christian principle of a reverence for life and Catholic social teachings.[69] ACR itself began in 1962 as Catholic Church Relief Fund, before changing its name in 1964 to Catholic Overseas Relief Committee, designating its clear focus on foreign aid rather than domestic relief. During the 1960s, ACR ran appeals that raised funds for prominent causes, including South Vietnamese refugees in 1966, Bihari drought victims in 1967, Biafran refugees in 1968 and West Bengali flood victims in 1969.[70] In its first five years, ACR raised over A$1.5 million that funded 'self-help' development projects in eighteen countries, including Papua New Guinea, Indonesia and the Solomon Islands, and provided emergency relief for victims of war and disasters in twenty-six countries.[71]

Unlike the ACC with its mix of church members, the ACR spoke exclusively for Catholics (broadly defined) and therefore could access the significant resources of the Catholic dioceses, religious orders, parishes, schools and newspapers across each state. For instance, the weekly Melbourne Catholic newspaper, *The Advocate*, ran cover stories urging readers to donate to its 'Aid for Pakistanis' appeal.[72] Although sectarianism was waning, legacy residential and educational segregation still existed to an extent. The ACR was therefore able to tap into existing Catholic social networks. In the 1971 census, there were over 3.4 million self-identified Catholics and Roman Catholics, making up approximately 27 per cent of the Australian population, second in number of adherents only to the Church of England (31 per cent).[73] Furthermore, on 3 and 10 October 1971, the Pope issued an appeal for believers to pray, fast and give alms in aid of Bangladeshi refugees. In his weekly address to pilgrims at St Peter's Square, Pope Paul urged believers 'to wake up the sense of humanity in the world to save the lives of countless human beings on the verge of death', specifically drawing attention to the '800,000 exhausted, sick and starving children' in Indian refugee camps.[74] Considering the supreme authority bestowed upon the pontiff within the Catholic tradition, these papal directives would have stimulated further acts of charity among devout Catholics in Australia.

---

[68] Ibid., 219.
[69] Paras and Stein, 'Bridging the Sacred and the Profane in Humanitarian Life', 215–18. For a general discussion on Caritas Internationalis, see Donal Dorr, 'Catholic Relief, Development Agencies and Deus Caritas Est', *Journal of Social Catholic Thought* 9 (2012): 285–314.
[70] *Canberra Times*, 5 November 1966, 20 April 1967, 2; 13; 6 July 1968; 3; 8 March 1969, 17.
[71] *Canberra Times* 2 May 1970, 15.
[72] *The Advocate*, 4 November 1971, cover.
[73] Commonwealth of Australia, *Census of Population and Housing, Bulletin 1. Summary of Population. Part 9. Australia*, 30 July 1971, 3.
[74] Anonymous, 'Pope Appeals for Aid to Bengali Children', *New York Times*, 4 October 1971, 3 and Anonymous, 'Pope and Synod Fast for Pakistani Refugees', *New York Times*, 11 October 1971, 5.

In view of these three factors – its distinctive collective identity, its large population in Australia relative to other denominations and the papal intervention – it is no surprise that Australian Catholics donated in record numbers directly to the agency in 1971; see Figure 3.2. The ACR received A$184,674 in calendar year 1971 and A$78,908 in 1972 from individuals and parishes earmarked explicitly for aid for Bangladeshi refugees. The ACR also received A$506,231 from its annual Lenten 'Project Compassion' appeal in 1972, run by the dioceses, much of which was earmarked for projects aiding Bangladeshi refugees and post-war reconstruction. For Catholics, Lent is a time of abstinence, fasting and repentance. The theme of Project Compassion in 1971 and 1972 was 'Share your Lent', a message well suited to a Catholic audience. With these donations, ACR funded 'special assistance to refugees' to the value of A$326,970 in 1971. In 1972, ACR reoriented its assistance towards reconstruction, allocating A$222,050 to rebuilding irrigation systems and schools and providing tools, fertilizer and cattle for farmers.[75] Furthermore, ACR also had access to Austcare funds; see Chapter 3. As will be recalled from Chapter 3, in 1971, Austcare ran its annual general appeal and a specific appeal for Bangladeshi refugees. Collectively, these two appeals raised over A$2 million of which $271,300 was distributed to the ACR for sponsored rehabilitation projects.

'Down to Earth Christianity'

Organized religious institutions, of course, do not represent the entirety of Christian giving. The Society for Those Who Have Less (henceforth 'the Society') is one example of a lay-led Christian charity that advocated and funded famine relief for Bangladeshi refugees. Established in 1962 amidst the activism surrounding the UN-initiated Freedom from Hunger Campaign (discussed in Chapter 6), the Society prioritized unglamorous yet practical solutions to tackle acute malnutrition in South Asia. Initially, the Society sent livestock and semen to promote agricultural development in India, Pakistan and Nepal. For instance, from 1964 to 1972, the Society shipped donated cross-bred cattle, sheep, horses, pigs, goats and day-old chicks, with a combined value of more than A$750,000 (or A$9.2 million in today's money).[76] By giving living animals, the Society contended it was providing a self-sustaining supply of high-protein foods.[77] During the 1970s, the Society added child sponsorship to its portfolio. The decision of the Society to reorient towards child welfare rather than focus exclusively on livestock and agricultural development was an attempt to broaden its appeal to the public. By the 1970s, it was commonplace for international aid organizations to initiate child sponsorship programmes to secure long-term, regular donations from individuals.[78] Arguably, for the Society, child sponsorships offered an additional revenue stream,

---

[75] All figures from Australian Catholic Relief, *Annual Report 1971* (Sydney: Devonshire Press), 1972 and Australian Catholic Relief *Annual Report 1972* (Sydney: Devonshire Press), 1973.
[76] The Society for Those Who Have Less, *Tenth Annual Report 1973*, 3, in Box 8, folder 9 'Annual Reports, 1964–80', in Papers of Leonard Stanley Reid, 1952–93. State Library of Victoria.
[77] Len Reid, *The Tragedy of Those Who Have Less* (Melbourne: Fraser & Morphet, 1973), 23.
[78] For an introduction to the pre-Second World War origins of child sponsorship schemes, see Joy Damousi, 'Humanitarianism and Child Refugee Sponsorship: The Spanish Civil War and the

thereby reducing its reliance on donations of livestock and allocations of funding from Australian Catholic Relief and left-wing Community Aid Abroad, an Australian agency that is examined in Chapter 6.

Society president, Len Reid, invoked Christian values and cultures of charity for the needy to galvanize ordinary Australians to think beyond themselves and help alleviate the suffering of others. Reid's form of Christianity was deliberately general and cross-denominational; his campaign targeted self-identifying if only of nominal Christians in Australia. Reid reminded Australians of the Christian values of service to God and helping the poor with humility and service. In his self-published book, Reid wrote, 'it is God's will and our privilege to help'.[79] The biblical principle of sacrificial giving was at the crux of Reid's activism. Broadly defined as giving beyond one's means, sacrificial giving is explicitly and implicitly referenced in the Hebrew and Christian bibles, most notably in Hebrews (13.16), 'Do not neglect to do good and to share what you have, for such sacrifices are pleasing to God'. Reid was inspired by Eastern philosophies, too. Quoting Mohandas Gandhi, Reid explained that whenever one person suffers voluntarily, it relieves someone else of suffering; 'everyone who fasts gives bread to another who needs it more – everyone who makes some sacrifice helps someone else somewhere'.[80] Reid was an agitator and sought to unsettle Australian complacency. At times, his rhetoric was confrontational. He argued that as a Christian community, 'we must take more responsibility for the great human problems that confront so many people around the world' and it is up to the non-government sector 'to campaign more vigorously. If necessary, they should crusade'.[81] He challenged Australians to put into action their Christian values. In his words, 'If Australia is to continue to call herself a Christian community, we can no longer procrastinate while millions face famine conditions'.[82]

Despite the zealotry, the Society was not an evangelical organization. Rather, its ethos was a reaction to mid-century consumerism, the rise of the technocrat in development circles and the self-serving pragmatism of government aid. The Christianity of the Society centred on grassroots activism. The Society was inspired by early Christians and avidly avoided the concentration of power that later beset the Church. Reid explains his guiding philosophy:

> A handful of Christians two thousand years ago changed pagan Rome within a generation. This is the type of dynamic, challenging, down to earth Christianity

---

Global Campaign of Esme Odgers', *Journal of Women's History* 32 (2020): 111–34; Emily Baughan, 'International Adoption and Anglo-American Internationalism, x.1918–1925', *Past & Present* 239 (2018): 181–217, especially 194–213 and Emily Baughan, *Saving the Children: Humanitarianism, Internationalism and Empire* (Berkeley: University of California Press, 2022), 28 and 188. For details on post-Second World War issues and the effects of child sponsorship programmes, see Brad Watson and Matthew Clarke, eds. *Child Sponsorship: Exploring Pathways to a Brighter Future* (London: Palgrave Macmillan UK, 2014).

[79] Reid, *The Tragedy of Those Who Have Less*, 23.
[80] Ibid., 7, 13, 63.
[81] Ibid., 25.
[82] Ibid., 62.

which is so urgently needed in Australia today. We must shake off the blinkers of materialism and self-interests and so broaden our outlook and vision.[83]

Reid bemoaned that since 'the postwar years we have given far too much importance to all those things which we can see and touch. We have become addicted to material possessions … consequently, we have less time for spiritual development'.[84] Notwithstanding these lamentations, Reid remained optimistic of the inherent virtues of individuals. To resolve the 'great human problems of those who have less', Reid believed 'we need only look unto ourselves to find our answer'.[85] When human behaviour disappointed Reid, he blamed the media for desensitizing us to tragedy. In *Ally*, the Society's monthly periodical, Reid described the displacement of Bangladeshis as 'the greatest human tragedy of this century'. Despite the constant reportage of the plight of the refugees in radio, print and TV news media, Reid decried that 'this has done little to motivate the better instincts deep down inside of us'.[86] In the same article, Reid reiterated, 'If ever a great human tragedy was needed to bring the best attributes within us to the surface, the present crisis in Bengal provides one.'[87] This assumption that individuals maintain the capacity to do good despite consistent evidence to the contrary indicates again the influence of Christianity on Reid. Specifically, Reid drew comfort from the Christian commitment to redemption and salvation of sinners, which is a core tenet of the religion.

Under Reid's leadership, the Society affirmed that humanitarianism was best left to individuals and was generally sceptical of professional aid workers and government meddling. Reid asserted that volunteers 'will always obtain a better utilization of funds expended and also do a far better job'. In the same report, Reid wrote,

> What Bangladesh requires, like so many other developing countries, is not too many experts, but practical people who can work with their own two hands and have a genuine desire to work amongst these people without fee or reward. Far too many people go to these [developing] countries as experts. However, the only real experts are the people motivated in the right spirit and who can improvise under local conditions.[88]

In this extract, Reid positioned the Society as oppositional to the rise of the technocrat and the expert class within large development organizations, although he seemed blind to the advantages of the professionalization of the NGO sector. Reid's belief in well-meaning, everyday people may be explained by his own life experiences. During the Second World War, Reid served as a fighter pilot and was awarded the Distinguished Flying Cross, for valour, courage or devotion to duty. After the war, he farmed dairy

---

[83] Ibid., 25.
[84] Ibid., 64.
[85] Ibid.
[86] Anonymous, presumably Len Reid, 'The Bengal Tragedy', *Ally*, December 1971, cover, in in Box 8, folder 7 'Ally, 1970–1979, in Papers of Leonard Stanley Reid.
[87] Ibid., 2.
[88] The Society, *Tenth Annual Report 1973*, 8.

cattle for twelve years. These varied experiences instilled in Reid an appreciation for individual responsiveness amidst challenging conditions. Reid was not a man of the book; instead, he learnt lessons during the hardships of war in the Pacific and farming in an inhospitable, drought-prone environment. As a lieutenant officer in the air force, Reid understood the importance of personal accountability and duty to others.

Politically, Reid was a small 'l' liberal, believing in the virtues of the individual and wary of government overreach. In the aid realm, Reid argued that government action was wasteful, poorly targeted and self-serving. Only the private sector, according to Reid, could aid in times of humanitarian crises. Government was restricted by 'red tape' and captive to political considerations. Furthermore, with a few exceptions, government aid is typically provided on a government-to-government basis, 'which means their aid does not penetrate the areas of greatest need, which is in the villages'.[89] As private agencies were not hindered by politics or bureaucracy, they were best placed to 'pioneer new programs which the government might find unacceptable'.[90] Given the antipathy of Reid towards government, it may seem inconsistent that he would serve three terms as a member of the Victorian legislative assembly and one term as a member of the Australian House of Representatives. However, when situated within his history of service and adherence to Christian values, arguably Reid entered politics to challenge the status quo of long-standing Liberal Party governments at the federal and state levels.

From 1958 to 1969, Reid served as the Victorian member of the legislative assembly for the seat of Dandenong, then an urban fringe industrial seat with large numbers of recent European immigrants. The 1966 census revealed that the City of Dandenong had a foreign-born population of 29 per cent, well above the national average of 18 per cent and greater than the Melbourne average of 26 per cent.[91] The large majority of these immigrants were European, particularly British and Irish (12 per cent), Dutch (5 per cent) and Italian (4 per cent).[92] The multinational composition of his electorate led Reid to establish and chair the All Nations Together Society. The organization, which operated from 1962 to 1971, aimed to assist migrants to integrate into Australian society and, importantly, help locally born Australians learn about the new residents. As was the case with the Society for Those Who Have Less, Reid's All Nations Together Society used simple but effective practices to aid mutual understanding. For instance, in 1962, Reid organized a concert to bring native-born and overseas-born residents together through the shared appreciation of music.[93] The concert proved a success, becoming an annual event in the local calendar. The theme of the 1963 concert was 'getting to know you'. At this point, the All Nations Together Society introduced a cash

---

[89] Anonymous, presumably Len Reid, 'Important Role of Voluntary Agencies', *Ally*, November 1972, 3.
[90] Ibid.
[91] O'Hanlon and Stevens, 'A Nation of Immigrants or a Nation of Immigrant Cities?' 563.
[92] Commonwealth of Australia, Census of Population and Housing, 30 June 1966, *Volume 4, Population and Dwellings in Local Government Areas, Part 2 Victoria* (Canberra: Government Printer, 1967), 66–7.
[93] 'In praktijk weinig contact tussen immigrant en Australiërs', 28 December 1962, *Dutch Australian Weekly*, 2.

prize for 'the best integrated family', the winning funds of which could be used to cover costs for education, language instruction or other 'family needs'.[94] From the example of the All Nations Together Society, Reid demonstrated his commitment to his local constituency and his credentials as an internationalist. Although Reid's methods were small in scale, they offered practical steps to enhance cross-cultural understanding during Australia's post-war mass immigration programme. Furthermore, the Victorian parliament proved conducive to the development of Reid as a humanitarian and activist. Indeed, along with a handful of parliamentary colleagues, Reid established the Society for Those Who Have Less in the Old Speaker's room at Parliament House in Melbourne.[95]

In 1969 Reid successfully contested the federal seat of Holt, an electorate in the outer south-eastern suburbs and urban fringe of Melbourne, which included his former state seat of Dandenong. Reid represented the Liberal Party, which at that point had been in government for twenty years. Yet Reid behaved more like an opposition MP, presenting a 'one man revolt against the McMahon ministry'.[96] According to commentators at the time, Reid's 'tireless work on Asian causes, especially Bangladesh' was widely admired and he enjoyed a 'great deal of goodwill from members of other parties'.[97] Reid was an outspoken critic of the parsimony and insensitivity of the Australian government during the Bhola cyclone in 1970. In his book, *The Tragedy of Those Who Have Less*, Reid recollected that he first learnt of the natural disaster while listening to the seven o'clock news bulletin. Reid remembered, 'My first reaction was: what can I do?' The following day, Reid sent urgent telegrams to the Australian prime minister (then John Gorton) and foreign minister (then William McMahon). In the cables, Reid urged the Australian government to send A$1 million immediately. The Australian government initially offered A$25,000, a miserly amount given the extent of destruction in Bangladesh. After much protest, including letters from Reid, the Australian government offered an additional in-kind donation of wheat, to the value of A$400,000.[98] But given the destructive nature of cyclones and the subsequent tidal bore, it is unlikely that a wheat consignment would overcome the resulting logistical barriers and reach those in most need.

In the ensuing weeks, news coverage and Pakistani reports revealed the extent of the devastation, both in terms of lives lost and physical destruction. Shocked by the accounts, Reid volunteered to visit the affected areas. It is unclear from the records whether Reid visited in his capacity as an Australian parliamentarian or in his role as president of the Society, which had committed to provide cattle and sheep to farmers who had lost their livestock. Presenting a description of selfless heroics, Reid wrote of his decision to visit Bangladesh: 'I could have found many reasons why I should not have undertaken such a visit. However, I was prepared to look beyond my personal

---

[94] 'Beurs en geldprijs voor immigranten familie' 25 October 1963, *Dutch Australian Weekly*, 4; 'Nederlands echtpaar wint prijs "Voor in stilte bewezen diensten"', 21 May 1965, *Dutch Australian Weekly*, 2.
[95] The Society, *Tenth Annual Report 1973*, 3.
[96] 'Interesting Seats: Holt, Victoria', *Canberra Times*, 30 November 1972, 18.
[97] 'Interesting Seats', 18.
[98] Reid, *The Tragedy of Those Who Have Less*, 10.

interests. I am now glad I made the effort.'⁹⁹ On return to Australia, Reid was now empowered with the knowledge of witnessing the devastation first-hand, which he used as evidence to make the case for greater Australian aid to the region. Because of his intimate knowledge of Bangladesh and tour of the worst affected areas, Reid positioned himself as an expert, not dissimilar to the ones he so despised within development circles. Nevertheless, Reid continued to lobby the Australian government for a cash donation of A$1 million in the following months. During a parliamentary debate on appropriations, Reid argued for 'a more humanitarian approach … if we are to come to grips with the problems in these [India and Pakistan] countries'.[100] Based on his visit to the region, Reid argued that the Bhola cyclone was the 'greatest catastrophe ever known', with at least two million fatalities, up to four million by some estimates.[101] In case these figures failed to shock his colleagues, Reid contextualized the death toll by drawing comparisons with the Second World War. Reid claimed that fatalities in Bangladesh after the cyclone were three times greater than the total of UK and US deaths after six years of combat. Despite the calamity in Bengal, Australian government and private donations to Bangladesh were a 'mere token which does little more than indicate a casual interest of the Government and the people of Australia'.[102]

A devout Christian, Reid framed his plea for greater assistance to Bangladesh in typical religious rhetoric. Reid asserted that it was our 'moral responsibility' to provide 'succour' to 'the aged and the needy in our great cities to the hungry people of India, from the orphans of East Pakistan … to the victims of racial discrimination'.[103] Revealingly, Reid implied that individuals would not spontaneously come together to tackle 'these great human problems'. Rather, Reid believed 'Australia needs strong moral leadership'. He indirectly criticized current leaders when he complained, 'if we had sufficient leaders I am sure many more would follow, because in the past Australians have always been known as generous and fair minded people'. It is evident that Reid was nostalgic, perhaps longing for a shared sense of responsibility that he witnessed during the Second World War. What is clear is his disappointment with 'the present generation [who] are not prepared to do more at their own particular level' and consequently recommended 'a crusade if this is the only way to get the people to accept greater responsibility for those who have less'. Interestingly, Reid endorsed commonwealth solidarity, arguing 'that we are expected on humanitarian grounds to go to the assistance of another Commonwealth country in its time of great need'.[104] For Reid, the Bhola cyclone (and the indifference of the Australian government) served as training ground for how he could combine his work as a humanitarian activist and politician. The blending of these two roles is rare: humanitarian activists seldom enjoy the privileges of public office; politicians typically avoid moral crusades for fear of alienating voters.

[99] Ibid.
[100] Len Reid, 'Appropriations Bill (No. 3) 1970–71', Australian House of Representatives, 22 April 1971, 1918.
[101] Ibid., 1919.
[102] Ibid., 1918.
[103] Ibid., 1919.
[104] Ibid.

When refugees began arriving in India en masse from April 1971, the Society was already well established in South Asia and able to provide practical assistance to refugees in Indian camps. In July 1971, Reid toured the affected region like he had done six months prior. He visited thirty refugee camps within fifty miles of Kolkata, with each camp approximately housing more than 10,000 refugees on average. He described the refugee camps in West Bengal: 'Conditions were bad. Sanitation, water and general facilities were woefully inadequate.' Reid recounted chaotic scenes where refugees, unable to secure a place in an overcrowded tent, would live anywhere they could find a piece of high land, including on roads, sheds, railway stations and factories.[105] At a parliamentary debate in August 1971, Reid presented a bleak depiction of life in the camps: 'The people are living under conditions far worse than those depicted in any picture or story one has seen or read.'[106] Along with journeys to Indian refugee camps, Reid's tour of South Asia included brief visits to Karachi to meet with Pakistani government officials and a five-day tour of Bangladesh. Here, Reid visited Bhola, Chattogram (Chittagong), Jashore (Jessore) and Dhaka, as well as meeting with East Pakistani government and military leaders, including the East Pakistani governor General Tikka Khan.[107] On arrival in Dhaka, Reid was greeted with much government fanfare and his tour was widely reported in local Bengali language newspapers.[108] As Reid had done previously in the aftermath of the Bhola cyclone, his tour of Bangladesh served his interests as president of the Society and member of the Australian parliament, moving between the two roles seamlessly. Indeed, the two roles were not only complementary but mutually beneficial. Reid used his official government status to gain entry to a region that at that time was closed to foreigners. Throughout his journey, Reid advanced his ideas for agricultural development, specifically by establishing modern dairy farms in the villages, and his increasing concern for children's welfare. On visiting a Swedish-run orphanage, Reid committed his organization to a cash donation.[109]

While Reid used his tour of India and Pakistan to promote the Society and collate evidence to lobby the McMahon government for more foreign aid (discussed next), the Pakistani government similarly used the visit of an Australian dignitary to further its own political agenda. In their coverage of Reid's tour, state-run newspapers made no mention of the ongoing conflict between the Pakistani armed forces and Mukti Bahini, opting instead to portray his trip as a review of the cyclone reconstruction programme. By way of example, compare the following narratives: in an address to the Australian parliament, Reid referenced his 'recent visit to quite a number of refugee camps in West Bengal' and reflected that 'India is doing a wonderful job in coping with the refugee

---

[105] Reid, *The Tragedy of Those Who Have Less*, 14–15.
[106] Len Reid, 'International Affairs', Australian House of Representatives, 23 August 1971, 551.
[107] Anonymous, 'Australian MP in Chattogram', *Purbadesh* (Dhaka), 14 July 1971. All Bengali language newspapers held in Box 6, Folder 9 'Folder 9. Press Information Department, Government of Pakistan, July 1971. Press clippings, with name of paper, place and date of publication', Papers of Leonard S. Reid. Translated into English by G. B. Nath.
[108] For example, Anonymous, 'Visit to Bhola by the Australian MP', *Purbadesh* (Dhaka), 12 July 1971; Anonymous, 'Visit of Australian MP to Bhola', *Dainik Pakistan* (Dhaka), 12 July 1971.
[109] Ibid.

problem and has most of her civil servants working around the clock'.[110] In contrast, the Pakistani-controlled *Azad* newspaper presented a very different narrative:

> Australian MP, Mr Len S. Reid, visited the Jhikargachha welcome (reception) centre today. Later he went to the Benapole border by car. Mr Reid observed the various facilities e.g., medical camp and residential rooms in the welcome centre. He spoke to the refugees returned from India and enquired about their wellbeing. It appeared that mothers with baby-in-arms, old and young, everybody seemed that they have breathed sighs of relief to have been able to come back to Pakistan.
>
> They informed the Australian MP that they had to spend their stay in so-called refugee camps in India amidst lots of suffering. A group of people belonging to the minority group [probably Hindus] informed Mr Reid that Indian military personnel held them hostage for two days at the border. On their firm insistence not to stay in India, they were allowed to cross the border in a designated corridor.
>
> Now having come back to their own homes they will engage in their respective occupations.
>
> Immediately upon arrival of Mr Reid at the reception centre, 23 refugees arrived there. Mr Reid was informed that just six hours prior to their arrival at the centre, the Indians mortar shelled the area. Mr Reid was taken to the place to show him the damage inflicted.[111]

In this extract, the newspaper brought into doubt the existence of Bangladeshi refugees in India. In fact, the account presents the Indian military as the perpetrators of violence from which Pakistan offered protection for its citizens. This article emphasized the welcome camps in Bangladesh for returning Bangladeshis over the refugee camps in India to strengthen and legitimize Pakistani rule in Bangladesh. The *Azad* was not alone; the *Paigham* newspaper similarly noted that Reid visited 'the welcome camps which houses the Pakistani citizens returning from India'.[112] Antara Datta contends that Pakistani press coverage was designed to divert international attention away from the refugee crisis in India and present Pakistani forces in a favourable light.[113] Reid therefore inadvertently became a pawn in the propaganda campaign of the Pakistani Information Service against India. This example illustrates how the intentions of the donor (in this case, Reid) can be undermined to serve the interests of a local actor, one which may be the antithesis of the objectives of the donor.

As a parliamentary member of the political party that governed Australia, Reid had direct access to the Prime Minister McMahon and Foreign Minister Bowen. Whether through correspondence, informal party room discussions or recorded parliamentary debates, Reid made repeated pleas for an increase in government foreign aid to India

---

[110] Len Reid, 'Question Emergency Relief Aid Speech', Australian House of Representatives, 27 October 1971.
[111] Anonymous, 'Australian MP's Visit to the Jhikargachha Welcome (reception) Centre', *Azad* (Dhaka), 13 July 1971.
[112] Anonymous, 'Australian MP Will Visit the Cyclone Affected Areas', *Paigham* (Dhaka), 11 July 1971.
[113] Datta, *Refugees and Borders in South Asia*, 77.

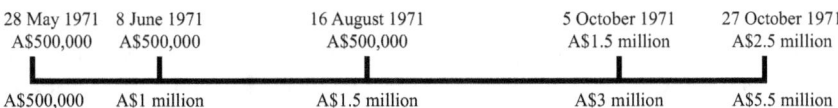

Figure 5.1 Timeline of Australian government cash and in-kind donations for Bangladeshi refugees by individual amount and date of authorization (top) and cumulative amount (bottom). Created by author.

in 1971 despite his earlier misgivings about official aid. His reasons for doing so were twofold: first, unlike private donations, government aid could be allocated immediately at scale and therefore provide a prompt response to an urgent crisis. Second, a sizeable government donation would elicit publicity locally and likely encourage Australian residents and organizations to offer donations as well. By early October, the Australian government had announced a series of cash and in-kind donations for Bangladeshi refugees. As illustrated in Figure 5.1, in late May, two months into the conflict, the Australian government announced its first donation, valued at A$500,000. Most of this grant (A$300,000) was earmarked for cholera and typhoid vaccines, medicines and plastic sheeting for emergency shelter. These supplies were airfreighted by a chartered Qantas Boeing 707s to Kolkata. Only A$50,000 was granted in cash and given to the Indian Red Cross.[114]

As the cholera epidemic worsened in the refugee camps, the Australian government authorized a further A$500,000, bringing the total to A$1 million on 8 June 1971. By mid-August, the Australian government announced a third grant of A$500,000. This donation provided rice for the refugees, a gift that Reid described as 'paltry' and 'would not feed the refugees for one day'.[115] With public interest in the plight of the Bangladeshi refugees escalating in September and October (discussed in more detail in Chapter 7), the Australian government doubled its financial commitment, offering an additional A$1.5 million for the refugees. Of this grant, A$1.25 million funded the purchase of Australian rice. The remaining A$250,000 was donated as cash to Indian humanitarian agencies and covered freight charges.[116]

This early October donation did not satisfy critics of the Australian government. Opposition and back-bench MPs argued that the cumulative amount of donations (cash and in-kind) of A$3 million was inadequate given the scale of the problem and recommended an additional cash donation of A$2 million.[117] In late October 1971,

---

[114] David Solomon, 'Aid Defended', *Canberra Times*, 7 June 1971, 1; AAP-Reuters, 'Hundreds Dying in Cholera Epidemic', *Canberra Times*, 3 June 1971, 5 and AAP-Reuters, 'Aid to Pakistan', *Papua New Guinea Post-Courier*, 28 May 1971, 7.

[115] Anonymous, '$1/2m of Rice Offered to India', *Canberra Times*, 19 August 1971, 1; Len Reid, 'International Affairs', 23 August 1971, 551.

[116] Ian Sinclair, 'Aid – East Pakistani Refugees', *Australian House of Representatives*, 5 October 1971, 1863, and Kim Beazley, 'Aid – East Pakistani Refugees', *Australian House of Representatives*, 5 October 1971, 1864–5.

[117] Len Reid, 'Aid to India and East Pakistan', *Australian House of Representatives*, 12 October 1971, 2141; Alan Jarman, 'Monetary Aid to Pakistan's Refugees', *Australian House of Representatives*, 12 October 1971, 2142; David Hamer, 'Monetary Aid to Pakistan's Refugees', *Australian House of Representatives*, 12 October 1971, 2143; Leonard Johnson, 'Monetary Aid to Pakistan's Refugees',

the Australian government allocated an extra A$2.5 million in aid, bringing the total amount to A$5.5 million. Once again, only a fraction of this second October donation (A$500,000) came in the form of cash, with the residual A$2 million still unused by the end of the conflict.[118] Some MPs argued that the Australian government should offer A$10 million in aid, a round number that captured the attention of the Australian public for the remainder of the year, as we will see in Chapter 7.[119] For Reid, he explained to parliament why Australian government grants were inadequate and ill-considered:

> I believe we are failing in our duty by not going to the assistance of these people in a more sacrificial way. For these reasons the Government's additional allocation of $2.5m is disappointing. It still only represents less than 0.5 per cent of the total amount of $1,200m that is needed each year to provide for the refugees. The United States of America has recently announced an additional contribution of $125m in cash. I must emphasise that cash is urgently needed because it enables the Indian Government to buy food items in India. It can be immediately used and no transport costs are involved. Britain has also provided an additional $17m and Sweden, a country approximately half our size, has provided $10m in cash and has already promised further large cash contributions. This is the type of aid that India and Pakistan need.[120]

Reid alleged that Australian government donations were self-serving, pragmatic and ineffectual. Arguably, Australian government aid in practice supported local rice growers and the national air carrier, Qantas, just as much, if not more than, the refugees in India. This extract also demonstrates the parsimony of Australian government aid, especially when compared with other countries. Furthermore, Reid also drew comparisons with past actions of the Australian government under different prime ministers. During 1965, the Menzies government allocated US$60 million to Indonesia, spread over three years, to assist with the recovery after the 1965 rebellion. Between 1965 and 1967, the Menzies/Holt governments provided A$25 million for the victims of the Bihar famine in India.[121] In doing so, Reid highlighted the significance of leadership in balancing moral obligations with limited financial means.

During October and November 1971, numerous MPs of all political backgrounds submitted to the Australian parliament petitions signed by Australian citizens. Len Reid was the most prolific, submitting signed petitions on eighteen occasions, or most sitting days. Reid tabled petitions on 5, 6, 23, 27 and 28 October; on 2, 3, 4, 9, 10, 11, 23 and 30 November; and on 1, 2, 7, 8 and 9 December 1971. He did so because of 'the

---

Australian House of Representatives, 12 October 1971, 2142'; Horace Garrick, 'Monetary Aid to Pakistan's Refugees', Australian House of Representatives, 13 October 1971, 2233; Don Chipp, 'Monetary Aid to Pakistan's Refugees', Australian House of Representatives, 13 October 1971, 2233;

[118] Len Reid, 'Emergency Relief Aid Speech', Australian House of Representatives, 27 October 1971, 2634.

[119] Kim Beazley, 'Aid to India and East Pakistan', Australian House of Representatives, 12 October 1971, 2141; Clyde Cameron, 'Aid to India and East Pakistan', Australian House of Representatives, 12 October 1971, 2141.

[120] Reid, 'Question Emergency Relief Aid Speech'.

[121] Ibid.

large amount of mail, telegrams and petitions that I and, I know, other honourable members have been receiving. I think it is important that the general public should show its concern by contacting the elected members of Parliament'.[122] The text of the petition lodged with parliament reads as follows:

1. It is obvious the people of Australia are vitally concerned about the welfare of some nine million East Pakistan refugees that have crossed the border into India. Also they are equally concerned about the desperate plight of millions of displaced persons in East Pakistan, many of whom are worse off than the refugees, as they are not even receiving relief supplies. The involvement of Australians is evidenced by their willingness to contribute substantial funds to voluntary agencies, to assist their work in these countries.
2. As some twenty million refugees and displaced persons are today facing acute problems of hunger and privation – nutrition and family problems – ultimate famine and death on an unprecedented scale – the Commonwealth Government must plan to come to their assistance in a more sacrificial way.[123]

Reid concluded that the petitioners 'humbly pray' that the Australian government donate A$10 million for immediate aid in India and East Pakistan and a further A$50 million over three years to assist with the rehabilitation of refugees in East Pakistan.[124] Arguably, Reid played a leading role in cajoling his colleagues to submit petitions. Of the 125 members of the Australian lower house, 59 parliamentarians submitted petitions at least once using similar language to Reid. The petition for additional government aid was a non-partisan issue as the fifty-nine parliamentarians

---

[122] Ibid.
[123] Len Reid, 'Aid for India and East Pakistan', Australian House of Representatives, 23 November 1971, 3450.
[124] Ibid. Other MPs who submitted petitions in similar wording include:
Frederick Collard and Dick Klugman on 7 October 1971; Kim Beazley, Clyde Cameron, Alan Jarman, David Hamer and Keith Johnson on 12 October 1971, 2141–3; Rex O'Connor, Chipp and Garrick on 13 October 1971, 2233; Malcolm Fraser, Tony Staley, Harry Jenkins on 14 October 1971, 2341–2; Frank Crean, Harry Webb, Malcom Fraser, Victor Garland, John Gorton, Kep Enerby, Harry Turner, Frank Stewart, Robert Solomon, Horrie Garrick, Bruce Lloyd, Gordon Scholes, Hector McIver, and Ray Whittorn, 'Petitions', Australian House of Representatives, 26 October 1971, 2471–6; Calwell, Anthony Street, Laurie Wallis, Neil Brown, Leonard Reynolds, 27 October 1971, 2565–7; John Fitzpatrick, Adrian Bennett, Frank Kirwan, Enderby, Jenkins and John Pettitt, 28 October 1971, 2661–4; Stephen Calder, Moss Cass, Leonard Johnson, Jim Cairns and Lionel Bowen, 2 November 1971, 2801–3; Neil Brown, Bruce Lloyd, Adrian Bennett and Gorton, 3 November 1971, 2891–3; Peter Howson and Brown, 4 November 1971, 3000–1; Fox and Hamer, 9 November 1971, 3124; Chipp, 10 November 1971, 3215; Dudley Erwin, Kirwan, Frank O'Keefe and Laurie Wallace, 11 November 1971, 3310–1; Hamer, Garrick and Edmund Fox, 9 November 1971, 3124–6; Edward Drury, Solomon, Enderby and Bruce Lloyd on 23 November 1971, 3348–50. In the Senate, Margaret Guilfoyle, 1959; Alexander Forbes, 24 November 1971, 3539; Garrick and Andrew Kennedy, 25 November 1971, 3633–5; Brown, Lloyd and Kennedy, 30 November 1971, 3786–7; Winton Turnbull, Wallis, Lloyd and Peter Howson, 1 December 1971, 3919–20; Lloyd, John McLeay, Wallis and Kennedy, 2 December 1971, 3972–4; Andrew Peacock, Crean, and Bruce, 7 December 1971, 4127–8; Malcolm MacKay, Bill Hayden, Leonard Reynolds, John Cramer, Michael MacKellar, Bury, Leslie Johnson, Charles Jones, Brendan Hansen, Charles Webb and McIvor, 8 December 1971, 4265–9; Francis Stewart, Leonard Johnson, Vincent Martin, Bill Morrison, James Cope and Lloyd, 9 December 1971, 4379–81.

represented the three major political parties in Australia. The most prolific included Bruce Lloyd (Country Party, rural Victoria), who submitted seven petitions, and Labor politicians Horrie Garrick (inner city Melbourne) and Laurie Wallis (outback South Australia), both of whom tabled four petitions each. Neil Brown and David Hamer, both suburban Melbourne Liberal Party colleagues of Reid, similarly tendered multiple petitions for the government to consider. What we have then is a broad-based groundswell of popular opinion for increased government assistance for Bangladeshi refugees, driven and inspired by Reid's brand of down-to-earth Christianity and activism. When the McMahon government ignored their pleas, individuals and NGOs resorted to their own methods in frustration of government inertia.

Conclusion

I began this chapter citing David King, the Christian scholar who urged researchers to consider *how* not *if* humanitarian organizations are religious. This chapter has demonstrated four ways that Christianity influenced humanitarian practices in the early 1970s. First, the radicalization of Christian thought within international federations in the mid-twentieth century trickled down to impact how lay individuals thought they *ought* to respond to the 1971 refugee crisis. Protestant and Catholic leadership in Geneva and in Rome, respectively, offered and legitimized theological frameworks that demanded economic redistribution, social justice and political liberation for the world's oppressed. For disaffected Australians, the radicalization of Christianity presented them with an alternative to individualist conservative politics, economic liberalism or godless communism. By making Christianity overtly political, religious leaders around the globe made faith a public action not only a private matter for believers. Second, religion was an effective tool to compel individuals to act charitably towards the refugees. As Len Reid made clear, feeling pity was irrelevant; what mattered was acting in a sacrificial way to ease the suffering of the refugees. Third, this chapter illustrated the universalizing appeal of Christianity in which the faithful helped anyone in need, not just co-religionists. Fourth, Protestant, Orthodox and Catholic umbrella organizations all benefitted from recently established aid agencies among their brethren. These religious humanitarian organizations had the resources and knowledge to spearhead fundraising campaigns and liaise both with global aid organizations as well as local agencies on the ground. Yet it is important to remember that formal religious organizations and their associated aid agencies do not tell the whole story. Citizen-driven Christianity, as evidenced by Len Reid's 'The Society for Those Who Have Less', reveals a desire for individuals to act and mobilize others to do the same that was independent of the church. Such grassroots activism was an outgrowth of the various rights-based movements underway in Western societies at the same time and will be examined in more detail in the next chapter.

6

The grassroots: Oxfam and the Freedom from Hunger Campaign

In a 1965 letter, the appraiser of Oxfam UK, Bernard Llewellyn, bemoaned to his Director Leslie Kirkley:

> Of course, Oxfam has a contribution to make – but in doing its primary job, not in this guise of a glorified Honey Bee [sic.] buzzing hither and thither, meddling in this and that, rather like an overgrown Lady Bountiful acting as a catalyst wherever possible, stirring up jealousies in other groups who are not so ubiquitously busy both saving the world and other organizations for themselves. *Just who do we think we are?* [italics added].[1]

For this aid agency, with its subsidiaries in the United States, Canada, Belgium and, from 1972, Australia, there seemed to be a crisis of confidence. Llewellyn wondered if all this humanitarian intervention merely resulted in 'meddling' and 'stirring up jealousies', with aid agencies staying busy simply to justify their continued existence and desire to impress donors. The quotation illustrates a degree of self-doubt in one of the most popular and effective humanitarian organizations in modern times. Nowadays, Oxfam manages a global annual budget of more than one billion euros, operates development programmes in seventy countries and has affiliated branches in twenty nations.[2] Yet in the mid-twentieth century, Oxfam's success was far from guaranteed. Llewellyn's insightful reflections were indicative of a broader malaise in the humanitarian sector in the 1960s and 1970s. Amidst a backdrop of decolonization, political radicalization, Western consumerism and individualism, grassroots organizations faced fundamental, if not existential, questions: Who should we help? How should we help? And why should we help? In this new world order, previous assumptions about religious or moral duty to provide charity to distant others were no longer applicable. Grassroots organizations, often nimble and responsive to popular

---

[1] Oxfam MSS PRG 2/4/1: Letter from Llewellyn to Kirkley, 15 July 1965, cited in Hilton, 'Oxfam and the Problem of NGO Aid Appraisal in the 1960s', 5.
[2] Oxfam International, *Oxfam Annual Report. April 2017 – March 2018*, accessed 22 March 2022, https://www-cdn.oxfam.org/s3fs-public/file_attachments/story/oxfam_annual_report_2017-2018_final_2.pdf.

sentiment, were best placed to adapt to these trends, even if their progress came at the expense of older, elitist associations.

This chapter examines two Australian branches of international grassroots organizations, Oxfam and the Freedom from Hunger Campaign. Oxfam in Australia was a slow starter. It took twenty years from humble beginnings as the Food for Peace campaign in 1952, a name change to Community Aid Abroad (CAA) in 1962, collaborating with Oxfam UK from 1965, to formal affiliation in 1972. The Bangladeshi refugee crisis proved pivotal in helping this Australian agency refine its mission, enhance its public profile and cement its relationships with partners abroad. Meanwhile, the Australian Freedom from Hunger Campaign (FFHC) enjoyed its most successful year in 1971 in eight years thanks in large part to the mobilization of volunteers who championed the cause in new and creative ways. Oxfam and the FFHC were significant organizations globally: together, they emphasized development rather than emergency relief, initiated educational programmes for Western donors, unashamedly politicized aid to foster solidarity between donors and recipients, and connect with rights-based movements that gained momentum during the 'long 1960s'.[3]

Community Aid Abroad: 'People to people' humanitarianism

CAA formally joined the Oxfam brand on 18 April 1972, but its origins could not have been more different from its parent organization. Although both agencies have Anglican roots, they subsequently moved in different directions: in the case of CAA, it turned towards secularism; for Oxfam, its members became influenced by Quakerism. Furthermore, CAA was established amidst the stability and prosperity of post-war Melbourne in a semi-rural retirement village, which, again, differs from the establishment of Oxfam during the Second World War when Britain was under siege and in the grip of privations. Despite these disparate beginnings, by the 1970s, Oxfam and CAA found themselves increasingly as natural allies: both organizations were oriented towards development and the proactive prevention of poverty rather than reactive emergency relief. They also embraced the political dimension of their work, endorsing liberation struggles and decolonization. This marriage only fractured in the late 1970s on the question of the independence of East Timor from Indonesia, a complex topic that warrants further research.[4]

---

[3] Arthur Marwick periodizes the long 1960s as beginning in 1958 and ending in 1974, see *The Sixties: Cultural Revolution in Britain, France, Italy, and the United States, c.1958-c.1974* (London: Bloomsbury Reader, 2012), 11-14. In their journal *The Sixties*, editors Jeremy Varon, Michael S. Foley and John McMillian define the decade as 1954 to 1975 to include antecedents and legacies, see 'Editorial: Time Is an Ocean: The Past and Future of the Sixties', *The Sixties* 1 (2008): 5.

[4] 'Oxfam and CAA', 4 July 1977 in Folder 1 'Community Aid Abroad (pre-1974): Correspondence with Community Aid Abroad regarding their programme and Oxfam's programme in India, Indonesia and elsewhere, Aug 1969-July 1977', MS. Oxfam PRG/3/3/2/65, Bodleian Libraries, University of Oxford.

CAA began with the actions of one man, a pensioner named Frank Gregory. During the (Anglican) Intercession Service every Wednesday at the St Laurence Settlement for Elderly People, Father Gerard Kennedy Tucker led the residents in prayer 'for the millions who were dying of starvation'.[5] For Gregory, prayer was insufficient. 'Should we not give of our substance?', he asked the priest in 1952. Thereafter, Gregory and his fellow pensioners gave two shillings (equivalent to 20 cents) each week to support the provision of high-protein food for patients at an Indian village hospital, not an insubstantial amount from a weekly pension rate of $6.75.[6] Word spread of the pensioners' donations, including to Miss Jean Mackenzie who lived in upper middle class Hawthorn. She contacted Father Tucker and asked him to visit her apartment to speak to her and her friends about his charity. Considered 'very charismatic' and 'always doing outrageous things', Tucker's address clearly made an impact.[7] Together, Tucker and Mackenzie formed the 'Food for Peace' campaign, the prevenient to CAA. To demonstrate her 'faith in the cause', Mackenzie quit her job, so that she could dedicate herself to promoting the fledgling charity. Initially, Food for Peace focused on famine relief in India and remained small in scale.[8] Geopolitically, Food for Peace advocated 'a fresh outlook, a new thinking about Asia and Asians' at a time when Australia was becoming enmeshed in East Asian affairs, particularly in conflicts such as the Korean War, Malayan Emergency and, later, the Vietnam War. It individualized charity, placing responsibility on citizens to act rather than waiting for government intervention or religious guidance. In their words, 'This is a personal thing, not something you can leave to Governments alone. And anyone who seeks it can find a way in which he or she can personally help … **as individuals**' [bold in original].[9] To be sure, Food for Peace did not approach every stratum in society for financial support, preferring to focus on the suburban and rural middle class. This orientation is evident at their campaign dinner in 1960, with the sixty guests including 'churchmen, educationalists, lawyers, doctors, journalists, farmers, businessmen and housewives'.[10]

Two major changes occurred in 1962. First, Jean Mackenzie, terminally ill with cancer, resigned from her position as secretary. Alongside Father Tucker, Mackenzie was instrumental in the early years of Freedom for Peace, organizing, advocating and travelling through India on long sojourns.[11] Tucker's 'idealistic young nephew', David Scott, was appointed Director, a paid position he held until 1970, a change that was indicative of the emerging professionalization of the organization.[12] Second, Food

---

[5] G. Kennedy Tucker, 'A Message from the Founder', *Now. The Journal of Community Aid Abroad*, No. 203, November-December 1971, in Folder 1 'Community Aid Abroad (pre-1974)'.

[6] Scott Christie, 'Inside Community Aid Abroad Part I: The Effervescent Agency with the Bubble-Up Philosophy', *Australian Social Work* 40 (1987): 31. Pension rates viewed online. Australian Government, *Social Security Guide*, section 5.2.2 'Age and Invalid pension – historical rates', accessed 22 March 2022, https://guides.dss.gov.au/guide-social-security-law/5/2/2/10.

[7] David Scott, interview with Ann Turner, 7 February 2001, accessed 16 November 2021, http://nla.gov.au/nla.obj-207214690, transcript, 21. NLA.

[8] Tucker, 'A Message from the Founder', *Now*.

[9] Anonymous, 'Food for Peace News', *Now*, September 1958, 6.

[10] Anonymous, 'What They Said at the Food for Peace Campaign Dinner', *Now*, No. 90, December 1960, 5.

[11] See, for example, Mackenzie's eight-month trip through India in 1959, Anonymous, 'Organizer appointed for Food for Peace Campaign', *Now*, No. 76, October 1959, 7.

[12] Scott, interview with Ann Turner, 21.

for Peace changed its name to Community Aid Abroad, signifying its commitment to stay community driven and internationally oriented and expanding its scope beyond famine relief. Seeking 'wider horizons', CAA acknowledged that 'the actual feeding of starving people is a short-term remedy'. Instead of famine relief, CAA would 'embrace health, education, agriculture and general community welfare'. Their revised mission concentrated on the 'guiding principle' of assisting 'people to help themselves'.[13] CAA worker Scott Christie recalled that throughout the 1960s, the philosophy of CAA centred on self-reliance, 'which is not necessarily the same as self-help or self-determination'.[14] In 1971, Acting Director of CAA, Adrian Harris, justified his priorities: 'Many countries have given help for specific refugee relief programmes but it would appear that the Indian Government needs help to develop an improved infrastructure to help its relief programme.'[15] In this remark, there was the implicit criticism that nations were too quick to donate goods, often in a rush for publicity, without thought of practical, albeit unglamorous, considerations, such as transport and logistics. Without sufficient infrastructure, donated goods failed to reach their intended beneficiaries, as we saw in Chapters 4 and 5.

Since its establishment in 1952, CAA always saw itself as different from mainstream humanitarian organizations. For one, it was the first home-grown international aid agency in Australia. As David Scott reflected in a 2001 interview, there were other humanitarian organizations in Australia at that time, but they were all branches of overseas agencies. For example, Save the Children Fund, Foster Parents' Plan, World Vision, CARE, and the Red Cross all had Australian offices.[16] But as a subservient affiliate, these offices were mandated to follow the vision, policies and strategies of the parent body. Conversely, CAA was uninhibited, free to shape the organization as it wished. This autonomy in the early years had practical implications. For CAA, unidirectional charity from Australia to the Global South was never the goal. Rather, they desired a reciprocal exchange that facilitated transnational relationships, which contested the conventional binary between donor and recipient. In early 1972, the slogan of CAA was, 'A people to people movement of aid and understanding'.[17] In a reflective four-part essay on Community Aid Abroad in 1988, Scott Christie explained the partnership as fundamentally dualistic:

> For sure, the contributions made by Community Aid Abroad supporters enable some of the poorest people in the world to improve their living standards by breaking the chains of oppression which have held back their personal and community development. However, that is only *one side* of the partnership.

[13] Anonymous, 'Community Aid Abroad. Campaign's New Name', *Now*, No. 108, July 1962, cover.
[14] Christie, 'Inside Community Aid Abroad Part I', 31.
[15] Adrian Harris, letter to Major General P. Cullen, 22 September 1971, File 13 'ACFOA Chairmen, Paul Cullen and Neil Batt, 1971–1977', Box 2, Series 'Setting up of ACFOA/Early ACFOA' Records of ACFOA.
[16] Scott, interview with Ann Turner, 41.
[17] Community Aid Abroad, 'Bangladesh Report. Brief Comments on Visit to Bangladesh by Adrian Harris', 5 March to 11 March 1972, Folder 5, 'General Correspondence: correspondence and papers relating to Community Aid Abroad's programme and activities, Apr 1971–July 1973', MS. Oxfam PRG/2/3/13/35, Bodleian Libraries, University of Oxford.

> The other side of the partnership consists of the opportunities for development which Community Aid Abroad provides for its supporters. Participation of people at the grass-roots level is a key element in the development process; this holds true for our supporters [donors] as well as for our project partners [recipients]. Recognition that the development process is as relevant for Australians as it is for, say, Indians, has influenced our thinking regarding the objectives, the structures and the programmes of our organization. [italics in original][18]

The language in this extract is dotted with references to postcolonialism and socialist leaning Third Worldism, ideologies that had by 1988 been dominant in development and aid circles for two decades. In this quotation, Christie asserted that Australians need development assistance too, thus undercutting any assumption of Western superiority, which had been at the core of European humanitarianism for centuries (see Chapter 2).

Rather than seeing aid as selfless charity, Christie reframed humanitarian action that emphasized what Westerners gained rather than gave. For Australians, partnering in development offered an opportunity to broaden one's horizons and learn about other cultures. He explained,

> It is absurd for people who support overseas aid programmes to regard themselves paternalistically as donors and the people who benefit from their contributions as 'recipients'. We need to open our eyes only a little to see something of what the people of Asia, Africa and Latin America can offer *us*: cultural and philosophical riches that go back thousands of years; perspectives on life that encourage us to see beyond the materialistic, acquisitive, dog-eat-dog aspects of our society – to see that development cannot be equated with the possession of a BMW, a swimming pool and an en suite toilet![19]

Once again, this extract critiques the perceived extravagances of Western capitalism. CAA wanted to change Australia as much as, if not more than, underdeveloped nations in the Global South. It was a cultural crusade that critiqued the value of material abundance that was so characteristic of developed nations experiencing post-Second World War prosperity. Arguably, Christie's comments may be viewed as reflecting a typical reaction to the excesses of late 1980s capitalism and the economic fallout from the Wall Street Crash in 1987. Yet the distinctive cultural and political stances of CAA were apparent to outsiders in the early 1970s. In 1971, Oxfam's International Secretary J. W. Jackson wrote in a position paper on the proposed union of Oxfam and CAA that the Australian agency may still view the British organization as a 'begging bowl charity' and cautioned that CAA was on a different path. He commented, 'they feel there is a greater need in Australia for them to educate their country's awakening

---

[18] Scott Christie, 'Inside Community Aid Abroad: Part IV. Development Is for Donors Too', *Australian Social Work* 41 (1988): 36.
[19] Christie, 'Inside Community Aid Abroad: Part IV', 36.

population to their interdependence not with the old world of Europe, but of the Pacific community of Asia'.[20] Thus, CAA leaders saw that Australia's future lay in the Asia-Pacific region, not Europe or America, and that it was up to this organization to shepherd the community through the transition.

Education and activism were key aspects to the CAA operation. Unlike the umbrella organizations of ACC and ACR, or the elite-run ACFOA and Austcare, CAA focused on community involvement in local groups. In 1971, there were 134 such groups, 84 of which were in Victoria. Jim Webb, then Director of CAA, lamented to his Oxfam colleagues that 'they cannot make much headway in other states however hard they try'.[21] By design, CAA local groups were responsible for specific development projects, and therefore, there was a tangible connection between funds raised and spent. Local groups received updates and reports from CAA headquarters and sometimes directly from the field, further consolidating close relationships between CAA members and their partners abroad. This arrangement created a sense of transparency and accountability, traits that were often perceived to be lacking in the NGO sector at this time. Participation was a crucial aspect of the local group format, especially when it came to education and knowledge exchange. Members learnt about history, politics and international relations in the Asia-Pacific to understand the root causes of inequality and poverty in the region. Philip Flood, Australian High Commissioner to Bangladesh (1973–6) and later Secretary of the Department of Foreign Affairs and Trade (1996–8), is credited as saying, 'Community Aid Abroad is the thinking person's aid organization'. CAA offered a 'strong educational program' with an 'intellectual component'.[22]

The formal union between CAA and Oxfam in April 1972 was seven years in the making. Oxfam records show the first correspondence between then Deputy Director Henry Fletcher and CAA chairman David Scott in early 1965. These early communications led to Oxfam lending £2,500 to CAA to help them expand their fundraising capacity. This loan was promptly repaid. Goodwill between the two organizations was further enhanced when CAA financially and practically contributed to several Oxfam projects in India (Bihar, Coimbatore and Bengaluru) and Africa (Kenya, Uganda and Biafra). Between 1966 and 1971, CAA allocated £40,449 to Oxfam projects, an amount equivalent in size to the contribution of Oxfam Belgique. Additionally, CAA and Oxfam shared knowledge through field collaborations and the exchange of staff between England and Australia. Meet-and-greet tours for senior management were commonplace in the late 1960s and early 1970s, trips that enabled the sharing of publications and ideas, all the while cementing personal relationships. In 1971 and 1972, CAA realigned itself from an exclusively development agency to one that supported Oxfam's emergency relief efforts in West Bengal, presumably to cement the newly formed alliance. As the Oxfam International Secretary wrote in a

---

[20] J. W. Jackson, Oxfam Memorandum, 'Oxfam and Community Aid Abroad', 25 August 1971, Folder 5 'General background', MS. Oxfam PRG/2/3/13/35.
[21] Oxfam, 'Notes on talk given to Div. heads by Jim Webb of CAA', 25 September 1971', Folder 5 'General background', MS. Oxfam PRG/2/3/13/35.
[22] Scott, interview with Ann Turner, 33.

1971 memorandum on the extent of the Oxfam–CAA relationship, it 'has touched upon virtually every aspect of the work of the two organizations'.[23]

As CAA and Oxfam became more entwined, management from both organizations wished to formalize their relationship, albeit for different reasons. CAA sought a merger to benefit from Oxfam's size and expertise in fundraising, publicity and educational programmes; Oxfam wished to align itself with an 'undoubtedly growing organization'. Realistically, it was also the only way Oxfam could enter the overcrowded Australian market that was characterized by 'the very high degree of competition'.[24] Oxfam's assessment of Australian conditions proved accurate and Australian aid agencies were not keen on the arrival of Oxfam. One month before the amalgamation, Austcare National Director, A. C. Prior, expressed concern to ACFOA Executive Director Geoffrey Solomon. He wrote,

> As stated in our discussions I am strongly of the opinion that the whole of the wider question of the introduction of OXFAM into the Australian fundraising field for overseas aid needs serious consideration and attention by ACFOA.[25]

Reading between the lines, the CAA–Oxfam union threatened the status quo in Australia, a situation that benefitted large organizations such as Austcare while sidelining smaller agencies such as CAA. Aside from serving as an opportunity to enter the Australian market, Oxfam sought a merger with CAA to offset some of the difficulties it was facing with the Canadian branch of the organization. At the time, Oxfam Canada, then under the influence of the radical left, disliked what it deemed as the paternalistic attitudes of Oxfam UK. As a result, during the late 1960s and early 1970s Oxfam Canada distanced itself from the parent organization, both in terms of rhetoric and practice in the field. In contrast to the Canadians, Oxfam no doubt viewed CAA as a reliable partner and donor and, importantly, as an organization that did not allow its internal politics to impact its relief projects in Bangladesh.[26]

The CAA/Oxfam response to the Bangladesh Liberation War

The Bangladesh Liberation War and reconstruction period was a turning point in the history of CAA. From 1971, this home-grown Australian NGO pivoted towards collaborating with international partners within the Oxfam family while turning its back on national networks. The reorientation of CAA towards international allies at this time was not inevitable. Rather, the evidence indicates that CAA struggled to

---

[23] J. W. Jackson, memorandum to Director, 25 August 1971, Folder 4 'General Background', MS. Oxfam PRG/2/3/13/35.
[24] Ibid.
[25] A. C. Prior, letter to Geoffrey Solomon, 2 March 1972, Folder 10 'Community Aid Abroad', Records of Community Aid Abroad, NLA.
[26] Maggie Black, *Cause for Our Times: Oxfam – the First Fifty Years* (Oxford: Oxford University Press, 1992), 172–3.

solicit donations during the 1971 war, and international collaborations presented CAA with an opportunity to regain relevance.

For CAA staff, the lack of donations during the 1971 war was a sensitive issue. Instead of using this organizational failure as cause for reflection or a chance for it to improve its fundraising initiatives, CAA staff blamed the Australian public. For example, in August 1971, Acting Director Adrian Harris wrote to Bill Kelly, the Secretary of the South Australian CAA office,

> We have been very concerned about the lack of interest in Australia in the situation in East Bengal and the plight of refugees in India. We feel Australia has made only a token gesture to help and we are trying to bring more pressure on the Government to increase our aid substantially.[27]

Adrian Harris repeated this sentiment three months later, this time writing in a report to the CAA national committee,

> Although we are not a relief agency it became apparent that, due to lack of interest in this country, Australia would make only a token contribution to the refugee problem. With cooperation from Oxfam, we have maintained a considerable campaign to draw attention to the plight of refugees. This includes sending 'Age' reporter, Max Beattie, to Bengal [covered in Chapter 7]. Writing and cabling many MPs and releasing press releases urging greater Australian assistance. CAA has received $15,000 from Austcare to be used by Oxfam for relief activity and sent another $20,000 from donations we have received.[28]

In this assessment, Harris repeatedly made two mistakes. First, he conflated the actions (or inactions) of the Australian government with public sentiment. As we will see in Chapter 7, public attitudes – as expressed in letters to MPs – vehemently opposed government policy towards Bangladeshi refugees in India. Second, Harris deduced that the failure of CAA to attract donations was due to public apathy. An alternative interpretation is that CAA failed to gain traction with their audience, whether it be by sending a confused message ('we are not a relief agency but …') or disseminating their publicity through the wrong media.

In 1971, CAA abandoned some of its long-held principles of reciprocal developmental aid in favour of dispensing charity so that it could piggyback on the successes of Oxfam UK in India. During the war, Oxfam funded the work of five Indian medical, welfare and sanitation teams in the refugee camps of West Bengal, a programme that benefitted 500,000 people. In September 1971, Oxfam Director Leslie Kirkley projected that the cost of supporting five teams in West Bengal would

---

[27] Adrian Harris, letter to Bill Kelly, 24 August 1971, folder 2 'S.A.', Box 5 'State Correspondence', Records of Community Aid Abroad, University of Melbourne Archives (hereafter UMA).

[28] Adrian Harris, Acting Director's Report for CAA National Committee Meeting, 17 November 1971, Folder 1 'Director's Reports 1967–1975', Box 4 'Reports', Records of Community Aid Abroad, UMA.

be £740,000.²⁹ In support of the Oxfam programme, CAA donated 5 tonnes of high-protein milk biscuits. These biscuits were purchased at cost by CAA and shipped to Mumbai free of charge by Air India.³⁰ The purchase and delivery of food aid, perhaps the archetype of emergency relief, demonstrates that CAA was willing to adapt its approach to aid, moving away from development assistance to one that aligned more closely to Oxfam's relief-oriented programme. Arguably, this ideological malleability was a rarity at a time of heightened political activism in Australia.

The reconstruction and rehabilitation period from 1972 to 1973 provided further opportunities for CAA to strengthen its international connections. In the minutes of the national committee meeting of CAA on 19 December 1971, it was noted that 'a suggestion was made that someone from CAA should visit Bangla Desh as soon as possible to gain firsthand information on the requirements for rehabilitation and development'. The committee also considered requesting an Australian tour of an Oxfam worker with recent experience in Bengal.³¹ It is noteworthy that in the same meeting, the national committee affirmed its desire to seek affiliation with Oxfam and accept its principles. The committee also announced five new appointments, including three field officers and two secretarial assistants, demonstrating that 1972 was a period of expansion for the organization.

In March 1972, the Oxfam family launched its Bangladesh appeal in which it endeavoured to raise A$2.5 million for the reconstruction of the young nation. CAA pledged to raise A$200,000 for this cause, the largest in its history.³² In a press release on 30 March 1972, CAA Director Jim Webb described the appeal as 'the most ambitious programme CAA has ever undertaken', further commenting, 'We must think big' [underline in original].³³ To reach this end, CAA launched its own fundraising appeal in Australia and sought evocative material from overseas partners to persuade donors. For example, Webb cabled a telegram to Oxfam's overseas aid director, Ken Bennett, with the message, 'CAA FULLY SUPPORTS BANGLA DESH PROGRAM STOP APPEAL LAUNCHED URGENTLY WANT PHOTOS STORIES WEBB+'.³⁴

The aim of raising A$200,000 was bold and, arguably, unrealistic. Between 1962 and 1972, CAA had raised A$1.2 million, which equated to an annual average of A$120,000.³⁵ In a letter to Ken Bennett, Webb confessed, 'We do hope to raise

---

[29] Leslie Kirkley, letter to Adrian Harris, 30 September 1971, Folder 5, MS. Oxfam PRG/2/3/13/35. For a first-hand reflection on Oxfam's work in India, see Julian Francis, 'Working with the Refugees, 1971', *Strategic Analysis* 45 (2021): 530–7.

[30] CAA Press Release, 'CAA Sends Australian High Protein Biscuits to Refugee Camps', 31 August 1971, Folder 5, MS. Oxfam PRG/2/3/13/35.

[31] Minutes of Meeting of National Committee, Community Aid Abroad, 19 December 1971, Folder 'Nat Exec. Minutes 1965–1973', Box 11 J. B. Webb (Director's Files), Records of Community Aid Abroad, UMA.

[32] Also note that Oxfam Canada raised C$590,000, one of its largest contributions in its history. O'Sullivan, *The NGO Moment*, 50.

[33] Jim Webb, press release, 'Urgent Appeal. Help Bangladesh Now', Folder 5. Press release also included in Folder 'Oxfam-Bangladesh 1973–74', Box 41 'CAA Oxfam', Records of Community Aid Abroad, UMA.

[34] Jim Webb, telegram to Ken Bennett, 29 March 1972, Folder 5, MS. Oxfam PRG/2/3/13/35.

[35] Jim Webb and Leslie Kirkley, press release, 'Directors Announce CAA and Oxfam Merger', 18 April 1972, Folder 5, MS. Oxfam PRG/2/3/13/35.

A$200,000, but have at this stage no idea of what will result.' Nevertheless, Webb concluded the letter on an up-beat tone, 'Things are looking up here. CAA Week will have quite an impact. We have already firm commitments for national TV and radio programmes'.[36] In a letter to Oxfam US Executive Director Thea Foster on 20 April, Webb continued to be positive, writing, 'We have no idea of the results our Bangla Desh Appeal will attain, but so far we have nearly $9,000 without having made any major effort.'[37] In the end, by May 1973, CAA had raised and transferred to Oxfam A$127,000 for Bangladeshi reconstruction, considerably below its aim of A$200,000 but still a significant increase from its annual average of A$120,000 for all projects.[38]

As a result of continued financial contributions from CAA, Oxfam assisted with the reconstruction of Bangladesh in myriad ways. On announcing their formal merger in April 1972, CAA and Oxfam declared that their first joint project would assist in the rehabilitation of Bangladesh, specifically in the areas of agriculture, ferries, communications and villages, all of which were decimated during the liberation war.[39] Of the A$127,000 raised during the CAA Bangladesh appeal in 1972, A$50,000 was allocated to the purchase of ferries for crossing the Brahmaputra River, part of a wider Oxfam project self-described as their 'piece de resistance' of the recovery programme.[40] At the time, ferries were the only means of river crossing for trucks carrying essential goods from ports to inland towns. An additional A$71,000 was transferred for the Bangladesh Rural Advancement Committee (BRAC) that aimed to address the low-lying and flood-prone Sulla district, which would prevent crop losses during the monsoon. The remaining funds were used for health schemes, such as nutritional programmes and anti-cholera vaccines.[41]

Working closely with Oxfam in Bangladesh from 1972, CAA was reinvigorated, turning what had been an underwhelming fundraising year in 1971 into the making of a confident, vibrant and internationally connected NGO. In practice, this meant that the Australian agency took independent action outside the agreed arrangements with Austcare and ACFOA on how to raise funds from the Australian public. After the disappointing allocation of donated funds from Austcare in 1971, the National Committee of CAA agreed to launch their own Bangladesh appeal once 'information on specific projects had been received by Oxfam'.[42]

Unsurprisingly, Paul Cullen was infuriated when he received news of an upcoming CAA appeal. As president of Austcare, chairman of ACFOA and president of the United Nations Association of Australia, Cullen sent a telegram to Oxfam headquarters

---

[36] Jim Webb, letter to Ken Bennett, 4 April 1972, Folder 5, MS. Oxfam PRG/2/3/13/35.
[37] Jim Webb, letter to Thea Foster, 20 April 1972, Folder 5, MS. Oxfam PRG/2/3/13/35.
[38] Jim Webb, letter to Major G. W. Acworth, Oxfam Field Secretary for Asia, 17 May 1973, Folder 5, MS. Oxfam PRG/2/3/13/35.
[39] Jim Webb and Leslie Kirkley, press release, 'Directors Announce CAA and Oxfam Merger', 18 April 1972, Folder 5, MS. Oxfam PRG/2/3/13/35.
[40] John Shiels, letter to Jim Webb, 11 August 1972, Folder 5, MS. Oxfam PRG/2/3/13/35.
[41] Marilyn Sanders, letter to Jim Webb, 29 May 1973, Folder 5, MS. Oxfam PRG/2/3/13/35; CAA, '1974 CAA Projects. Review Supplement', June 1975, Folder 1, MS. Oxfam PRG/3/3/2/65.
[42] Minutes from Meeting of National Committee, Community Aid Abroad, 8 March 1972, Folder 9 'Community Aid Abroad', Records of Community Aid Abroad, NLA.

expressing his outrage at the proposed CAA appeal for Oxfam projects in Bangladesh. The telegram is reproduced in full as it captures a moment when the genteel mask typical of the humanitarian sector dropped and true rivalries were revealed. The cable read as follows:

> UNDERSTAND THAT COMMUNITY AID ABROAD PROPOSES LAUNCHING A SPECIAL APPEAL THROUGHOUT AUSTRALIA FOR OXFAM PROJECTS IN BANGLADESH WITH AGREEMENT AND COOPERATION OF OXFAM STOP MUST ADVISE YOU THAT REPURCUSSIONS[sic] OF THIS WILL REACT AGAINST SUCCESS OF FUND RAISING EFFORTS OF CURRENTLY ESTABLISHED ORGANISATIONS IN AUSTRALIA STOP INTRODUCTION OF MAJOR BODY OF YOUR STANDING CAN ONLY REACT AGAINST THE TRUE INTEREST OF BANGLADESH AND WHOLE AID PROGRAMME STOP STRONGLY URGE THAT BEFORE TAKING THIS DRASTIC STEP OF INTERVENTION IN AUSTRALIAN AID FIELD THAT FULL DISCUSSION WITH EXISTING AUSTRALIAN ORGANISATIONS CONSIDERING THAT OBJECTIVE SHOULD BE THAT MAXIMUM FUNDS SHOULD BE RAISED FOR BANGLADESH AND OTHER PROJECTS.[43]

Unlike telegrams of the time that were typically clear and concise, this telegram was lengthy and, towards the end, confusing. The writing style suggests that Cullen did not proofread before sending, indicating a degree of impulsivity that may have been caused by feelings of rage. As telegram rates were charged by the word, such verbosity came at a cost to Cullen. In the early 1970s, Australian telegram rates were 48 cents for the first twelve words, 4 cents per word thereafter. At 104 words in length, this telegram cost at least A$4.16, double if posted as an urgent telegram.[44] In 2023 currency, the tariff for this telegram was A$51, a pricey fee for basic correspondence, although perhaps not for an individual of Cullen's means. In any case, the length and rancour of this telegram reveal that the schedule of the fundraising appeals was so delicately poised that Cullen was determined to protect the status quo from a large, international player such as Oxfam.

That same day, Geoffrey Solomon of ACFOA telephoned Jim Webb of CAA at the behest of Austcare. In Webb's notes from the conversation, he articulated the position of CAA but did not provide insight into the perspective of ACFOA. These notes adopted a conciliatory tone, suggesting that CAA had no choice but to seek funds from the public to support its Bangladesh projects. To quell opposition from ACFOA and others, Webb assured Solomon that CAA would not adopt an aggressive marketing strategy, which could contribute to donor compassion fatigue. Specifically, Webb stated that CAA would not hold a door knock, engage public relations firms or commission advertising. Instead, CAA would rely on press statements to secure funds.

---

[43] Paul Cullen, telegram to Oxfam GB, 1 March 1972 (also noted as 29 February 1972), Folder 10 'Community Aid Abroad', Records of Community Aid Abroad, NLA.

[44] Telegram rates deduced from Anonymous, 'Phone Calls, Rents Rise', *Canberra Times*, 2 August 1975, 1.

Webb justified the CAA appeal on the basis that it 'cannot hold off until May' to receive donations from the Austcare general appeal.[45]

The conversation between Solomon and Webb did not ease tensions, however. The following day, Cullen wrote a terse letter to Webb. In the letter, Cullen dismissed the assurances of Webb from the previous telephone conversation, asserting that 'we are nearing our critical annual appeal period. This is April and May'. Cullen hoped the Austcare appeal would raise between A$1 and A$2 million, funds that would ultimately benefit reconstruction in Bangladesh. The tone of the letter deteriorated towards the concluding paragraphs, with Cullen making thinly veiled threats to CAA. He wrote,

> We believe that any appeal by CAA in our period – a period well recognised by ACFOA – would be detrimental to our result. Furthermore, it would be detrimental to an extent far beyond what your appeal might raise.
>
> Accordingly we do urge that you agree not to make any public appeal – with or without OXFAM – until the end of May.
>
> May I refer to the donation we made to OXFAM last year.[46]

In this extract, Cullen illustrated the power he held across the Australian humanitarian sector. Although it is not made explicit, one could draw the conclusion that if CAA were to persist with its appeal, Austcare would withhold funds from CAA following its appeal. Cullen warned CAA against cannibalizing behaviour, arguing that running a separate CAA appeal would disadvantage the humanitarian sector overall. In reply, Jim Webb challenged Cullen on his allegations. Whereas Cullen insisted that the months of April and May were set aside for the Austcare appeal, Webb insisted that 'the ACFOA calendar lists it [the Austcare appeal] as May 21–28 in most States'. As the CAA week was scheduled for 9 to 16 April, Webb contended there would be no overlap in public appeals, thus negating any claim that the CAA appeal would hurt Austcare.[47]

Given the competitive nature of fundraising and the overcrowded humanitarian aid sector in Australia, it is understandable that individual agencies would exchange forthright letters on occasion. What changed this series of letters to something unusual is that Paul Cullen sought the support of other agencies to sideline CAA. Foolishly, Cullen approached Phyllis Frost, the President of the Australian FFHC, an organization particularly close to CAA. FFHC and CAA shared a vision and a politics that made them strategic partners. So when Frost received Cullen's letter, she forwarded it to CAA, which is how this letter was ultimately archived within the records of CAA. In the letter, Cullen included copies of correspondence between him and CAA as well as with Oxfam. Indicating an absence of political antennae, Cullen wrote, 'May I suggest that because of our common interests generally, and in several States specifically, that

---

[45] Anonymous, 'Conversation between Mr. J. Webb, Community Aid Abroad, and Mr. Solomon, ACFOA', 1 March 1972, Folder 10 'Community Aid Abroad', Records of Community Aid Abroad, NLA.

[46] Paul Cullen, letter to Jim Webb, 2 March 1972, Folder 10 'Community Aid Abroad', Records of Community Aid Abroad, NLA.

[47] Jim Webb, letter to Paul Cullen, 3 March 1972, Folder 10 'Community Aid Abroad', Records of Community Aid Abroad, NLA.

Freedom From Hunger Campaign should send a cable to OXFAM in similar terms.'[48] From this point, correspondence between Austcare and CAA became acrimonious, illustrative of ill will and divergent philosophies between the two organizations.

CAA leaders were most irate because Austcare contacted Oxfam directly at a time when negotiations of the merger had reached their crescendo after years of discussions. From the documents, it appears that Cullen contacted Oxfam without the knowledge of CAA, reinforcing the impression that Austcare sought to marginalize CAA from discussions by withholding information. In response to the telegram from Cullen, Oxfam replied 'WE HAVE NO DESIRE TO JEOPARDISE ANY HELP FOR BANGLADESH. HAVE ASKED CAA TO DISCUSS WITH YOU IN VIEW OF ITS AUTONOMOUS STATUS.'[49] It is clear in this telegram that Oxfam wished to avoid being embroiled in any local dispute between Australian humanitarian agencies, particularly since Oxfam at that time had no authority over CAA policies. Critically, Oxfam informed CAA of its correspondence with Cullen. The response from CAA Chairman David Scott to Cullen was blistering. He wrote,

> Dear Paul,
>
> We have received a cable from Oxfam advising us that you have cabled to them criticising our appeal for Oxfam projects in Bangladesh. Apparently you have alleged that Oxfam intervention will reduce funds raised by established Australian agencies.
>
> *I fail to see how our domestic business is any of your concern and would like an explanation of your action.* CAA, which was established long before Austcare, has provided support for Oxfam projects for many years and is regarded as part of the Oxfam family.
>
> Your action is all the more incomprehensible in the light of our recent telephone conversation. At the time I explained to you that CAA was not proposing to launch any major organised appeal …
>
> You will recall that last year when the needs of refugees were so acute and Austcare launched an additional appeal, we gave our name in support of the appeal and a number of CAA supporters and groups gave donations to the Austcare appeal …
>
> It seems to me that you are regarding Bangladesh as Austcare's preserve and I think your attitude on this and your action in contacting Oxfam after our conversation are unjustifiable. [italics added][50]

In this letter, Scott also noted that the hunger strikers (covered in Chapter 7) initially desired to raise money for CAA. However, CAA directed these protesters to the Australian FFHC for whom they raised A$50,000 and, as Phyllis Frost observed, 'were

---

[48] Paul Cullen, letter to Phyllis Frost, 2 March 1972, Folder 10 'Community Aid Abroad', Records of Community Aid Abroad, NLA.
[49] Oxfam GB, telegram to Paul Cullen, 3 March 1972, Folder 10 'Community Aid Abroad', Records of Community Aid Abroad, NLA.
[50] David Scott, letter to Paul Cullen, 2 March 1972, Folder 10 'Community Aid Abroad', Records of Community Aid Abroad, NLA.

responsible for the best publicity that Freedom from Hunger had ever received'.[51] Scott noted this example as further evidence of their 'cooperative attitude'. It also documents allegiances within the Australian aid sector in which like-minded individuals coalesced around shared visions for the future. Humanitarian aid was no longer a monolithic enterprise to ease the suffering of others. Rather, by the 1970s, the aid sector was fractured, increasingly polarized and operated within a politicized space. These themes are also evident in the records of the Australian FFHC, which is the focus of the next section.

Freedom from Hunger Campaign

The FFHC originated from the UN's Food and Agriculture Organization (FAO), the oldest and largest UN agency that was informed by starvation in war-torn Europe and Asia as well as the 1943 Bengal famine. When the FAO was officially established in October 1945, the new UN agency had a grand vision: not only would the FAO work to 'secure adequate supply of food for every man' but also 'secure adequate livelihoods' and care for the welfare of farmers.[52] The fact that the antecedents of the FAO coincided with the Bengal famine would have ramifications throughout the 1950s. The anthropogenic catastrophe provided the training ground for the next generation of nutritional scientists in India, who would later serve in the FAO and champion the cause of a citizen-driven Freedom from Hunger Campaign.[53] Most notably, Binay Ranjen (B. R.) Sen served as India's Director-General of Food during the Bengal famine and would be the first Director-General of the FAO from outside the UK or United States, serving in this role from 1956 to 1967. The Kolkata-raised, Oxford-educated Sen was shaped by his encounters with hunger in his native Bengal, reflecting in 1982, 'All my life I had been in the midst of hunger and poverty in all its stark reality.'[54] Despite this bleak existence, Sen remained optimistic, believing that the twentieth-century advances in science, social hygiene and agriculture could mitigate future risks of famine. For Sen, the explosive rate of population growth witnessed mid-century created a sense of urgency for the implementation of hunger alleviation programmes.[55] As with many newly established UN agencies, the FAO encountered budgetary restraints, limiting its capacity to achieve its lofty goal of hunger prevention. In its early years, the FAO faced criticism, even ridicule, as evidenced by this stinging rebuke in *The Economist* in 1952: 'For some time the practical businessman with a

---

[51] Ibid.
[52] Amalia Ribi Forclaz, 'From Reconstruction to Development: The Early Years of the Food and Agriculture Organization (FAO) and the Conceptualization of Rural Welfare, 1945–1955', *International History Review* 41 (2019): 351–2; Corinne A. Pernet and Amalia Ribi Forclaz, 'Revisiting the Food and Agriculture Organization (FAO): International Histories of Agriculture, Nutrition and Development', *International History Review* 41 (2019): 346.
[53] For a discussion on the causes and impacts of the Bengal famine, see Cormac Ó Gráda, '"Sufficiency and Sufficiency and Sufficiency": Revisiting the Bengal Famine of 1943–44', *UCD Centre for Economic Research Working Paper Series*, University College Dublin, 2010, 32–3.
[54] B. R. Sen, *Towards a Newer World* (Dublin: Tycooly International, 1982), 137.
[55] D. John Shaw, *World Food Security* (London: Palgrave Macmillan, 2007), 78.

wide experience of rice and the rice trade has tended to recede into the background and his place has been taken by the civil servant who cannot be expected to appreciate the finer points of an extremely complex trade.' The journal continued, lamenting in a surly tone that 'The Food and Agriculture Organization is a permanent institution devoted to proving that there is not enough food in the world.'[56] For *The Economist*, the FAO represented the worst aspects of government overreach and meddling in the private sphere of commerce.

The intrinsic problem with Intergovernmental organization (IGO) – that they are dependent on the member states that fund them – was evident in the case of the FAO. But rather than shrinking its ambitions, under the leadership of Sen, the FAO reimagined their funding streams. After a brainstorming session with US President Dwight Eisenhower, Sen proposed a worldwide campaign to combat hunger, modelled along the lines of previously successful 'International Year of …' campaigns of the UN, with public participation as its distinctive feature.[57] Sen cobbled together a supportive coalition of UN agencies, governments and civil society groups.[58] He recalled, 'Never before has any World Campaign so permeated society at all levels in such a short time. The main reason is that hunger has a unique universal appeal. Nothing touches the conscience of man as much as hunger.'[59] Sen secured backing among influential world leaders, including Pope John, French President Charles de Gaulle and Queen Elizabeth II, who referenced the FFHC in her widely consumed Christmas message to the Commonwealth in 1963.[60] Coinciding with the First Development Decade in 1960, the global FFHC was officially launched in India amidst much fanfare. The location of the launch should come as no surprise. Aside from being the birthplace and training ground of Sen, in the preceding years, the Indian national had argued passionately that the FFHC should focus its attention on Asia and, to a lesser extent, Latin America. Indeed, in his first official trip as Director-General of the FAO, Sen visited Dhaka, revealing the high priority the agency placed on hunger alleviation in Bengal. The focus on India also made sense from a strategic and marketing perspective: the subcontinent had experienced a famine in living memory, and Europeans, Canadians and Australians were familiar with donating to famine relief in the region. Indian projects under the FFHC rubric proved widely popular, with significant funding contributions by the Netherlands with Australia in second place. Other major donors included the UK, Ireland, Canada, France, Denmark, West Germany, Japan and Finland.[61] The FFHC found strongest support among development-oriented NGOs.[62] Not only did these charities and clubs align politically with the objectives of the FFHC, but they also

---

[56] Anonymous, 'Asia's Rice Shortage', *The Economist*, 23 August 1952, 30.
[57] Benjamin Siegal, '"The Claims of Asia and the Far East": India and the FAO in the Age of Ambivalent Internationalism', *International History Review* 41 (2019): 441; B. R. Sen, *The Basic Freedom – Freedom from Hunger* (Geneva: FAO, 1963), 15.
[58] Hieke Wieters, 'On Fishing in Other People's Ponds: The Freedom from Hunger Campaign, International Fundraising and the Ethics of NGO Publicity', in *Humanitarianism and the Media: 1900 to the Present*, ed. Johannes Paulmann (New York: Berghahn Books, 2019), 188.
[59] Sen, *Towards a Newer World*, 144.
[60] Ibid.
[61] Siegal, '"The Claims of Asia and the Far East"', 442–3; O'Sullivan, *The NGO Moment*, 62.
[62] Hilton, 'Oxfam and the Problem of NGO Aid Appraisals in the 1960s', 3.

shared a similar approach that rejected paternalism in favour of education to foster solidarity between donor and recipient. Sen wrote,

> The Freedom from Hunger Campaign is intended to be primarily educational in character – to make the Governments and peoples all over the world aware of the nature of the problem so that integrated efforts can be made both nationally and internationally to overcome it ... Action projects have an important part to play by providing a means through which developed countries can express their solidarity with the developing countries.[63]

Originally the FFHC was scheduled to run for five years, climaxing in 1963, but its success led to an additional five-year term, which was renewed again for a second decade in 1970. Despite the success of the FFHC across many countries, the US government became oppositional during the 1960s. In a Cold War environment, the American government advocated 'trade not aid' and ideologically was wary of solidarity movements that could in time usher in communist uprisings.[64]

By the time of the Bangladesh Liberation War and refugee flight in 1971, the FFHC was well established, demonstrating the long roots of its activism that stretched back to the 1940s. It is fitting that the FFHC was spearheaded by an Indian with past humanitarian experience during the Bengal famine of 1943, a region that would face famine conditions in 1971. It is also apt that a leading donor for Indian FFHC projects during the 1960s was Australia, second only to the Netherlands.[65] The networks between Australia, India and the FFHC would re-emerge in 1971 during the Bangladeshi refugee crisis. Beyond specific connections between individuals and locales, the establishment of the FFHC left a greater legacy on 1970s aid campaigns. It bridged the gap between private philanthropy, development NGOs and the UN. The FFHC pioneered new ways of fundraising and created a sense of shared humanity that harnessed the power of various youth groups, civic clubs, religious organizations and voluntary bodies.[66] During these formative years, national chapters were established and allowed time to grow in influence and resources. At its peak, there were over a hundred nations involved; among these, Australia, Canada and the UK were the strongest.[67]

Like the establishment of CAA, the founding of the Australian FFHC committee was closely associated with organized religion. In February 1961, Methodist Reverend W. J. Hobbin formed the Australian branch, receiving bipartisan support from political, academic and civic leaders. During the 1960s, the Australian FFHC enjoyed widespread

---

[63] Sen, *Towards a Newer World*, 148.
[64] Siegal, '"The Claims of Asia and the Far East"', 441 and Wieters, 'On Fishing in Other People's Ponds', 190.
[65] Siegal, '"The Claims of Asia and the Far East"', 427 and 443.
[66] Matthew Bunch, 'All Roads Lead to Rome: Canada, the Freedom from Hunger Campaign and the Rise of NGOs, 1960–1980', PhD Diss., University of Waterloo, 2007, 239.
[67] Bunch, 'All Roads Lead to Rome', 240; Agnieszka Sobocinska, 'Popular Causes: The Volunteer Graduate Scheme, the Freedom from Hunger Campaign and Altruistic Internationalism', *Journal of Australian Studies* 43 (2019): 509.

appeal in large part to the ways in which the organization politicized hunger and funded media-friendly small-scale projects in Asia. Like other national committees, the Australian FFHC drew in the public as well. The Australian FFHC made inroads into schools, thereby targeting children (and indirectly their parents and teachers) and gaining access to a hitherto underutilized market for funds and a source of free labour. In NSW in 1963, nearly three thousand schools ran fundraising campaigns, raising A£18,000. Other innovative forms of fundraising included doorknock appeals. Again, in NSW in 1963, some seventy thousand volunteers raised A£257,000 using this method. The Australian FFHC supported performative fundraising, including fasting and austerity lunches in which the money saved on food was donated to the FFHC. Through symbolic deprivation, individuals demonstrated solidarity and empathy with the world's poor. As we will see in the case of the FFHC relief for Bangladeshi refugees, performative acts of solidarity provided readymade human-interest stories for newspapers, magazines and television, and as a result, served to create free publicity for the cause. By the 1970s, the FFHC was the most known humanitarian agency in Australia and, along with the Australian Red Cross, the most admired charity.[68]

The 1971 Appeal

Unlike CAA or the Red Cross, the Australian FFHC was primarily a fundraising organization. It did not have operational staff and instead chose to allocate raised funds to support financially existing projects run by local humanitarian agencies. Thus, when we explore the role of the Australian FFHC during the 1971 war, we gain insights into donation practices among the public. As we will see again in Chapter 7, this section moves away from generic descriptions of the public or citizenry and instead examines precisely who donated to the Bangladeshi refugee crisis. By breaking down donations according to location, we can then introduce census data, including age, income and occupation. This analysis therefore provides insights into the socioeconomic characteristics of individuals most affected by the unfolding refugee crisis. This section also analyses methods of fundraising. Although the Australian FFHC had its origins in relatively passive doorknock appeals, in 1971, this organization increasingly harnessed the power of youthful political activism to solicit donor dollars. Specifically, the FFHC endorsed and encouraged the public performance of humanitarian fundraising.

One of the main differences between the Australian FFHC and its competitors at this time was its human capital. At the time of the Bangladeshi refugee crisis, the Australian FFHC had run successive, annual doorknock campaigns each spring for a decade and had trained a legion of dedicated professional staff and volunteers. Not surprisingly, by 1971, the Australian FFHC oozed confidence, which was in contrast to the insecurity of the Australian Red Cross and anxieties of ACFOA and Austcare. Its national publicity officer, Leo Kelly, articulated the self-assurance of the organization when he reported in December 1971, 'The Australian Freedom from Hunger Campaign's 1971 Appeal

---

[68] Ibid., 522. Note that Australia changed its currency from pounds to dollars in February 1966.

was a foregone "success" almost before it started.' Kelly attributed the effectiveness of the 1971 appeal to several factors.

First, the 'horror' of the Bangladeshi refugee crisis 'drew public attention as nothing else could to the world hunger situation generally and the lack of properly deployed aid which contributed to its cause'. Second, the hunger strikers who protested inadequate government aid further drew public interest in the cause, which is the subject of Chapter 7. Third, the grassroots campaign was driven by 'dedicated' state directors, regional directors, local committee members and rank-and-file volunteers. Fourth, the FFHC engaged in a multimedia 'publicity blitz', some of which included celebrity endorsements. Lastly, citizens spontaneously initiated 'happenings in suburban areas and country towns', which reflected 'the vast creative potential of the public' amidst mass mobilization, discussed later. Collectively, these factors dovetailed to create a conducive environment for the Australian FFHC to maximize fundraising during a crisis.[69]

As a development-oriented organization with permanent staff, the FFHC benefitted from existing connections and relationships with Indian relief organizations and their staff. For example, in the Records of the Australian Freedom from Hunger Campaign, there were numerous cables exchanged between Alan Smith, National Executive Officer of FFHC, and J. B. Singh of CARE/AgriIndia in New Delhi. These cables document the flow of funds from Australia to India in June, July, September, October and November 1971.[70] But the Australian did not offer his Indian counterpart a blank cheque. Questions of use of donated funds were ever present. According to Smith, in a cable date-stamped 26 October 1971, the Australian public was 'demanding' the information. While the Australian Red Cross requested information on how donated funds were used for publicity purposes and subsequent fundraising campaigns, it seems that a similar request from the Australian FFHC committee was motivated to placate donor demands. By putting the desires of the benefactor front and centre, the Australian FFHC contributed to the sense that their financial sponsors maintained a measure of control over the recipient population. This power dynamic was eerily like the paternalistic imperial relationships so admonished by FFHC founders.

Singh acquiesced to the publicity demands of Smith. In a campaign newsletter dated 10 November 1971, the Victorian branch of the Australian FFHC committee reported to its supporters on '*Our* Pakistani Refugee Project' [italics added]:

> *Our* refugee project is being implemented in conjunction with the Indian Freedom from Hunger Campaign. No 'handouts' are involved. The *refugees themselves* are building semi-permanent shelters from adequate materials provided by the campaign. All work is carried out under the supervision of the Indian FFHC … Perhaps the finest feature of our project is that it involves the *refugees themselves* in the solution of their immediate need for proper shelter. It also lifts them above

---

[69] Leo Kelly, 'Publicity Officers Report, December 1971', Folder 107 '1972 States/General, 1971/State Directors' Conference, Action for World Development', Box 19, Australian Freedom from Hunger Campaign. Records of AFFHC.

[70] Folder 315, 'Cables', Box 56 and Folder 357 'Cables', Box 62, Records of AFFHC.

the morale-shattering boredom of sitting down and doing nothing – until they die. [italics added][71]

In this extract, metropolitan chairman Jim James and country chairman Thomas Tehan claimed ownership of the relief efforts on two occasions. Moreover, James and Tehan wrote repeatedly that the refugees were responsible for their own uplift rather than lazily accepting free gifts. James and Tehan also noted that the work of the refugees was supervised by the Indian FFHC, a further denigration to the Bangladeshi refugees who were perceived as incompetent and untrustworthy. Interestingly, James and Tehan insisted there were no 'handouts', a mid-twentieth-century term that gained widespread traction after its use by American President Lyndon Baines Johnson in his War on Poverty.[72] Handouts henceforth became a catch-all label for those who despised welfare or anti-poverty measures. In the American context, handouts became a shorthand way to express a desire to help the deserving poor, for example, the working class, while at the same time refusing to aid the undeserving poor, such as those who were long-term unemployed, homeless or drug addicts. As a term, 'handout' signalled a moral crusade that sought to cajole aid recipients into desired behaviours. It echoed the aspirations and preferred outcomes of Christian uplift from the early twentieth century, albeit cloaked in mid-century secular language.[73]

From its origin, FFHC founder B. R. Sen created a global campaign that would educate and mobilize citizens to address the political and economic causes of hunger and malnourishment. This approach proved successful in Australia, and in 1971, the Australian FFHC raised over A$1,333,000, a remarkably high figure given that the organization was restricted to a one-day appeal on 28 September 1971. In comparison, Austcare raised A$2 million across two appeals throughout the year. Arguably, the Australian FFHC was so successful in 1971 because it had laid the foundations for over a decade that understood aid as a political issue and empowered citizens from all sectors of society to engage in individual acts of activism and fundraising. By framing aid as a political issue, the FFHC connected charity with other protest movements that gained momentum in Australia around the same time. As Jon Piccini writes, 'In the 1970s more Australians were talking about a wider array of rights than ever before.'[74]

To educate and mobilize citizens, the Australian FFHC published and distributed a monthly periodical, *Hungerscope*. As was the case in the eighteenth and nineteenth

---

[71] Australian FFHC Victorian State Committee, 'Campaign News' 10 November 1971, Folder 522 '1971 State Corres. Vic.', Box 81, Records of AFFHC.

[72] Michael L. Gillette, *Launching the War on Poverty: An Oral History* (New York: Oxford University Press, 2010), 117 and 206.

[73] Martin Carcasson, 'Negotiating the Paradoxes of Poverty: Presidential Rhetoric on Welfare from Johnson to Clinton', PhD Diss. (Texas A & M University, 2004), 20, 51–4.

[74] Jon Piccini, *Human Rights in Twentieth Century Australia* (Cambridge: Cambridge University Press, 2019), 155. Most prominent campaigns included anti-conscription and anti-Vietnam War [see Nick Irving, 'Anti-conscription Protest, Liberal Individualism and the Limits of National Myths in the Global 1960s', *History Australia* 14 (2017): 187–201] and student activism [see Kate Murphy, '"In the Backblocks of Capitalism": Australian Student Activism in the Global 1960s', *Australian Historical Studies* 46 (2015): 252–68].

centuries, print media was a central apparatus through which humanitarian organizations could build a constituency of committed activists and reach new audiences. In the case of *Hungerscope*, the magazine included inspirational stories of individuals raising funds through various activities that could serve as models for others to emulate. For example, during their annual appeal in 1971, school students participated in 'starvathons' to raise money. Such publicity stunts were performed at Hawthorn and Macleod primary schools in Melbourne's eastern suburbs and at Devonport Secondary College in northern Tasmania. These schools raised modest sums: $30 at Hawthorn, $71 at Macleod and $200 at Devonport. But from the perspective of FFHC, these school fundraisers were invaluable as a source of media exposure. By using children, FFHC prepared human-interest stories, ready for publication in metropolitan and community newspapers with the potential to influence citizen readers as well as political leaders.[75]

Furthermore, the activism of young people had ripple effects throughout the community. Victorian State Director Ron Butt wrote to the national committee,

> SCHOOL MAILING. We believe our 1971 School mailing 'hit the spot'. Hundreds of schools phoned or wrote asking for posters, leaflets, display kits, slides etc. The financial response this year has been staggering in its proportions.
>
> THE FASTERS. These remarkable young people acted as a real catalyst within the community. They had tremendous value in the fields of:-
> PUBLICITY
> FUNDRAISING
> CHURCH AND SCHOOL FUNDRAISING
> POLITICAL INFLUENCE (capitalization and underlining in original)[76]

The mobilization of children and youth was not unique to the Australian FFHC. The British office of FFHC similarly harnessed the idealism of youth to promote their cause while at the same time attempting to mould British young people into model citizens, creating the next generation of international humanitarians.[77] Adolescent Canadians,

---

[75] For coverage of Victorian school starvathons, see 'Boys Give Up Lunch for Others', *Melbourne Herald*, 30 September 1971; 'Just Rice For Lunch. Children Give $71 towards Hunger Appeal', *Diamond Valley News*, 28 September 1971; '"Refugee Lunch" Ends Fast', *Melbourne Sun-News Pictorial*, 6 October 1971. All press clippings in Folder 399 'Vic Press Clippings 1971', Box 66, Records of the Australian Freedom from Hunger Campaign (henceforth AFFHC). For Tasmanian coverage, see 'After Their Fast', *Launceston Examiner*, 5 October 1971 in Folder 434, '1971 Interstate Press Clippings (TAS)', Box 71, Records of AFFHC.

[76] Australian Freedom from Hunger Campaign, Victorian State Committee. 'Brief Report on the 1971 Appeal by State Director Ron Butt, 25/11/1971', Folder 107, Box 19, Records of AFFHC. State donation figures from 'Report on Recommendations from State Directors' Meeting – December 12 and 13' in Folder 107, Box 19, Records of AFFHC.

[77] Anna Bocking-Welch, 'Youth against Hunger: Service, Activism and the Mobilisation of Young Humanitarians in 1960s Britain', *European Review of History* 23 (2016): 154–70; Anna Bocking-Welch, 'Imperial Legacies and International Discourses; British involvement in the United Nations Freedom from Hunger Campaign', *Journal of Imperial and Commonwealth History* 40 (2012): 879–96.

too, participated in the Miles for Millions walkathon in the 1960s and 1970s, raising millions of dollars to address global hunger and poverty. These empathetic and optimistic 'milers', as they were known, were not just participants in a worthy cause; they were fundamental to the organizing of fundraising events for a wider social movement that challenged global inequalities.[78]

Like CAA, the FFHC was most successful in the state of Victoria. Ron Butt proudly declared that his branch had received the highest number of donations since 1963. With $523,000 donated by mid-December 1971, Victoria represented nearly half of all donations received but accounted for 28 per cent of the national population.[79] The fact that the Victorian branch of the FFHC received donations at nearly twice the rate that one would expect from their population size can be explained by two reasons. First, the Victorian branch leveraged their established resources, such as experienced professional staff, well-connected volunteers and widely distributed publications. Other states, such as Queensland, Tasmania and South Australia, lacked the social infrastructure necessary to maximize fundraising during a crisis. Second, the Victorian branch used its relationship with CAA, another organization highly concentrated in the southern state. As noted earlier, CAA directed the hunger strikers to direct their fundraising activities towards FFHC. The hunger strikers and the media circus that ensued is the subject of Chapter 7. For the moment though, it is worthwhile noting the ways in which CAA and FFHC interacted and cross-fertilized, ensuring that both organizations maximized their fundraising capacity throughout 1971 and 1972.

Records of the Australian FFHC also provide financial contributions at the level of suburbs and country towns. Using socio-economic statistics from the 1971 census, we can then draw inferences about the types of people who donated cash to the FFHC. Table 6.1 lists the top fifteen municipalities by total donations received. It also lists the proportion of the labour force population who were classified as 'white collar' and the average weekly rent for households. Occupation and rent are used as indicators of the class background and degree of affluence of residents. The municipality of Camberwell was by far the leading donor area. This municipality in 1971 included wealthy suburbs of Toorak as well as Camberwell. The industrial satellite town of Geelong was second, which was anomalous given its low rate of white-collar workers and lower incomes, as suggested by average weekly rents. The next eight municipalities were all along the middle class south-eastern suburban corridor, except for Melbourne, whose population lived mostly in the suburb of Carlton, adjacent to Melbourne University. The low rents in this area were most likely the result of a mix of cheap student housing and old workers' cottages. The poor area of Sunshine, in Melbourne's outer northern suburbs, was listed as the eleventh highest donating municipality. Home to many labourers as well as suffering high rates of unemployment, the presence of Sunshine on this list

---

[78] Tamara Myers, 'Local Action and Global Imagining: Youth, International Development and the Walkathon Phenomenon in Sixties' and Seventies' Canada', *Diplomatic History* 38 (2012): 282, 292.
[79] Report on Recommendations from State Directors, 13 December 1971, 3, Folder 107, Box 19, Records of AFFHC. Proportion of population calculated from Australian Bureau of Statistics, *1971 Census. Bulletin 3 Demographic Characteristics. Part 2 Victoria* (Canberra: AGPS, 1972), 2 and Australian Bureau of Statistics, *1971 Census. Bulletin 3 Demographic Characteristics. Part 9 Australia* (Canberra: AGPS, 1972), 2.

Table 6.1 Top Fifteen Donating Municipalities in Victoria against Economic Background

Rank	Municipality	Money received ($)	% White collar	Av. weekly rent ($)
1	Camberwell	27,900	34.62	22.72
2	Geelong	17,205	14.64	14.38
3	Prahran	16,367	25.92	20.17
4	Melbourne	16,120	24.35	15.88
5	Waverley	15,351	27.22	22.64
6	Moorabbin	12,633	19.59	20.46
7	Heidelberg	11,261	22.97	20.66
8	Doncaster	10,742	31.65	22.7
9	Kew	10,581	35.32	22.97
10	Box Hill	9,847	24.87	21.04
11	Sunshine	9,621	7.53	14.62
12	Malvern	9,550	29.90	21.28
13	Brighton	8,703	35.70	22.59
14	Knox	7,065	15.90	17.8
15	Ballarat	5,227	18.05	12.68

* White collar includes professional and administrative work; proportion calculated from labour force population, not total adult population.
Source: Amounts donated from Australian Freedom from Hunger Campaign, Victorian State Committee, 'List of Money Received from Municipalities as at 10th December 1971', in Folder 522, Box 81, Records of AFFHC. Occupations and weekly rent data from Census of Population and Housing, 'Bulletin 7. Characteristics of the Population and Dwellings Local Government Areas. Part 2. Victoria (Canberra: AGPS, 1973).

was unexpected and appeared atypical. When most of the municipalities listed were broadly middle class, why did the working-class residents of Sunshine and Geelong donate to the FFHC? This question is even more confounding when situated within the context of patterns of giving in Australia. In contemporary studies, there is a clear correlation between personal income and amount donated to charities; there is also a strong correlation between education (and presumably occupation) and donations to charities.[80] As the left-leaning Australian Council of Social Service reported in 2004, 'income is a critical factor in the giving of money and overlays other factors'.[81]

Arguably, there are two reasons that explain the above-average donations from Geelong and Sunshine. First, local schoolchildren and young people played a significant role in persuading residents to support the 1971 FFHC appeal. The idealism and earnestness of children and young people 'cut through', to use a marketing phrase, to residents in a way not possible for organization-led campaigning, which sometimes trigger feelings of suspicion (e.g. how much of my money is spent on administration?)

---

[80] Myles McGregor-Lowndes, Marie Crittall, Denise Conroy and Robyn Keast, *Individual Giving and Volunteering: Giving Australia 2016 Report* (Brisbane: Australian Government Department of Social Services, 2017), xxi.
[81] Australian Council of Social Service, *Giving Australia: Research on Philanthropy in Australia* (Canberra: AGPS, 2005), 9.

and parochialism (e.g. we should look after our own first before sending money overseas). Students from both Sunshine High School and Geelong's Gordon Institute of Technology initiated a range of fundraising activities, such as public fasting, walkathons, dances, car washes and raffles.⁸² Rather than simply asking directly for money, these children and youth offered a performance of some kind in exchange for donations. The performative nature of school fundraisers was critical as donors could *see* how their donations were educating young people to become compassionate and civic minded, traits that engendered positive reinforcement through the gifting of donations.

Second, the Communist Party of Australia (CPA) took a keen interest in events in Bangladesh. Not surprisingly, the CPA viewed the war for independence as a class struggle in which Bangladeshis had been exploited economically for years by the 'comprador bourgeois elements who have ruled in Pakistan'.⁸³ The CPA was politically aligned with the Maoist elements within the Bangladesh liberation movement and supported the socialist agenda of Sheikh Mujibur Rahman and the Awami League. Throughout 1971, the weekly newspaper of the CPA, the *Tribune*, provided extensive coverage on the war. Importantly, the newspaper went beyond the shock imagery and human-interest stories that dominated mainstream newspapers and instead opted for lengthy articles that contextualized the conflict.⁸⁴ The newspaper also provided space for individuals to announce publicly offers of assistance to the liberation movement by supporting the communist parties of India and East Bengal.⁸⁵

Communists in Australia were no fringe movement. Australian communists reached their zenith in the late 1940s and, over decades, had a pervasive influence on the local trade union movement. In the following decades, the CPA was challenged by the centre-left Australian Labor Party for leadership of the Australian working class. Still, in the early 1970s, the CPA remained a political force that shaped left-wing thinking on a range of issues, such as the peace movement, indigenous rights and migrant settlement.⁸⁶ Consequently, within communist circles, the Bangladeshi independence war was a major talking point and an issue that likely emanated out to factory floors around Australia. By framing the Bangladesh war as part of a broader

---

[82] Victorian Freedom from Hunger Campaign, *News Bulletin*, December 1971, in Folder 522, Box 81, Records of AFFHC.
[83] Anonymous, 'Pakistan-India-Ceylon: A Sub-Continent in Turmoil', *Communist Party Tribune*, 7 April 1971, 9.
[84] See Denis Freney, 'East Bengal: Profile of Revolt', 19 May 1971, 9; Denis Freney, 'Pakistan: The Politics of a Human Disaster', 16 June 1971, 9; Anonymous, 'Bangladesh Call for Liberation', 18 August 1971, 8; Anonymous, 'CPA backs Bangladesh', 1 September 1971, 10; multiple articles, 20 October 1971, 1, 9, 11; Anonymous, 'Bangla Desh action c'ttee', 17 November 1971, 12; W. E. Gollan, 'Revolutionary perspectives in Bangla Desh', 8 December 1971, 9 and Anonymous, 'The "three wars" in India-Pakistan', 14 December 1971, 9.
[85] T. Gergos, Mt Waverley, 'Pakistan', 16 June 1971, 2; Mark Lang, Carnegie, 'Pakistan', 23 June 1971, 2; Anonymous, 'Pakistan: seamen's relief offer', 3 November 1971, 12.
[86] Douglas Jordan, 'Conflict in the Unions: The Communist Party of Australia, Politics and the Trade Union Movement, 1945–1960', PhD Diss., Victoria University, 2011, 69; Stuart Macintyre, *The Party: The Communist Party of Australia from Heyday to Reckoning* (Sydney: Allen & Unwin, 2022).

working-class struggle, Australian left-wing activists could appeal to the concerns of factory workers and labourers who may not ordinarily identify with overseas aid appeals. In short, the Australian FFHC appeal was so successful in Sunshine and Geelong because of individual activists who attracted supported from two traditionally disempowered groups: children and the working class.

Conclusion

'Just who do we think we are?', asked Bernhard Llewellyn to Oxfam, the question with which I started this chapter. Llewellyn's question was not rhetorical, and no doubt many humanitarian NGOs struggled to find an answer. For grassroots organizations such as CAA/Oxfam and the FFHC, they knew who they were by virtue of who they were not. They rejected elitism, paternalism and political neutrality. By extension, CAA and the FFHC encouraged 'people to people humanitarianism', reciprocity and mutual understanding. But CAA and the FFHC were not immune from change themselves. As we have seen in this chapter, both organizations became increasingly secular and overtly political in their orientation. CAA and the FFHC both began the 1960s viewing humanitarian aid through a political lens; by the time of the Bangladeshi reconstruction in 1972, they were ensconced in wider struggles for rights and freedom. In the words of Alan Smith, 'liberation is the new term for development'.[87] It seems that this humanitarian aligned himself with Third World liberation struggles and the emancipation of peoples oppressed by centuries of colonial domination and economic exploitation.

CAA and the FFHC introduced new forms of fundraising and consciousness raising at a time when citizens embraced a more active role in public life than in previous decades. This mattered because these two grassroots organizations cooperated to democratize humanitarian aid by transferring much responsibility to local groups and individuals. In doing so, CAA and the FFHC tapped into previously underutilized populations for support, such as children, youth and the working class. By empowering these groups, CAA and the FFHC provided a platform for these marginalized individuals to express outrage at systemic inequality, social justice and government indifference. As Food for Peace commented in 1958, aid 'is a personal thing, not something you can leave to governments alone'. This early sentiment shaped what would become Oxfam Australia and its close ally, the FFHC. But by enabling individuals, CAA and the FFHC inadvertently encouraged citizens to take matters into their own hands, operating well beyond the realms of established humanitarian NGO practice. Such individual humanitarianism will be the subject of the next chapter.

---

[87] Alan Smith, letter to Fran Newell, 25 November 1971, in Folder 116, Box 20, Records of AFFHC.

7

The individuals: Moira Dynon, Paul Poernomo and citizen letters of protest

While the NGOs covered in this book could all be classified as citizen-driven, in this chapter we see citizen-driven aid taken to its natural extreme: the lone humanitarian who often acted in isolation or with a handful of supporters. This chapter examines three examples of such individual humanitarianism. First, it explores the actions of Moira Dynon, a well-connected upper middle class Melbourne housewife with an established record of providing aid to India and speaking out on a range of social and political issues since the 1950s. Next, this chapter examines Paul Poernomo, a hunger striker who sought to raise awareness and funds for refugees in India. Lastly, it analyses the 2,500 letters written by citizens to Australian Opposition Leader Gough Whitlam, pleading him to increase Australian government aid to Bangladeshi refugees in India.

This chapter demonstrates the challenges faced by individual humanitarians. Dynon and Poernomo endured hostile acts from government as well as significant demands on their time and resources. In spite of these hardships, individual humanitarians maintained advantages over traditional aid organizations, such as their capacity to generate publicity, elicit sympathetic media coverage of their activities and create a public following. Despite acting on their own with a handful of supporters, this chapter illustrates the impact of these individuals at various levels: the community at large, the NGO sector and government policy. Although such do-gooders were maligned in the past for their ineptitude, ushering in the wave of professionalization and introduction of the technocrat of the mid-twentieth century, in the 1970s these individual humanitarians used their alleged amateurism to their advantage. With nothing personal to gain from lobbying their cause, these citizens became the epitome of authenticity, an increasingly admired and rare trait in a materialistic world.

Moira Dynon, a Catholic internationalist

Moira Dynon was an energetic member of civil society and passionate about many causes. In the 1950s and 1960s, Dynon was a member of the local branch of the Australian Association for the United Nations, the Australian Asian Association, the Catholic Women's League and, at different times, both the Liberal Party and Australian Labor Party. She advocated for the marginalized Japanese children fathered by Australian servicemen, supported migrant welfare services and opposed the continuance of the Asian-exclusive white Australia immigration policy.[1] Dynon found the activities of these NGOs frustrating however, feeling the 'need was for something more definite and practical'.[2] When famine struck India in 1964, Dynon established the Aid India campaign to help prevent starvation.[3] Dynon explained that she felt compelled to 'do what she could, in her own way, to bring immediate aid to those, particularly the disadvantaged, who needed help at once'.[4] Over the next six years, the Aid India campaign shipped processed milk equivalent to twenty-five million pints, valued at over A$800,000.[5] Figure 7.1 shows a photograph of Dynon checking a consignment of 115 tonnes of powdered milk, valued at A$50,000, at her home before sea passage to India in 1966.

During the 1960s Dynon established a keen understanding of what worked, both rhetorically in Australia and practically in India, which augured well for her response to the 1971 refugee crisis. In her decades of campaigning, Dynon proved herself to be an engaging public speaker, making speeches across Australia on topics including anti-communism (1959), Australian-Japanese children (1964), international cooperation and development (1965), food relief for India (1966, 1968) and women's equality (1970).[6] In these engagements, Dynon not only developed her skills in oratory but also learned how to sell her message and differentiate the Aid India campaign from the many other worthy humanitarian organizations. Dynon distinguished her campaign from others by emphasizing the person-to-person nature of this aid, therefore arguing that every individual could, and should, make a difference to ease avoidable suffering. By focusing on friendship, goodwill and cooperation, Dynon stressed the importance of personal relationships, which implicitly contrasted her campaign from the dehumanizing forces of modern bureaucracies and professionalized NGOs. Dynon also proved to be a tireless worker, willing to travel great distances to spread her message. Rather than limiting herself to the major cities, Dynon ventured to many country towns and regional centres, areas often overlooked by elites. Furthermore, Dynon understood the importance of mobilizing children in her campaigns. From 1964 to 1970, Dynon secured support from the Victorian Education Department for her to approach schools to participate in the food appeal and offered informative talks to schoolchildren in her 'spare time'.[7] Husband John Dynon reflected on the impact

---

[1] John F. Dynon, *Moira Dynon: An Inspiring Life* (Melbourne: Jacinta Efthim, 2020), 151, 155, 176–81. For background on Australia's immigration policies, see Rachel Stevens, *Immigration Policy from 1970 to the Present* (New York: Routledge, 2016), 26–30 and Rachel Stevens, 'After the "Great White Walls" Came Down: Debating the Ethnicity of Immigrants in Australia and the USA, 1980–1990', *Immigrants & Minorities* 32 (2014): 267–70.
[2] Dynon, *Moira Dynon*, 198.
[3] This organization involved numerous name changes and for brevity I will refer to Dynon's NGO as Aid India campaign. From 1964 to 1965, the NGO was called Aid for India meeting; from 1966 to 1968, it was called Aid for India campaign; from late 1969, the name changed again to Aid India campaign. Within this organization the Victorian branch also ran the Milk for India campaign in which citizens could donate cans of powdered or condensed milk.
[4] Dynon, *Moira Dynon*, 186.
[5] 'Malvern housewife fights against Indian starvation', 28 October 1971, *The Advocate*, 9.
[6] For transcripts of these speeches, see https://moiradynon.com.au/category/talks/.
[7] 'Malvern housewife fights against Indian starvation'.

Figure 7.1 Mrs M. Dynon checks a load of milk at her Melbourne home. Photographer: Keith Byron, NAA: A1501, A6702/3.

of accessing schools on the campaign, writing: 'Thousands who were children at Australian schools … would have memories of gifting tins of processed milk. In the community, there existed a genuine love of giving to this cause.'[8]

Dynon also adopted a pragmatic approach to aid, choosing to donate high-protein processed and powdered milk products that would be most useful for the recipients. Her belief in the value of milk products was summed up in its campaign slogan, 'Feeling sorry won't help, MILK will!'[9] Dynon wrote in a letter to her husband, 'It seems incredible that the milk can be made to go so far and to do so much for so many needy children, women, and refugees'. She reiterated this point in a subsequent letter, 'it is amazing how far the milk powder gifts are stretched'. Revealingly, Dynon

---

[8] Dynon, *Moira Dynon*, 322, 349.
[9] Campaign poster, unfiled correspondence, Dynon family papers. At the time of publication, the Dynon family papers were being transferred to the National Library of Australia, see MS 10714.

also commented that details of the distribution of milk products 'should keep the critics quiet'.[10] As has been shown throughout this book, in the mid-twentieth century humanitarian organizations were placed under public scrutiny in which donors insisted on transparency and accountability in the sector. In practice, this meant that relief organizations professionalized and employed technical, salaried staff and commissioned external reviews. Dynon's approach, in contrast, seems amazingly simple: she asked and continued to ask recipients what goods would be most useful and appropriate for local conditions.[11] To ensure cost-effectiveness and avoid wasteful spending, Dynon negotiated free international shipping, first with the Menzies government and from 1967 with the Shipping Corporation of India.

Dynon routinely described consignments of powdered milk as an expression of friendship to India, and her desire to strengthen and promote understanding between the people of India and Australia.[12] To reach these goals, Dynon led by example. She completed two solo trips of India in the late 1960s and a third trip in August and September 1971 at the height of the Bangladeshi refugee crisis. During these trips, Dynon met with Indian humanitarian workers in New Delhi and Kolkata, and Indian politicians, including Indira Gandhi, in 1967.[13] These meetings enabled Dynon to foster relationships directly with those responsible for distributing aid. The familiarity of Dynon with Indian cultures helped her educate Australian audiences on the importance of fostering goodwill with Indians. Indeed, during her second trip Dynon wrote in a letter to her husband, John, 'You know, I always feel so at home with Bengalis.' Dynon commented that 'Calcutta was so interesting, so busy and so wonderful. I hated leaving there this morning.'[14] Dynon urged Australian citizens and leaders that 'we owe a special duty to our neighbour, India, the world's largest democracy – and I believe it [providing aid] is a simple exercise in political wisdom'.[15] By emphasizing India's democratic tradition, Dynon was implicitly comparing India favourably with authoritarian and atheist regimes, such as the People's Republic of China. Dynon made this case explicit in an address to Bairnsdale in country Victoria in February 1971. She said:

> In Asia, democracy of any sort is a rare jewel. When the people of the largest nation in the world are forced to live in accordance with the thoughts of Chairman Mao, we should be truly grateful that the second largest [nation], thinking what thoughts it chooses, goes freely to the polls. Especially in this region of military and princely dictatorships, and rubber stamp parliaments, India *merits the respect for all those who value freedom for her faith*, amply demonstrated in the past, that the basis of power is not force, but the free will of the people. [italics added][16]

---

[10] Dynon, *Moira Dynon*, 304, 314.
[11] Ibid., 193.
[12] Ibid., 194.
[13] Ibid., 256.
[14] Ibid., 303.
[15] Ibid., 325.
[16] Moira Dynon, 'India Today', address in Bairnsdale, Victoria, 25 February 1971, accessed 26 November 2022, www.moiradynon.com.au.

In these comments, Dynon presented the recipient of humanitarian aid as one worthy of respect and admiration, not pity. Contrary to typical depictions of the passive, helpless victim in need of salvation, Dynon argued that while many Indians may be impoverished and in need of food aid, that country has achieved political freedom unlike other decolonized states in Asia. Dynon conveyed to her listeners that India and Australia had far more in common (freedoms of expression, association and religion) than they had in opposition, particularly within the context of creeping communism in south-east Asia.

Dynon's Aid India campaign was important for three reasons: first, it demonstrated how a charismatic, energetic and determined woman could create the networks to establish a significant humanitarian programme without the challenges of a traditional charity or NGO. Second, by the time of the 1971 Bangladeshi refugee crisis, Dynon had the logistical and social infrastructure in place to enable a swift response to the humanitarian crisis. Third, the campaign served as the gateway to developing Dynon's understanding of India and its specific needs. Therefore, building on the foundations of years of networking, advocacy and fundraising, Dynon was prepared to respond to calls for assistance after the Bhola cyclone hit Bangladesh in November 1970.

Aid for Bangladesh

Dynon campaigned to raise awareness and funds on three related but distinct causes from 1970 to 1972: cyclone victims in Bangladesh, Bangladeshi refugees in India and reconstruction efforts in newly independent Bangladesh. Although ostensibly campaigning for three distinct causes, in this section I will analyse Dynon's humanitarian work from late 1970 to early 1972 collectively. Table 7.1 lists donated cash and in-kind donations by date, destination, contents and approximate value. It should be noted that donations to West Bengal were specifically earmarked for distribution among refugees rather than Indian women and children, which had been the case since 1964. Looking at Table 7.1, one could assume that donations sent equated to donations received. Yet the experience of Dynon reveals the barriers (official, logistical, political and accidental) to ensuring that aid reached their intended recipients.

By the early 1970s Dynon had encountered interference and obstruction from the Holt, Gorton and McMahon federal governments (1966–72), reversing the friendly relations under the Menzies government (1949–66). In an undated handwritten note, Dynon outlined the various tactics she suspected the government was employing to undermine her humanitarian work. She wrote:

1. Obvious hostility at Federal Government and top departmental levels and obvious resentment of our influence.
2. "This campaign has got to be stopped"
3. E.P.D.R. [East Pakistan Disaster Relief]
   a. Delay
   b. Receipt wrongly made out

Table 7.1 Cash and In-Kind Donations, December 1970 to March 1972

Date	Destination	Contents	Value (in A$)
3/12/1970	East Pakistan	Cheque	3000
3/12/1970	East Pakistan	565 cartons baby food and 10 cartons powdered milk	N/A
7/1/1971	East Pakistan	Cheque	3000
21/3/1971	West Bengal	41 cartons powdered milk	410
		439 cartons of baby food, soup, 13 × 56lb bags of milk;	
27/4/1971	West Bengal	powdered milk	N/A
21/5/1971	West Bengal	Powdered milk and food stuffs	4000
24/6/1971	West Bengal	Milk products, baby food and blankets	N/A
30/6/1971	West Bengal	200 cartons condensed milk	N/A
30/7/1971	West Bengal	260 cartons macaroni, 70 cartons soup, 100 cartons broth	N/A
18/8/1971	West Bengal	5 crates foodstuffs	N/A
8/11/1971	West Bengal	Cheque	1000
29/2/1972	Bangladesh	1 case tinned food, 20 cases Carnation milk, 28 bags sugar, 8 bags children's clothes and blankets	9000
3/3/1972	Bangladesh	738 cartons broth and soup	2000

Source: Dynon family papers.

    c. Commonwealth Bank "trick"
    d. If so, a well-aimed smear campaign could be contemplated even although charges could be refuted
4. Telephone tapped
5. Slow mail – some mail from India not received[17]

Individually, each of these items may seem inconsequential, but when written down as a list, Dynon believed that a concerted effort was at play, particularly by figures in the Department of Foreign Affairs (DFA), to stymie her humanitarian activities. Dynon's fear that her telephone was tapped may seem far-fetched, but at the time many political activists were under surveillance by the Australian Security Intelligence Organisation, the Australian equivalent of MI5 that was established in 1949 to counter communist infiltration and other subversive activities.[18] John Dynon similarly believed that his wife had been subject to a smear campaign in which the Aid India campaign had been maligned in the press. He wrote:

---

[17] Moira Dynon handwritten notes, undated. Folder 'Personal (Esp. re: East Pakistan Emergency Correspondence)', Dynon family papers.
[18] John Blaxland, *The Protest Years: The Official History of ASIO, 1963–1975* (Sydney: Allen & Unwin, 2015), chapters 3 and 4.

There were the continual references in some of the press throughout Australia to the effect that quantities of the milk had been left uncollected on the docks in India or had got into wrong hands. The source of these allegations could not be ascertained, and they appeared to be mischievous allegations made for dubious reasons.[19]

These examples illustrate the potential problems that individual humanitarians encounter, particularly when their work runs contrary to government policy. Arguably, it is much easier for governments to intimidate individuals into silence than large organizations, especially those that are embedded within a larger international federation, such as the Red Cross or Oxfam. Regrettably, in this instance government hostility went far beyond reputational damage for Dynon and her campaign, resulting in failures to provide aid in time for those in most need.

Table 7.1 shows that Dynon fundraised promptly in the wake of the Bhola cyclone. On 3 December 1970, Dynon sent two letters to the Australian Deputy High Commissioner in Dhaka Jim Allen. In the first, Dynon enclosed a copy of a cheque for A$3,000 made payable to the DFA, which would then be dispensed to the Deputy High Commission in Dhaka for relief purposes. In the second, Dynon listed the material aid that she had shipped. On 8 December, Allen sent a letter to Dynon confirming receipt of these letters and acknowledged that 'gifts of foodstuffs and money which are now on their way to Dacca'.[20] In these letters Dynon expressly asked Allen to distribute the donated aid 'at your discretion, on the principle of need'.[21] On 7 January 1971, Dynon sent another letter to Allen, this time offering an additional cash donation of A$3,000 and outlined her plans to ship further material aid the following week. In this correspondence, Dynon routinely asked Allen to provide a receipt on arrivals of goods and funds, and some indication of how the relief was used, 'as such receipt is required by our Honorary Treasurer for audit purposes'.[22]

For the Bhola cyclone campaign, Dynon broke with her traditional practice of liaising directly with local humanitarian organizations and instead channelled aid through DFA. The inclusion of the governmental department proved to be her undoing. For months Dynon telephoned and corresponded with DFA officials in Melbourne and Canberra on the whereabouts of cash and in-kind donations. A Canberran DFA officer within the aid policy section, M. R. Casson, confirmed to Dynon on 13 January 1971 that her second cheque for A$3,000, issued on 7 January 1971, had been 'mislaid and an intensive search has failed to recover them [sic]'.[23] Casson advised Dynon to

---

[19] John Dynon, 'The Later Years: 1971 to 1976', draft of chapter for biography, Dynon family papers.
[20] Jim Allen, letter to Moira Dynon, 8 December 1970, filed in folder '1970 E. Pak Relief', Dynon family papers.
[21] Moira Dynon, letter to Jim Allen, re: cheque, 3 December 1970, filed in folder '1970 E. Pak Relief', Dynon family papers.
[22] Ibid. and Moira Dynon, letter to Jim Allen, re: cheque, 7 January 1971, filed in folder '1970 E. Pak Relief', Dynon family papers.
[23] M. R. Casson, DFA, letter to Moira Dynon, 13 January 1971, filed in folder '1970 E. Pak Relief', Dynon family papers.

cancel the cheque and reissue a new one, a procedure that Dynon later described as the 'Commonwealth Bank trick'.[24] Alarmingly, on 7 January 1971 Allen sent a letter to DFA confirming that he had not received the first cheque of A$3,000 or the consignment of baby food.[25] A foreign affairs officer in Melbourne, A. H. Maudouit, then forwarded Allen's letter to Dynon on 10 March 1971. Predictably, Dynon was outraged by DFA ineptitude, writing on 19 March 1971:

> It is with deep concern that I note that in his memorandum dated 7th January 1971 … Mr Allen said: 'So far we have seen no sign either of (a) the consignment of baby food or of (b) the cheque for $(A)3000.00' …
>
> I am well aware that in recent months circumstances in East Pakistan have been very difficult. However, there appears to have been a very long delay in the transfer to Mr Allen of funds which were urgently needed for relief. Indeed I have received no information from Mr Allen as to the exact date on which the amounts were received, or in fact that he has received them … I have seen no other correspondence from Mr Allen except for the letter dated 8 December.[26]

Dynon was clearly frustrated with the silence from Allen in Dhaka and the failure of DFA officials to provide information on the locations and uses of donated aid. Such information was vital for the day-to-day running of this campaign. As Dynon explained to Maudouit in the same letter, she felt a responsibility to donors to be able to trace the impact of donations, an obligation that DFA was impeding. Dynon was presumably infuriated by dismissive remarks from DFA. For example, in response to the letter from Dynon on 19 March, Maudouit assured Dynon, 'most of the queries you raise will be resolved as the result of the present enquiries now being undertaken by the department'.[27] It is improbable that Dynon would have found such assurances any comfort, particularly since it was DFA itself that had caused the significant delays in the transfer of relief.

The persistence of Dynon with an obstructionist government department ultimately yielded results. In April 1971 Dynon received her first correspondence from Allen in 1971. In a letter dated 26 February 1971, Allen confirmed he had received the two cash donations of A$3,000. The food consignments, however, were proving difficult to track. Allen supposed that the first consignment of goods was misappropriated in Singapore en route to Dhaka and suspected that the aid ended up in the hands of a British military aid team. Allen assured Dynon that even though he was 'not in a position to say just where the consignment … was finally used, I have no doubt in my own mind that it was put to good use somewhere'.[28] Furthermore, Allen presented the

---

[24] Dynon handwritten notes, undated. Folder 'Personal (Esp. re: East Pakistan Emergency Correspondence)', Dynon family papers.
[25] Jim Allen, letter to DFA, 7 January 1971, filed in folder '1970 E. Pak Relief', Dynon family papers.
[26] Moira Dynon, letter to A. H. Maudouit, DFA, 19 March 1971, filed in folder '1970 E. Pak Relief', Dynon family papers.
[27] A. H. Maudouit, letter to Moira Dynon, 23 March 1971, filed in folder '1970 E. Pak Relief', Dynon family papers.
[28] Jim Allen, letter to Moira Dynon, 26 February 1971, received April 1971, filed in folder 'Aust Govt EPDR correspondence', Dynon family papers.

situation as unavoidable: 'One just has to accept that that sort of thing was part of the rush and confusion that prevailed during those first few days after the cyclone struck.'[29] Allen was even less optimistic about the second consignment of goods shipped on 14 January 1971. At the time of writing this letter, 26 February, Allen feared that 'we are going to have a good deal of trouble with such a large number of small packages' and recommended that, in future, Dynon contain 'small packages within large, strongly constructed crates'. Even then Allen was pessimistic because 'these [secured crates] are frequently broken open and pilfered in transit'.[30] On 28 April 1971, Allen updated Dynon on the whereabout of the second consignment: 'I am afraid there seems to be a hoodoo on relief efforts from Melbourne.' The cargo boat containing the aid was unable to dock at Chittagong 'owing to political unrest at the time' and was rerouted to Penang, Malaysia, 'where it will wait until Chittagong starts functioning as a port again'.[31] In the end, the donated goods did not arrive for a further five months, nine months after shipment.[32] This circuitous journey illustrates that the giving of aid is arguably the easiest part of the humanitarian process, particularly in recipient countries affected by disasters and war, and with weak government structures. Allen's explanation, that the cargo ship could not dock at Chittagong port due to 'political unrest', was a euphemism for the raging civil war. By late April, Pakistani armed forces had captured urban centres and disrupted international transport links. Throughout the Bangladesh Liberation War foreigners were forbidden from entry and this ban probably extended to foreign vessels. When donated material aid did arrive, there remained opportunities for wrongful acquisition (as was the case with the first consignment) or theft.

Even cash donations can ultimately be used for other purposes if deemed suitable by the local actors responsible for disbursement. In the case of the two cheques of A$3,000 donated for cyclone victims in December 1970 and January 1971, Allen wrote to Dynon in October 1971 recommending that these funds be used to support internally displaced villagers who were seeking sanctuary in Nagori, a town 15 miles northwest of Dhaka. Allen explained to Dynon that thousands of destitute people, 'mostly Hindus and some Christians and Muslims', had gathered at a Roman Catholic mission in Nagori after fleeing their villages destroyed by the Pakistani Army. He acknowledged that although 'to some extent help has reached the people in the cyclone area', in his view the refugees in Nagori were more worthy of the aid because they 'have nothing. Their plight, quite literally, is desperate.' Allen compared conditions in Nagori with the refugee camps in West Bengal, which Dynon had recently visited and concluded: 'I am sure you will agree that no human need anywhere could be greater than the need in some of these refugee centres.' Reflecting on the politically sensitive situation of the time, Allen suggested that Dynon reply by telegram with the singular word 'AGREE' to avoid raising concerns from the authorities.[33] Presumably, Dynon

[29] Ibid.
[30] Ibid.
[31] Jim Allen, letter to Moira Dynon, 28 April 1971, unfiled correspondence, Dynon family papers.
[32] Jim Allen, letter to Moira Dynon, 30 September 1971, unfiled correspondence, Dynon family papers.
[33] Jim Allen, letter to Moira Dynon, 12 October 1971, unfiled correspondence, Dynon family papers.

did agree. In February 1972 Allen corresponded with Dynon once more with an exasperated tone: 'At long last, the money that you collected and sent 15 months ago for cyclone relief has now been spent on relief work which, though not connected with the cyclone, was every bit as urgent.'[34]

In this letter and a subsequent letter dated 25 June 1972, Allen included photographic slides and written reports on the running of the refugee centres penned by local workers. Allen appreciated the significance of providing humanitarian organizations with visual and textual evidence of impact, both to satisfy donor needs and assist with future fundraising efforts. Interestingly, these materials were to be shared with the Australian Red Cross – which, at that stage, was working closely with the Bangladesh Red Cross – indicating that the issue of a dearth of publicity materials was still plaguing this giant of Australian humanitarianism (see Chapter 4). Of the donated A$6,000, approximately two-thirds were allocated to Nagori and used to purchase food (specifically wheat and pulses) and clothing.[35] Local relief worker Regin Corraya wrote that the goods purchased 'thus saved several thousands of lives from the hand of death and cool'.[36] Corraya also provided accounts that show that Allen transferred the funds in nine instalments from mid-November 1971 to 9 January 1972. Why Allen decided to pay in instalments is not clear, although it could have been a strategy to prevent pilfering. In addition to the Nagori camp, the remaining one-third of donated funds supported a second refugee operation in Jhalokati, eighty miles south of Dhaka. Local worker Noel Niren Malakar offered an extensive inventory of goods purchased, including men's, women's, and children's clothing (singlets, lungis, saris, chadors). Like Nagori, Allen transferred the funds in instalments rather than as a lump sum.

The itemized accounting of expenditures in both camps documents remarkably little waste. The only egregious use of funds was the A$10 spent on 'entertainment costs' in Nagori. Even the transportation costs were miniscule: A$130 for three trips to Jhalokati and A$130 for transport to Nagori. These expenses pale in comparison to the freight charges incurred by the Australian government when it donated in-kind aid, which was A$710,000 for refugees in India in 1971 and a further A$500,000 for aid donated during the 1972 Bangladeshi reconstruction.[37] In this example we see the advantages of small-scale humanitarianism over state-based ones. Dynon used her pre-existing relationships to organize free international freight with the Shipping Corporation of India and gratis distribution in-country via Jim Allen. Of course, the aid was delayed and used for purposes not originally intended at the time of donation, but the effects of the relief were undeniable. As Corraya wrote, 'Every dollar was spent in meeting real human needs.'[38] Malakar likewise expressed, 'by your

[34] Jim Allen, letter to Moira Dynon, 19 February 1972, unfiled correspondence, Dynon family papers. Also, copies are held at the National Library of Australia in MS 3118 'Mrs Dynon'.
[35] Noel Niren Malakar, letter to Moira Dynon, 23 February 1972, unfiled correspondence, Dynon family papers. Also, copies held at the National Library of Australia in MS 3118 'Mrs Dynon'.
[36] Sylvester Regin Corraya, letter to Moira Dynon, 2 February 1972, unfiled correspondence, Dynon family papers. Also, MS 3118 'Mrs Dynon'.
[37] Australian Parliament, House of Representatives, 22 October 1972, 3424.
[38] Corraya, letter to Moira Dynon, unfiled correspondence, Dynon family papers. Also, MS 3118 'Mrs Dynon'.

relief many people have been benefitted and they convey their endless gratitude to you'.[39]

During the 1971 refugee crisis, most international aid was directed towards the refugees in India because East Pakistan remained closed to foreigners. Moira Dynon's campaign capitalized on this pivot to India, and she made effective use of her networks in West Bengal where most refugees had settled. Since 1969 Dynon collaborated with the West Bengal Council of Women (WBCW) and throughout 1971 she corresponded extensively with WBCW workers. A junior member of staff, Utpala Misra, sent to Dynon long letters describing the causes of Bangladeshi displacement and conditions in the refugee camps. Misra also sent photographs and local press clippings, which Dynon found to be 'a great help in my [fundraising] efforts'.[40] She provided details on how the donations were distributed, information that would assist with further fundraising efforts. The WBCW eschewed dispensing the aid in the highly publicized refugee camps near Kolkata. Instead, the WBCW travelled one-and-a-half days from Kolkata to the remote and under-resourced refugee camp in Murshidabad.[41] The letters from India were more than merely informative. Indeed, the written descriptions of starvation and massacres had a potent emotional impact on Dynon. She wrote, 'I can fully understand how you feel. My heart aches for you, my other Bengali friends, and the suffering of children and people. Please be assured that I am doing everything I can.'[42] In this written correspondence then, we see the benefits of people-to-people humanitarianism in action, such as the unfiltered accounts of life in the refugee camps, the minimization of political meddling and directing donations to those most in need.

The disadvantage of this direct approach, however, was that the humanitarian work was not automatically subject to media coverage or publicity. This problem was highlighted by Misra: 'Most foreign aid comes to India either through the church or through official agencies. You must be one of the rare exceptions handing over things to Indian welfare organisations direct. Result – you get no publicity!'[43] Rather than accepting the situation or waiting for Dynon to organize her own publicity, Misra arranged publicity with the Australian Deputy High Commissioner in Kolkata, Douglas Sturkey. Misra explained to Dynon that because she had previously met Sturkey, who 'proved such a friendly spirit', she and WBCW president, Mrs N. Mukherji, 'decided to go whole-hog, photographed him "handing over" the cases to me, and lo and behold, we are in the newspapers today!'[44] For his part, Sturkey also corresponded with Dynon about the publicity stunt. Almost sheepishly, Sturkey asked for forgiveness rather than permission, writing:

---

[39] Malakar, letter to Moira Dynon, unfiled correspondence, Dynon family papers. Also, MS 3118 'Mrs Dynon'.
[40] Moira Dynon, letter to Utpala Misra, 21 June 1971, unfiled correspondence, Dynon family papers.
[41] Utpala Misra, letter to Moira Dynon, 20 August 1971, unfiled correspondence, Dynon family papers.
[42] Ibid. and Utpala Misra, letter to Moira Dynon, 3 July 1971, unfiled correspondence, Dynon family papers.
[43] Misra, letter to Dynon, 20 August 1971.
[44] Ibid.

With some trepidation lest I was treading on your toes I agreed to Mrs N. Mukherji's suggestion that I formally hand over to the West Bengal Council of Women the five crates of foodstuffs so kindly sent by your Aid India Campaign for the benefit of the refugees. Together with Mrs S. Misra I prepared the attached press release and issued it together with the enclosed set of photographs. I do hope that your Campaign will not feel that I have intruded in any way into your work. Mrs Mukherji and Mrs Misra were anxious that we should get as much publicity for you as possible.[45]

In response, Dynon politely expressed gratitude for the 'interest' shown by the Deputy High Commissioner and thanked him for sharing the press release and photographs, which 'will be of considerable interest to supporters of the campaign'.[46] The formal language used by Dynon in this letter may be because she did not know the Australian diplomat well. Alternatively, the letter conveyed an unease in Dynon about whipping up publicity for the sake of self-congratulation. While many humanitarian organizations were frequently seeking public recognition of their work, Dynon seemed uninterested in such obvious self-promotion. Arguably, Dynon's Catholic faith instilled in her a sense of obligation and duty to help those in distress. Dynon also had other methods at her disposal aside from publicity gimmicks, including educating schoolchildren and delivering speeches at public events.

Throughout this book I have outlined how humanitarian NGOs sought to raise public awareness of the 1971 refugee crisis and solicit donations from citizens. Methods of persuasion included launching public appeals, distributing posters and brochures, and using media to promote their cause. The approach of Dynon was different. She believed that speaking tours would educate people and unleash the possibility of changing public attitudes and behaviours. Dynon addressed diverse audiences, from young schoolchildren to the elderly in care homes. Importantly, Dynon allowed time after delivering her speech to answer audience questions. The dialogic nature of these exchanges not only helped Dynon correct misunderstandings, but it also placed the audience on equal footing with her. To reach many people across all sectors of society, Dynon was often on the road and away from her family, and her itinerary was exhausting. From family papers, it can be deduced that in 1971 Dynon made sixteen public addresses, a figure that no doubt underestimates the extent of her travels. For example, if mid-July 1971 was indicative of Dynon's typical movements, then she possibly made three addresses per week, each some distance from the next. On 14 July 1971, Dynon made a public speech in Ringwood, an outer suburb of Melbourne. On 20 July, Dynon spoke in country town Daylesford, two hours' drive north-west of Melbourne. The next day, Dynon addressed the public in Ballarat, a regional city fifty kilometres south-west of Daylesford.

---

[45] Douglas Sturkey, letter to Moira Dynon, 18 August 1971, filed in folder 'Bengal 1971 Crisis. Correspondence with MPs', Dynon family papers.
[46] Moira Dynon, letter to Douglas Sturkey, 16 September 1971, filed in folder 'Bengal 1971 Crisis. Correspondence with MPs', Dynon family papers.

It is evident from letters written by the public that Dynon was a persuasive and engaging public speaker. For example, eight-year-old Richard from Yarra Valley Church of England School in Ringwood, Victoria, sent this letter of thanks:

Dear Mrs Dynon,

Our class, P3, would like to thank you for coming out to visit us. Your talk was most interesting. And thank you for answering all our questions. We are very pleased to be able to help the Indian children.

Yours faithfully
Richard (P3)[47]

It is noteworthy that Dynon not only presented a talk to schoolchildren, but she also answered 'all our questions'. Rather than delivering information from the position of an aloof technocrat, Dynon's presentation and oratory skills ensured that her message was understood and also remembered. Similarly, on 1 June 1971 Dynon received a letter of gratitude and cheque for A$25 from Jean Towans, representing the Kangaroo Ground Presbyterian Ladies' Guild in country Victoria. Towans wrote:

We all thank you most sincerely for coming out to speak to us today. We know that your time is most valuable, and we do appreciate your coming so much. We also found your talk most informative. With every good wish for your campaign and kindest regards.[48]

In this example, we see how Dynon used her informative talks to solicit funds for the Bangladeshi refugee campaign. At a time when humanitarian NGOs embraced mass marketing, Dynon conversely opted for a localized and targeted approach. Arguably, Dynon's methods of persuasion – to inform and educate – was more effective than attempting to evoke pity and guilt, the typical communications strategy of the post-war NGO. The connection between small-scale talks and fundraising was made explicit by a teacher at Dynon's alma mater, Catholic girls' school Loreto Mandeville Hall, in Melbourne:

Dear Mrs Dynon,

Thank you so much for coming to speak at Monday's assembly. We all greatly appreciated what you said, and it certainly affected the girls suitably, as we have had direct giving appeals on both Monday and Tuesday and raised $80. I cannot recall ever having had an appeal of this type, when one gets no personal return, achieving anything like this success before.
We shall pray for the success of your [public] meeting [discussed below] on Friday and shall send a few girls to represent us.

With gratitude,
Yours sincerely in Christ,
(Sr) Anne McPhee[49]

[47] Unfiled correspondence, Dynon family papers.
[48] Ibid.
[49] 20 October 1971, filed in folder '9A Melbourne Town Hall 22–10–71', Dynon family papers.

This letter demonstrates the impact Dynon had on those she addressed. Her capacity to change attitudes and, more importantly, behaviours cannot be underestimated. Scholars have written extensively on the visual representations of humanitarian objects (see Chapter 2). Depictions of aid recipients were often clichéd, enabling the viewer to disengage from the cause. In contrast, Dynon communicated with the intention of eliciting a change in the behaviour of her audience members. By focusing on the potential of the individual to assist, Dynon implicitly held her audience to account and instilled in them a sense of duty to help the refugees.

The numerous talks presented by Dynon mattered because she was able to establish an emotional connection between her campaign and the audience. In this book I have argued that a sense of connection and knowing the other was a central feature of grassroots NGOs and individual acts of humanitarianism. In the case of Dynon, her connection with the public was evidenced in letters received. For example, Indian High Commissioner to Australia, A. M. Thomas, commented that he planned to use some of Dynon's ideas in his own speeches. He wrote: 'I went through the notes that you prepared for your Bairnsdale address with great interest. You have prepared it very well in your inimitable style. I am sure the address would have had a tremendous effect … Some of your ideas I myself will be using in a speech that I am to make to the Sydney Rotary Club.'[50] Others disclosed personal information in their letters, indicating a degree of trust between the writer and Dynon. On 11 June 1971, Melbourne woman Florence Suters sent a cheque of $5 to the campaign, a figure she deemed 'a rather small donation'. Suters was at pains to explain to Dynon her personal situation: 'My husband passed away last week and certain things have to be settled. But I would feel that I was letting my loved one down if I did not make some effort to help.'[51] Meanwhile, elderly residents at the Brotherhood of St Lawrence village reflected that the work of Dynon helped create an emotional bridge between them and children in the Indian camps. Eleanor Lindsay wrote:

> Dear Mrs Dynon,
>
> Miss Maxwell and I do sincerely thank you for the snapshot you sent us of "our" Indian children in camp. We feel so acutely for them, and the so many in the world in such dire distress and need, and we are grateful to you for this channel through which we can send, at least, a little help.[52]

The use of the possessive adjective 'our' in this extract may seem paternalistic, reflecting almost the women's sense of ownership of the children. A more generous interpretation is that Dynon helped create in these elderly women a valued, emotional connection, one not dissimilar to child sponsorship schemes employed by numerous humanitarian NGOs.

---

[50] 11 March 1971, filed in folder 18 'India Govt', Dynon family papers.
[51] Unfiled correspondence, Dynon family papers.
[52] 16 March 1971, unfiled correspondence, Dynon family papers.

The extract also shows that aside from delivering public speeches, Dynon offered to send relevant information to interested citizens. Like her talks, the posted material was well received. Bernadette Galbally wrote to Dynon on 23 June 1971:

Dear Moira,

Very many thanks indeed for going to the trouble of sending us the information regarding the aid to India campaign. I will certainly pass on the information contained in it. Please accept this small donation towards this truly worthy cause.[53]

School students contacted Dynon requesting information on her campaign. For example, senior high school student Robyn Madigan wrote to Dynon, 'to ask you if you could possibly send me any information available on the work that you do in India and Pakistan'. Madigan was preparing her last term assignment in her final year in which she selected the topic, 'The Plight of the Indian and Pakistani Refugees'.[54] Similar to her speeches, the purpose of Dynon sending information was to educate the Australian public on the intellectual, cultural, religious and political contributions of Eastern cultures on Western civilization as well as the specific challenges facing the people of South Asia. As such, Dynon was anxious to depict the recipients of aid not as passive victims but as individuals from a civilization worthy of admiration. Furthermore, Dynon's ability to distil complex information to a variety of audiences was testament to her vast knowledge of South Asian societies. For Dynon, such knowledge came after many years of working exclusively in the Indian humanitarian space, her multiple trips to that country to establish relationships and liaising with Indian government officials, particularly the Indian High Commissioner to Australia. Dynon also read widely on the history and politics of India and Pakistan, as evidenced by her copious notes on the readings.[55]

Ostensibly, the work and campaigning of Dynon may seem apolitical with its emphasis on education and advocacy rather than protest, which is the subject of the next section. However, beneath Dynon's genteel veneer was an astute activist who understood the most effective ways to disseminate her views. For example, Dynon led the organization of a public meeting 'to call for realistic emergency relief for Pakistani refugees in India' on Friday 22 October 1971, from noon to 2 pm at Melbourne Town Hall. The choice of date is significant: by 22 October, public awareness of the refugee crisis was peaking, shifting into political outrage at the perceived indifference of the Australian government. The meeting included nineteen speakers from across the humanitarian sector and religious leaders, many of whom have appeared elsewhere in this book. Speakers included Ron Butt (FFHC), Brendan O'Dwyer (ACFOA), David Scott (CAA/Oxfam), Len Reid (the Society) as well as leaders from the Anglican, Methodist, Presbyterian and Catholic churches, and Reform Judaism. In organizing the meeting, Dynon allocated time limits for each speaker: humanitarians were allocated five minutes, religious leaders six minutes and community activists three minutes. One

---

[53] Unfiled correspondence, Dynon family papers.
[54] Unfiled correspondence, Dynon family papers.
[55] Unfiled correspondence, Dynon family papers.

such activist, Steve Rooney, had participated in a public hunger strike in September and October, discussed next, revealing the popularity and importance he had earnt within five weeks of protest.

The public meeting had a clear political bent in which the causes of the war were contextualized, and perpetrators of violence identified and blamed. Dynon argued in her address that the 'savagery' of the Pakistani armed forces had 'unleashed Bengali nationalism', turning what was a 'seething ferment' of calls for self-rule into an eruption. Dynon believed that 'Bangla Desh independence is now inevitable', a provocative claim that would upset American and Pakistani officials. Although Dynon placed responsibility on the Pakistani 'junta' for offering a political settlement satisfactory to the people of Bangladesh, she still asserted that the nations of the world had an obligation to ease the immediate suffering of the refugees. Dynon believed it behoved Australians citizens 'to jolt our government out of its complacency' and demand 'massive aid and a political settlement'.[56] As an outcome of the public meeting, the two hundred attendees agreed to hold a protest rally in Melbourne on Monday 25 October at 5 pm, which in turn triggered subsequent rallies on Friday 29 October and Monday 1 November.[57] These three rallies, however, attracted very different crowds: the rallies on 25 October and 1 November attracted a mainstream mass of people with the goal of encouraging citizens to write to their MPs for more government aid; the 29 October rally, conversely, attracted twenty socialists who were seeking funds to buy ammunition for the Mukti Fauj liberation army.[58] These rallies document two different approaches to enacting change: one, demanding immediate change through disruptive protest (such as buying ammunition in the above example, or staging hunger strikes, discussed next); two, seeking gradual reform within the parliamentary system (such as writing to MPs). The remainder of this chapter will cover both methods in turn.

Paul Poernomo and the hunger strikers

As a form of political protest, hunger strikes have a long history in the modern era. Johanna Siméant documents the first known instances of collective protest fasts in colonial America in the 1770s. These protests in Virginia, Rhode Island and Massachusetts were religious in tone and the strikers sought divine intervention against their colonial rulers. In the late nineteenth century, hunger strikes emerged within the penitentiary system in Tsarist Russia, most famously by Leon Trotsky in 1898. Trotsky's adherents would similarly fast for political purposes, this time while interned in the gulags of Stalinist Russia in the 1930s. Elsewhere in the 1930s and during the Second World War, imprisoned communists in France, China and Albania staged hunger

---

[56] Moira Dynon, text of comments for public meeting at Melbourne Town Hall', filed in folder 9A, Dynon family papers.
[57] 'Thousands may join in Canberra aid protest', *The Age*, 26 October 1971, 10; Peter Johnson, 'Bangla Desh their cause', *The Sun*, 30 October 1971, 11; 'Rally aims at $20m. Aid', *The Sun*, 1 November 1971, 24.
[58] Ibid. and 'Actions on Bangla Desh', 20 October 1971, *The Tribune*, 11.

strikes.⁵⁹ Meanwhile in British history, the suffragettes starved for political inclusion in 1909. Britain would bear witness to hunger strikes across its empire, especially in Ireland and India, during their independence struggles.⁶⁰ Mohandas Gandhi was perhaps the most prolific practitioner of hunger strikes in the early twentieth century, performing at least fifteen separate fasts, which ranged in duration from five days to three weeks. Gandhi of course was a transnational activist, fasting in South Africa for civil rights for Hindus and, later, in British India for self-rule.⁶¹ Gandhi was the apotheosis of determined, non-violent protest, inspiring future activists during the protest movements of the 1960s and 1970s in the West.⁶² This mainstreaming of hunger strikes has its own critics, though. For example, Siméant laments the 'banalization' of this form of protest. An alternative perspective is that from the 1960s fasting as an act of dissent had gained widespread legitimacy.⁶³ Consequently, hunger strikes evolved from being a tactic used primarily in prisons and among those most marginalized in society, to a method that could be employed in communal spaces to draw the public's attention to a cause.

As hunger strikes moved beyond the penal system to the public realm, protesters now had another audience aside from authority figures: the third-party bystander. Even if the bystander was only imagined or had to be created, the hunger strike now took on a performative aspect. By depriving themselves of nourishment, the emaciated and weak body of the hunger striker became the stage on which protesters could denounce injustice all the while forcing onlookers to bear witness or evoke sympathy. As Siméant explains, the personal suffering of the hunger striker renders indifference impossible, for the public or the state.⁶⁴ Furthermore, the potential for martyrdom – intrinsic to any high-risk protest – creates a spectacle, a drama unfolding. By depriving themselves of food day after day in public spaces, fasters become physically weaker but symbolically more powerful. Hunger strikes are generally successful because this method empowers people who are otherwise powerless. It is a confrontational form of protest in which violent acts are directed towards the self. The internalized enactment of violence in public spaces compels the attention of passers-by and provokes action from authorities.⁶⁵

On Saturday 11 September 1971, Indonesian-born poet Paul Poernomo began a hunger strike on the steps of the Melbourne General Post Office (GPO). Initially his goal

---

⁵⁹ Johanna Siméant, 'From Fast to Hunger Strike', in *Bodies in Protest: Hungry Strikes and Angry Music*, ed. Johanna Siméant and Christophe Traïni (Amsterdam: Amsterdam University Press, 2016), 19–20.
⁶⁰ Kevin Grant, *Last Weapons: Hunger Strikes and Fasts in the British Empire, 1890–1948* (Oakland: University of California Press, 2019); James Vernon, *Hunger: A Modern History* (Cambridge, MA: Harvard University Press, 2009), 43.
⁶¹ Siméant, 'From Fast to Hunger Strike', 21–2.
⁶² Sean Scalmer, 'Nonviolent Activism and the Media. Gandhi and Beyond', in *Routledge Companion to Media and Activism*, ed. Graham Meikle (New York: Routledge, 2018), 38–9.
⁶³ Siméant, 'From Fast to Hunger Strike', 22–4.
⁶⁴ Johanna Siméant, 'The Meaning of Bodily Violence', in *Bodies in Protest: Hungry Strikes and Angry Music*, ed. Johanna Siméant and Christophe Traïni (Amsterdam: Amsterdam University Press, 2016), 35–46, 39.
⁶⁵ Sharman Apt Russell, *Hunger: An Unnatural History* (New York: Basic Books, 2005), 73; Stephen J. Scanlan, Laurie Cooper Stoll and Kimberly Lumm, 'Starving for Change: The Hunger Strike and Nonviolent Action, 1906–2004', *Research in Social Movements, Conflicts and Change* 28 (2008): 275 and 310.

was to raise awareness and funds for Bangladeshi refugees; by 20 September Poernomo raised the stakes, insisting he would only end his strike once the Australian government provided A$10 million in aid for Bangladeshi refugees.[66] This singular act of defiance by one man in Melbourne was not spontaneous but contextually contingent. First, on 11 September *The Age*, Melbourne's newspaper of record, published the first of three special reports from its correspondent in Kolkata, Max Beattie, whose trip was funded by Community Aid Abroad (CAA), see Chapter 6.[67] Australian newspaper coverage of the Bangladeshi refugee crisis typically involved publishing syndicated articles by *New York Times* correspondent Sydney Schanberg, *The Times* (London) correspondent Peter Hazelhurst or anonymous reports from Reuters or Associated Press. Unlike these syndicated articles, Beattie's reports were written deliberately for an Australian reader and, consequently, awarded prime positioning within the newspaper, including one cover story. *The Age* published subsequent detailed reports by Beattie on Tuesday 14 September, Saturday 18 September and Monday 20 September, the last of which included the inflammatory cover headline, 'Two million children are fighting for life'.[68] It is therefore probable that Beattie's provocative report on the 'Lost Millions of Calcutta' impacted Poernomo, galvanizing him to act.

Second, Paul Poernomo was an atypical Melburnian, a man whose character had been shaped by years of government surveillance, ostracization and a deep commitment to spirituality. When Paul Poernomo migrated to Australia, he was never supposed to settle permanently. Until 1973, Asian migration to Australia was technically prohibited but still possible under specific conditions. Poernomo entered Australia as part of the government's Colombo Plan, the multilateral aid programme that offered scholarships to Asian students to study in Western countries who, after graduation, would return to their home country. In Poernomo's case, he was one of 5,500 students who entered Australia between 1951 and 1965, three-quarters of whom were from Malaya, Indonesia, India, Pakistan or Ceylon.[69] Poernomo arrived in 1957 to study a five-year electrical engineering course at Footscray Technical College in Melbourne. In his first three years of study, Poernomo passed his examinations although he never excelled. From 1960 Poernomo's mental health began to unravel, affecting his studies. Once Poernomo started failing some subjects in 1960, the Australian government took greater interest in his life.

Because Poernomo had entered Australia at the request of the Australian government, the authorities had the power to deport him should his progress at college be deemed unsatisfactory. In 1961, Poernomo's health deteriorated further, suffering an 'acute depression' at the end of the year, which affected his short-term memory and ability to concentrate.[70] The Australian government placed Poernomo under the

---

[66] 'After 8 Days, He Keeps Fasting', *The Herald*, 20 September 1971, 3.
[67] Max Beattie, 'The Tragedy of Bengal', *The Age*, 11 September 1971, 11.
[68] Max Beattie, 'The Tragedy of Bengal', 14 September 1971, 8; 18 September 1971 and Max Beattie, '100,000 child refugees dead', *The Age*, 20 September 1971, cover.
[69] Daniel Oakman, *Facing Asia: A History of the Colombo Plan*, 2nd edn (Canberra: ANU Press, 2010), 179.
[70] H. A. Bland, Secretary Department of Labour and National Service, letter to Australian Embassy, Djakarta, 5 March 1962, in NAA: A1838, 2010/5/12/32.

care of a psychiatrist, R. E. G. MacLean, who was tasked with evaluating Poernomo's capacity to complete his studies. MacLean indicated that Poernomo suffered from bipolar disorder (though that term was not used) because he had 'a cyclical tendency to emotional swings such that when his emotional state is "up" he is able to be the cheerful and extroverted entertainer, but when his emotional state is "down" he is, as he is now, somewhat depressed'. The psychiatrist described the depression as 'mild' but resistant to treatment, such as the use of antidepressants and talk therapy. The psychiatrist would later describe Poernomo as a 'recurrent depressive and is difficult to help'.[71] The Australian government continued to surveil Poernomo's academic progress and monitor his mental health, including whether the student attended his medical appointments.[72]

When Poernomo failed all five of his subjects in 1962, the Department of External Affairs (DEA) terminated his scholarship (including his living allowance) and began arrangements for his return to Indonesia.[73] Rather than repatriate, Poernomo unsuccessfully lodged an application to stay in Australia as a private student. Poernomo had received approval from the college to stay enrolled as a private student, but the Indonesian government insisted that their citizen return 'as soon as possible'.[74] Sensing resistance from Poernomo, the DEA attempted to induce Poernomo to return home by offering to pay his passage.[75] The Australian Department of Immigration became involved in this saga, too, as Poernomo was now an unwelcome immigrant. On 6 August 1963, the Commonwealth Migration Officer 'instructed' Poernomo to accept the government's offer to organize repatriation.[76] Immigration officials booked Poernomo 'on the first available boat which was scheduled to leave on 2 October'. But Poernomo resisted again: if he could not stay as a private student, then he would marry an Australian on 23 September, before his scheduled boat departure.[77] On 25 September, Poernomo advised the immigration department that he had married an Australian and applied for permanent residency.[78] During his permanent residency interview with Australian immigration officials, Poernomo remarked that he had no intention of returning to Indonesia. Poernomo explained that he would struggle to find employment without his diploma, he did 'not like present conditions in Indonesia' and

---

[71] Cable from Department of External Affairs liaison officer Miss Emily Dick to Mr L. Smith, 1 October 1962, in NAA: A1838, 2010/5/12/32.

[72] Dr R. MacLean, psychiatrist superintendent, letter to Dick, undated, likely October 1962, in NAA: A1838, 2010/5/12/32.

[73] J. K. Waller, First Assistant Secretary, Department of External Affairs (DEA), letter to Mr Poernomo Soerodipoero (Paul), 9 April 1963, in NAA: A1838, 2010/5/12/32; P. H. Cook, Acting Secretary, Department of Labour and National Service, letter to the Secretary, DEA, 11 June 1963, in NAA: A1838, 2010/5/12/32.

[74] Ali Marsaban, Cultural Attaché, Embassy of Indonesia, Sydney, letter to the Secretary, Department of Labour and National Service, 30 July 1963, in NAA: A1838, 2010/5/12/32.

[75] A. F. Blackburn, Australian Embassy Djakarta, letter to the Secretary, Department of Labour and National Service, 17 June 1963, in NAA: A1838, 2010/5/12/32.

[76] P. R. Heydon, Secretary, Department of Immigration, letter to the Secretary, DEA, 6 August 1963, in NAA: A1838, 2010/5/12/32.

[77] Heydon, cable to Mr Blackburn, 16 September 1963, in NAA: A1838, 2010/5/12/32.

[78] J. Weeden, Director, Commonwealth Office of Education, letter to the Secretary, DEA, 2 October 1963, in NAA: A1838, 2010/5/12/32.

that his father, who had fifteen other children, could not financially support him. In the interview Poernomo revealed that he was estranged from his family, too.[79] Despite his best efforts, Poernomo failed to convince officials of the genuineness of his marriage and, consequently, the immigration department withheld a permanent residency visa for twelve months pending further inquiries.[80] In the end, the department delayed issuing a visa for eighteen months, granting Poernomo permanent residency on 23 July 1965.[81] By 1971, Poernomo was thirty-six, divorced and moved between semi-skilled jobs as an engineering draughtsman, clerk, writer and poet.[82]

The backstory of Poernomo is important for many reasons. It shows the strength of character of Poernomo, which enabled him to withstand intense government pressure over many years, as had befallen Moira Dynon. It demonstrates that Poernomo had the ingenuity to find a legitimate avenue to permanent residency even when existing government policy was hostile to his presence in Australia. But in resisting government requirements, Poernomo attracted the attention of authorities. Because Poernomo had been surveilled, he had a file that officials could later draw upon when he began his hunger strikes in 1971. Government records show that the DFA 'traced' Poernomo on 21 October 1971 and prepared 'background' material on him on 22 October.[83] But unlike Dynon, Poernomo was a loner, and his social network appears limited. Poernomo was therefore not the typical counterculture revolutionary. Perhaps because he defied stereotypes, the Melbourne public found Poernomo enigmatic, worthy of admiration and imitation.

Poernomo began his hunger strike on the steps of the GPO, located at the corner of Elizabeth and Bourke streets, one of Melbourne's busiest intersections. The choice of location was deliberate: in recent years, the steps of the GPO became the 'in' place to stage demonstrations or air grievances against the state.[84] The GPO was symbolic of state power; on a practical level, the GPO distributed (on behalf of the Commonwealth postmaster general) conscription forms for national service in Vietnam.[85] At the time, military conscription and Australia's involvement in the American war in Vietnam was the cause célèbre. In 1970 and 1971, Melbourne staged its largest demonstration in its history, including some 100,000 protesters on 30 June 1971.[86] As the 'unofficial "demo-centre"', the postmaster general tolerated protesters, unless violent or offensive.[87] Its

---

[79] Tabbiner, memo to T. Smith, 14 November 1963, in NAA: A1838, 2010/5/12/32.
[80] Heydon, letter to Secretary, DEA, 4 December 1963, in NAA: A1838, 2010/5/12/32.
[81] Heydon, letter to Secretary, DEA, 23 July 1965, in NAA: A1838, 2010/5/12/32.
[82] Memo, Department of Immigration, Brisbane, undated, NAA: J25, 1970/7223; John Lewis, 'Paul Tells of Agony and Ecstasy of His Nine-day Fast', *The Age*, 22 September 1971, 4; 'Hunger hurts …', *The Herald*, 24 September 1971, 3.
[83] Memo, 21 October 1971, in NAA: A1838, 2010/5/12/32; Memo, 22 October 1971, in NAA: A1838, 2010/5/12/32.
[84] Simon Townley, 'GPO Takes on a New Trend', *The Herald*, 28 September 1971, 11.
[85] Sean Scalmer, *Dissent Events: Protest, the Media, and the Political Gimmick in Australia* (Sydney: UNSW Press, 2002), 57.
[86] 'June 30: The Moratorium nation-wide', *The Tribune*, 7 July 1971, 10; for historical background, see Jon Piccini, Evan Smith and Matthew Worley, 'Introduction: The History of the Far Left in Australia since 1945', in *The Far Left in Australia since 1945*, ed. Jon Piccini, Evan Smith and Matthew Worley (New York: Routledge, 2018), 2–8.
[87] Townley, 'GPO Takes on a New Trend', *The Herald*, 28 September 1971, 11.

central location, symbolism and connection to dissent made the GPO an ideal location to raise public awareness of the refugee crisis and solicit funds from passers-by, which would then be channelled to the FFHC (see Chapter 6). One passer-by, nineteen-year-old truck driver Steve Rooney from the outer eastern suburb of Belgrave, was so moved by Poernomo's appeal that he, too, began fasting at the GPO. They were later joined by twenty-year-old student Geoff Evans of Malvern, a well-to-do inner south-eastern suburb, and Paul Smith, a bookseller from Flemington in the inner north-west.[88] In the weeks that followed, fasters would come and go with varying degrees of commitment. The one constant was Poernomo.

Media coverage of the fasters was slow to materialize. The first press report came eight days after Poernomo began his strike in the centrist broadsheet, *The Herald*. The next day, centre-left broadsheet with the largest metropolitan readership, *The Age*, included the headline, 'Paul tells of agony and ecstasy of his nine-day fast'. It is noteworthy in these two articles that the editors of the newspapers chose to focus on Poernomo and not his imitators. The newspapers also included sympathetic photographs of Poernomo: *The Herald* depicted Poernomo stoically seated cross-legged in a Gandhian-like pose while a passer-by donated coins into his collection tin; *The Age* meanwhile photographed Poernomo holding his FFHC collection tin. In both articles the journalists emphasized the duration of Poernomo's fast, eight and nine days respectively. Therefore, the hunger strike only became newsworthy once the fast had extended beyond a week. In subsequent articles in both newspapers, journalists stressed the physical challenges of sustaining a fast. *The Herald* ran the headline, 'Hunger hurts ...' while *The Age* used the title, 'Fasting Paul feels the pangs of starvation'.[89] Both articles included photographs of Poernomo lying down and in a weak state. Poernomo temporarily broke his fourteen-day fast on 26 September. Once again, this was captured by the press with a photograph of Poernomo and a reference to his bodily pain. The headline stated, 'Paul ends the pangs with a great plate of porridge'.[90] This article reported that while Poernomo rested, Steve Rooney continued the fast at the GPO with his younger brother, Jim. The Rooney brothers, however, were merely supporters to Poernomo's one-man mission. The editorial decisions of the newspapers to focus on Poernomo rather than all fasters – some of whom were demonstrably fickle – humanized this story of protest. Poernomo persisted because of his faith, commenting, 'I spend a lot of time meditating ... I think about God', he said.[91] By juxtaposing the visible discomfort of Poernomo with his devotion to faith, the Melbourne public gained insight into a complex man who put the needs of Bangladeshi refugees ahead of his own.

Coverage of Poernomo in *The Age* narrated how the Indonesian had captured the hearts of Melburnians. In his first article on the hunger strike, journalist John Lewis described how Poernomo had overcome initial resistance. He wrote:

---

[88] *The Herald*, 20 September 1971, 3.
[89] *The Herald*, 24 September 1971, 3; Gary Dean, 'Fasting Paul Feels the Pangs of Starvation', *The Age*, 25 September 1971, 5.
[90] John Lewis, 'Paul Ends the Pangs with a Great Plate of Porridge', *The Age*, 27 September 1971, 4.
[91] *The Age*, 22 September 1971, 4.

After morale-deflating doubts earlier in the fast, suddenly the Javanese-born clerk can see he is achieving something. The people of Melbourne have warmed to him. He says he can see it in their smiles as they pass by him. He can see it as the donations begin to make the little tins look inadequate.[92]

In a later article Lewis observed that the fast 'has drawn an extraordinary response from the people of Melbourne – most have reacted warmly to him and donated money, sometimes everything they had in their pockets and sometimes the rings from their fingers'.[93] During the fourteen-day fast, Poernomo and his supporters raised over A$20,000.[94] Lewis conceded that although most of the public were supportive, Poernomo on occasion faced intimidation and taunts. Some individuals teased Poernomo with hamburgers, while others threatened physical violence, such as beatings. On the previous Saturday, Lewis reported the most serious incident that involved five drunken men, one of whom drew a knife on Poernomo. Fortuitously, three sailors walking by intervened and diffused the situation. The drunken men retreated, and the sailors slept beside the fasters for the rest of the night. These anecdotes of Poernomo braving dangerous city streets during his hunger strike only added to his heroic appeal.

After a brief respite, Poernomo recommenced his fast on Tuesday 28 September. This second hunger strike, however, abruptly ended on Friday 1 October at the hands of federal police. Although the postmaster general traditionally condoned protests at the GPO, it appears in this instance that the Commonwealth attorney general, Senator Ivor Greenwood, personally intervened, most likely at the behest of the prime minister. Greenwood cited an obscure federal law for the basis of the arrest of the fasters. According to the *Post and Telegraph Act 1901*, s115(1)(b) and s115(2), any person who wilfully obstructs the course of business of the post office is liable for a penalty; any person committing an offense may be required to leave the post office; should they refuse to leave, police officers are required to remove such persons.[95] It proved to be a tactical error for the Australian government. Although the government was acting in accordance with the law, they proved themselves to be tone-deaf to public sentiment. When Poernomo and five of his supporters were arrested and escorted to waiting police wagons, 'afternoon shoppers hurled abuse' at the police and thirty Melbourne University students sat on the steps all night in protest.[96] Tabloid newspaper *The Sun* also led with the story, reporting people 'rushed forward and put coins in the group's collection boxes as police led the fasters away'.[97] The next day, fifteen new hunger strikers appeared on the GPO steps to replace the arrested fasters and to show the futility of police intervention.[98]

---

[92] Ibid.
[93] *The Age*, 27 September 1971, 4.
[94] Ibid.
[95] *Post and Telegraph Act 1901* (Cth), accessed 26 December 2022, http://www5.austlii.edu.au/au/legis/cth/num_act/pata1901121901213/.
[96] 'Police Arrest Six Fasters after GPO Vigil Raid', *The Age*, 2 October 1971, cover.
[97] Wayne Grant, 'Police Arrest Fasters on GPO Steps', *The Sun*, 2 October 1971, cover.
[98] 'Hamer: Let the Fast 6 Off', *The Herald*, 2 October 1971, cover.

The Australian government wanted to silence the hunger strikers by arresting them, but their actions only increased the press coverage of the protest and widened the appeal of the fasters. All newspapers carried this story on their front page, including, for the first time, *The Sun*, a conservative tabloid. Letters to the editor indicate further community support for the hunger strike. Michael Neil of working class Brunswick described the arrests as 'vindictive' and commended the fasters whose actions 'remind us of our responsibility within our global village' and represent 'the only significant symbol of caring that has spontaneously appeared to goad our conscience into action'. Ross Hamilton of West Brunswick described his rage about the arrests of the fasters: 'For as far back as I can remember, I have never been so infuriated by the actions of my fellow Australians.' Hamilton ridiculed the federal police officers and implied racist undertones for the inadequate Australian government aid for Bangladeshi refugees. He wrote, 'I hope you all sleep well tonight. Try not to worry too much about those millions starving in Pakistan – after all, they're not Australians – they're not even white!'[99] Meanwhile, the editor of *The Herald* described the arrests as 'altogether indefensible' and 'a ridiculous misuse of authority by Commonwealth police'.[100] Following public outrage at the arrests, Victorian Liberal Acting Premier Dick Hamer also objected, sending a telegram early on Saturday 2 October to the prime minister with the message:

> URGENTLY REQUEST YOU INTERVENE IN ARREST OF FASTERS AT MELBOURNE GPO TO HAVE CHARGES DROPPED. THEY HAVE STIRRED OUR CONSCIENCE AND GREATLY AIDED FREEDOM FROM HUNGER CAMPAIGN IN THIS STATE.[101]

The Australian government acquiesced, dropping all charges against the fasters later that day. Press reports indicated that McMahon and Greenwood initially resisted succumbing to popular will, fearing such a capitulation would set a precedent for subsequent protests at the GPO. In the end, the prime minister and attorney general agreed that dropping all charges 'was the only way out of some bad public relations'.[102]

Although the authorities may have appeased public sentiment on the issue of arrests, government officials still demanded that the remaining hunger strikers leave the GPO. To reach that end, the postmaster general installed a collection box for donations and permitted one poster and a progress total to be placed beside it.[103] The fasters also found a new site for their protest, this time on the steps of St Paul's Anglican Cathedral at the busy intersection of Flinders and Swanston streets in central Melbourne. The church proved to be a hospitable environment with the dean of St Paul's, Reverend Thomas, personally endorsing the actions of the hunger strikers. The steps of the cathedral would house the fasters for at least another month.[104]

---

[99] 'Fasters Arrest Infuriates', *The Age*, 4 October 1971, 9.
[100] 'Over-Kill at GPO Steps', *The Herald*, 4 October 1971, 4.
[101] *The Herald*, 2 October 1971, cover.
[102] John Sorell, 'Arrests Interrupted the Senator's Weekend', *The Herald*, 4 October 1971, 2.
[103] 'GPO Box Will Replace Fasters', *The Age*, 8 October 1971, 3.
[104] *The Age*, 3 November 1971, cover.

Figure 7.2 A hunger demonstration was held outside Parliament House Canberra, 26 October 1971. Photographer: Phil Thomson. Source: *Sydney Morning Herald*.

Meanwhile, Poernomo and his flock travelled to the national capital, Canberra, on Monday 4 October. The following day Poernomo, Steve Rooney and Geoff Evans began another hunger strike in front of the steps to Parliament House. Figure 7.2 shows a slender Poernomo posing for photographers outside parliament; in the background a crowd of supporters brave the wet weather. The journey of the hunger strikers to the capital coincided with the sitting of parliament in which members of both chambers discussed increasing aid to refugees in India. On Wednesday 6 October, the strikers experienced their first tangible victory: a government decision to double the official aid to the refugees from A$1.5 million to A$3 million. The hunger strikers welcomed this increase but insisted that they would continue their fasts until the government guaranteed at least A$10 million. As a 'red-eyed' Geoff Evans reflected, 'If the government was at all humane, we would not have to be here.'[105] Len Reid, the Christian charity leader and MP (see Chapter 5), believed that the actions of the fasters 'caused the government to add $500,000 to the aid it had planned'. He explained: 'I feel that the part of these people have played over the past three weeks at the Melbourne GPO and now here [in Canberra] has had a lot of influence on the government.'[106] Poernomo

---

[105] 'Refugee aid', *The Sun*, 6 October 1971, 2.
[106] '$1.5 mil. More Hunger Relief', *The Sun*, 6 October 1971, cover.

fasted for sixteen days in Canberra before a doctor ordered he be taken to hospital for 'malnutrition, dehydration and exposure'.[107] On release from hospital, Poernomo recommenced his fast for a further fourteen days. Again, Poernomo broke his fast, this time for one week, before commencing another hunger strike at the Sydney GPO on 8 November 1971. He had new associates in Sydney – Robert Myall, seventeen, from Melbourne and Keri Baba, twenty-eight, a former student, along with many other unnamed young activists – who fasted with him until another police arrest on 12 November. Once again, the fasters were forced from the GPO and a collection tin was installed in their place, a photograph of which covers this book. The hunger strikers continued their fast on the steps of St Andrew's Anglican Church in central Sydney.[108]

The impact of Poernomo is undeniable though hard to quantify. Steve Rooney told reporters in Canberra that because of the fast, 20,000 people had written to the prime minister urging him to increase aid to refugees. An additional five thousand people had signed their petition to MPs and five hundred people had written to Foreign Minister Nigel Bowen. Rooney believed the letter writers 'were mainly from Melbourne people', reflecting the extent to which Poernomo had captured the attention of residents of that city. In Canberra, Poernomo inspired young people. *The Age* quoted 'a pretty brunette faster named Angela': ' "He never complained, he talked about others, never of himself ... He is the most incredible person I have ever met." '[109] In a letter to the editor, Dorothy Roberts of suburban Bayswater commented:

> Millions of destitute refugees who have crossed into India during the past few months must feel that the attitude taken by the rest of the world has been to 'pass by on the other side'.
>
> Perhaps they could detect a faint hope that their plight may at last be beginning to be recognised if they were to know that a young man thousands of miles away from them was willing to forfeit his life by emulating their extremity in an attempt to obtain more generous aid for them.
>
> By personal suffering Paul Poernomo and his fellow fasters have brought the tragedy of East Pakistan right to the steps of our Parliament House.[110]

On 27 October 1971, the Australian government increased their aid contribution again, this time to A$5.5 million.[111] At the same time, the Melbourne fasters had raised A$35,918, a figure that would increase to nearly A$50,000 by year's end. It is evident that Poernomo's activism had a tangible result. But these state and private donations were always seen as insufficient by Poernomo and his followers. From the beginning Poernomo demanded at least A$10 million in government aid and he encouraged his

---

[107] 'Faster Will Return, Say Friends', *The Age*, 22 October 1971, 3.
[108] 'More Fasters', *Canberra Times*, 8 November 1971, 3; 'Fasters Happy', 11 November 1971, 3; 'Fasters Move', 13 November 1971, 1; 'Fasters' 17 November 1971, 3; 'Stolen', 19 November 1971, 3.
[109] 'Faster Will Return, Say Friends', *The Age*, 22 October 1971, 3.
[110] 'World Seeks to Ignore the Refugees', *The Age*, 26 October 1971, 9.
[111] 'Australia to raise aid total to $5.5m', *The Age*, 28 October 1971, cover; Victorian Freedom from Hunger Campaign, *News Bulletin*, December 1971, pp. 9–12, in Folder 522 '1971 State Correspondence Vic', Box 81, Records of the AFFHC.

fellow citizens to similarly petition their political leaders to reach that goal. The final section of this chapter examines such letters.

Dear Mr Whitlam

The National Archives of Australia holds the records of Gough Whitlam, Australia's twenty-first prime minister (1972–5) and arguably the country's most controversial political leader. From 1967 to 1972, Whitlam served as Opposition Leader of the Labor Party, during which time he became increasingly popular with an electorate weary of twenty-three years of conservative rule. These records hold over 2,500 letters from constituents to Whitlam urging the expectant prime minister to increase aid to Bangladeshi refugees in India. This trove of citizen letters on one subject is rare. By comparison, the papers of Prime Minister McMahon, held at the National Library of Australia, are only partially open to the public. My request to access the folder of constituency correspondence on Pakistani refugees in 1971 was declined by the McMahon family lawyers in 2018.[112] Although I could access constituent correspondence to Prime Minister McMahon from 1971 to 1972, these letters covered an array of subjects. In this subseries, I found just 108 citizen letters on Bangladeshi refugees, a fraction of the likely number of letters received.[113]

The relative openness of the Whitlam letters offers a window into the world views of Australians during one of the most turbulent times in its history. Political historian Sean Scalmer argues that 1971 was the most tumultuous year in Australia's delayed adoption of 1960s protest movements. According to press coverage, Scalmer calculated over 350 separate incidents of collective action, a figure higher than other years. Furthermore, these protests were increasingly adversarial, disruptive and radical than conciliatory demonstrations of the 1960s, such as teach-ins.[114] When situated within this political context, citizen letters provide insight into Australian advocacy that goes beyond the traditional agitators, such as university students, feminists and minority rights activists.[115] These activists may have attracted the most commentary, but numerically

---

[112] Folder 71 'Pakistani Refugees, 1971', Subseries [unnumbered] 'Constituency correspondence: Sequence 2 (1961–1981)', Series 8 'Member for Lowe, 1949–1981', Papers of Sir William McMahon, MS 3926, NLA.
[113] See Subseries 17/8 'Correspondence, 1971–1972', Series 17 'Prime Minister', 1967–72, MS 3926.
[114] Scalmer, *Dissent Events*, 38 and 57.
[115] There is extensive research conducted on student and minority rights activism. For student activism, see Kate Murphy, 'Student Activism at the University of New England in Australia's "Long 1960s"', *Journal of Australian Studies* 43 (2019): 174–87; Kate Murphy, 'In the Backblocks of Capitalism: Australian Student Activism in the Global 1960s', *Australian Historical Studies* 46 (2015): 252–68; Lewis D'Avingdor, 'Participatory Democracy and New Left Student Movements: The University of Sydney, 1973–1979', *Australian Journal of Politics and History* 61 (2015): 233–47; Alan Barcan, *From New Left to Factional Left: Fifty Years of Student Activism at Sydney University* (Melbourne: Australian Scholarly, 2011). For women's liberation, see Susan Magarey, 'Beauty Becomes Political: Beginnings of the Women's Liberation Movement in Australia', *Australian Feminist Studies* 33 (2018): 31–44; Michelle Arrow and Angela Woollacott, eds. *Everyday Revolutions: Remaking Gender, Sexuality and Culture in 1970s Australia* (Canberra: ANU Press, 2019). For gay liberation, see Robert Reynolds and Shirleene Robinson, *Gay and Lesbian, Then and Now: Australian Stories from a Social Revolution* (Melbourne: Black, 2016); Graham Willett, *Living Out Loud: A History of Gay and Lesbian Activism in Australia* (Sydney: Allen & Unwin, 2000). For

they represent a small minority of the population. Conversely, constituent letters written by Australians of diverse origins enable us to analyse how these individuals understood the refugee crisis and in what ways they thought governments and citizens should intervene.

Historians of humanitarianism have moved beyond analysing the actions of elites, diplomats and NGOs to examine the actions of individuals in their everyday lives. As Tehila Sasson observes, 'by the 1970s boycotts were everywhere' in which empowered consumers used the marketplace as a space of protest.[116] Aside from the Nestlé boycott, consumers also deliberately avoided South African made products in opposition to its apartheid regime.[117] Consumer behaviours are an important local act of resistance in which otherwise disempowered individuals can express their solidarity with oppressed populations around the globe.[118] But consumer boycotts are not the only method of localized humanitarianism available to citizens. Constituent letters that demanded change or expressed objections to those in power can, too, be read as everyday acts of humanitarianism. As 'hidden transcripts', constituent letters can undermine dominant political narratives or official ideologies advocated by elites or the state.[119] These letters grant us direct access to the diversity and complexity of public opinion, eschewing ill-defined categorizations of 'the public' or 'the silent masses'. With expanding access to secondary and higher education in Australia since the late nineteenth century, letter writing became an egalitarian social practice available to most.[120] Consequently, constituent letters offer access to the thoughts and feelings of under-represented groups, including women and children, as well as often overlooked rural denizens.

The arrival of 2,500 citizen letters for Whitlam was anomalous in two regards. First, the scale was unprecedented. In the UK, MPs typically received between one and three constituent letters per week until the early 1960s; by 1970, most MPs received between twenty-seven and seventy-five constituent letters per week.[121] Australia's longest serving prime minister, Robert Menzies, received 22,000 letters over an eighteen-year period, or 1,222 letters per year.[122] Conversely, Whitlam received 2,517 letters over a three-month period, the bulk of which were sent in October, see Figure 7.3.

---

indigenous activism, see Richard Broome, *Fighting Hard: The Victorian Aborigines Advancement League* (Canberra: Aboriginal Studies Press, 2015); Jennifer Clark, *Aborigines & Activism: Race, Aborigines & the Coming of the Sixties to Australia* (Perth: UWA Press, 2008).

[116] Tehila Sasson, 'Milking the Third World? Humanitarianism, Capitalism and the Moral Economy of the Nestlé Boycott', *American Historical Review* 121 (2016): 1196, 1199. See also Hilton et al., 'History and Humanitarianism', e27–8.

[117] Simon Stevens, 'Boycotts and Sanctions against South Africa: An international history, 1946–1970' (PhD diss., Columbia University, 2016), 118–61; O'Sullivan, *Ireland, Africa and the End of Empire*, 132–57.

[118] Rob Skinner, 'Humanitarianism and Human Rights in Global Anti-Apartheid', in *A Global History of Anti-Apartheid*, ed. A. Konieczna and R. Skinner (Cham: Springer International, 2019), 35–6, 56.

[119] Martin Lyons, *Dear Prime Minister: Letters to Robert Menzies 1949–1966* (Sydney: New South, 2021), 23.

[120] Isobelle Barrett Meyering, 'The Margaret Bailey Case: High School Activism, the Right to Education and Modern Citizenship in Late 1960s Australia', *History Education Review* 48 (2019): 186.

[121] Oonagh Gay, 'MPs Go Back to Their Constituencies', *Political Quarterly* 76 (2005): 58.

[122] Lyons, *Dear Prime Minister*, 25. Note this is unlikely to be the full extent.

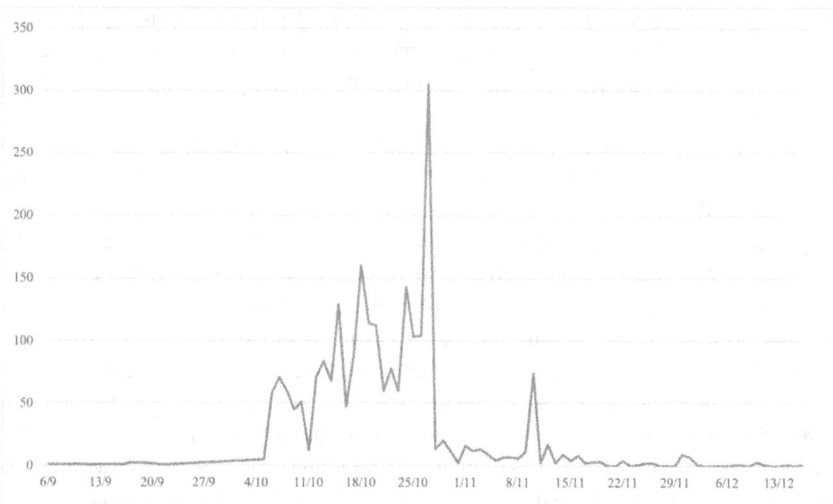

Figure 7.3 Citizen letters by number and date of sending in DD/MM format, 1971. NAA: M157, 33/33/PART21 to 26.

The peak day – with 305 letters sent – was Wednesday 27 October, the day when the McMahon government announced an extra A$2 million in aid for the refugees. Rather than quietening public opposition to government policy, the announcement of the McMahon government to increase aid only triggered further criticism. Arguably, the data demonstrates the impact of the hunger strikers on public awareness of the refugee crisis and their propensity to act. Figure 7.3 shows that letters sent increased after the police arrests of hunger strikers on 1 October, which produced front-page headlines in all Melbourne-based newspapers on 2 October and 4 October. As the hunger strikers relocated to Canberra, media coverage became national in scope and their audience grew significantly, particularly in New South Wales (NSW). Consequently, most residents of the most populous state of NSW sent their letters after 22 October.

The second way in which these letter writers diverged from past practice relates to gender. In single-authored letters where the writer revealed their gender, 74 per cent were female. By way of comparison, women accounted for less than 30 per cent of letters written to Menzies between 1949 and 1966.[123] The gender split of letter writers only reveals part of the story: 13 per cent of letters were sent from couples or households, typically nuclear families. Rather than seeing letter writing to politicians as a solitary act, in more than one in ten cases it was an interpersonal activity. Presumably, in drafting the letters, husbands, wives, sons and daughters discussed – even debated – what to include in their letter and how best to persuade Whitlam.

Despite the large numbers of letters, it is possible to identify recurring themes based on the identification of keywords, see Table 7.2. In the letters, many citizens began

---

[123] Ibid., 226.

Table 7.2 Keywords from Letters

Identity		How much?		Influences	
Australia/n, citizen	1224	Massive	1047	Media	517
Wealth*	1173	$30 million	639	Faith	292
Neighbours	58	Per person/head = $12 m	299	Moral/responsibility	266
Asia	30	$10 million	258	Paul	50

Note: The asterisk represents the inclusion of synonyms, e.g. wealth, generous, affluent, in the count.
Source: NAA: M157, 33/33/PART21 to 26.

with the phrase, 'As a citizen …' or 'As an Australian …'. These expressions indicate awareness of the power of the individual, particularly the voting individual within a parliamentary democracy. Reference to being an Australian reflects the influence of post-imperial 'new nationalism' over the dominion or 'colonial nationalism' of old.[124]

Relatedly, letter writers understood Australia as part of Asia, referring to India and Bangladesh as geographic neighbours, which, again, was contrary to conventional understandings of Australia as isolated and insular.[125] This sense of proximity consequently necessitated humanitarian action. Many writers also identified Australia as a wealthy, prosperous, rich or affluent nation. Implicit in such statements was an awareness of stark global inequalities. If Australia was a rich country and therefore in a position to donate aid to the refugees, it begged the question: how much should the country give? Nearly half of the writers expressed disapproval of current government levels of aid, with 1,031 letters containing adjectives such as stingy, miserly, meagre, niggardly and selfish. Forty-two per cent of writers argued that Australian aid should be 'massive', as Dynon advocated in her Melbourne Town Hall speech in October. When they offered specific amounts, 639 writers recommended A$30 million (or six times the existing level), 299 writers reasoned that A$1 per head (or A$12 million) was fair. Only 258 (roughly 10 per cent) advocated A$10 million, the same figure as advocated by the hunger strikers.

When writing to Whitlam, citizens explained what motivated them and how they sourced information. Over five hundred writers mentioned explicit media coverage of the crisis, including TV, newspapers and radio reports. During 1971 the national broadcaster, the Australian Broadcasting Corporation, screened fifty-eight extended segments on the Bangladesh Liberation War and refugee crisis. Through the moving image, television networks introduced a new way of visualizing suffering: with a brutal realism, such expedited footage invited the viewer to intervene.[126] Religion also played an important role, which reinforces my argument of the persistence of faith within

---

[124] Stuart Ward, 'The "New Nationalism" in Australia, Canada and New Zealand: Civic Culture in the Wake of the British World', in *Britishness Abroad: Transnational Movements and Imperial Culture*, ed. Kate Darian-Smith, Patricia Grimshaw and Stuart Macintyre (Melbourne: Melbourne University Press, 2007), 243–314.

[125] James Jupp, 'From "White Australia" to "Part of Asia": Recent Shifts in Australian Immigration Policy towards the Region', *International Migration Review* 29 (1995): 210.

[126] Emma Hutchison, 'Humanitarian Emotions through History: Imaging Suffering and Performing Aid', in *Emotional Bodies: The Historical Performativity of Emotions*, ed. Dolores Martín-Munro and Beatriz Pichel (Urbana: University of Illinois, 2019), 235; Lasse Heerten, 'Biafras of the

humanitarian circles, see Chapter 5. In the letters, citizens described themselves as Christian or part of a Christian nation. Some mentioned Catholicism explicitly and others referred to church or prayer in a general sense. Faith was also used by some to chide the Opposition Leader into action. For example, Miss Josephson of Brisbane wrote, 'Australia – a so-called Christian nation – must prove to the world that she is willing to contribute her share.'[127] Mrs Constance Putt of Melbourne lambasted the Australian government, which she described as 'so meagre as to be insulting, coming as it does from such a privileged, affluent and so-called "Christian" country'.[128] The more secular terms of 'morality' or having a 'moral responsibility' to assist those in distress were also mentioned, even if the Christian ethics underpinning these values were not identified. Fifty people also mentioned Paul Poernomo by name, indicating the direct impact he had on public attitudes towards the refugee crisis.

The value of the letters is that they give us access to the internal states of under-represented groups, such as children. Primary school-aged children sent letters of protest, demonstrating remarkable clarity in understanding complex global problems. For example, on 13 October Phyllis Frendo from a coal mining town in country Victoria handwrote:

> Dear Mr Whitlam,
>
> I was very disappointed in what I have heard. I don't think you are giving much support in helping the 'Freedom from Hunger Campaign'. We poor ones seem to be helping the 'Freedom from Hunger Campaign' more than you rich ones.
>
> A disappointed 11-year-old,
> Phyllis Frendo[129]

Phyllis was correct in observing that working-class citizens were financially supporting the FFHC more than many affluent residents, see Table 6.2 in Chapter 6. Her clarity of expression is refreshing but not uncommon among her peers. On 18 October, Paul Keen from Canberra also expressed his displeasure:

> Dear Mr Whitlam,
>
> I am not satisfied with the money you are giving the refugees. You should send 8 million dollars. Please send clothes.
> Thank you for reading my letter.
> I remain,
>
> Yours sincerely,
> Paul Keen[130]

Mind: French Postcolonial Humanitarianism in Global Conceptual History', *American Historical Review* 126 (2021): 1462.
[127] NAA: M157, 33/33PART25.
[128] Ibid.
[129] NAA: M157, 33/33PART22.
[130] NAA: M157, 33/33PART24.

Paul did not identify his age, however given that the letter was written in pencil, and by the imprecise nature of the handwriting, it is likely that he was around nine years old. Paul lived in Downer, then a working-class suburb in the north of Canberra. On the same day in a neighbouring suburb, ten-year-old Belinda Babovic also wrote to Whitlam in pencil, and sparsely used pen for emphasis on particular words. In the extract below, bold text is used in place of pen:

Dear Mr Whitlam,

I have been watching the TV and I have been seeing the <u>East Pakistan Refugees, **sick, dying**</u> and they are hungry which you can tell because they are so skinny and look so sad as you would know. I have been **PRAYING** that our Prime Minister will donate <u>more</u> money for the <u>PAKISTAN Refugees</u> who are sick and dying.
<u>Please</u> donate as much as you can. You may need help one day, too.
Please [in double sized font] help them. Please Help.
Thank you for reading this letter.

Sincerely
Belinda Babovic
(10 years old) [underline and capitalization in original][131]

Four other children aged nine to ten years of age from the neighbouring Canberran suburbs of Downer and Watson wrote to Whitlam on 18 October. One child wrote, 'the children of Rosary School have been giving money for the refugees' while another beseeched, 'I am praying very hard that you will help donate many more dollars to the refugee camp in East Pakistan. My friends would like you to do this.'[132] Given that only six children from neighbouring suburbs wrote to Whitlam on the same date, it is probable that they were friends and acted outside of classroom directives. Had they acted on instruction from a teacher, we would see at least thirty letters (a standard classroom size in Australia) in this archival file. There is also no reference to a teacher in their letters. The fact that these nine- and ten-year-old children most likely acted independently of adult influence demonstrates the impact this refugee crisis had on their young minds during a period of heightened political activism in Australia's recent history. Access to (young) children's writing is notoriously difficult, often reliant on classroom assessments or essay competitions, tasks that inherently skew children's writing towards meeting adult expectations.[133] There were occasions when schoolchildren wrote to Whitlam as a class activity, for example, the grade 6 class from St Patrick's Primary School in industrial Geelong West in Victoria, the grade 5 class from St Columban's School in Mayfield, adjacent to the port town of Newcastle in NSW, and the year 11 class from Christian Brothers' College in regional Toowoomba

---

[131] NAA: M157, 33/33PART25.
[132] Michael Cosgrove, NAA: M157, 33/33PART25; Wendy Corbin, NAA: M157, 33/33PART25.
[133] See, for example, Rachel Stevens, 'Understanding British Return Migration: The Australian Department of Immigration, British Youth Cultures and the Failed Promotional Tour of Australia in 1960', in *When Migrants Fail to Stay New Histories on Departures and Migration*, ed. Ruth Balint, Joy Damousi and Sheila Fitzpatrick (London: Bloomsbury, 2023), forthcoming.

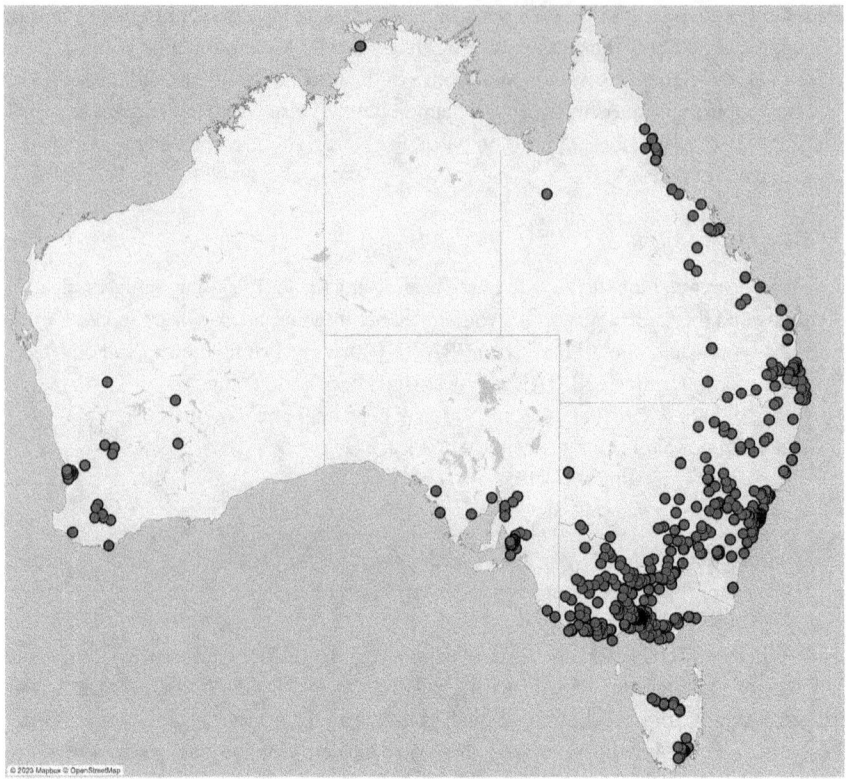

Figure 7.4 Geographical distribution of letters from citizens to Whitlam.
Source: NAA: M157, 33/33/PART21 to 26.

in Queensland.[134] Alternatively, sometimes a class would select one student to write on behalf of the class, for instance, the year 9 class at St Mary's College in Leederville, suburban Perth.[135] As was the case with households and couples who wrote to Whitlam, the fact that students wrote to Whitlam, either among friends or as a class, further demonstrates the collaborative nature of this form of humanitarian activism, which is in contrast to the typically solitary acts of consumer boycotts.

Figure 7.4 maps the location of each letter writer using the latitude and longitude coordinates of the sender's return address. This geospatial data reveals two seemingly paradoxical findings: the disproportionate concentration of letter writers in two states (Victoria and NSW); and the geographical dispersal of letter writers within these two states. First, Victorians were over-represented in the trove of letters. With 28 per cent of the national population, 39 per cent of letters came from this state. Less strikingly, NSW accounted for 38 per cent of letter writers, slightly above its proportion of the

[134] NAA: M157, 33/33PART24; NAA: M157, 33/33PART25; NAA: M157, 33/33PART26.
[135] NAA: M157, 33/33PART21.

Table 7.3 Letter Writers, Population Distribution and TV Access, Urban/Rural Divide, Victoria and NSW

		Percentage of letters	Percentage of population	Percentage with TV access in dwelling
Victoria	Urban	67	88	90
	Rural	33	12	80
	Total	100	100	100
NSW	Urban	71	79	87
	Rural	29	11	79
	Total	100	100	100

Source: NAA: M157, 33/33/PART21 to 26; Australian Bureau of Statistics, *1971 Census*.

national population (36 per cent). Conversely, letter writers in Queensland and Western Australia – traditionally the two most politically conservative states – were most under-represented. Despite accounting for 14 per cent of the national population, only 7 per cent of letters came from Queenslanders; a similar rate of under-representation occurred in Western Australia. The concentration of Victoria, especially, and NSW, to a lesser extent, can be explained by the activism and advocacy of Dynon, Poernomo and a media culture supportive of their causes.

The geographic distribution within the states of Victoria and NSW is perplexing. Table 7.3 shows that 33 per cent of letters from Victorians came from rural or regional areas despite being home to only 12 per cent of the state's residents. Similarly, 29 per cent of letters from NSW were written by country denizens even though they amounted to 11 per cent of the total population of that state.

The over-representation of rural citizens is counter-intuitive and runs contrary to conventional ideas about the urban–rural binary. As in most developed nations, Australia, too, has a long-entrenched schism between the city and the country. In a vast country with inadequate infrastructure, urban primacy was – and remains – an economic necessity for settlers. The concentration of settlement in a handful of colonial capital cities has resulted in Australia being one of the most (sub-)urbanized countries in the world.[136] Despite romanticized depictions of the bush, rural Australia has been plagued with challenges, from an unforgiving climate, an inhospitable geography, economic decline, government neglect and an absence of basic services.[137] Cultural assumptions about the city–country dichotomy persist even if they were originally

---

[136] Andrew Spencer, Jeremy Gill and Laura Schmahmann, 'Urban or suburban? Examining the density of Australian cities in global context', 7th State of Australian Cities Conference, 9–11 December 2015, Gold Coast, Australia, 2015, 12.

[137] For historiography on Australian portrayals of the bush, see Richard Waterhouse, 'Australian Legends: Representations of the Bush, 1813–1913', *Australian Historical Studies* 31 (2000): 201–21; Bill Garner, 'Bushmen of the *Bulletin*: Re-examining Lawson's "Bush Credibility" in Graeme Davison's "Sydney and the Bush"', *Australian Historical Studies* 43 (2012): 452–65; Graeme Davison, 'Sydney and the Bush: An Urban Context for the Australian Legend', *Australian Historical Studies* 18 (1978): 191–209.

imported from Britain, with modernity connected to progressive urban lifestyles, learning and communication, and rurality associated with tradition and, depending on one's perspective, backwardness, limitation and ignorance.[138] Yet, humanitarianism is fundamentally a modern idea and practice, as explored in Chapter 2. The over-representation of country-based letter writers therefore undermines ingrained cultural assumptions that equate rural with provincialism, narrow-mindedness and conservatism.

Table 7.3 also includes a column that lists access to television within the home. Fortuitously, the Australian 1971 census included a question on television access. It should be noted that Australia did not have access to colour television until 1975, much later than many other comparable Western nations. According to census data, rural dwellers were twice as likely not to have access to television, with one in five homes not having a TV set. Television ownership serves as a symbol of modernity; it also had a very practical impact, providing moving imagery of the war in Bangladesh and the refugee crisis. The relationship between TV ownership and humanitarian activism can only be inferred as a correlation – not causation – from the archival and census data. Nevertheless, the combined data suggests that the introduction of television was not as revolutionary as some scholars have argued and implies the continued centrality of radio and print news media in rural communities.[139]

Conclusion

In the historiography of humanitarianism, much scholarship has focused on the influence of media in shaping popular ideas about charity. Arguably, historians can only infer such impact. In contrast, this chapter has examined empirically the influence of individual acts of humanitarianism. It contends that by informing, moving and, importantly, conversing with their audiences, Dynon and Poernomo shaped public sentiment and motivated their onlookers to act as well. The disproportionate number of Victorians who wrote to Whitlam is quantitative evidence of the influence of Dynon and Poernomo. Other methods, such as NGOs publishing shock imagery in visual media, was probably less effective due to its unidirectional nature and the capacity of the viewer to avert their gaze. When we ask, 'why do individuals care about the suffering of distant others?' this chapter concludes that inspiration is a more activating emotion than shame or pity.

This chapter also highlights the cross-fertilization across networks of solidarity and the interaction of local and national scales of humanitarian activism. Moira Dynon and Paul Poernomo directed their supporters to donate to allied NGOs, such

---

[138] Kate Murphy, *Fears and Fantasies: Modernity, Gender and the Rural-Urban Divide* (New York: Peter Lang, 2010), introduction; Raymond Williams, *The Country and the City* (London: Chatto and Windus, 1973), 1, 297.

[139] Herteen, 'Biafras of the Mind', 1462; Bertrand Taithe, 'Compassion Fatigue: The Changing Nature of Humanitarian Emotions', in *Emotional Bodies: The Historical Performativity of Emotions*, ed. Dolores Martín-Munro and Beatriz Pichel (Urbana: University of Illinois Press, 2019), 253–4.

as the FFHC or Australian Catholic Relief. These individuals encouraged a culture of dissent (albeit through very different behaviours), which in turn contributed to the unprecedented number of constituent letters written in protest to Opposition Leader Whitlam. Christian humanitarian Len Reid, MP, was correct to credit Poernomo with the increase in Australian foreign aid to the refugees in India. Although it is comforting to present a celebratory narrative of two individuals, it is important to note that Dynon and Poernomo paid a high price for their activism. Both Dynon and Poernomo faced resistance and intimidation from an unfriendly government. Privately they also suffered the health consequences of an excessive workload (in the case of Dynon) and malnutrition (in the case of Poernomo).[140] Their sacrifices demonstrate how the bravery of the few emboldens the many.

---

[140] Dynon, 'The Later Years: 1971 to 1976', Dynon family papers.

8

Conclusion

On 19 January 1975, Gough Whitlam visited Bangladesh, the first and only Australian prime minister to do so. At a state banquet held in his honour, Whitlam remarked to his host, Bangladeshi Prime Minister Sheikh Mujibur Rahman,

> Bangladesh has no firmer friend than Australia. Our affection for your country and its people has been deep and continuing. Australia followed with close interest and deep concern the tragic events that led to the birth of your nation ... Australia gave early recognition to the new republic [of Bangladesh]. This recognition was followed by a prompt commitment to assist in the rehabilitation, development and welfare of your people. That commitment was given by the previous Australian government and unhesitatingly reaffirmed by the present [Whitlam] government. Australian policy has reflected the sympathy and affection for Bangladesh felt on both sides of the Australia parliament, among all parties and in all parts of society.[1]

Although Whitlam correctly identified that 'all parts of [Australian] society' had felt sympathy for the Bangladeshi cause, he understated the intensity of such sentiment. Meanwhile, Whitlam exaggerated the degree of support offered by the Australian government at the time. Whitlam also omitted how citizens and NGOs extensively lobbied political leaders to change policy, with some success. This extract demonstrates why it is so important for historians to interrogate the histories constructed by political leaders, whether they be in the form of memoirs or public speeches after the fact. Given the prevalence of state-centric accounts, along with archived state documents, it is little wonder the limited scholarship on the Bangladesh Liberation War that does exist in English typically focuses on the actions of governments. Histories written by Gary Bass, Sonia Cordera, Srinath Raghavan and Simon Smith provide important entry points into understanding international responses to an often-overlooked war of independence. However, these accounts do not tell the whole story. In the case of Australia at least, the intentions and actions of citizens proved more consequential than government policy. Indeed, citizens led politicians during a distinct period of heightened public activism alongside timid political leadership.

---

[1] Gough Whitlam, 'Speech by the Prime Minister of Australia, the Hon E. G. Whitlam, QC at a Banquet Given by the Prime Minister of Bangladesh in Dacca on 19 January 1975', Box 0149, Whitlam Prime Ministerial Collection, 2.

A common theme that runs throughout this book is that of resistance. After decades of instability and poverty due to the Depression and two world wars, Australians naturally welcomed the security and material abundance that came with the economic boom years of the mid-twentieth century. But as indicated by Liisa Malkki in her study of female Finnish Red Cross workers, financial security and political stability can only provide limited levels of satisfaction and do little to stymie the mundane routinization or loneliness of everyday life.[2] When Australians read or heard about Bangladeshi refugees facing a cholera outbreak in June or a freezing winter in October, these challenges were viewed as symbolic of systemic problems in the new world order. The Bangladeshi refugees in India were daily reminders that society had become too materialistic and that individuals showed a callous disregard for the suffering of others. In this context, citizen-driven aid should be seen as another example of the protest movements and counterculture of the 1960s and 1970s.[3] In their calls to aid Bangladeshi refugees, Australian citizens implicitly, and at times explicitly, rejected the emotionally vapid post-Second World War consumerism and, instead, sought to build connections with the recipients of aid. Well-travelled, informed and frustrated with government inertia, Australian citizens from a cross-section of society challenged their political leaders to address global economic inequalities and mitigate injustice, particularly in the decolonizing states of Asia.

Australian citizens during the 1971 crisis also disregarded the dominant frame of post-Second World War geopolitics, namely, the Cold War binary. The evidence presented in this book shows a blanket absence of citizen concern about the Cold War as it related to the refugee crisis. To be sure, the Bangladesh Liberation War was not a neat conflict between capitalist and communist belligerents. The Indian state was officially non-aligned but was closer to the USSR than the United States and had an active communist party within its own borders. Meanwhile, the Awami League was overtly socialist in its doctrine, which contrasted with the close alliance between West Pakistan and the United States. If Australian citizens were to adhere blindly to Cold War logic, then it would follow that they would support West Pakistan or at least abstain from aligning with either side. The reasons for Australians shelving Cold War calculations are arguably twofold: first, as Agnieszka Sobocinska has shown in her analysis of applications to the Volunteer Graduate Scheme (VGS), from the 1950s, young Australians expressed anticolonial attitudes; by 1971, many of these graduates would be at the peak of their careers, shaping humanitarian operations and public discourse – for example, Jim Webb, director of Community Aid Abroad (CAA) and former VGS worker.[4] Second, Australia's military involvement in the American war in Vietnam soured popular attitudes towards 'hot' conflicts in the Cold War and, in particular, demonstrated the futility in trying to suppress national liberation struggles

---

[2] Liisa Malkki, *The Need to Help: The Domestic Arts of International Humanitarianism* (Durham, NC: Duke University Press, 2015), 3–10, 22.
[3] For an excellent discussion of the connection between Cold War politics, economic security and counterculture, see Jeremy Suri, 'AHR Forum: The Rise and Fall of an International Counterculture, 1960–1975', *American Historical Review* 114 (2009): 67–8.
[4] Sobocinska, *Saving the World?* 109.

led by local socialists. Like Martyn Lyons and his study of constituent letters to Robert Menzies, this study has shown that citizens were not passive repositories of official ideology and thus presents an alternative political history that sidelines rather than centres the Cold War.[5]

Citizen-Driven Humanitarianism takes as its vantage point a comparison of multiple NGOs within one national context facing a specific crisis that demanded a response. Rather than looking at a specific NGO over time or examining several NGOs during a series of episodes, this book illustrates the advantages of employing a deep, yet narrow, analysis to a field of research. In examining civil society actors at multiple levels – the internationally connected, the national federations, grassroots organizations and individual activists – this book highlights the shifting contours and trajectories of the NGO sector in Australia, much of which is applicable to other Western nations. Most notably, the NGO sector in the 1970s was overcrowded, with each agency competing for brand awareness, differentiation, donor dollars and access to the corridors of power. Along with fighting for survival, NGOs also differed in ideology and fundamental ideas about who aid organizations should help and why. In this congested landscape, some NGOs thought it best to cooperate and pool resources for maximum benefit, such as Oxfam UK and CAA, the Australian Freedom from Hunger Campaign [FFHC] and CAA, and Austcare and ACFOA. The tense environment in which Australian humanitarian organizations operated came to a climax in early 1972 when Oxfam UK indirectly entered the Australian market much to the chagrin of Austcare's founder Paul Cullen. His overreaction to the CAA proposal to run an appeal for the Bangladesh reconstruction effort in early 1972 reflects a deeply divided sector that could not even agree on the causes of the Bangladeshi exodus and the best methods to help. By comparing the paths that different NGOs took in 1971, we see how the decisions made by specific organizations were merely one option among others. Comparative forms of writing history are therefore one of the most effective ways to instil contingency in our narratives of past events.

By looking at multiple actors across various scales, we can also see the ways in which humanitarian organizations and individuals interacted, which in turn influenced the collective humanitarian response. Figure 8.1 illustrates the creation and operation of networks of solidarity during the Bangladeshi refugee crisis in the form of a scaled Venn diagram.

This diagram has three elements. First, the relative significance and power of each humanitarian actor in the Australian landscape is represented by its size and the thickness of its outline. Second, each humanitarian actor is positioned in proximity to allies and at a distance from oppositional competitors. Lines connect humanitarian actors who shared a relationship: the thickness of the line depicts the strength of the relationship between humanitarian actors, and conversely, a thin line represents a weak association. Third, each humanitarian actor discussed in this book is clustered within one of three ideological orientations within a set: state aligned (dotted line), religious (dash line) and activist (solid line). Because some humanitarian actors had

---

[5] Lyons, *Dear Prime Minister*, 229.

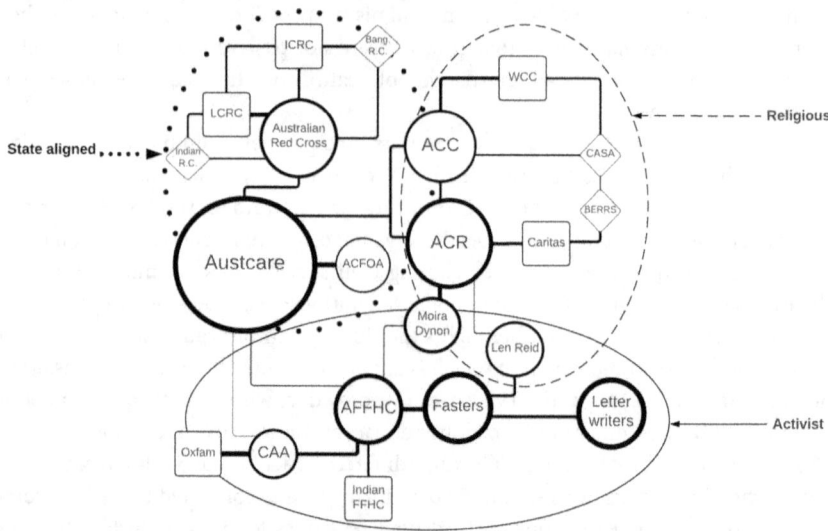

Figure 8.1 Inter-network cluster analysis. Created by author.

more than one ideological orientation, there are sets that overlap. For example, Len Reid was an activist as well as religious and, therefore, occupies the intersection of both the religious and activist sets.

Figure 8.1 presents a tangled Australian aid network. The relationships were closest when ideological dispositions were shared across organizations – for example, among the Australian Council of Churches (ACC) and Australian Catholic Relief (ACR) – and between organizations and their international parent bodies – such as CAA and Oxfam, or throughout the Red Cross movement. Austcare was the largest humanitarian organization, but it was not as influential as it believed it should be. Alongside Austcare, many other aid agencies forged an independent path, such as the Australian FFHC. Figure 8.1 also documents the layers of interaction between individuals, national organizations and international federations. For instance, devout Catholic Moira Dynon was widely covered in the local Catholic press, which no doubt helped ACR fundraise for Bangladeshi refugees, money that was later forwarded to Caritas Internationalis and from there, onto the Bangladesh Ecumenical Relief and Rehabilitation Service (BERRS). Although Figure 8.1 depicts networks of solidarity, it likewise represents disunity, too. The working relationship between CAA and Austcare was weak at best, hostile at worst; there was no connection between the fasters and any of the state-aligned or religious humanitarian organizations, including ACFOA, Austcare, the Australian Red Cross, ACC and ACR. Despite the absence of an alliance between the fasters and these foremost aid agencies, the hunger strikers connected with other like-minded individuals, such as inspiring the letter writers. Moreover, the fasters aligned themselves with organizations of a similar ideological mindset, such as the Australian FFHC and CAA.

Figure 8.1 is designed as a scaled Venn diagram, so that each set or cluster represents its influence relative to others. In other words, the activist cluster is larger than the religious cluster, which in turn is larger than the state-aligned cluster. The difference in cluster size is not overwhelming, but it is significant. In Chapters 3 and 4, I demonstrated that the behaviours of the federations and the Red Cross detracted from the overall effectiveness of state-aligned humanitarian assistance to Bangladeshi refugees. In Chapter 5 and in the first section of Chapter 7, I showed that religious humanitarians enhanced their effectiveness primarily from their commitment to ecumenicalism and collaborative consultation with local communities in India and Bangladesh. In Chapters 6 and 7, I illustrated how activists drove the Australian humanitarian response to the Bangladeshi refugee crisis. They were able to do so due to the numbers of citizens involved, their emotional commitment to the cause and radicalism that imbued the political climate at that time.

In addition to charting the development of Australian humanitarianism in the third quarter of the twentieth century, this book makes three interventions into Western humanitarian historiography. First, throughout this book, I have argued that elite and established NGOs encountered citizen blowback from their push towards professionalization and de-politicization. Instead of capitulating to the discourse and practices of the modern NGO, empowered citizens created their own forms of humanitarianism that satisfied their desires for proximity and knowing the recipients of aid. If eighteenth- and nineteenth-century humanitarianism was characterized by distance, then late-twentieth-century charity could be categorized by a degree of intimacy in which individual humanitarians sought relationships and knowledge from the people they sought to help. This book presents a narrative of citizens taking back control and power from organizations that were increasingly seen as too closely associated with states and intergovernmental bodies. Anne-Meike Fechter has shown in her contemporary ethnographic research in Cambodia that caring became a form of establishing connection and, by extension, facilitating a sense of belonging in the recipient community.[6] Rather than seeing recipients as fundamentally different from the donor, individual humanitarians typically created a sense of familiarity by building bridges across significant social, cultural and ethnic divides. As such, Fechter challenges the 'distant stranger' or 'exotic other' as the archetypal humanitarian object; instead, she shows that familiarity, mutual appreciation and direct relationships are equally, if not more, important for motivating and attracting individual humanitarians.[7]

The second intervention is that when one looks beyond the established, elite-run NGOs, we see the persistence of Christianity in shaping ideas and rationales that underpinned international humanitarianism. In Chapter 5, I demonstrated that activist Christians were the new outsiders; their politics of aggressive economic redistribution made them natural allies of the New Left; their sympathy for the marginalized – based on biblical foundations of the upside-down kingdom – begot aid that was universal in

---

[6] Anne-Meike Fechter, 'Brokering Transnational Flows of Care: The Case of Citizen Aid', *Ethnos* 85 (2020): 299, 301.

[7] Anne-Meike Fechter, 'Development and the Search for Connection', *Third World Quarterly* 40 (2019): 1816, 1828.

scope.[8] Similarly, Len Reid argued openly for a down-to-earth Christianity. Grassroots organizations, including CAA/Oxfam and the Australian FFHC, while ostensibly secular, also had deep Christian roots at their core. The beliefs of CAA and the FFHC were similarly based on the Christian ethics of social justice and duty, even if only implicitly. In Chapter 7, devout Catholic Moira Dynon was unwavering in her commitment to reduce hunger in South Asia and empowered women and children to do the same. Paul Poernomo, while not Christian, similarly drew upon his spirituality to sustain him and his followers to continue their fasts for a cause greater than themselves. In the citizen letters of protest sent to Whitlam, hundreds of letter writers explicitly identified themselves as Christian, Catholic or living in a Christian country. This book has shown that even if religious identities became less salient after the 1950s, this did not equate to a decline in religiously informed behaviour.

The myth of secularism is problematic because it too narrowly defines religiosity as based on regular church attendance, church membership or daily prayer. Once we expand the definition of religion to include cultural assumptions about morality, justice and equality, we see that faith continued to influence how individuals understood global problems and impacted humanitarian practices. Furthermore, secularism as an idea is powerful because it is closely associated with modernity and scientific rationalism, values that were embraced by the post-Second World War NGO. Arguably, the broad appeal of secularism is also due to what it is not: it is free from connotations of bigotry, abuses of power and traditional social values that marginalize women, homosexuals and believers of other faiths. But regrettably, the church does not have a monopoly on such failings. We must remind ourselves that secularism is not a neutral position but in fact promotes, what Alistair Ager and Joey Ager term, a 'liberal materialism' that deems reasonable only that which is materially verifiable.[9] It is important that historians recognize the contributions of Christians to the understanding and practice of humanitarianism and not be dissuaded by counterclaims that associate Christianity with intolerance, violence or the excesses of their missionary pasts. Indeed, during the mid-twentieth century, Christians of various persuasions were pioneering champions of solidarity. As Diarmaid Kelliher observes, solidarity movements are underpinned by the twin philosophies of the New Left and Christian thinking.[10] It is therefore possible if not popular to accept the diversity and complexity of what it means to be a person of faith in the modern world.

Particularly for historians of humanitarianism, or international historians interested in cross-cultural encounters, it is important to remember what religion can offer. It presents us with a compelling explanation of why individuals mobilized for a cause when they themselves had nothing to gain. In *Other People's Struggles*, political theorist Nicholas Owen explores who he terms 'the conscience constituent', who is distinct from the 'beneficiary constituent', who is an individual who does stand to gain from

---

[8] Ross Langmead, 'Refugees as Guests and Hosts: Towards a Theology of Mission among Refugees and Asylum Seekers', *Religion, Migration and Identity* 43 (2016): 175.
[9] Alistair Ager and Joey Ager, 'Faith and the Discourse of Secular Humanitarianism', *Journal of Refugee Studies* 24 (2011): 459.
[10] Diarmaid Kelliher, 'Historicising Geographies of Solidarity', *Geography Compass* 12 (2018): 1.

social movements.[11] Faith, it has been shown in this book, was a powerful motivating force for individuals from a range of backgrounds to advocate for significantly greater levels of humanitarian assistance for Bangladeshi refugees. Faith is also important for humanitarian practitioners who often find themselves working in deeply religious communities. A recent global analysis of 2,000 censuses, surveys and population registers found that 80 per cent of the world's population identified with a religious group, a figure that would be even higher if we examined just the Global South.[12] As we saw in Chapter 4, foreign aid workers were expelled from the mostly Hindu-dominated refugee camps in part because the Indian government determined there was a clash of cultures.[13] For humanitarians working at the operational level, religious literacy is crucial to enable them to engage effectively with the recipients of aid. Religion also presents a method to approaching post-conflict recovery and reconciling the brutalities of war with the ongoing necessity of everyday survival. For those forced into exile or who witnessed atrocities, theology can provide an important source of succour and offer meaning to the incomprehensible, cathartic avenues that are unavailable to secularists.[14] The marginalization of religion within humanitarian discourse is, to adopt Erin Wilson's terminology, 'an ontological injustice' that denies 'views of alternative worlds'.[15] In other words, the hegemony of secularism in many humanitarian NGOs not only negates alternative views of the world (epistemological injustice) but also fails to acknowledge that different people inhabit different worlds (ontological injustice). For individual humanitarians, Bangladeshi recipients of aid and local Indian welfare agencies, faith served as a guiding light. Rather than seeing religion as oppositional to rational, scientifically based humanitarianism, historians of humanitarianism should view faith as complementary and an enduring component of the humanitarian spirit.

The third intervention is by drawing attention to the central role played by individuals from a cross-section of society. Recently, Agnieszka Sobocinska wrote, 'we still know very little about the public's engagement with foreign aid and international development before the 1980s'.[16] This book begins to fill this lacuna. In the case of Australian aid for Bangladeshi refugees in 1971, the suburban and rural backgrounds of the activists, letter writers and donors to the FFHC can all be viewed as symptoms of 'the politics of the street' rather than reflecting perspectives of depersonalized organizations.[17] Throughout this book, I have been keen to draw attention to the role of individuals: their backgrounds, attitudes, blind spots, motivations and strategies. What we find is that leadership matters in inspiring citizens, and that leadership itself comes in many forms. Paul Poernomo, for example, was hardly a typical poster boy of the counterculture movement, and his background could be summarized as a series

---

[11] Nicholas Owen, *Other People's Struggles: Outsiders in Social Movements* (Oxford: Oxford University Press, 2019), 1–20.
[12] Alistair Ager and Joey Ager, *Faith, Secularism, and Humanitarian Engagement: Finding the Place of Religion in the Support of Displaced Communities* (New York: Palgrave Macmillan, 2015), 7.
[13] Ibid., 9.
[14] Ager and Ager, 'Faith and the Discourse of Secular Humanitarianism', 461.
[15] Erin Wilson, ' "Power Differences" and "the Power of Difference": The Dominance of Secularism as Ontological Injustice', *Globalizations* 14 (2017): 1076, 1083.
[16] Sobocinska, *Saving the World?* 15.
[17] O'Sullivan, *Ireland, Africa and the End of Empire*, 152.

of failures, underachievement and mundanity. Yet his quiet commitment to a public fast struck a chord with the public, and sympathy with his cause only grew after his arrest by federal police. Meanwhile, Moira Dynon travelled the country, speaking about the riches of South Asian culture and what Western civilization could gain from Eastern practices as well as what it could give. In a distinctly female approach to dialogue, Dynon engaged with her audience as equals, sharing her message and encouraging conversation. Her goal was to stimulate curiosity about different societies. This approach was not about instilling a sense of shared humanity that held an implicit assumption about Western superiority. Rather, Dynon (as well as CAA and the FFHC) endeavoured to communicate an appreciation of difference not sameness. This was more than just compassion; it was about respect for others and an acknowledgement that Asian cultures had much to offer Westerners dissatisfied with the rise in consumerism, individualism and the continued warmongering of the Cold War.

Effective leadership is as much about empowering others as it is to lead by example. In the cases of Len Reid and Dynon, both used their platforms to argue that every individual had an obligation to mitigate inequality and prevent suffering. Such empowerment had clear effects, as shown by the letter writers and donors. Data documented in this book demonstrates that groups hitherto marginalized from positions of power, such as the working class, women, children and youth, actively engaged with the cause to aid Bangladeshi refugees, as well as related issues, including decolonization, economic inequality and mass violence against minorities. Particularly in Chapters 6 and 7, *Citizen-Driven Humanitarianism* has been careful to eschew vague, ill-defined terms to describe citizens, such as 'the public', 'the masses' or 'ordinary people'. By integrating census data to this research, we gain insight into the demographics of people most likely to fundraise and advocate for Bangladeshi refugees. In addition to asking who was motivated to provide aid for Bangladeshi refugees, I also asked, how were they mobilized? The research in this book indicates that media were important sources of information for citizens, but that television may not be as significant a factor as one would readily assume. As has been explained previously, faith was a critical motivating force, as were the hunger strikers who protested in the cities across the triangle of power in Australia: Melbourne, Canberra and Sydney.

Lastly, by considering where citizen donors and activists lived, we can glean insights into how solidarity emerged as a process. This book contends that place of residence had powerful impacts, creating specific sites of protest; see Figure 7.3. As geographers Gavin Brown and Helen Yaffe have found in the case of anti-apartheid protests in London, we see in the case of Australian aid for Bangladeshi refugees that solidarity emerged in more than one place simultaneously; it was multidirectional, complex and multilayered in which ideas rapidly moved between hubs (cities) and spokes (towns). Brown and Yaffe write that unlike charity, solidarity forms when citizens perceive oppression and injustice and *identify* with external suffering. Possibly, the extent to which Australian citizens identified with Bangladeshi refugees and their quest for liberation holds a mirror to a deep, unspoken discontent within Australian society.[18]

---

[18] Gavin Brown and Helen Yaffe, 'Practices of Solidarity: Opposing Apartheid in the Centre of London', *Antipodes* 46 (2014): 37.

Western democracies have a habitual concern about the rise of populist political parties, specifically those targeting far-right constituencies. Over the past eight years, arguably, anxieties about political populism reached their zenith after the election of Donald Trump in the United States and the successful Brexit campaign in the UK. As troubling as these elections were, they do not represent the entirety of political behaviour in Western democracies. *Citizen-Driven Humanitarianism* highlights that populism is not intrinsically a force of evil. In the case of Australian citizens, they effectively moved government policy towards a more compassionate position for Bangladeshi refugees even though these political leaders had little to gain (electorally or geopolitically) from such a change. This instance of citizens leading the political establishment was not an aberration, even if it was rare. After the 2004 Indian Ocean tsunami that killed over 200,000 people and displaced 1.5 million people in Indonesia, Sri Lanka, the Maldives, the Seychelles, India and Thailand, the Australian government spent A$60 million on immediate emergency relief. The government offered an additional A$15 million in grants and funding for the World Bank and Asian Development Bank. The combined A$75 million donated by the Australian government pales in comparison to the A$330 million donated by Australian citizens to humanitarian NGOs.[19] As was the case during the Bangladesh Liberation War, Australian citizen donations occurred at a time of extended, conservative political rule, and at the subsequent federal election, a reformist Labor party won government. Thus, during periods of political disaffection and a widespread perception that the incumbent government does not reflect the will of the people, Australian citizens have demonstrated a capacity to outperform government action. Too often, populism is associated with politicians acquiescing to the demands of a vocal and extreme minority for electoral advantage. If our political leaders instead sought out and listened to the quiet voices of decency, then we could find a path towards policies that treat refugees not as criminals but with magnanimity.

---

[19] Australian Government AusAid, *Australia's Response to the Indian Ocean Tsunami. Report for the Period Ending 30 June 2005* (Canberra: Commonwealth of Australia, 2005), iii–3, 13.

Bibliography

Archival material

Archives of the Australian Baptist Missionary Society
Australian Council of Churches Records
Australian Council for Overseas Aid Records
Australian Freedom from Hunger Campaign Records
Australian Red Cross – National Office Records
Casey Family Papers
Community Aid Abroad Archives, National Library of Australia and University of Melbourne Archives
Dodge family Papers
Dynon Family Papers
International Committee of the Red Cross Archives
Letter 1972 [manuscript], correspondence between Jim Allen and Moira Dynon
National Archives of Australia
National Archives (UK)
Near East Relief Committee Records
Oxfam Archive, Oxford University
Papers of Leonard Stanley Reid
Papers of Rt Hon. Malcolm John Fraser
Papers of Sir William McMahon
Save the Children Fund Archive, University of Birmingham
United Nations High Commission for Refugees Archives
Whitlam Prime Ministerial Collection
World Council of Churches Archives

Oral history interviews

David Scott, interview with Ann Turner, 2001
James Lawrence Allen, interviewed by Mel Pratt, 1976
Major-General Paul Cullen, interviewed by Diana Ritch, 1983
Phillip Flood, interviewed by Gregory Wood, 2012
Sir Geoffrey Newman-Morris, interviewed by Amy McGrath, 1980
Sir Keith Shann, interviewed by Ken Henderson, 1985

Periodicals

Adelaide Advertiser
Ally (The Society for Those Who Have Less)

Austcare News Bulletin
Australian Jewish News
Canberra Times
Catholic Leader
Communist Party Tribune
Diamond Valley News
Dutch Australian Weekly
Farrago
Hansard (Parliament of Australia)
International Review of the Red Cross
Launceston Examiner
Melbourne Herald
Melbourne Sun-News
National Times
New York Times
Now, Incorporating Food for Peace News
Now, the Journal of Community Aid Abroad
Papua New Guinea Post-Courier
Sydney Morning Herald
The Age
The Advocate (Melbourne Catholic newspaper)
The Argus
The Australian
The Catholic Worker
The Economist
The Guardian
The Lutheran
The Telegraph (Brisbane)
The West Australian
UNHCR Bulletin
Vision Magazine
World Union of Students News Service
Woroni

Works cited

Adelman, Jeremy. 'Is Global History Still Possible, or Has It Had Its Moment?' *Aeon* (2017). Accessed 6 May 2023, https://aeon.co/essays/is-global-history-still-possible-or-has-it-had-its-moment.

Ager, Alistair, and Joey Ager. 'Faith and the Discourse of Secular Humanitarianism'. *Journal of Refugee Studies* 24 (2011): 456–72.

Ager, Alistair, and Joey Ager. *Faith, Secularism, and Humanitarian Engagement: Finding the Place of Religion in the Support of Displaced Communities*. New York: Palgrave Macmillan, 2015.

Aker, Jenny. 'Cash or Coupons? Testing the Impacts of Cash versus Vouchers in the Democratic Republic of Congo'. *Center for Global Development Working Paper* 320 (2013): 1–51.

Akmam, Wardatul. 'Atrocities against Humanity during the Liberation War in Bangladesh: A Case of Genocide'. *Journal of Genocide Research* 4 (2002): 543–59.

Allana, Gulam. *Pakistan Movement: Historic Documents*. Karachi: University of Karachi, 1967.

Allen, Margaret. '"White Already to Harvest". South Australian Women Missionaries in India'. *Feminist Review* 65 (2000): 92–107.

Andrade, Tonio. 'A Chinese Farmer, Two African Boys, and a Warlord: Toward a Global Microhistory'. *Journal of World History* 21 (2010): 573–91.

Arrow, Michelle. *Friday on Our Minds: Popular Culture in Australia since 1945*. Sydney: University of New South Wales Press, 2009.

Aslanian, Sebouh David, Joyce E. Chaplin, Ann McGrath and Kristin Mann. 'AHR Conversation. How Size Matters: The Question of Scale in History'. *American Historical Review* 118 (December 2013): 1431–72.

Australian Bureau of Statistics. '2016 Census Data Summary: Religion in Australia'. Accessed 13 March 2022. https://www.ausstats.abs.gov.au/Ausstats/subscriber.nsf/0/E3E51096DAC0AD7CCA25814D00240616/$File/religion,%202016%20census%20data%20summary%20(updated).pdf.

Australian Bureau of Statistics. 'Historical Data'. https://www.abs.gov.au/websitedbs/censushome.nsf/home/historicaldata?opendocument.

Australian Bureau of Statistics. 'People and Communities'. https://www.abs.gov.au/People-and-Communities.

Australian Bureau of Statistics. *1971 Census of Population and Housing*. Canberra: Australian Government Publishing Service, 1971. https://www.abs.gov.au/AUSSTATS/abs@.nsf/DetailsPage/2105.01971?OpenDocument.

Australian Bureau of Statistics, 'Average Weekly Earnings. June 1971'. Accessed 24 February 2022. https://www.ausstats.abs.gov.au/ausstats/free.nsf/0/743DBDA3F3F797D0CA25751600108605/$File/63020_JUN1971.pdf.

Australian Catholic Relief. *Annual Report 1971* (Sydney: Devonshire Press, 1972).

Australian Catholic Relief. *Annual Report 1972* (Sydney: Devonshire Press, 1973).

Australian Charities and Not-for-profits Commission (ACNC), *Australian Charities Report, 8th Edition*, 7 June 2022. Accessed 12 May 2023. https://www.acnc.gov.au/tools/reports/australian-charities-report-8th-edition.

Australian Council of Social Service. *Giving Australia: Research on Philanthropy in Australia*. Canberra: AGPS, 2005.

Australian Curriculum, Assessment and Reporting Authority. 'National Report on Schooling in Australia Data Portal'. Accessed 14 April 2022, https://www.acara.edu.au/reporting/national-report-on-schooling-in-australia/national-report-on-schooling-in-australia-data-portal/student-numbers#view1.

Australian Government. *Social Security Guide*. Accessed 22 March 2022. https://guides.dss.gov.au/guide-social-security-law/5/2/2/10.

Australian Government AusAid. *Australia's Response to the Indian Ocean Tsunami: Report for the Period Ending 30 June 2005*. Canberra: Commonwealth of Australia, 2005.

Australian Taxation Office. *Taxation Statistics 1983–84*. Canberra: Australian Government Publishing Service, 1986.

Backhuis, Per Catharina. '"Noble Helpers of Evil Exploiters?" Contesting and Negotiating West German Mass Tourism to the Global South, 1970–1985'. *Journal of Tourism History* 14 (2022): 47–69.

Baker, Kevin. *Paul Cullen, Citizen and Soldier: The Life and Times of Major-General Paul Cullen AC, CBE, DSO and Bar, ED, FCA*. Sydney: Rosenberg, 2005.

Bal, Ellen. 'Becoming the Garos of Bangladesh: Policies of Exclusion and the Ethnicisation of a "Tribal" Minority'. *South Asia: Journal of South Asian Studies* 30 (2007): 439–55.

Ballantyne, Tony. 'Moving Texts and "Humane Sentiment": Materiality, Mobility and the Emotions of Imperial Humanitarianism'. *Journal of Colonialism and Colonial History* 17, no. 1 (2016): 1–21. Accessed 23 April 2021. doi:10.1353/cch.2016.0000.

Barnett, Michael. *Empire of Humanity: A History of Humanitarianism*. Ithaca, NY: Cornell University Press, 2011.

Barnett, Michael, and Janice Gross Stein, *Sacred Aid: Faith and Humanitarianism*. New York: Oxford University Press, 2012.

Barrett Meyering, Isobelle. 'The Margaret Bailey Case: High School Activism, the Right to Education and Modern Citizenship in Late 1960s Australia'. *History Education Review* 48 (2019): 183–97.

Bass, Gary J. *Freedom's Battle: The Origins of Humanitarian Intervention*. New York: Vintage Books, 2008.

Bass, Gary J. *The Blood Telegram: Nixon, Kissinger, and a Forgotten Genocide*. New York: Alfred A. Knopf, 2013.

Baughan, Emily. 'International Adoption and Anglo-American Internationalism, c.1918–1925'. *Past & Present* 239 (2018): 181–217.

Baughan, Emily. *Saving the Children: Humanitarianism, Internationalism and Empire*. Berkeley: University of California Press, 2022.

Baughan, Emily, and Juliano Fiori. 'Save the Children, the Humanitarian Project, and the Politics of Solidarity: Reviving Dorothy Buxton's Vision'. *Disasters* 39 (2015): s129–s145.

Beachler, Donald. 'The Politics of Genocide Scholarship: The Case of Bangladesh'. *Patterns of Prejudice* 41 (2007): 467–92.

Beck, Luke. 'The Theological Underpinnings of Australia's Constitutional Separation of Church and State Provision'. *Australian Journal of Politics & History* 64 (2018): 1–17.

Bell, David. 'This Is What Happens When Historians Overuse the Idea of the Network', *The New Republic*, 26 October 2013.

Benthall, Jonathan. 'The Care of Orphans in the Islamic Tradition, Vulnerable Children, and Child Sponsorship Programs'. *Journal of Muslim Philanthropy and Civil Society* 3 (2019): 4–24.

Benvenuti, Andrea. 'Difficult Partners: Indo-Australian Relations at the Height of the Cold War, 1949–64'. *Australian Journal of Politics and History* 57 (2011): 53–67.

Berg, Maxine. 'Introduction: Global Microhistory of the Local and the Global'. *Journal of Early Modern History* 27 (2023): 1–5.

Black, Maggie. *Cause for Our Times: Oxfam – the First Fifty Years*. Oxford: Oxford University Press, 1992.

Blaxland, John. *The Protest Years: The Official History of ASIO, 1963–1975*. Sydney: Allen & Unwin, 2015.

Blood, Archer. *The Cruel Birth of Bangladesh: Memoirs of an American Diplomat*. Dhaka: University Press Limited, 2002.

Bocking-Welch, Anna. 'Imperial Legacies and International Discourses; British Involvement in the United Nations Freedom from Hunger Campaign'. *Journal of Imperial and Commonwealth History* 40, no. 5 (2012): 879–96.

Bocking-Welch, Anna. 'Youth against Hunger: Service, Activism and the Mobilisation of Young Humanitarians in 1960s Britain'. *European Review of History* 23, nos. 1–2 (2016): 154–70.

Bose, Sarmila. *Dead Reckoning: Memories of the 1971 Bangladesh War*. London: Hurst, 2011.
Bose, Sarmila. 'History on the Line: Fragments of Memories: Researching Violence in the 1971 Bangladesh War'. *History Workshop Journal* 73 (2012): 285-95.
Bose, Sarmila. 'The Question of Genocide and the Quest for Justice in the 1971 War'. *Journal of Genocide Research* 13, no. 4 (2011): 393-419.
Boucher, Ellen. *Empire's Children: Child Emigration, Welfare, and the Decline of the British Empire*. Cambridge: Cambridge University Press, 2015.
Brown and Helen Yaffe. 'Practices of Solidarity: Opposing Apartheid in the Centre of London'. *Antipodes* 46 (2014): 34-52.
Brushett, Kevin. 'Partners in Development? Robert McNamara, Lester Pearson, and the Commission on International Development, 1967-1973'. *Diplomacy and Statecraft* 26 (2015): 84-102.
Buch, Neville Douglas. 'American Influence on Protestantism in Queensland since 1945'. PhD Diss., University of Queensland, 1994.
Bunch, Matthew. 'All Roads Lead to Rome: Canada, the Freedom from Hunger Campaign and the Rise of NGOs, 1960-1980'. PhD Diss., University of Waterloo, 2007.
Burke, Roland. *Decolonization and the Evolution of International Human Rights*. Philadelphia: University of Pennsylvania Press, 2013.
Butt, Aqil. *Secession and Security: Explaining State Strategy against Separatists*. Ithaca, NY: Cornell University Press, 2017.
Cabanes, Bruno. *The Great War and the Origins of Humanitarianism, 1918-1924*. Cambridge: Cambridge University Press, 2014.
Carcasson, Martin. 'Negotiating the Paradoxes of Poverty: Presidential Rhetoric on Welfare from Johnson to Clinton'. PhD Diss., Texas A & M University, 2004.
Carey, Hilary. *Empire of Hell: Religion and the Campaign to End Convict Transportation in the British Empire, 1788-1875*. Cambridge: Cambridge University Press, 2019.
Chacko, Priya. 'Indian Foreign Policy and the Ambivalence of Postcolonial Modernity', PhD Diss., University of Adelaide, 2007.
Chavura, Stephen, John Gasgoine and Ian Tregenza, *Reason, Religion and the Australian Polity: A Secular State?* London: Routledge, 2019.
Chilton, Hugh. *Evangelicals and the End of Christendom: Religion, Australia and the Crises of the 1960*. New York: Routledge, 2020.
Christiansen, Samantha. 'From Student Activists to Muktibahini: Students, Mass Violence and the Bangladesh Liberation War'. In *Genocide and Mass Violence in Asia: An Introductory Reader*, edited by Frank Jacob, 78-97. Berlin: De Gruyter, 2019.
Christie, Scott. 'Inside Community Aid Abroad Part I: The Effervescent Agency with the Bubble-up Philosophy'. *Australian Social Work* 40 (1987): 31-2.
Christie, Scott. 'Inside Community Aid Abroad: Part IV. Development Is for Donors Too'. *Australian Social Work* 41 (1988): 36-7.
Clark, J. C. D. 'Secularization and Modernization: The Failure of a "Grand Narrative"'. *Historical Journal* 55 (2012): 161-94.
Commonwealth of Australia, Census of Population and Housing, 30 June 1966. *Volume 4, Population and Dwellings in Local Government Areas, Part 2 Victoria*. Canberra: Government Printer, 1967.
Commonwealth of Australia. *Bulletin 4. Birthplace. Part 9. Australia*. Sydney: Ambassador Press, 1973.
Cordera, Sonia. 'India's Response to the 1971 East Pakistan Crisis. Hidden and Open Reasons for Intervention'. *Journal of Genocide Research* 17 (2015): 45-62.

Crouthamel, Jason, and Peter Leese, eds. *Psychological Trauma and the Legacies of the First World War*. Cham: Palgrave Macmillan/Springer International, 2017.

Cruickshank, Joanna. 'Religious Freedom in "the Most Godless Place under Heaven": Making Policy for Religion in Australia'. *History Australia* 18 (2021): 42–52.

Curtis, Heather D. *Holy Humanitarians: American Evangelicals and Global Aid*. Cambridge, MA: Harvard University Press, 2018.

D'Costa, Bina. *Nationbuilding, Gender and War Crimes in South Asia*. London: Routledge, 2011.

Damousi, Joy. 'Humanitarianism and Child Refugee Sponsorship: The Spanish Civil War and the Global Campaign of Esme Odgers'. *Journal of Women's History* 32 (2020): 111–34.

Damousi, Joy. 'Humanitarianism in the Interwar Years: How Australians Responded to the Child Refugees of the Armenian Genocide and the Greek-Turkish Exchange'. *History Australia* 12 (2015): 95–115.

Damousi, Joy. *The Humanitarians: Child War Refugees and Australian Humanitarianism in a Transnational World, 1919-1975*. Cambridge: Cambridge University Press, 2022.

Damousi, Joy. 'World Refugee Year 1959–60: Humanitarian Rights in Postwar Australia'. *Australian Historical Studies* 51 (2020): 212–27.

Datta, Antara. *Refugees and Borders in South Asia: The Great Exodus of 1971*. New York: Routledge, 2012.

Davey, Eleanor. *Idealism beyond Borders: The French Revolutionary Left and the Rise of Humanitarianism, 1954–1988*. Cambridge: Cambridge University Press, 2015.

David, Huw T. 'Transnational Advocacy in the Eighteenth Century: Transatlantic Activism and the Anti-Slavery Movement'. *Global Networks* 7 (2007): 367–82.

Davies, Thomas. 'Rethinking the Origins of Transnational Humanitarian Organizations: The Curious Case of the International Shipwreck Society'. *Global Networks* 18 (2018): 461–78.

de Vries, Jan. 'Playing with Scales: The Global and the Micro, the Macro and the Nano'. *Past & Present* 242, Supplement 14 (November 2019): 23–36.

Debnath, Angela. 'British Perceptions of the East Pakistan Crisis 1971: "Hideous Atrocities on Both Sides"'. *Journal of Genocide Research* 13, no. 4 (2011): 421–50.

Desgrandschamps, Marie-Luce. 'Dealing with "Genocide": The ICRC and the UN during the Nigeria–Biafra War, 1967–70'. *Journal of Genocide Research* 16 (2014): 218–97.

Dowlah, Caf. *The Bangladesh Liberation War, the Sheikh Mujib Regime, and Contemporary Controversies*. Lanham, MD: Lexington Books, 2016.

Dynon, John. *Moira Dynon: An Inspiring Life*. Melbourne: Jacinta Efthim, 2020.

Dynon, Moira. 'Australian-Japanese Children in Japan'. Address, Melbourne, February 1964.

Edgar, Lynn, Valérie Gorin and Dolores Martín-Moruno, eds. *Making Humanitarian Crises: Emotions and Imagery*. Cham: Springer, 2022.

Edwards, Benjamin. *WASPS, Tykes and Ecumaniacs: Aspects of Australian Sectarianism, 1945–1981*. Sydney: Acorn Press, 2008.

Favez, Jean-Claude. *The Red Cross and the Holocaust*. Cambridge: Cambridge University Press, 1999.

Fazakarley, Jed. 'Multiculturalism's Categories and Transnational Ties: The Bangladeshi Campaign for Independence in Britain, 1971'. *Immigrants and Minorities* 34 (2016): 49–69.

Fechter, Anne-Meike. 'Brokering Transnational Flows of Care: The Case of Citizen Aid'. *Ethnos* 85 (2020): 293–308.

Fechter, Anne-Meike. 'Development and the Search for Connection'. *Third World Quarterly* 40 (2019): 1816–31.
Fechter, Anne-Meike, and Anke Schwittay. 'Citizen Aid: Grassroots Interventions in Development and Humanitarianism'. *Third World Quarterly* 40 (2019): 1769–80.
Fehrenbach, Heide, and Davide Rodogno, eds. *Humanitarian Photography: A History*. Cambridge: Cambridge University Press, 2015.
Feldman, Shelley. 'Displacement and the Production of Difference: East Pakistan/Bangladesh, 1947–1990'. *Globalizations* 19 (2022): 187–204.
Ferris, Elizabeth. 'Faith and Humanitarianism: It's Complicated'. *Journal of Refugee Studies* 24 (2011): 606–25.
Fischer-Tiné, Harald. 'Marrying Global History with South Asian History: Potential and Limits of Global Microhistory in a Regional Inflection'. *Comparativ* 2 (2017): 52–77.
Flegar, Veronika. 'UNHCR's Shifting Frames in the Social Construction of Disabled Refugees: Two Case Studies on the Organization's Work During the World Refugee Year (1959–1960) and the International Year of Disabled Persons (1981)'. *Diplomatica* 1 (2019): 157–79.
Flood, Philip. *Dancing with Warriors: A Diplomatic Memoir*. Melbourne: Australian Scholarly, 2011.
Foley, Griff. 'Action for World Development: An Australian Initiative in Development Education'. *Journal of Christian Education* 21 (May 1978): 5–21.
Forsyth, David P. *The Humanitarians: The International Committee of the Red Cross*. Cambridge: Cambridge University Press, 2005.
Francis, Julian. 'Working with the Refugees, 1971'. *Strategic Analysis* 45 (2021): 530–7.
Franke, Mark F. N. 'Responsible Politics of the Neutral: Rethinking International Humanitarianism in the Red Cross Movement via the Philosophy of Roland Barthes'. *Journal of International Political Theory* 6 (2010): 142–60.
Franks, Suzanne. 'How Famine Captured the Headlines'. *Media History* 12 (2006): 291–312.
Frost, Nick. 'Historical Themes in Child Welfare: The Emergence of Early Child Welfare Structures'. In *The Routledge Handbook of Global Child Welfare*, edited by Pat Dolan and Nick Frost, 19–31. New York: Routledge, 2017.
Gamsa, Mark. 'Biography and (Global) Microhistory'. *New Global Studies* 11 (2017): 231–41.
Gandhi, Indira. *India and BanglaDesh: Selected Speeches and Statements, March to December 1971*. New Delhi: Orient Longman 1972.
Ganguly, Sumit, and Manjeet S. Pardesi. 'Explaining Sixty Years of India's Foreign Policy'. *India Review* 8 (2009): 4–19.
Ganter, Regina. *The Contest for Aboriginal Souls*. Canberra: ANU Press, 2018.
Gatrell, Peter. *Free World? The Campaign to Save the World's Refugees, 1956–63*. Cambridge: Cambridge University Press, 2011.
Gatrell, Peter. 'The World-Wide Web of Humanitarianism: NGOs and Population Displacement in the Third Quarter of the Twentieth Century'. *European Review of History: Revue européenne d'histoire* 23 (2016): 101–15.
Gay, Oonagh. 'MPs Go Back to Their Constituencies'. *Political Quarterly* 76, no. 1 (2005): 57–66.
Ghobrian, John-Paul A. 'The Secret Life of Elias of Babylon and the Uses of Global Microhistory'. *Past & Present* 222 (2014): 51–93.
Ghobrial, John-Paul A., ed. 'Global History and Microhistory'. *Past & Present Supplement* 14 (2019): 1–383.

Ghobrial, John-Paul A. 'Introduction: Seeing the World Like a Microhistorian'. *Past & Present* 242, Supplement 14 (2019): 1–22.
Ghosh, Papiya. 'Partition's Biharis'. *Comparative Studies of South Asia, Africa and the Middle East* 17 (1997): 21–34.
Gibson, Campbell and Kay Jung. *Historical Census Statistics on the Foreign-born Population of the United States, 1850 to 2000*. Washington, DC: US Census Bureau, 2006.
Gillette, Michael L. *Launching the War on Poverty: An Oral History*. New York: Oxford University Press, 2010.
Glover, Nikolas. 'Between Order and Justice: Investments in Africa and Corporate International Responsibility in Swedish Media in the 1960s'. *Enterprise & Society* 20 (2019): 401–44.
Goldworthy, David. *Facing North: A Century of Australian Engagement with Asia*. Melbourne: Melbourne University Press, 2001.
Goltermann, Svenja. *The War in Their Minds. German Soldiers and Their Violent Pasts*. Ann Arbor: University of Michigan Press, 2017.
Goren, Valérie. 'Advocacy Strategies of Western Humanitarian NGOs from the 1960s to the 1990s'. In *Humanitarianism & Media: 1900 to the Present*, edited by Johannes Paulmann, 201–21. New York: Berghahn Books, 2019.
Götz, Norbert. 'Rationales of Humanitarianism: The Case of British Relief to Germany, 1805–1815'. *Journal of Modern European History* 12 (2014): 186–99.
Götz, Norbert, Georgina Brewis and Steffen Werther. *Humanitarianism in the Modern World: The Moral Economy of Famine Relief*. Cambridge: Cambridge University Press, 2020.
Grant, Kevin. 'Anti-Slavery, Refugee Relief, and the Missionary Origins of Humanitarian Photography ca. 1900–1960'. *History Compass* 15 (2017): 1–24.
Grant, Kevin. *Last Weapons: Hunger Strikes and Fasts in the British Empire, 1890–1948*. Oakland: University of California Press, 2019.
Gray, Asta *Travelling Rough on the Hippie Trail: Drugs, Danger and Dysentery*. Santa Cruz: CreateSpace, 2016.
Griffen-Foley, Bridget. *Australian Radio Listeners and Television Viewers: Historical Perspectives*. Cham: Palgrave Pivot, 2020.
Gupta, Dipak K. 'The Naxalites and the Maoist Movement in India: Birth, Demise and Reincarnation'. *Democracy and Security* 3 (2007): 157–88.
Gurry, Meg. *India and Australia: Mapping the Journey*. Melbourne: Melbourne University Press, 2015.
Haider, Zagrul. 'A Revisit to the Indian Role in the Bangladesh Liberation War'. *Journal of Asian and African Studies* 44 (2009): 537–51.
Hakan Yavuz, M and Hakan Erdagöz. 'The Tragedy of the Ottomans: Muslims in the Balkans and Armenians in Anatolia'. *Journal of Muslim Minority Affairs* 39 (2019): 273–81.
Hammerstad, Anne. *The Rise and Decline of a Global Security Actor: UNHCR, Refugee Protection and Security*. Oxford: Oxford University Press, 2014.
Hannig, Florian. 'Negotiating Humanitarianism and Politics: Operation Omega's Border-Breaching Missions during the East Pakistan Crisis of 1971'. In *Dilemmas of Humanitarian Aid in the Twentieth Century*, edited by Johannes Paulmann, 329–43. Oxford: Oxford University Press, 2016.

Hannig, Florian. 'The Biafra Crisis and the Establishment of Humanitarian Aid in West Germany'. In *German Philanthropy in Transatlantic Perspective*, edited by Gregory R. Witkowski and Arnd Bauerkämper, 205–25. Cham: Springer 2016.

Hannig, Florian. 'The Power of the Refugees. The 1971 East Pakistan Crisis and the Origins of UN's Engagement with Humanitarian Aid'. In *The Institution of International Order: From the League of Nations to the United Nations*, edited by Simon Jackson and Alanna O'Malley, 111–35. New York: Routledge, 2018.

Haokip, Thongkholal. 'Inter-Ethnic Relations in Meghalaya'. *Asian Ethnicity* 15 (2014): 302–16.

Haug, Hans. *Humanity for All: The International Red Cross and Red Crescent Movement*. Berne: Paul Haupt, 1993.

Heaslip, Graham, Ira Haavisto and Gyöngyi Kovács 'Cash as a Form of Relief'. In *Advances in Managing Humanitarian Operations*, edited by Christopher W. Zobel, Nezih Altay and Mark P. Haselkorn, 59–78. Cham: Springer, 2018.

Heerten, Lasse. *The Biafran War and Postcolonial Humanitarianism: Spectacles of Suffering*. Cambridge: Cambridge University Press, 2017.

Heerten, Lasse. 'Biafras of the Mind: French Postcolonial Humanitarianism in Global Conceptual History'. *American Historical Review* 126 (2021): 1448–84.

Heerten, Lasse, and A. Dirk Moses. 'The Nigeria-Biafra War: Postcolonial Conflict and the Question of Genocide'. *Journal of Genocide Research* 16 (2014): 169–203.

Heidt, Mari Rapela. 'Development, Nations, and "The Signs of the Times": The Historical Context of Populorum Progressio'. *Journal of Moral Theology* 6 (2017): 1–20.

Heraclides, Alexis, and Ada Dialla. *Humanitarian Intervention in the Long Nineteenth Century. Setting the Precedent*. Manchester: Manchester University Press, 2015.

Hilton, Matthew. 'Commentary: Politics Is Ordinary: Non-Governmental Organizations and Political Participation in Contemporary Britain'. *Twentieth Century Britain* 22 (2011): 230–68.

Hilton, Matthew. 'International Aid and Development NGOs in Britain and Human Rights since 1945'. *Humanity: An International Journal of Human Rights, Humanitarianism, and Development* 3 (2012): 449–72.

Hilton, Matthew. 'Ken Loach and the Save the Children Film: Humanitarianism, Imperialism, and the Changing Role of Charity in Postwar Britain'. *Journal of Modern History* 87 (2015): 357–94.

Hilton, Matthew. 'Oxfam and the Problem of Aid Appraisal in the 1960s'. *Humanity. The International Journal of Human Rights, Humanitarianism and Development* 9 (Spring 2018): 1–18.

Hilton, Matthew, Emily Baughan, Eleanor Davey, Bronwen Everill, Kevin O'Sullivan and Tehila Sasson. 'History and Humanitarianism: A Conversation'. *Past & Present* 241 (2018): e1–e38.

Hollinger, David A. 'After Cloven Tongues of Fire: Ecumenical Protestantism and the Modern American Encounter with Diversity'. *Journal of American History* 98 (2011): 31–48.

Hopgood, Stephen, and Leslie Vinjamuri. 'Faith in Markets'. In *Sacred Aid: Faith and Humanitarianism*, edited by Michael Barnett and Janice Gross Stein, 38–65. New York: Oxford University Press, 2012.

Hudson, Wayne. *Australian Religious Thought*. Melbourne: Monash University Publishing, 2016.

Humphries, Jane. *Childhood and Child Labour in the British Industrial Revolution* Cambridge: Cambridge University Press, 2010.

Hunt, Lynn. *The Invention of Human Rights. A History*. New York: W. W. Norton, 2007.

Hutchison, Emma. 'Humanitarian Emotions through History: Imaging Suffering and Performing Aid'. In *Emotional Bodies. The Historical Performativity of Emotions*, edited by Dolores Martín-Munro and Beatriz Pichel, 219–41. Urbana: University of Illinois Press, 2019.

Ignatieff, Michael. *The Warrior's Honor: Ethnic War and the Moral Conscience*. London: Chatto & Windus, 1998.

Iriye, Akira, Petra Goedde and William I. Hitchcock, eds. *The Human Rights Revolution*. New York: Oxford University Press, 2012.

Irving, Nick. 'Anti-Conscription Protest, Liberal Individualism and the Limits of National Myths in the Global 1960s'. *History Australia* 14 (2017): 187–201.

Irwin, Julia F. *Making the World Safe: The American Red Cross and a Nation's Humanitarian Awakening*. New York: Oxford University Press, 2013.

Islam, Md. Maidul. 'Secularism in Bangladesh: An Unfinished Revolution'. *South Asia Research* 38 (2018): 20–39.

Jacob, Frank. 'Genocide and Mass Violence in Asia: An introduction'. In *Genocide and Mass Violence in the Age of Extremes*, edited by Frank Jacob, 1–12. Berlin: De Gruyter, 2019.

Jalal, Ayesha. *The Struggle for Pakistan*. Cambridge, MA: Harvard University Press, 2014.

Jensen, Steven L. B. *The Making of International Human Rights: The 1960s, Decolonization and the Reconstruction of Human Values*. Cambridge: Cambridge University Press, 2016.

Jensz, Felicity. *German Moravian Missionaries in the British Colony of Victoria, Australia, 1848–1908*. Leiden: Brill, 2010.

Jones, Andrew. 'The Disasters Emergency Committee (DEC) and the Humanitarian Industry in Britain, 1963–85'. *Twentieth Century British History* 26 (2015): 573–601.

Jordan, Douglas. 'Conflict in the Unions: The Communist Party of Australia, Politics and the Trade Union Movement, 1945–1960'. PhD Diss., Victoria University, 2011.

Jupp, James. 'From "White Australia" to "Part of Asia": Recent Shifts in Australian Immigration Policy towards the Region'. *International Migration Review* 29 (1995): 207–22.

Kaell, Hillary. 'Pilgrimage in the Jet Age: The Development of the American Evangelical Holy Land Travel Industry, 1948–1978'. *Journal of Tourism History* 2 (2010): 23–38.

Kaiserfeld, Thomas. 'From Sightseeing to Sunbathing: Changing Traditions in Swedish Package Tours; from Edification by Bus to Relaxation by Airplane in the 1950s and 1960s'. *Journal of Tourism History* 2 (2010): 149–63.

Karim, Md. Redowanul. 'The Role of the Arab World in the Liberation War of Bangladesh'. *International Journal of Innovative Science and Research Technology* 4 (2019): 331–41.

Kelliher, Diarmaid. 'Historicising Geographies of Solidarity'. *Geography Compass* 12 (2018): 1–12.

Kilby, Patrick. *NGOs and Political Change a History of the Australian Council for International Development*. Canberra: ANU Press, 2015.

King, David P. 'World Vision: Religious Identity in the Discourse and Practice of Global Relief and Development'. *Review of Faith and International Affairs* 9 (2011): 21–8.

King, David P. *God's Internationalists: World Vision and the Age of Evangelical Humanitarianism*. Philadelphia: University of Pennsylvania Press, 2019.

Klose, Fabian. 'The Colonial Testing Ground: The International Committee of the Red Cross and the Violent End of Empire'. *Humanity* 2 (2011): 107–26.
Köhn, Holger. 'Jewish Life in Camps after 1945. Displaced Persons Camps in the US Zone of Germany'. In *Catastrophes*, edited by Andreas Hoppe, 63–80. Cham: Springer, 2016.
Kunter, Katharina. 'Global Reach and Global Agenda: The World Council of Churches'. In *The Changing World Religion Map: Sacred Places, Identities, Practices and Politics*, edited by Stanley D. Brunn and Donna Gilbreath, 2909–23. Dordrecht: Springer, 2015.
Kunter, Katharina. 'Revolutionary Hopes and Global Transformations: The World Council of Churches in the 1960s'. *Kirchliche Zeitgeschichte* 30 (2017): 342–7.
Laderman, Charlie. *Sharing the Burden: The Armenian Question, Humanitarian Intervention and Anglo-American Visions of Global Order*. Oxford: Oxford University Press, 2019.
Lago, Enrico Dal and Kevin O'Sullivan. 'Introduction: Towards a New History of Humanitarianism'. *Moving the Social* 57 (March 2016): 5–20.
Lake, Meredith. *The Bible in Australia: A Cultural History*. Sydney: NewSouth Press, 2018.
Langmead, Ross. 'Refugees as Guests and Hosts: Towards a Theology of Mission among Refugees and Asylum Seekers'. *Religion, Migration and Identity* 43 (2016): 171–88.
La Porte, Pablo. 'Humanitarian Assistance during the Rif War (Morocco, 1921–6): The International Committee of the Red Cross and "an Unfortunate Affair"'. *Historical Research* 89 (2016): 114–35.
Laqua, Daniel. 'The Tensions of Internationalism: Transnational Anti-Slavery in the 1880s and 1890s'. *International History Review* 33 (2011): 705–26.
Laqua, Daniel. 'Inside the Humanitarian Cloud: Causes and Motivations to Help Friends and Strangers'. *Journal of Modern European History* 12 (2014): 175–85.
Laylock, Joanne, and Francesca Piana, eds. *Aid to Armenia: Humanitarianism and Intervention from the 1890s to the Present*. Manchester: Manchester University Press, 2020.
Lerner, Adam B. 'Collective Trauma and the Evolution of Nehru's Worldview: Uncovering the Roots of Nehruvian Non-Alignment'. *International History Review* 41 (2019): 1276–300.
Lloyd, Lorna. '"What's in a Name?" The Curious Tale of the Office of High Commissioner'. *Diplomacy & Statecraft* 11 (2000): 47–78.
Lloyd, Lorna and Alan James. 'The External Representation of the Dominions, 1919–1948: Its Role in the Unravelling of the British Empire'. *British Year Book of International Law* 67 (1997): 479–501.
Loescher, Gil. *The UNHCR and World Politics: A Perilous Path*. Oxford: Oxford University Press, 2001.
Loescher, Gil. 'UNHCR's Origins and Early History: Agency, Influence, and Power in Global Refugee Policy'. *Refuge* 33 (2017): 77–86.
Loewenstein, Richard J. 'Dissociation Debates: Everything You Know Is Wrong'. *Dialogues in Clinical Neuroscience* 20 (2018): 229–42.
Lowe, Kimberly. 'Humanitarianism and National Sovereignty: Red Cross Intervention on Behalf of Political Prisoners in Soviet Russia, 1921–3'. *Journal of Contemporary History* 49 (2014): 652–74.
Lowe, Kimberly. 'The League of Red Cross Societies and International Committee of the Red Cross: A Re-Evaluation of American Influence in Interwar Internationalism'. *Moving the Social* 57 (2017): 37–56.

Lyons, Martin. *Dear Prime Minister: Letters to Robert Menzies 1949–1966*. Sydney: New South, 2021.

Maclean, Kama. *British India, White Australia: Overseas Indians, Intercolonial Relations and the Empire*. Sydney: UNSW Press, 2020.

Macintyre, Stuart. *The Party: The Communist Party of Australia from Heyday to Reckoning*. Sydney: Allen & Unwin, 2022.

Maclean, Kama. 'A Colonial in the Colonies: Governor Casey, Mahatma Gandhi and the Endgame of Empire'. *Journal of Colonialism and Colonial History* 19 (2018): 1–31.

Magnússon, Sigurður Gylfi. 'Far-Reaching Microhistory: The Use of Microhistorical Perspective in a Globalized World'. *Rethinking History* 21 (2017): 312–41.

Mahalanabis, D., Choudhuri, A. B., Bagchi, N. G., Bhattacharya. A. K., Simpson, T. W. 'Oral Fluid Therapy of Cholera among Bangladesh Refugees'. *WHO South-East Asia Journal of Public Health* 1 (2012): 105–12.

Maksudyan, Nazan. *Orphans and Destitute Children in the Late Ottoman Empire*. Syracuse, NY: Syracuse University Press, 2014.

Maksudyan, Nazan. 'The Orphan Nation: Gendered Humanitarianism for Armenian Survivor Children in Istanbul, 1919–1922'. In *Gendering Global Humanitarianism in the Twentieth Century*, edited by Esther Möller Johannes Paulmann and Katharina Stornig, 117–42. Cham: Palgrave Macmillan, 2020.

Malkki, Liisa. *The Need to Help: The Domestic Arts of International Humanitarianism*. Durham, NC: Duke University Press, 2015.

Marshall, Dominque. 'Humanitarian Sympathy for Children in Times of War and the History of Children's Rights, 1919–1959'. In *Children and War: A Historical Anthology*, edited by James Marten and Robert Coles, 183–99. New York: New York University Press, 2002.

Martin, Fiona. 'The Socio-Political and Legal History of the Tax Deduction for Donations to Charities in Australia and How the "Public Benevolent Institution" Developed'. *Adelaide Law Review* 38 (2017): 195–221.

Marwick, Arthur. *The Sixties: Cultural Revolution in Britain, France, Italy, and the United States, c.1958–c.1974*. London: Bloomsbury Reader, 2012.

Maul, Daniel Roger. 'The Rise of a Humanitarian Superpower: American NGOs and International Relief, 1917–1945'. In *Internationalism, Imperialism and the Formation of the Contemporary World*, edited by Miguel Bandeira Jerónimo and José Pedro Monteiro, 127–46. Cham: Palgrave Macmillan, 2018.

McGregor-Lowndes, Myles, Marie Crittall, Denise Conroy and Robyn Keast. *Individual Giving and Volunteering. Giving Australia 2016 Report*. Brisbane: Australian Government Department of Social Services, 2017.

Medick, Hans. 'Debatte: Turning Global? Microhistory in Extension'. *Historische Anthropologie* 24 (2016): 241–52.

Mestyan, Adam. 'Domestic Sovereignty, A'yan Developmentalism, and Global Microhistory in Modern Egypt'. *Comparative Studies in Society and History* 60 (2018): 415–45.

Mookherjee, Nayanika. *The Spectral Wound: Sexual Violence, Public Memories, and the Bangladesh War of 1971*. Durham, NC: Duke University Press, 2015.

Mookherjee, Nayanika. '1971: Pakistan's Past and Knowing What Not to Narrate'. *Comparative Studies of South Asia, Africa and the Middle East* 39 (2019): 212–22.

Mookherjee, Nayanika. 'Historicising the Birangona: Interrogating the Politics of Commemorating the Wartime Rape of 1971 in the Context of the 50th Anniversary of Bangladesh'. *Strategic Analysis* 45 (2021): 588–97.

Moniz, Amanda B. *From Empire to Humanity: The American Revolution and the Origins of Humanitarianism*. Oxford: Oxford University Press, 2016.

Morris, Jeremy. 'Secularization and Religious Experience: Arguments in the Historiography of Modern British Religion'. *Historical Journal* 55 (2012): 195–219.

Morris-Suzuki, Tessa. 'Unconventional Warfare: The International Committee of the Red Cross and Humanitarian Dilemmas in Korea 1950–53'. *History Australia* 10 (2013): 15–34.

Moses, A. Dirk. 'The United Nations, Humanitarianism and Human Rights: War Crimes/ Genocide Trials for Pakistani Soldiers in 1971'. In *Human Rights in the Twentieth Century*, edited by Stefan-Ludwig Hoffman, 258–80. New York: Cambridge University Press, 2011.

Moses, A. Dirk, and Lasse Heerten, 'The Nigeria-Biafra War: Post-Colonial Conflict and the Question of Genocide'. *Journal of Genocide Research* 16 (2014): 169–203.

Moses, A. Dirk, Marco Duranti and Roland Burke, ed. *Decolonization, Self-Determination and the Rise of Global Human Rights Politics*. Cambridge: Cambridge University Press, 2020.

Moshman, David. 'Conceptual Constraints on Thinking about Genocide'. *Journal of Genocide Research* 3 (2001): 431–50.

Moyn, Samuel. *The Last Utopia: Human Rights in History*. Cambridge, MA: Harvard University Press, 2010.

Moyn, Samuel. *Not Enough: Human Rights in an Unequal World*. Cambridge, MA: Harvard University Press, 2018.

Mullins, Patrick. *Tiberius with a Telephone: The Life and Stories of William McMahon*. Melbourne: Scribe, 2019.

Murphy, Kate. *Fears and Fantasies: Modernity, Gender and the Rural-Urban Divide*. New York: Peter Lang, 2010.

Murphey, Rhoads. *A History of Asia*, 5th edn. London: Longman, 2005.

Murphy, Kate. '"In the Backblocks of Capitalism": Australian Student Activism in the Global 1960s'. *Australian Historical Studies* 46 (2015): 252–68.

Musson, Janice. 'Britain and the Recognition of Bangladesh in 1972'. *Diplomacy & Statecraft* 19, no. 1 (2008): 125–44.

Naqvi, Tahir. 'Migration, Sacrifice and the Crisis of Muslim Nationalism'. *Journal of Refugee Studies* 25 (2012): 474–90.

Nash, David. 'Reconnecting Religion with Social and Cultural History: Secularization's Failure as a Master Narrative'. *Cultural and Social History* 1 (2004): 302–25.

O'Brien, Glen. 'Anti-Americanism and the Wesleyan-Holiness Churches in Australia'. *Journal of Ecclesiastical History* 61 (2010): 314–43.

Ó Gráda, Cormac. '"Sufficiency and Sufficiency and Sufficiency": Revisiting the Bengal Famine of 1943–44'. *UCD Centre for Economic Research Working Paper Series*, University College Dublin, 2010.

O'Hanlon, Seamus. *City Life: The New Urban Australia*. Sydney: New South, 2018.

O'Hanlon, Seamus, and Rachel Stevens. 'A Nation of Immigrants or a Nation of Immigrant Cities? The Urban Context of Australian Multiculturalism, 1947–2011'. *Australian Journal of Politics and History* 63 (2017): 556–71.

Oakman, Daniel. *Facing Asia: A History of the Colombo Plan*, 2nd edn. Canberra: ANU Press, 2010.

Oppenheimer, Melanie. *The Power of Humanity: 100 Years of Australian Red Cross 1914–2014*. Sydney: HarperCollins, 2014.

Oppenheimer, Melanie, Susanne Schech, Romain Fathi, Neville Wylie and Rosemary Cresswell, 'Resilient Humanitarianism? Using Assemblage to Re-Evaluate the History of the League of Red Cross Societies'. *International History Review* 43 (2021): 579–97.

Orchard, Phil. *Protecting the Internally Displaced*. London: Routledge, 2019.

O'Sullivan, Kevin. *Ireland, Africa and the End of Empire: Small State Identity in the Cold War 1955–75*. Manchester: Manchester University Press, 2012.

O'Sullivan, Kevin. 'A "Global Nervous System": The Rise and Rise of European Humanitarian NGOs, 1945–1985'. In *International Organizations and Development, 1945–1999*, edited by Marc Frey, Sönke Kunkel, Corinna Unger, 196–219. London: Palgrave Macmillan, 2014.

O'Sullivan, Kevin. 'The Search for Justice: NGOs in Britain and Ireland and the New International Economic Order, 1968–82'. *Humanity* 6 (2015): 173–87.

O'Sullivan, Kevin. *The NGO Moment: The Globalisation of Compassion from Biafra to Live Aid*. Cambridge: Cambridge University Press, 2021.

Owen, Nicholas. *Other People's Struggles: Outsiders in Social Movements*. Oxford: Oxford University Press, 2019.

Oxfam International, *Oxfam Annual Report. April 2017 – March 2018*. Accessed 22 March 2022. https://www-cdn.oxfam.org/s3fs-public/file_attachments/story/oxfam_annual_report_2017-2018_final_2.pdf.

Paipais, Vassilios. 'Reinhold Niebuhr and the Christian Realist Pendulum'. *Journal of International Political Theory* 17, no. 2 (June 2021): 185–202.

Paras, Andrea, and Janice Gross Stein. 'Bridging the Sacred and the Profane in Humanitarian Life'. In *Sacred Aid: Faith and Humanitarianism*, edited by Michael Barnett and Janice Gross Stein, 211–39. New York: Oxford University Press, 2012.

Paulmann, Johannes, ed. *Humanitarianism and Media: 1900 to the Present*. New York: Berghahn Books 2018.

Paulsen, Eric. 'The Citizenship Status of the Urdu-Speakers/Biharis in Bangladesh'. *Refugee Survey Quarterly* 25, no. 3 (2006): 54–69.

Peach Ceri. 'Contrasting Patterns of Indian, Pakistani and Bangladeshi Settlement in Britain'. *Migracijske teme* 13 (1997): 15–36.

Peppiatt, David, John Mitchell and Penny Holzmann. *Cash Transfers in Emergencies: Evaluating Benefits and Assessing Risks*. London: Overseas Development Institute, 2001.

Perez SJ, Pradeep. 'Bangladesh'. In *Christianity in South and Central Asia*, edited by Kenneth R. Ross, Daniel Jeyaraj and Todd M. Johnson, 184–96. Edinburgh: Edinburgh University Press, 2019.

Pernet, Corinne A., and Amalia Ribi Forclaz. 'Revisiting the Food and Agriculture Organization (FAO): International Histories of Agriculture, Nutrition and Development'. *International History Review* 41 (2019): 345–50.

Piccini, Jon, Evan Smith and Matthew Worley. 'Introduction: The History of the Far Left in Australia since 1945'. In *The Far Left in Australia since 1945*, edited by Jon Piccini, Evan Smith and Matthew Worley, 1–18. New York: Routledge, 2018.

Piccini, Jon. *Human Rights in Twentieth Century Australia*. Cambridge: Cambridge University Press, 2019.

Piggin, Stuart, and Robert Linder. *The Fountain of Public Prosperity: Evangelical Christians in Australian History, 1740–1914*. Melbourne: Monash University, 2018.

Pilkington, Richard. 'In the National Interest? Canada and the East Pakistan Crisis of 1971'. *Journal of Genocide Research* 13, no. 4 (2011): 451–74.

Pinkerton, Alasdair. 'A New Kind of Imperialism? The BBC, Cold War Broadcasting and the Contested Geopolitics of South Asia'. *Historical Journal of Film, Radio and Television* 28 (2008): 537–55.

Pinkerton, Alasdair. 'The BBC in South Asia: From the End of Empire to the Cold War'. In *Diasporas and Diplomacy: Cosmopolitan Contact Zones at the BBC World Service (1932–2012)*, edited by M. Gillespie and A. Webb, 140–62. London: Routledge, 2012.

Piotrowicz, Wojciech D. 'In-Kind Donations, Cash Transfers and Local Procurement in the Logistics of Caring for Internally Displaced Persons. The Case of Polish Humanitarian NGOs and Ukrainian IDPs'. *Journal of Humanitarian Logistics and Supply Chain Management* 8 (2018): 374–97.

Pollock, Linda. 'Childhood, Parents and the Family, 1500–1900'. In *The Routledge Handbook of Global Child Welfare*, edited by Pat Dolan and Nick Frost, 3–18. New York: Routledge, 2017.

Prakash, Teesta. 'Strategic Reassessments: Aid and Bureaucracy in Australia-India Relations 1951–70'. *Australian Journal of Politics and History* 67 (2021): 2–15.

Pringle, Yolana. 'Humanitarianism, Race and Denial: The International Committee of the Red Cross and Kenya's Mau Mau Rebellion'. *History Workshop Journal* 84 (2017): 89–107.

Putnis, Peter. 'Reuters and the Idea of a British Commonwealth News Agency in the Aftermath of World War II'. *Media History* 27 (2021): 314–30.

Quirk, Joel, and David Richardson. 'Anti-slavery, European Identity and International Society: A Macro-Historical Perspective'. *Journal of Modern European History* 7 (2009): 69–92.

Raghavan, Srinath. *1971: A Global History of the Creation of Bangladesh*. Cambridge, MA: Harvard University Press, 2013.

Rahman, Md. Mahbubar, and Willem Van Schendel. '"I Am Not a Refugee": Rethinking Partition Migration'. *Modern Asian Studies* 37 (2003): 551–84.

Raiser, Konrad. 'The World Council of Churches and International Civil Society'. *Ecumenical Review* 46 (1994): 38–44.

Redclift, Victoria. 'Abjects or Agents? Camps, Contests and the Creation of "Political Space"'. *Citizenship Studies* 17 (2013): 308–21.

Rees, Yves. 'Reading Australian Modernity: Unsettled Settlers and Cultures of Mobility'. *History Compass* 15: e12489 (2017): 1–13. Accessed 9 October 2022. https://doi.org/10.1111/hic3.12429.

Reid, Len. *The Tragedy of Those Who Have Less*. Melbourne: Society 'For Those Who Have Less', 1973.

Reinisch, Jessica. 'Internationalism in Relief: The Birth (and Death) of UNRRA'. *Past & Present* 210 (2011): 258–89.

Ribi Forclaz, Amalia. *Humanitarian Imperialism: The Politics of Anti-Slavery Activism, 1880–1940*. Oxford: Oxford University Press, 2015.

Ribi Forclaz, Amalia. 'From Reconstruction to Development: The Early Years of the Food and Agriculture Organization (FAO) and the Conceptualization of Rural Welfare, 1945–1955'. *International History Review* 41 (2019): 351–71.

Rodogno, Davide. *Against Massacre: Humanitarian Interventions in the Ottoman Empire, 1815–1914*. Princeton, NJ: Princeton University Press, 2011.

Rowe, Paul S. 'The Global – and Globalist – Roots of Evangelical Action'. *Review of Faith and International Affairs* 17 (2019): 36–49.
Roy, Haimanti. *Partitioned Lives: Migrants, Refugees, Citizens in India and Pakistan, 1947–65*. Oxford: Oxford University Press, 2013.
Russell, Sharman Apt. *Hunger. An Unnatural History*. New York: Basic Books, 2005.
Rutledge, Martha. 'Cohen, Sir Samuel Sydney (1869–1948)'. In *Australian Dictionary of Biography*. Accessed 24 February 2022. https://adb.anu.edu.au/biography/cohen-sir-samuel-sydney-5718/text9671.
Said, Edward. *Orientalism*. New York: Random House, 1978.
Saikia, Yasmin. 'Beyond the Archive of Silence: Narratives of Violence of the 1971 Liberation War of Bangladesh'. *History Workshop Journal* 58, no. 1 (2004): 275–87.
Saikia, Yasmin. 'Insāniyat for Peace: Survivors' Narratives of the 1971 War of Bangladesh'. *Journal of Genocide Research* 13 (2011): 475–501.
Saikia, Yasmin. 'War as History, Humanity in Violence: Women, Men and Memories of 1971, East Pakistan/Bangladesh'. In *Sexual Violence in Conflict Zones. From the Ancient World to the Era of Human Rights*, edited by Elizabeth Heineman, 152–69. Philadelphia: University of Pennsylvania Press, 2011.
Saikia, Yasmin, *Women, War, and the Making of Bangladesh*. Durham, NC: Duke University Press, 2011.
Saikia, Yasmin. 'War as History, Humanity in Violence: Women, Men and Memories of 1971, East Pakistan/Bangladesh'. In *Sexual Violence in Conflict Zones: From the Ancient World to the Era of Human Rights*, edited by Elizabeth Heineman, 152–69. Philadelphia: University of Pennsylvania Press, 2011.
Salmanova, Ulduz. 'The Coal Mines Regulation Act of 1862: The Beginnings of the Child Labour Debate in Australia'. *Journal of the History of Childhood and Youth* 13 (2020): 359–83.
Salvatici, Silvia. '"Help the People to Help Themselves": UNRRA Relief Workers and European Displaced Persons'. *Journal of Refugee Studies* 25 (September 2012): 428–51.
Salvatici, Silvia. *A History of Humanitarianism, 1755–1989: In the Name of Others*. Manchester: Manchester University Press 2020.
Sasson, Tehilia. 'From Empire to Humanity: The Russian Famine and the Imperial Origins of International Humanitarianism'. *Journal of British Studies* 55, no. 3 (2016): 519–37.
Sasson, Tehila. 'Milking the Third World? Humanitarianism, Capitalism, and the Moral Economy of the Nestlé Boycott'. *American Historical Review* 121 (2016): 1196–224.
Scalmer, Sean. *Dissent Events: Protest, the Media, and the Political Gimmick in Australia*. Sydney: UNSW Press, 2001.
Scalmer, Sean. 'Nonviolent Activism and the Media: Gandhi and Beyond'. In *Routledge Companion to Media and Activism*, edited by Graham Meikle, 38–46. New York: Routledge, 2018.
Scanlan, Stephen J. and Laurie Cooper Stoll and Kimberly Lumm. 'Starving for Change. The Hunger Strike and Nonviolent Action, 1906–2004'. *Research in Social Movements, Conflicts and Change* 28 (2008): 275–323.
Schrover, Marlou, Teuntje Vosters and Irial Glynn, 'NGOs and West European Migration Governance (1860s until Present): Introduction to a Special Issue'. *Journal of Migration History* 5 (2019): 189–217.
Sen, B. R. *The Basic Freedom – Freedom from Hunger*. Geneva: FAO, 1963.
Sen, B. R. *Towards a Newer World*. Dublin: Tycooly International Publications, 1982.
Sensen, Oliver. *Kant on Human Dignity*. Berlin: De Gruyter 2011.
Shah, Aqil. *The Army and Democracy*. Cambridge, MA: Harvard University Press, 2014.

Shahnawaz, A. Mantoo. 'Bihari Refugees Stranded in Bangladesh since 1971'. *Journal of South Asian Studies* 1, no. 2 (2013): 123–9.
Shamshad, Rizwana. *Bangladeshi Migrants in India*. New Delhi: Oxford University Press, 2017.
Shaw, D. John. *World Food Security*. London: Palgrave Macmillan, 2007.
Siegal, Benjamin. '"The Claims of Asia and the Far East": India and the FAO in the Age of Ambivalent Internationalism'. *International History Review* 41 (2019): 427–50.
Siméant, Joanna. 'From Fast to Hunger Strike'. In *Bodies in Protest: Hungry Strikes and Angry Music*, edited by Johanna Siméant and Christophe Traïni, 17–24. Amsterdam: Amsterdam University Press, 2016.
Siméant, Joanna. 'The Meaning of Bodily Violence'. In *Bodies in Protest. Hungry Strikes and Angry Music*, edited by Johanna Siméant and Christophe Traïni, 35–46. Amsterdam: Amsterdam University Press, 2016.
Simpson, Bradley. 'Self-Determination, Human Rights, and the End of Empire in the 1970s'. *Humanity* 4 (2013): 239–60.
Simonow, Joanna. 'The Great Bengal Famine in Britain: Metropolitan Campaigning for Food Relief and the End of Empire, 1943–44'. *Journal of Imperial and Commonwealth History* 48 (2020): 168–97.
Singh, Sinderpal. *India in South Asia: Domestic Identity Politics and Foreign Policy from Nehru to the BJP*. New York: Routledge, 2013.
Singh, Zorawar Daulet. *Power and Diplomacy: India's Foreign Policies during the Cold War*. New Delhi: Oxford University Press, 2019.
Sisson, Richard and Leo E. Rose. *War and Secession: Pakistan, India, and the Creation of Bangladesh*. Berkeley: University of California Press, 1990.
Skinner, Rob. 'Humanitarianism and Human Rights in Global Anti-Apartheid'. In *A Global History of Anti-Apartheid*, edited by A. Konieczna and R. Skinner, 33–65. Cham: Springer International, 2019.
Skinner, Rob and Alan Lester, 'Humanitarianism and Empire: New Research Agendas'. *Journal of Imperial and Commonwealth History* 40 (2012): 729–47.
Sluga, Glenda. *Internationalism in the Age of Nationalism*. Philadelphia: University of Pennsylvania Press, 2013.
Smith, Ric. *India, the United States, Australia and the Difficult Birth of Bangladesh*. Canberra: Australian Institute of International Affairs, 2019.
Smith, Simon C. 'Coming Down on the Winning Side: Britain on the South Asia Crisis, 1971'. *Contemporary British History* 24, no. 4 (2010): 451–70.
Sobocinska, Agnieszka. *Visiting the Neighbours: Australians in Asia*. Sydney: University of New South Wales Press, 2014.
Sobocinska, Agnieszka. 'Popular Causes: The Volunteer Graduate Scheme, the Freedom from Hunger Campaign and Altruistic Internationalism in Australia'. *Journal of Australian Studies* 43 (2019): 509–24.
Sobocinska, Agnieszka. *Saving the World? Western Volunteers and the Rise of the Humanitarian-Development Complex*. Cambridge: Cambridge University Press, 2021.
Sobocinska, Agnieszka, and Richard White. 'Travel and Connections'. In *The Cambridge History of Australia*, vol. 2, edited by Alison Bashford and Stuart McIntyre, 472–93. Cambridge: Cambridge University Press, 2015.
Spencer, Andrew, Jeremy Gill and Laura Schmahmann. 'Urban or Suburban? Examining the Density of Australian Cities in Global Context'. 7th State of Australian Cities Conference, 9–11 December 2015, Gold Coast, Australia, 2015.

Steinacher, Gerald. *Humanitarians at War: The Red Cross in the Shadow of the Holocaust.* Oxford: Oxford University Press, 2017.

Stevens, Rachel. 'After the "Great White Walls" Came Down: Debating the Ethnicity of Immigrants in Australia and the USA, 1980–1990'. *Immigrants & Minorities* 32 (2014): 262–92.

Stevens, Rachel. *Immigration Policy from 1970 to the Present.* New York: Routledge, 2016.

Stevens, Rachel. 'Humanitarianism from the Suburbs: Australian Refugee Relief and Activism during the 1971 Bangladeshi Liberation War'. *Australian Journal of Politics and History* 65 (2019): 566–83.

Stevens, Rachel. 'Understanding British Return Migration: The Australian Department of Immigration, British Youth Cultures and the Failed Promotional Tour of Australia in 1960'. In *When Migrants Fail to Stay New Histories on Departures and Migration*, edited by Ruth Balint, Joy Damousi and Sheila Fitzpatrick. London: Bloomsbury, 2023, forthcoming.

Stevens, Rachel, and Seamus O'Hanlon. 'Intimate Oral Histories: Intercultural Romantic Relationships in Postwar Australia'. *Australian Historical Studies* 49 (2018): 359–77.

Stevens, Simon. 'Boycotts and Sanctions against South Africa: An International History, 1946–1970'. PhD Diss., Columbia University, 2016.

Stone, Dan, ed. *The Historiography of Genocide.* London: Palgrave Macmillan, 2008.

Suri, Jeremy. 'AHR Forum: The Rise and Fall of an International Counterculture, 1960–1975'. *American Historical Review* 114 (2009): 45–68.

Swain, Shurlee. 'Do You Want Religion with That? Welfare History in a Secular Age'. *History Australia* 2 (2005): 79.1–8.

Swartz, Rebecca. *Education and Empire: Children, Race and Humanitarianism in the British Settler Colonies, 1833–1880.* Cham: Palgrave Macmillan, 2019.

Swain, Shurlee. 'A Long History of Faith-Based Welfare in Australia: Origins and Impact'. *Journal of Religious History* 41 (2017): 81–96.

Swenson, Sara Ann. 'Compassion without Pity: Buddhist Dāna as Charity, Humanitarianism, and Altruism'. *Religion Compass* 14 (2020): 1–10.

Taithe, Bertrand. 'Compassion Fatigue: The Changing Nature of Humanitarian Emotions'. In *Emotional Bodies. The Historical Performativity of Emotions*, edited by Dolores Martín-Munro and Beatriz Pichel, 242–62. Urbana: University of Illinois Press, 2019.

Taithe, Bertrand. 'Demotic Humanitarians: Historical Perspectives on the Global Reach of Local Initiatives, 1940–2017'. *Third World Quarterly* 40 (2019): 1781–98.

Talbot, Ian. 'Partition of India: The Human Dimension'. *Cultural and Social History* 6 (2009): 403–10.

Taylor, Becky. 'A Change of Heart? British Policies towards Tubercular Refugees during 1959 World Refugee Year'. *Twentieth Century British History* 26 (March 2015): 97–121.

Thackeray, David. *Forging a British World of Trade. Culture, Ethnicity and Market in the Empire-Commonwealth.* Oxford: Oxford University Press, 2019.

Thompson, Andrew C. 'The Protestant Interest and the History of Humanitarian Intervention, c.1685–1756'. In *Humanitarian Intervention: A History*, edited by Brendan Simms and D. J. B. Trim, 67–88. Cambridge: Cambridge University Press, 2011.

Thompson, Michael G. *For God and Globe: Christian Internationalism in the United States between the Great War and the Cold War.* Ithaca, NY: Cornell University Press, 2016.

Thulin, Mirjam & Björn Siegel. 'Transformations and of *shtadlanut* and *tzedakah* in the Early Modern and Modern Period'. *Jewish Culture and History* 19 (2018): 1–7.

Trim, D. J. B. 'If a Prince Use Tyrannie towards His People: Interventions on Behalf of Foreign Populations in Early Modern Europe'. In *Humanitarian Intervention: A History*, edited by Brendan Simms and D. J. B. Trim, 29–66. Cambridge: Cambridge University Press, 2011.

Trivellato, Francesca. 'Microstoria/Microhistoire/Microhistory'. *French Politics, Culture and Society* 33 (2015): 122–34.

Trivellato, Francesca. 'What Differences Make a Difference? Global History and Microhistory Revisited'. *Journal of Early Modern History* 27 (2023): 7–31.

Turner, Louis, and John Ash. *The Golden Hordes: International Tourism and the Pleasure Periphery*. London: Constable, 1975.

Tusan, Michelle. 'Humanitarianism, Genocide and Liberalism'. *Journal of Genocide Research* 17 (2015): 83–105.

Tusan, Michelle. *The British Empire and the Armenian Genocide: Humanitarianism and Imperial Politics from Gladstone to Churchill*. London: Bloomsbury, 2017.

Twomey, Christina. 'Framing Atrocity: Photography and Humanitarianism'. *History of Photography* 36 (2015): 255–64.

Twomey, Christina, and Andrew J. May. 'Australian Responses to the Indian Famine, 1876–78: Sympathy, Photography and the British Empire'. *Australian Historical Studies* 43 (2012): 233–52.

Twomey, Christina and Jodie Boyd. 'Class, Social Equity and Higher Education in Postwar Australia'. *Australian Historical Studies* 47 (2016): 8–24.

Uddin, Sufia. *Constructing Bangladesh: Religion, Ethnicity and Language in an Islamic Nation*. Chapel Hill: University of North Carolina Press, 2006.

UNHCR, *Report of the United Nations High Commissioner for Refugees on the Activities of the United Nations Focal Point for Assistance to Refugees from East Bengal in India*, 23 June 1972. Geneva: UNHCR, 1972.

UNHCR, *State of the World's Refugees 2000. Fifty Years of Humanitarian Action*. Geneva: UNHCR, 2000.

United States Census Bureau. 'Statistical Abstract of the United States: 2012. Section 1. Population. Table 75. Self-Described Religious Identification of Adult Population'. https://www.census.gov/library/publications/2011/compendia/statab/131ed/populat ion.html

van Bergen, L. 'Medical Care as the CARROT: The Red Cross in Indonesia during the War of Decolonization, 1945–1950'. *Medicine, Conflict and Survival* 29 (2013): 216–43.

van Dam, Peter. 'No Justice without Charity: Humanitarianism after Empire'. *International History Review* 44 (2020): 653–74.

van Dijk, Boyd. 'Internationalizing Colonial War: On the Unintended Consequences of the Interventions of the International Committee of the Red Cross in South-East Asia, 1945–1949'. *Past & Present* 250 (February 2021): 243–83.

van Schendel, Willem. *The Bengal Borderlands: Beyond State and Nation in South Asia*. London: Anthem Press, 2005.

Varon, Jeremy, Michael S. Foley and John McMillian. 'Editorial: Time Is an Ocean: the Past and Future of the Sixties'. *The Sixties* 1 (2008): 1–7.

Vernon, James. *Hunger: A Modern History*. Cambridge, MA: Harvard University Press, 2009.

Vignaux, Barbara. 'L'Agence France-Presse en guerre d'Algérie'. *Vingtième Siècle. Revue d'histoire* 3 (2004): 121–30.

Waldron, Jeremy. 'Dignity and Rank'. In *Dignity, Rank, and Rights*, edited by Meir Dan-Cohen, 13–47. New York: Oxford University Press, 2012.

Ward, Stuart. 'The "New Nationalism" in Australia, Canada and New Zealand: Civic Culture in the Wake of the British World'. In *Britishness Abroad: Transnational Movements and Imperial Culture*, edited by Kate Darian-Smith, Patricia Grimshaw and Stuart McIntyre, 243–314. Melbourne: Melbourne University Press, 2007.

Watenpaugh, Keith. *Bread from Stones: The Middle East and the Making of Modern Humanitarianism*. Oakland: University of California Press, 2015.

Watson, Brad, and Matthew Clarke, eds. *Child Sponsorship: Exploring Pathways to a Brighter Future*. London: Palgrave Macmillan UK, 2014.

White, Richard. *A History of Getting Away*. Melbourne: Pluto Press, 2005.

Widmer, Sabina. 'Neutrality Challenged in a Cold War Conflict: Switzerland, the International Committee of the Red Cross, and the Angolan War'. *Cold War History* 18 (2018): 203–20.

Wieters, Hieke. *The NGO Care and Food Aid from America 1945-80: 'Showered with Kindness'?* Manchester: Manchester University Press, 2017.

Wieters, Hieke. 'On Fishing in Other People's Ponds: The Freedom from Hunger Campaign, International Fundraising and the Ethics of NGO Publicity'. In *Humanitarianism and the Media: 1900 to the Present*, edited by Johannes Paulmann, 185–200. New York: Berghahn Books, 2019.

Wilkinson, Olivia. *Secular and Religious Dynamics in Humanitarian Response. Routledge Research in Religion and Development*. Oxford: Routledge, 2020.

Willebrands, J. C., and E. C. Blake. 'Patterns of Relationships between the Roman Catholic Church and the World Council of Churches'. *Ecumenical Review* 24 (1972): 247–9.

Williams, Raymond. *The Country and the City*. London: Chatto and Windus, 1973.

Williams, Roy. *In God they Trust? The Religious Beliefs of Australian Prime Ministers, 1901–2013*. Sydney: Bible Society, 2013.

Wilson, Erin. '"Power Differences" and "the Power of Difference": The Dominance of Secularism as Ontological Injustice'. *Globalizations* 14 (2017): 1076–93.

Winter, Christine. 'Limits of Impartiality: The Delegates of the International Committee of the Red Cross in Australia during the Second World War'. *History Australia* 10 (2013): 56–74.

Wright, Matthew. 'The Pearson Commission, Aid Diplomacy and the Rise of the World Bank, 1966–1970', PhD Diss., University of Durham, 2017.

Wylie, Neville. 'The Sound of Silence: The History of the International Committee of the Red Cross as Past and Present'. *Diplomacy & Statecraft* 13 (2002): 186–204.

Wylie, Neville, Melanie Oppenheimer and James Crossland, 'The Red Cross Movement: Continuities, Changes and Challenges'. In *The Red Cross Movement: Myths, Practices and Turning Points*, edited by Neville Wylie, Melanie Oppenheimer and James Crossland, 1–26. Manchester: Manchester University Press, 2020.

Zalmanovich, Tal. '"What Is Needed Is an Ecumenical Act of Solidarity:" The World Council of Churches, the 1969 Notting Hill Consultation on Racism, and the Anti-Apartheid Struggle'. *Safundi* 20 (2019): 174–92.

Index

abolitionism 34–6
accountability 1, 118, 132, 154
activism (*see also* youth activism) 2, 22, 42, 47, 53–6, 132, 145
Ahmed, Tajuddin 13
Aid India Campaign 152–66
Allen, James (Jim) 157–60
altruistic internationalism 52
American Committee for Armenian and Syrian Relief (ACASR) 38
Amnesty International 45
Anglicanism (*see also* Church of England) 102–8, 128, 165, 173, 175
Arab response 23
Armenia 38
'Eastern Question' 39
Asia-Pacific region 132, 179, 194–5
Australian-Asian Association 151
Australian Broadcasting Corporation 179
Australian Catholic Relief (ACR) 56–60, 112–16, 190
Australian Council of Churches (ACC) 56–60, 99, 104–12, 190
Australian government
  aid for Bangladeshi refugees 118, 122–3, 178–9
  aid for Bhola cyclone victims 118–20
  aid for Bihar famine victims 124
  logistical support for NGOs 63–6
  official position during war 23, 28
  official recognition of Bangladesh 187
  relations with India 23–9
Australian Jewish Welfare Society (AJWS) 67
Australian Labor Party (ALP) 62, 126, 149, 151
Australian Red Cross Society
  alliances 190
  background 79
  comparison with ACC 108
  cooperation with Dynon 160

medical personnel 88–90
publicity demands 91–3, 97
reconstruction in Bangladesh 94–8
unwanted in-kind donations 84–7
Awami League 10–13, 17–19, 20, 28, 149, 188

Bangladesh Ecumenical Relief and Rehabilitation Service (BERRS) 72, 113, 190
Bangladesh, recognition of 187
Bangladesh Red Cross Society 81, 94–7, 160
Baptist Church, Australia 69, 72, 104
Baptist missionaries 94
Baptist World Aid 72
Barwick, Garfield (Sir) 62
Beattie, Max 134, 168
Beer, Henrik 75, 85, 89, 92–3
Bengal famine 24, 140–2
Bhola cyclone 7, 1, 61, 119–21, 155–7
Bhutto, Zulfiqar Ali 11
Biafra 16, 48, 78, 97
Bignami, Enrico 94
Biharis 18, 95–8
Blood, Archer 17–18
Bowen, Nigel (Sir) 28, 63, 112, 122, 175
boycotts, consumer 177
British Broadcasting Corporation (BBC) 46–8, 91
British Red Cross Society 79, 84
Brotherhood of St Lawrence 164
Bury, Leslie 28

camps 15, 64–70, 82, 109–10, 121, 159–61
Canadian government 22–3
Caritas Internationalis 56, 60, 114, 190
Casey, Richard (Sir) 25
Catholic Social Studies Movement (CSSM) 113

Catholic Women's League 151
Catholicism (*see also* Australian Catholic
    Relief) 2, 60, 165, 180
  newspapers 190
  school system 102, 113, 163
charity 27–34, 45, 53, 99, 114–16, 127–31,
    191
child nutrition programme 82, 85
children
  emigration schemes 36
  fundraising 143, 150
  labour 36
  letter writing 180–1, 190
  rescue 38
  sponsorship 115, 164
  western imagination 37
cholera 15, 61, 71, 107
Christian Agency for Social Action
    (CASA) 70–2, 106, 108–10
Christian Children's Fund 58
Christian ethics 56–7, 100, 180, 192
Christian internationalism 35, 56, 99
Christian nation 100–4, 179–80, 192
Church Acts 102
Church of England (*see also* Anglicanism)
    102
citizen
  activism 150, 189
  Christian citizenship 111–12
  definition 2
  donations 143
  'happenings' 144
  model 146
city/country dichotomy (*see* urban/rural
    divide)
class 147–50
class struggle 149–50
Cohen, Samuel (Sir) 67
Cold War 2, 4–5, 19–20, 27–8, 43, 46, 91,
    142, 188–9, 194
Colombo Plan 168
Commission on Churches on International
    Affairs (CCIA) 105
commonwealth solidarity 120
communism 8, 46, 126, 155
Communist Party of Australia
    (CPA) 149–50
community development 130
community-driven 130

compassion 23–4, 32–3, 71–2, 99,
    149, 194–5
compassion fatigue 61, 137
conscription, Vietnam War 170
conservatism 59, 183–4
consumerism 116, 188, 194
counterculture 52, 100, 170, 188, 192
coup (*see* military coup)
Crawford, John (Jack) (Sir) 61
Cullen, Paul (Major General)
  ACFOA chairman 63
  ACFOA dispute with DFA 65–7
  Austcare tour of India 70–1
  disbursement of aid 72
  dispute with CAA/Oxfam 136–40, 189
  personal history 67–8
  personality 64, 68, 73

decolonization 41, 56, 64–5, 127–8, 188
  ICRC involvement 77–8
  WCC support 105–6
democracy 2, 27, 29, 91, 154, 179
depoliticization 22–3, 55, 59, 191
development 53, 55–9, 61–2, 76, 111,
    116, 128
Development Decade 42, 141
diaspora, South Asian 22
Disasters Emergency Committee (DEC)
    48, 61
displaced persons (DPs) 41, 105
donations 59–61, 69 (*see also* fundraising)
  Australian Catholic Relief 115
  cash vs material donations 85–6, 123–4,
    155
  contemporary field 31–2
  lack of, CAA 134
  Red Cross 79–80, 94
doorknock appeals 69, 137, 143
Douglas-Home, Alec (Sir) 21
duty 33, 79, 112, 154, 162–4, 192
dysentery 109

economic redistribution 29, 126, 191
educational programmes 128, 142,
    154, 162–5
ecumenism/ecumenicalism 103–7, 112–13,
    191
elites 6, 9, 11, 13, 38, 41, 53, 56–7, 152, 191
elitism 150

emergency relief 40–1, 55–8, 128, 135, 165, 195
ethnic chauvinism 9
ethnic cleansing (*see also* genocide) 7, 96
European Children Fund 38
evangelicalism 58, 72, 100–4, 113
evangelism (*see also* proselytization) 58, 112
Evans, Geoff 171, 174
everyday humanitarianism 177
expert class (*see also* technocrat) 117
External Affairs, Australian Department of 24–6, 61–2, 169–70

famine relief 24, 40, 115, 129–30, 152
fasting (*see also* hunger strikes) 115, 143, 149, 167–71
Flood, Philip 132
Food for Peace campaign 128–9
Food and Agriculture Organization (FAO) 140–1
Foreign Affairs, Australian Department of 62, 85, 156–60
foreign aid workers 88–9, 109–10, 193
freight 66, 71, 72, 123, 160
Frost, Phyllis 138–9
fundraising 37, 47–8, 92, 106, 126, 135, 142–50, 155, 161–3

Gandhi, Indira 19, 23, 26, 90–3, 154
Gandhi, Mohandas 25, 116, 167, 171
generosity (*see also* sacrificial giving) 99, 108
genocide 17–19, 96
global history 3–5
global inequality 50, 53, 147, 150, 167, 179, 188
global microhistory 3–5
Global South 106, 130–1, 193
Good Samaritan 101
Great Commission 101

Hamer, Richard (Dick) (Sir) 173
Harris, Adrian 130
Hazelhurst, Peter 95
Hebrews 116
historiography 2, 16, 184, 191–2
Holocaust 17, 78, 97
human rights 15, 29, 32, 45–6, 105
    Universal Declaration of 105

humanitarian intervention 39–49
humanitarianism
    definition 32
    histories 55
    religious origins 33–4
    sector in Australia 56–61
hunger 144, 192
hunger strikes
    allies 190
    arrest by federal police 172–3
    history 166–7
    news coverage of 171–5
    symbolism 167

idealism 42, 146, 148
Immigration, Australian Department of 169–70
imperialism, European 34, 53, 64, 73, 77
Indian Catholic Relief Services 71
individualism 100, 105, 127
Indian government 19–20, 106, 130, 165
    aid provided to refugees 82, 124
    expulsion of BBC 91, 193
    expulsion of foreign aid workers 89–90, 110, 193
    Ministry of Rehabilitation 83
    postcolonial nationalism 90–1
Indian High Commission, Australia 70, 164
Indian Red Cross Society 76, 80–6, 91–5, 110, 123
industrialization 8, 35, 103
International Committee for the Red Cross (ICRC) 77–8, 81, 94–8
International Federation of Red Cross and Red Crescent Societies (*see* League of Red Cross Societies)
international humanitarian law 77
International Refugee Organization (IRO) 40
international war crimes tribunals 17
internationalists 56, 62, 64, 68, 99, 119, 151–2
Iqbal, Muhammad (Sir) 5
Islam, Amirul 13
Israeli government 23

Japanese-Australian children 50–1, 151–2
Japanese Red Cross Society 94

jet age 49
Jinnah, Muhammad Ali 9
Johnson, Lyndon Baines 20, 145
journalists 13–14, 89, 109, 129, 171
Judeo-Christian ethics 57

Kashmir dispute 91
Kennedy Tucker, Gerard (Father) 129
Khan, Ayub 10
Khan, Sadruddin Aga (Prince) 43
Khan, Safdar Ali 75
Khan, Tikka 121
Khan, Yahya 11, 75
Kirkley, Leslie 127, 134
Kissinger, Henry 21

Lahore Resolution 5
language movement 8
League of Nations 38, 68
League of Red Cross Societies (LRCS)
    background 78–9
    response to refugee crisis 75–6, 79–93
Leviticus 100
Liberal Party of Australia 62, 118–19, 126, 151
liberalism 46, 118, 126
liberation struggle (*see also* national liberation movements) 128, 150
literacy rates 36, 53
Llewellyn, Bernard 127
logistics 130, 155–9
Luke 101
Lutheran Church, Australia 72, 104
Lutheran World Relief 105

Mackenzie, Jean 129
magazines (*see* periodicals)
Maitra, S. S. (Major General) 84, 89
Maoism 149
marginalization 150, 191
Mark 101
martial law 7, 10
Mascarenhas, Anthony 21–2
materialism/materialistic 52, 117, 131, 151, 188
Matthew 101
McMahon, William (Sir) 29, 63, 112, 119, 121–2, 155, 173, 176

Médecins Sans Frontières (MSF) 47, 78
mental illness 168–9
Menzies, Robert (Sir) 26, 124, 154–5, 177–8, 189
Methodist Church, Australia 99, 102, 142, 165
microhistory 3–5
middle class 36, 49–50, 147–50
military coup, Pakistan 7
milk 152–4
Minogue, Noreen 84, 88, 94
minority rights 73, 101, 111
missionaries 24, 100, 159
mobilization 145, 152
modernity 53, 91, 184, 191–2
morality 127
Mountbatten, Louis (Viceroy) 5
Mountbatten Plan 5
Mukti Bahini 14, 121
Mukti Fauj 166
Muslim solidarity 6

Naidu, Padmaja 93
national liberation movements 41, 46, 73, 105–6, 150, 188
nationalism 6–11, 19, 29, 91
nationalist histories 18 (*see also* historiography)
Naxalites 20
Near East Foundation (NEF) 38
Nehru, Jawaharlal 25, 90
neo-imperialism 90, 98
Newman-Morris, Geoffrey (Sir) 86, 89, 93
news coverage 21, 48–9, 61, 95, 105, 107, 117
    influencing public opinion 179
    Pakistan coverage of Reid's tour 121–2
    tabloids 172–3
newspapers (*see* news coverage)
Nigerian Civil War (*see* Biafra)
Nixon, Richard 20–1, 42
non-aligned movement 90, 188
non-violent protest 167

Operation Omega 22
Operation Searchlight 12, 80
oppression 126, 177, 194
orientalism 39

orphanages 38, 102
Orthodox Church 39, 60, 104, 126
Ottoman Empire 18, 39
oppression 130, 194
overseas development assistance (ODA) 42
Oxfam Belgique 132
Oxfam Canada 133
Oxfam US 136

pacificism 91, 100, 105, 149
Pakistan Movement 5
Pakistani People's Party 11
Pakistani Red Cross Society 75, 81
pan-Islamic solidarity (*see* Muslim solidarity)
paternalism 45, 133, 142, 144, 150, 164
Partition of India 5
peace movement (*see* pacificism)
People's Republic of China 21, 27, 90, 154–5
people-to-people humanitarianism 24, 128–30, 150–2, 161
periodicals 145–6
petitions 35, 53, 124–6, 175
photography (*see also* visual representations) 47, 135
pity 71, 126, 155, 163, 184
pleasure periphery 51–2
Plimsoll, James (Sir) 26
Pope Paul VI 113–14
postcolonialism 7, 46, 71, 73, 76, 90–3, 131
poverty 128
PRC (*see* People's Republic of China)
Presbyterian Church, Australia 102, 163, 165
press coverage (*see* news coverage)
press releases/statements 96, 134–5, 137, 162
prisoners of war (POWs) 40, 77
professionalization 1, 53–7, 67, 117, 129, 151–2
proselytization (*see also* evangelism) 99
protest movements 2, 22, 53, 145, 167, 176, 188
public opinion 35, 53, 90, 126, 134, 177
public relations (*see also* publicity) 95, 111, 137, 173

publicity 37, 41, 70, 92, 96–8, 108–10, 133, 144, 160–1
publicity stunts 22, 92, 146, 161

Qantas Airways 64, 71–2, 123–4
Quakerism 128

Radcliffe, Cyril (Sir) 6, 8
radicalism (*see also* radicalization) 22, 73, 112–13, 126, 191
  Australian aid sector 58–9
  East Pakistanis 13
  Maoists 20
  Oxfam Canada 133
  protests 176
  WCC 105–6
radicalization (*see also* radicalism) 55, 111–12, 126–7
Rahman, Mujibur (Sheikh) 10, 29, 94, 149, 187
rape 13, 18
Rawls, John 45
Ray, Siddhartha Shankar 28
Razakars 14
reciprocal/reciprocity 130, 134, 150
Red Cross (international movement)
  background 76–8
Reform Judaism 68, 165
rehabilitation 70, 72, 96, 108, 115, 125, 135–6
Reid, Len 116
  background 118–19
  down to earth Christianity 115–18, 192
  parliamentary speeches 120
  public meeting 165
  support of hunger strikers 174, 185
  visit to Pakistan 121
relationships 190–1
  Aid India/Dynon 152, 154, 160, 165
  FFHC 144
  Oxfam movement 128–32
  Red Cross 97–8
  symbiotic relationships 40, 43, 52, 90
religious cultures 100, 191–2
religious nationalism 6

responsibility 93–101, 120, 129, 145, 150, 173, 179
Reuters 49, 91, 168
rights-based movements 126, 145
riots 7–8
Robert-Tissot, Jean-Pierre 75, 84
Rooney, Jim 171
Rooney, Steve 166, 171, 174–5
Royal Australian Air Force (RAAF) 64
rural 126, 177, 183–5

sacrificial giving 116, 124–6
Save the Children Fund 37, 56, 130
scales 2–4, 184, 189
Scott, David 62, 129–30, 165
SEATO defence pact 20
secessionism 8, 22–3, 46
Second Indo-Pakistani War 1965 6, 8, 20, 26
Second Vatican Council 103
secular/faith dichotomy 57
sectarianism 60, 103
secularization 2, 192–3
    secularization thesis 103–4
self-reliance 130
Sen, Binay Ranjen (B. R.) 140–2
schoolchildren 148–50, 163–5, 181–2
schools 143, 148, 153
Scott, David 129, 139
Shann, Keith (Mick) (Sir) 65
Shaw, Patrick 27
Shipping Corporation of India 154, 160
Singh, Swaran 15
Six Points movement 10
slavery 34–5
Smith, Paul 171
Social Gospel 99
social justice 29, 126, 150, 192
social movements 147, 192–3
socialism 91, 105–6, 113, 188
solidarity 42, 128, 142–3, 177, 184, 189, 190–2
Solomon, Geoffrey 62, 133, 137–8
speaking tours 162–5
Stubbings, Leon 85, 88
Sturkey, Douglas 70, 161–2
suffering 126, 152, 167, 194
surveillance 156
Swedish Red Cross Society 80, 94

Tange, Arthur (Sir) 26–7
technocrat (*see also* expert class) 116–17, 163
telecommunications 36
telethon, charity 48
television 47–8, 110, 117, 143, 179–85, 194
Third Worldism 78, 111, 131
tourism (*see also* travel) 49–50
trade union movement 149–50
transnationalism 1–2, 19, 35–6, 130
transparency 1, 55, 57, 73, 132, 154
travel 36
typhoid 71

UK (*see* United Kingdom)
UNHCR (*see* United Nations High Commissioner for Refugees)
Union of Soviet Socialist Republics 20, 90, 188
United Kingdom government 21–2
    colonialism 90
United Nations Association of Australia 69, 136
United Nations Children's Emergency Fund (UNICEF) 40, 53, 72, 82
United Nations High Commissioner for Refugees (UNHCR) 1, 15, 40, 43–5, 59, 72, 80
United Nations Relief and Rehabilitation Administration (UNRRA) 40
United States government 20–1, 66, 142
urban/rural divide 182–3
USSR (*see* Union of Soviet Socialist Republics)

visual representations (*see also* photography) 47, 164, 179, 184
Volunteer Graduate Scheme (VGS) 52, 62, 188
volunteerism 23, 53, 76, 117, 128, 143

walkathons 147, 149
Webb, Jim 132, 135, 137–8, 188
West Bengal Council of Women (WBCW) 161–2
white Australia policy 25, 152
white collar 147–8
Whitlam, Gough 28, 151, 176–7, 187
working class 148–50, 181

World Christian Action, Division of 99, 104
World Council of Churches (WCC) 105–6
World Food Programme 82
World Lutheran Federation 113
World Refugee Year (WRY) 41, 56, 68–9

World Vision 58, 130

youth 142, 148–9
youth activism 52, 143, 146, 194

Zedong, Mao 21, 154–5

www.ingramcontent.com/pod-product-compliance
Lightning Source LLC
Chambersburg PA
CBHW071830300426
44116CB00009B/1501